International Finance

BPP
UNIVERSITY

Seventh Global Edition

The McGraw-Hill/Irwin Series in Finance, Insurance, and Real Estate

Stephen A. Ross
Franco Modigliani Professor of Finance and Economics
Sloan School of Management
Massachusetts Institute of Technology
Consulting Editor

International Finance

Seventh Global Edition

Cheol S. Eun
Georgia Institute of Technology

Bruce G. Resnick
Wake Forest University

International Finance 7th Global Edition
Cheol S. Eun and Bruce G. Resnick
ISBN-13 9780077161613
ISBN-10 0077161610

Published by McGraw-Hill Education
Shoppenhangers Road
Maidenhead
Berkshire
SL6 2QL
Telephone: 44 (0) 1628 502 500
Fax: 44 (0) 1628 770 224
Website: wwww.mcgraw-hill.co.uk

British Library Cataloguing in Publication Data
A catalogue record for this book is available from the British Library

Library of Congress Cataloguing in Publication Data
The Library of Congress data for this book has been applied for from the Library of
Congress

Commissioning Editor: Tom Hill
Marketing Manager: Vanessa Boddington
Content Product Manager: Alison Davis

ISBN-13 9780077161613
ISBN-10 0077161610

Printed and bound in Singapore by Markono Print Media Pte Ltd

To Elizabeth

C.S.E.

To Donna

B.G.R.

About the Authors

Cheol S. Eun,
Georgia Institute of Technology

Cheol S. Eun (Ph.D., NYU, 1981) is the Thomas R. Williams Chair and Professor of Finance at the Scheller College of Business, the College of Management, Georgia Institute of Technology. Before joining Georgia Tech, he taught at the University of Minnesota and the University of Maryland. He also taught at the Wharton School of the University of Pennsylvania, Korea Advanced Institute of Science and Technology (KAIST), Singapore Management University, and the Esslingen University of Technology (Germany) as a visiting professor. He has published extensively on international finance issues in such major journals as the *Journal of Finance, JFQA, Journal of Banking and Finance, Journal of International Money and Finance, Management Science,* and *Oxford Economic Papers.* Also, he has served on the editorial boards of the *Journal of Banking and Finance, Journal of Financial Research, Journal of International Business Studies,* and *European Financial Management.* His research is widely quoted and referenced in various scholarly articles and textbooks in the United States as well as abroad.

Dr. Eun is the founding chair of the *Fortis/Georgia Tech Conference on International Finance.* The key objectives of the conference are to promote research on international finance and provide a forum for interactions among academics, practitioners, and regulators who are interested in vital current issues of international finance.

Dr. Eun has taught a variety of courses at the undergraduate, graduate, and executive levels, and was the winner of the Krowe Teaching Excellence Award at the University of Maryland. He also has served as a consultant to many national and international organizations, including the World Bank, Apex Capital, and the Korean Development Institute, advising on issues relating to capital market liberalization, global capital raising, international investment, and exchange risk management. In addition, he has been a frequent speaker at academic and professional meetings held throughout the world.

Bruce G. Resnick,
Wake Forest University

Bruce G. Resnick is the Joseph M. Bryan Jr. Professor of Banking and Finance at the Wake Forest University School of Business in Winston-Salem, North Carolina. He has a D.B.A. (1979) in finance from Indiana University. Additionally, he has an M.B.A. from the University of Colorado and a B.B.A. from the University of Wisconsin at Oshkosh. Prior to coming to Wake Forest, he taught at Indiana University for ten years, the University of Minnesota for five years, and California State University for two years. He has also taught as a visiting professor at Bond University, Gold Coast, Queensland, Australia, and at the Helsinki School of Economics and Business Administration in Finland. Additionally, he served as the Indiana University resident director at the Center for European Studies at the Maastricht University, the Netherlands. He also served as an external examiner to the Business Administration Department of Singapore Polytechnic and as the faculty advisor on Wake Forest University study trips to Japan, China, and Hong Kong.

Dr. Resnick teaches M.B.A. courses at Wake Forest University. He specializes in the areas of investments, portfolio management, and international financial management. Dr. Resnick's research interests include market efficiency studies of options and financial futures markets and empirical tests of asset pricing models. A major interest has been the optimal design of internationally diversified portfolios constructed to control for parameter uncertainty and exchange rate risk. In recent years, he has focused on information transmission in the world money markets and yield spread comparisons of domestic and international bonds. His research articles have been published in most of the major academic journals in finance. His research is widely referenced by other researchers and textbook authors. He is an associate editor for the *Emerging Markets Review, Journal of Economics and Business,* and the *Journal of Multinational Financial Management.*

Preface

Our Reason for Writing this Textbook

Both of us have been teaching international financial management to undergraduates and M.B.A. students at Georgia Institute of Technology, Wake Forest University, and at other universities we have visited for three decades. During this time period, we conducted many research studies, published in major finance and statistics journals, concerning the operation of international financial markets. As one might imagine, in doing this we put together an extensive set of teaching materials that we used successfully in the classroom. As the years went by, we individually relied more on our own teaching materials and notes and less on any one of the major existing textbooks in international finance (most of which we tried at some point).

As you may be aware, the scope and content of international finance have been fast evolving due to deregulation of financial markets, product innovations, and technological advancements. As capital markets of the world are becoming more integrated, a solid understanding of international finance has become essential for astute corporate decision making. Reflecting the growing importance of international finance as a discipline, we have seen a sharp increase in the demand for experts in the area in both the corporate and academic worlds.

In writing *International Finance*, Seventh Global Edition, our goal was to provide well-organized, comprehensive, and up-to-date coverage of the topics that take advantage of our many years of teaching and research in this area. We hope the text is challenging to students. This does not mean that it lacks readability. The text discussion is written so that a self-contained treatment of each subject is presented in a *user-friendly* fashion. The text is intended for use at both the advanced undergraduate and M.B.A. levels.

The Underlying Philosophy

International Finance, Seventh Global Edition, like the first six editions, is written based on two tenets: emphasis on the basics and emphasis on a managerial perspective.

Emphasis on the Basics

We believe that any subject is better learned if one first is well grounded in the basics. Consequently, we initially devote several chapters to the fundamental concepts of international finance. After these are learned, the remaining material flows easily from them. We always bring the reader back, as the more advanced topics are developed, to their relationship to the fundamentals. By doing this, we believe students will be left with a framework for analysis that will serve them well when they need to apply this material in their careers in the years ahead.

We believe this approach has produced a successful textbook: *International Finance* is used in many of the best business schools in the world. Various editions of the text have been translated into Spanish and two dialects of Chinese. In addition, local co-authors have assisted in preparing a Canadian, Malaysian, and Indian adaptations.

Seventh Edition Organization

International Finance, Seventh Global Edition, has been completely updated. All data tables and statistics are the most current available when the text went to press. Additionally, the chapters incorporate several new International Finance in Practice boxes that contain real-world illustrations of chapter topics and concepts. In the margins below, we highlight specific changes in this edition.

This part lays the macroeconomic foundation for all the topics to follow.

Recent economic developments such as the global financial crisis and sovereign debt crisis of Europe.

Updated coverage of monetary developments, including the euro zone crisis.

Updated balance-of-payments statistics.

Review of corporate governance systems in different countries, the Dodd-Frank Act, and managerial implications.

Part ONE
Foundations of International Financial Management 2

1   Globalization and the Multinational Firm 4

2   International Monetary System 29

3   Balance of Payments 64

4   Corporate Governance around the World 83

This part describes the market for foreign exchange and introduces currency derivatives that can be used to manage foreign exchange exposure.

Fully updated market data and examples. New section on non-deliverable forward contracts.

Integrated coverage of key parity conditions and currency carry trade.

Fully updated market data and examples.

Part TWO
The Foreign Exchange Market, Exchange Rate Determination, and Currency Derivatives 110

5   The Market for Foreign Exchange 112

6   International Parity Relationships and Forecasting Foreign Exchange Rates 139

7   Futures and Options on Foreign Exchange 172

This part describes the various types of foreign exchange risk and discusses methods available for risk management.

Systematic coverage of foreign currency transaction exposure management and a new case application.

Conceptual and managerial analysis of economic exposure to currency risk.

Part THREE
Foreign Exchange Exposure and Management 196

8   Management of Transaction Exposure 198

9   Management of Economic Exposure 231

10   Management of Translation Exposure 252

A Managerial Perspective

The text presentation never loses sight of the fact that it is teaching students how to make managerial decisions. *International Finance,* Seventh Global Edition, is founded in the belief that the fundamental job of the financial manager is to maximize shareholder wealth. This belief permeates the decision-making process we present from cover to cover. To reinforce the managerial perspective, we provide numerous "real-world" stories whenever appropriate.

This part provides a thorough discussion of international financial institutions, assets, and marketplaces.

Fully updated market data and statistics. Updated discussion on Basel 2.5 and III capital adequacy standards. Updated discussion on the causes and consequences of the global financial crisis. New Finance in Practice box on the Libor scandal. New section on BBA Libor.

Fully updated market data and examples. Updated empirical coverage of the features, characteristics, and regulations governing dollar denominated foreign bonds, Eurobonds, and global bonds.

Fully updated market data and statistics. Updated discussion of market consolidations and mergers.

Fully updated market data and statistics.

Updated statistical analysis of international markets and diversification with small-cap stocks.

This part covers topics on financial management practices for the multinational firm.

Updated trends in cross-border investment and M&A deals. Updated political risk scores for countries.

New analysis of home bias and the cost of capital around the world.

Updated discussion of multilateral netting systems available for commercial use.

Fully updated comparative national income tax rate table with updated examples. New Finance in Practice box reading on transfer pricing.

Pedagogical Features

Chapter Outline—At the beginning of each chapter, a chapter outline is presented to provide a roadmap of concepts to be learned in that chapter.

Exhibits—Within each chapter, extensive use is made of graphs and tables to illustrate important concepts.

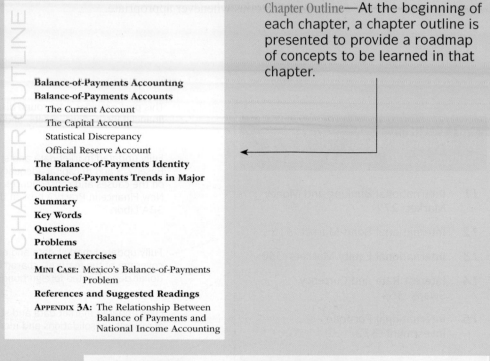

EXHIBIT 2.3   The Value of the U.S. Dollar since 1960[a]

[a]The value of the U.S. dollar represents the nominal exchange rate index (2005 = 100) with weights derived from trade among 21 industrialized countries.
Source: International Financial Statistics.

Examples—These are integrated throughout the text, providing students with immediate application of the text concepts.

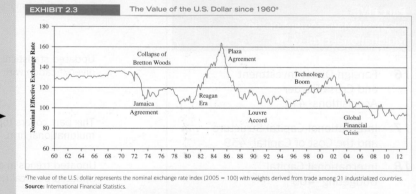

EXAMPLE | 11.1: Rollover Pricing of a Eurocredit

Teltrex International can borrow $3,000,000 at LIBOR plus a lending margin of .75 percent per annum on a three-month rollover basis from Barclays in London. Suppose that three-month LIBOR is currently $5\frac{17}{32}$ percent. Further suppose that over the second three-month interval LIBOR falls to $5\frac{1}{8}$ percent. How much will Teltrex pay in interest to Barclays over the six-month period for the Eurodollar loan?

Solution: $3,000,000 × (.0553125 + .0075)/4 + $3,000,000 × (.05125 + .0075)/4 = $47,109.38 + $44,062.50 = $91,171.88

International Finance in Practice Boxes—Selected chapters contain International Finance in Practice boxes. These real-world illustrations offer students a practical look at the major concepts presented in the chapter.

FX Market Volumes Surge

The FX market is growing at record levels, according to figures released by the CME Group, the largest regulated foreign exchange market in the world.

Last month the CME Group reported average daily notional volume at a record level of $121 billion, up 82 percent compared to a year earlier.

With a number of indicators at play like the news of Greece's credit concerns and the continued appetite for high-yielding currencies like the Australian dollar and the Canadian dollar, the CME saw record volumes and notional values in the euro and Australian and Canadian dollars. Euro FX futures and options saw total average daily volume of 362,000 contracts with total notional ADV of slightly over $67 billion.

Australian dollar futures and options climbed to nearly 119,000 contracts in average daily volume with almost $11 billion in total notional ADV, and Canadian dollar futures and options surpassed 88,000 contracts in ADV and $8 billion in total notional ADV.

With foreign currency futures going from strength to strength, the CME Group recently published a white paper outlining the benefits of FX futures.

"These contracts provide an ideal tool to manage currency or FX risks in an uncertain world," it said. "Product innovation, liquidity, and financial surety are the three pillars upon which the CME Group has built its world-class derivatives market. The CME Group provides products based on a wide range of frequently transacted currencies, liquidity offered on the state-of-the-art CME Globex electronic trading platform, and financial sureties afforded by its centralized clearing system."

Source: *Global Investor,* March 2010.

---

www.theice.com

This is the website of the Intercontinental Exchange (ICE). Several FX futures contracts are traded on their electronic trading platform.

www.numa.com/ref/exchange.htm

This is the website of The Numa Directory. It provides the website address of most of the stock and derivative exchanges in the world.

Annotated Web Resources—Web links located in the margins within each chapter serve as a quick reference of pertinent chapter-related websites. Each URL listed also includes a short statement on what can be found at that site.

In More Depth—Some topics are by nature more complex than others. The chapter sections that contain such material are indicated by the section heading "In More Depth"' and are in *blue type*. These sections may be skipped without loss of continuity, enabling the instructor to easily tailor the reading assignments to the students. End-of-chapter Questions and Problems relating to the In More Depth sections of the text are also indicated by *blue type*.

In More Depth

European Option-Pricing Formula

In the last section, we examined a simple one-step version of binomial option-pricing model. Instead, we could have assumed the stock price followed a multiplicative binomial process by subdividing the option period into many subperiods. In this case, S_T and C_T could be many different values. When the number of subperiods into which the option period is subdivided goes to infinity, the European call and put pricing formulas presented in this section are obtained. Exact European call and put pricing formulas are:[5]

$$C_e = S_t e^{-r_f T} N(d_1) - E e^{-r_i T} N(d_2) \qquad (7.12)$$

and

$$P_e = E e^{-r_i T} N(-d_2) - S_t e^{-r_f T} N(-d_1) \qquad (7.13)$$

The interest rates r_i and r_f are assumed to be annualized and constant over the term-to-maturity T of the option contract, which is expressed as a fraction of a year.

Invoking IRP, where with continuous compounding $F_T = S_t e^{(r_i - r_f)T}$, C_e and P_e in Equations 7.12 and 7.13 can be, respectively, restated as:

$$C_e = [F_T N(d_1) - E N(d_2)] e^{-r_i T} \qquad (7.14)$$

and

$$P_e = [E N(-d_2) - F_T N(-d_1)] e^{-r_i T} \qquad (7.15)$$

where

$$d_1 = \frac{\ln(F_T/E) + .5\sigma^2 T}{\sigma\sqrt{T}}$$

and

$$d_2 = d_1 - \sigma\sqrt{T}$$

$N(d)$ denotes the cumulative area under the standard normal density function from $-\infty$ to d_1 (or d_2). The variable σ is the annualized volatility of the change in exchange rate $\ln(S_{t+1}/S_t)$. Equations 7.14 and 7.15 indicate that C_e and P_e are functions of only five variables: F_T, E, r_i, T, and σ. It can be shown that both C_e and P_e increase when σ becomes larger.

Ancillary Materials

To assist in course preparation, the following ancillaries are offered on the Online Learning Center—www.mcgraw-hill.co.uk/textbooks/eun:

- **Solutions Manual**—Includes detailed suggested answers and solutions to the end-of-chapter questions and problems, written by the authors.
- **Lecture Outlines**—Chapter outlines, learning objectives, and teaching notes for each chapter.
- **Test Bank**—True/false and multiple-choice test questions for each chapter. Available as Word documents and in computerized EZ Test format.
- **PowerPoint Presentations**—PowerPoint slides for each chapter to use in classroom lecture settings.

The site also includes the International Finance Software that can be used with this book. This Excel software has four main programs:

- A currency options pricing program allows students to price put and call options on foreign exchange.
- A hedging program allows the student to compare forward, money market instruments, futures, and options for hedging exchange risk.
- A currency swap program allows students to calculate the cash flows and notional values associated with swapping fixed-rate debt from one currency into another.
- A portfolio optimization program based on the Markowitz model allows for examining the benefits of international portfolio diversification.

The four programs can be used to solve certain end-of-chapter problems (marked with an Excel icon) or assignments the instructor devises. A User's Manual and sample projects are included on the website.

Acknowledgments

We are indebted to the many colleagues who provided insight and guidance throughout the development process. Their careful work enabled us to create a text that is current, accurate, and modern in its approach. Among all who helped in this endeavor for the seventh global edition:

Richard Ajayi
University of Central Florida

Lawrence A. Beer
Arizona State University

Nishant Dass
Georgia Institute of Technology

John Hund
Rice University

Irina Khindanova
University of Denver

Gew-rae Kim
University of Bridgeport

Jaemin Kim
San Diego State University

Yong-Cheol Kim
University of Wisconsin, Milwaukee

Yen-Sheng Lee
Bellevue University

Charmen Loh
Rider University

Atsuyuki Naka
University of New Orleans

Richard L. Patterson
Indiana University, Bloomington

Adrian Shopp   H. Douglas Witte
Metropolitan State University of Denver   *Missouri State University*

John Wald
University of Texas at San Antonio

Many people assisted in the production of this textbook. At the risk of overlooking some individuals, we would like to acknowledge Brian Conzachi for the outstanding job he did proofreading the entire manuscript and Chee Ng for his excellent work proofreading selected chapters. Additionally, we thank Yusri Zaro for his hard work checking the accuracy of the solutions manual. Rohan-Rao Ganduri, Kristen Seaver, Milind Shrikhande, Jin-Gil Jeong, Sanjiv Sabherwal, Sandy Lai, Jinsoo Lee, Hyung Suk Choi, Teng Zhang, and Victor Huang provided useful inputs into the text. Professor Martin Glaum of the Giessen University (Germany) also provided valuable comments.

We also wish to thank the many professionals at McGraw-Hill/Irwin for their time and patience with us. Charles Synovec, executive brand manager, and Noelle Bathurst and Sarah Otterness, development editors have done a marvelous job guiding us through this edition, as has Judi David, as content project manager.

A very special thanks go to Julie Byrne, University College Dublin, and Agustino Manduchi, Jönköping University, for their contributions to this Global Edition.

Last, but not least, we would like to thank our families, Christine, James, and Elizabeth Eun and Donna Resnick, for their tireless love and support, without which this book would not have become a reality.

We hope that you enjoy using *International Finance,* Seventh Global Edition. In addition, we welcome your comments for improvement. Please let us know either through McGraw-Hill/Irwin, c/o Editorial, or at our e-mail addresses provided below.

Cheol S. Eun
cheol.eun@scheller.gatech.edu

Bruce G. Resnick
resnickbg@wfu.edu

What's Special about I

Foreign Exchange
and Political Risks

https://www.cia.gov/library/
publications/the world-
factbook

Website of *The World Factbook*
published by the CIA provides
background information, such
as geography, government,
and economy, of countries
around the world.

CHAPTER

1

Gl
Mu

assemb
made c
and Ind
single c
   Rece
allows
instanc
as stoc
In part
other f
additio
Petrole
ing the
Consec
investo

¹This info

4

some economists estimate that privatization improves efficiency and reduces operating costs by as much as 20 percent.

There is no one single way to privatize state-owned operations. The objectives of the country seem to be the prevailing guide. For the Czech Republic, speed was the overriding factor. To accomplish privatization en masse, the Czech government essentially gave away its businesses to the Czech people. For a nominal fee, vouchers were sold that allowed Czech citizens to bid on businesses as they went on the auction block. From 1991 to 1995, more than 1,700 companies were turned over to private hands. Moreover, three-quarters of the Czech citizens became stockholders in these newly privatized firms.

In Russia, there has been an "irreversible" shift to private ownership, according to the World Bank. More than 80 percent of the country's nonfarm workers are now employed in the private sector. Eleven million apartment units have been privatized, as have half of the country's 240,000 other business firms. Additionally, via a Czech-style voucher system, 40 million Russians now own stock in over 15,000 medium- to large-size corporations that recently became privatized through mass auctions of state-owned enterprises.

In China, privatization has proceeded by way of listing state-owned enterprises (SOEs) on the organized exchanges, thereby making SOEs eligible for private ownership. In the early 1980s, China launched two stock exchanges—the Shanghai Stock Exchange and the Shenzhen Stock Exchange—as a part of concerted efforts toward market-oriented reform. Since their inception, the Chinese stock markets have grown at a phenomenal pace, becoming some of the largest stock markets in Asia in terms of capitalization. Currently, more than 2,000 companies are listed on China's stock exchanges. China's stock markets now play a vital role in privatization of SOEs, raising new capital for business investments and ventures, and propagating corporate ownership among citizens. Foreigners may also participate in the ownership of Chinese firms mainly by investing in the so-called B-shares listed on the Shanghai or Shenzen stock exchanges or in those shares that are directly listed on the Hong Kong Stock Exchange (H-shares), New York Stock Exchange, or other international exchanges. It is noted that A-shares of Chinese firms are mostly reserved for domestic investors. While individual and institutional investors are now actively investing in Chinese shares, the Chinese government still retains the majority stakes in most public firms.

For some countries, privatization has meant globalization. For example, to achieve fiscal stability, New Zealand had to open its once-socialist economy to foreign capital. Australian investors now control its commercial banks, and U.S. firms purchased the national telephone company and timber operations. While workers' rights have changed under foreign ownership and a capitalist economy, New Zealand now ranks high among the most competitive market environments. Fiscal stability has also been realized. In 1994, New Zealand's economy grew at a rate of 6 percent and inflation was under control. As can be seen from the experiences of New Zealand, privatization has spurred a tremendous increase in cross-border investment.

Global Financial Crisis of 2008–2009

The subprime mortgage crisis in the United States that began in the summer of 2007 led to a severe credit crunch, making borrowing and refinancing difficult for households, firms, and banks. The credit crunch, in turn, escalated to a full-blown global financial crisis in 2008–2009. The defining moment of the crisis came on September 14, 2008, when Lehman Brothers, a major U.S. investment bank with a global presence, went bankrupt. The abrupt failure of an iconic U.S. bank touched off a major crisis of confidence in financial markets and institutions around the world. Stock prices fell precipitously. Output fell and unemployment rose sharply. As shown in Exhibit 1.5, the Dow Jones Industrial Average (DJIA), a popular U.S. stock market index, fell rapidly from a peak of 14,164 reached on October 9, 2007, to a trough of 7,062 on February 27, 2009, a 50 percent decline, while the U.S. unemployment rate began to rise from 4.4 percent

EXHIBIT 1.5

U.S. Unemployment Rate and Dow Jones Industrial Average (DJIA)

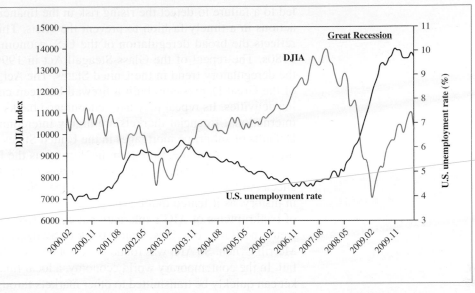

Source: Bloomberg.

in May 2007 to reach 10.1 percent in October 2009. At the same time, international trade has been shrinking rapidly. The crisis engulfed not only the advanced economies, such as the United States, Japan, and the European Union, but also many emerging economies, including Brazil, China, and Russia, albeit less severely. The world was sliding into the "Great Recession," the most serious, synchronized economic downturn since the Great Depression.

Subprime mortgages are a financial instrument designed to facilitate home ownership for low and modest income households. Most subprime mortgages are adjustable-rate mortgages and are refinanced relatively frequently. Mortgage banks raise funds for making subprime loans mainly by securitization. Once subprime mortgage loans are originated, they are pooled and packaged into a variety of mortgage-backed securities and sold to various institutional investors in the United States and abroad. Subprime mortgages worked as designed while house prices were rising during 1996–2005. But as U.S. interest rates began to rise in early 2004 due to the tightening monetary policy of the Federal Reserve, house prices stopped rising and began to decline in 2006. Subsequently, subprime borrowers started to default, spreading risk among investors and eroding the bank capital base in the United States and abroad.

What caused the global financial crisis? While it may be early to provide a definitive answer for this important question, it is possible to identify several factors that are likely to have contributed to the crisis. First, households and financial institutions borrowed too much and took too much risk. This excessive borrowing and risk taking is, in turn, attributable to the ample supply of liquidity and credit that is due to (i) the "easy money" policy of the Federal Reserve Bank, a legacy of its former chairman, Allan Greenspan, and also (ii) the massive inflow of foreign money associated with the recycling of trade surpluses of Asian countries, including China, Japan, and Korea, and the oil-exporting countries in the Middle East. Second, the crisis was amplified many-fold and transmitted globally by securitization. Securitization allows loan originators to avoid bearing the default risk, which leads to a compromised lending standard and increased moral hazard. Also, financial engineers designed opaque and complex mortgage-based securities that could be used for excessive risk-taking. These securities were traded infrequently and were often difficult to value. Third, the "invisible hands" of free markets apparently failed to self-regulate its excesses, contributing to the banking crisis. At the same time, "light touch" regulations by government agencies, such as the Securities and Exchange Commission (SEC) and the Federal Reserve, led to a failure to detect the rising risk in the financial system and to take regulatory actions in a timely fashion to prevent the crisis. This laissez-faire regulatory stance reflects the broad deregulation of the U.S. economy that has taken place since the 1980s. The repeal of the Glass-Steagall Act in 1999 is the *prima facie* example of the deregulatory trend in the United States. The Act, which was adopted in the wake of the Great Depression, built a firewall between commercial and investment banking activities. Its repeal may have encouraged banks to take risks excessively. Fourth, international financial markets are highly interconnected and integrated nowadays. Defaults of subprime mortgages in the United States came to threaten the solvency of the teachers' retirement program in Norway as the latter invested in U.S. mortgage-backed securities. The U.S. government was compelled to rescue AIG, a U.S. insurance company, with a $180 billion package, the most costly bailout of a single firm in history, as it feared that if AIG were allowed to fail, it might start a chain reaction of bankruptcies of AIG's international counterparties that included Goldman Sachs, Deutsche Bank, Barclays, Union Bank of Switzerland (UBS), Société Générale, and Merrill Lynch. So AIG was found to be not only too big, but also too interconnected to fail. In the contemporary world economy, a local financial shock originating in a market can quickly be transmitted to other markets through contagion and other channels. No market or institution is an island in an integrated world.

Facing the severe credit crunch and economic downturn, the U.S. government took forceful actions to save the banking system and stimulate the economy. As a matter of fact, the government acted as the lender of last resort as well as the spender of last resort to keep the economy floating. Specifically, the Bush administration-implemented Troubled Asset Relief Program (TARP), which was enacted in October 2008. Seven hundred billion dollars of the TARP fund were injected into the financial system to buy nonperforming assets and mortgage-related securities from banks and also to directly strengthen banks' capital reserves. The Obama administration, in turn, implemented an $850 billion economic stimulus program to boost economic activities and create jobs. Many governments around the world, notably the U.K., France, Germany, China, and Korea, implemented similar stimulating measures. In addition, to prevent future financial crises and costly bailouts, the U.S. government adopted much tighter rules of finance in July 2010. Among other things, the new rules prohibit banks from making risky investments with their own money, which may endanger the core capital of banks. In addition, a new independent Consumer Financial Protection Bureau was set up to protect consumers from predatory lending. Also, a new Financial Stability Oversight Council of regulators chaired by the Treasury secretary would be responsible for carefully monitoring the **systemic risk** affecting the entire financial market.

Lastly, it is noteworthy that during the course of the global financial crisis of 2008–2009, the G-20, composed of both leading developed countries, such as Germany, Japan, and the United States, and major developing countries, such as Brazil, China, India, Korea, and South Africa, has emerged as the premier forum for discussing international economic issues and coordinating financial regulations and macroeconomic policies. We will revisit and discuss these and other related issues in greater detail in Chapter 11.

Multinational Corporations

In addition to international trade, foreign direct investment by MNCs is a major force driving globalization of the world economy. According to a UN report, there are about 60,000 MNCs in the world with over 500,000 foreign affiliates.[9] Since the 1990s, foreign direct investment by MNCs grew at the annual rate of about 10 percent. In comparison, international trade grew at the rate of 3.5 percent during the same period.

[9]The source for this information is the United Nations' *World Investment Report*, various issues.

Multinationals More Efficient

Foreign-owned manufacturing companies in the world's most highly developed countries are generally more productive and pay their workers more than comparable locally owned businesses, according to the Organisation for Economic Co-operation and Development.

The Paris-based organization also says that the proportion of manufacturing under foreign ownership in European Union countries rose substantially during the 1990s, a sign of increasing economic integration.

In a report on the global role of multinationals, the OECD points out that for some countries, the level of production abroad by foreign subsidiaries of national businesses was comparable to total exports from these countries.

The finding underlines the increasing importance in the world economy of large companies with bases scattered across the globe.

Gross output per employee, a measure of productivity, in most OECD nations tends to be greater in multinationals than in locally owned companies, the report says.

This is partly a factor of the multinationals being bigger and more geared to operating according to world-class levels of efficiency. But it also reflects their ability to transfer new thinking in production technologies through an international factory network.

Reflecting the greater efficiencies, workers in foreign-owned plants tend to earn more money than those in locally owned ones.

In Turkey, employees of multinationals earn double the wages of their counterparts. The equivalent figure in the UK is 23 percent and in the US it is 9 percent.

In the EU in 1998, a quarter of total manufacturing production was controlled by a foreign subsidiary of a bigger company compared to 17 percent in 1990. The figure has probably increased since then, and is expected to climb further as the impact of the euro tightens the link between member countries' economies.

Measuring Globalisation: The Role of Multinationals in OECD Economies. For details see www.oecd.org

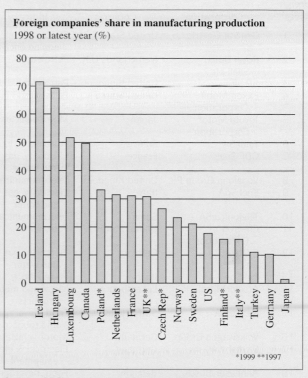

Foreign companies' share in manufacturing production
1998 or latest year (%)

*1999 **1997

Source: OECD, Activities of Foreign Affiliates database.

Source: Peter Marsh, *Financial Times*, March 20, 2002, p. 6. Reprinted with permission.

As indicated in the International Finance in Practice box, "Multinationals More Efficient," MNCs are reshaping the structure of the world economy.

A **multinational corporation (MNC)** is a business firm incorporated in one country that has production and sales operations in many other countries. The term suggests a firm obtaining raw materials from one national market and financial capital from another, producing goods with labor and capital equipment in a third country, and selling the finished product in yet other national markets. Indeed, some MNCs have operations in dozens of different countries. MNCs obtain financing from major money centers around the world in many different currencies to finance their operations. Global operations force the treasurer's office to establish international banking relationships, place short-term funds in several currency denominations, and effectively manage foreign exchange risk.

Exhibit 1.6 lists the top 40 of the largest 100 MNCs ranked by the size of foreign assets. The list was compiled by the United Nations Conference on Trade and Development (UNCTAD). Many of the firms on the list are well-known MNCs

www.unctad.org/wir

This UNCTAD website provides a broad coverage of cross-border investment activities by multinational corporations.

EXHIBIT 1.6 The World's Top 40 Nonfinancial MNCs Ranked by Foreign Assets, 2011

Ranking by Foreign assets	Corporation	Country	Industry	Assets (in $ Billions)		Sales (in $ Billions)		Employment (in Thousands)	
				Foreign	Total	Foreign	Total	Foreign	Total
1	General Electric Co	United States	Electrical & electronic equipment	502.61	717.24	77.48	147.30	170.00	301.00
2	Royal Dutch Shell plc	Netherlands/U.K.	Petroleum	296.45	345.26	282.67	470.17	75.00	90.00
3	BP plc	United Kingdom	Petroleum	263.58	293.07	308.44	386.46	68.01	83.43
4	Exxon Mobil Corporation	United States	Petroleum	214.13	331.05	310.09	433.53	49.50	82.10
5	Toyota Motor Corporation	Japan	Motor vehicles	214.12	372.57	142.89	235.20	123.66	325.91
6	Total SA	France	Petroleum	211.31	228.04	197.48	256.73	61.07	96.10
7	GDF Suez	France	Electricity, gas and water	194.42	296.65	82.73	126.04	110.55	218.87
8	Vodafone Group Plc	United Kingdom	Telecommunications	171.94	186.18	65.45	74.09	75.48	83.86
9	Enel SpA	Italy	Electricity, gas and water	153.67	236.04	66.82	110.53	36.66	75.36
10	Telefonica SA	Spain	Telecommunications	147.90	180.19	63.01	87.35	231.07	286.15
11	Chevron Corporation	United States	Petroleum	139.82	209.47	139.34	236.29	31.00	61.00
12	E.ON AG	Germany	Electricity, gas and water	133.01	212.50	90.96	157.01	43.76	78.89
13	Eni SpA	Italy	Petroleum	122.08	198.70	106.24	153.63	45.52	78.69
14	ArcelorMittal	Luxembourg	Metal and metal products	117.02	121.88	93.68	93.97	197.15	260.52
15	Nestlé SA	Switzerland	Food, beverages and tobacco	116.13	121.26	92.17	94.19	318.30	328.00
16	Volkswagen Group	Germany	Motor vehicles	115.08	221.49	173.39	221.49	277.11	501.96
17	Siemens AG	Germany	Electrical & electronic equipment	112.36	141.75	87.42	102.49	244.00	360.00
18	Anheuser-Busch InBev NV	Belgium	Food, beverages and tobacco	106.34	112.43	34.94	39.05	108.45	116.28
19	Honda Motor Co Ltd	Japan	Motor vehicles	105.15	143.20	78.13	100.59	109.40	179.06
20	Deutsche Telekom AG	Germany	Telecommunications	102.05	170.34	44.89	81.53	113.57	235.13
21	Pfizer Inc	United States	Pharmaceuticals	100.39	188.00	40.49	67.43	64.42	103.70
22	Mitsubishi Corporation	Japan	Wholesale trade	98.17	153.01	47.16	254.72	17.62	58.72
23	EDF SA	France	Electricity, gas and water	95.00	322.08	35.49	90.78	28.90	156.17
24	Daimler AG	Germany	Motor vehicles	94.16	205.91	120.64	148.10	103.69	271.37
25	Iberdrola SA	Spain	Electricity, gas and water	88.05	134.70	23.21	44.90	19.44	31.89
26	Sanofi	France	Pharmaceuticals	85.77	139.23	42.09	46.41	55.38	113.72
27	Fiat S.p.A.	Italy	Motor vehicles	85.24	111.25	69.92	82.79	134.44	197.02
28	ConocoPhillips	United States	Petroleum	82.68	153.23	85.68	230.86	8.53	29.80
29	BMW AG	Germany	Motor vehicles	79.35	171.57	77.79	95.66	73.32	100.31
30	EADS N.V.	France	Aircraft	77.79	122.99	61.67	68.29	84.72	133.12
31	Hutchison Whampoa Limited	Hong Kong, China	Diversified	77.29	92.79	23.48	30.02	206.99	250.00
32	General Motors Co	United States	Motor vehicles	77.09	144.60	69.05	150.28	106.00	207.00
33	Ford Motor Company	United States	Motor vehicles	77.00	179.25	65.10	136.26	85.00	164.00
34	Wal-Mart Stores Inc	United States	Retail & Trade	74.66	180.66	109.23	421.85	800.00	2100.00
35	Sony Corporation	Japan	Electrical & electronic equipment	73.84	161.61	55.54	82.18	109.20	168.20
36	France Telecom S.A.	France	Telecommunications	73.08	133.56	23.82	62.94	66.70	171.95
37	Nissan Motor Co Ltd	Japan	Motor vehicles	71.91	134.58	90.88	119.08	82.22	155.10
38	Xstrata PLC	Switzerland	Mining & quarrying	71.77	74.83	30.43	33.88	38.25	40.39
39	Procter & Gamble Co	United States	Diversified	68.08	138.35	48.71	82.56	94.62	129.00
40	Anglo American plc	United Kingdom	Mining & quarrying	68.04	72.44	28.64	30.58	94.00	100.00

Source: *World Investment Report 2012*, UNCTAD.

with household names because of their presence in consumer product markets. For example, General Electric (GE), General Motors, British Petroleum (BP), Toyota, BMW, Sony, Wal-Mart Stores, Procter & Gamble, Nestlé, Pfizer, and Siemens are names recognized by most people. By country of origin, U.S. MNCs, with 22 out of the total of 100, constitute the largest group. France has 16 MNCs and the U.K. 13 in the top 100, followed by Germany with 12, Japan with 6 and Switzerland with 5. It is interesting to note that some Swiss firms are extremely multinational. Nestlé, for instance, derives about 98 percent of its sales from overseas markets, and employs about 318,000 workers, 97 percent of its total employment, outside Switzerland. Obviously, MNCs make a significant contribution to the creation of job opportunities around the world.

MNCs may gain from their global presence in a variety of ways. First of all, MNCs can benefit from the economy of scale by (i) spreading R&D expenditures and advertising costs over their global sales, (ii) pooling global purchasing power over suppliers, (iii) utilizing their technological and managerial know-how globally with minimum additional costs, and so forth. Furthermore, MNCs can use their global presence to take advantage of underpriced labor services available in certain developing countries, and gain access to special R&D capabilities residing in advanced foreign countries. MNCs can indeed leverage their global presence to boost their profit margins and create shareholder value.

In recent years, companies are increasingly using offshore outsourcing as a way of saving costs and boosting productivity. For example, when Microsoft entered the video game market, it decided to **outsource** production of the Xbox gaming console to Flextronics, a Singapore-based contract manufacturer. Flextronics, in turn, decided to manufacture all Xbox consoles in China. This outsourcing decision allows Microsoft, a company mainly known for its strength in software, to benefit from the manufacturing and logistics capabilities of Flextronics and low labor costs in China. Like Microsoft, many companies around the world are using outsourcing to enhance their competitive positions in the marketplace.

SUMMARY

This chapter provided an introduction to *International Financial Management*.

1. It is essential to study "international" financial management because we are now living in a highly globalized and integrated world economy. Owing to the (a) continuous liberalization of international trade and investment, and (b) rapid advances in telecommunications and transportation technologies, the world economy will become even more integrated.

2. Three major dimensions distinguish international finance from domestic finance. They are (a) foreign exchange and political risks, (b) market imperfections, and (c) an expanded opportunity set.

3. Financial managers of MNCs should learn how to manage foreign exchange and political risks using proper tools and instruments, deal with (and take advantage of) market imperfections, and benefit from the expanded investment and financing opportunities. By doing so, financial managers can contribute to shareholder wealth maximization, which is the ultimate goal of international financial management.

4. The theory of comparative advantage states that economic well-being is enhanced if countries produce those goods for which they have comparative advantages and then trade those goods. The theory of comparative advantage provides a powerful rationale for free trade. Currently, international trade is

4. Bretton Woods system: 1945–1972.

5. Flexible exchange rate regime: Since 1973.

We now examine each of the five stages in some detail.

Bimetallism: Before 1875

Prior to the 1870s, many countries had **bimetallism**, that is, a double standard in that free coinage was maintained for both gold and silver. In Great Britain, for example, bimetallism was maintained until 1816 (after the conclusion of the Napoleonic Wars) when Parliament passed a law maintaining free coinage of gold only, abolishing the free coinage of silver. In the United States, bimetallism was adopted by the Coinage Act of 1792 and remained a legal standard until 1873, when Congress dropped the silver dollar from the list of coins to be minted. France, on the other hand, introduced and maintained its bimetallism from the French Revolution to 1878. Some other countries such as China, India, Germany, and Holland were on the silver standard.

The international monetary system before the 1870s can be characterized as "bimetallism" in the sense that both gold and silver were used as international means of payment and that the exchange rates among currencies were determined by either their gold or silver contents.[1] Around 1870, for example, the exchange rate between the British pound, which was fully on a gold standard, and the French franc, which was officially on a bimetallic standard, was determined by the gold content of the two currencies. On the other hand, the exchange rate between the franc and the German mark, which was on a silver standard, was determined by the silver content of the currencies. The exchange rate between the pound and the mark was determined by their exchange rates against the franc. It is also worth noting that, due to various wars and political upheavals, some major countries such as the United States, Russia, and Austria-Hungary had irredeemable currencies at one time or another during the period 1848–1879. One might say that the international monetary system was less than fully *systematic* up until the 1870s.

Countries that were on the bimetallic standard often experienced the well-known phenomenon referred to as **Gresham's law**. Since the exchange ratio between the two metals was fixed officially, only the abundant metal was used as money, driving more scarce metal out of circulation. This is Gresham's law, according to which "bad" (abundant) money drives out "good" (scarce) money. For example, when gold from newly discovered mines in California and Australia poured into the market in the 1850s, the value of gold became depressed, causing overvaluation of gold under the French official ratio, which equated a gold franc to a silver franc 15½ times as heavy. As a result, the franc effectively became a gold currency.

Classical Gold Standard: 1875–1914

Mankind's fondness for gold as a storage of wealth and means of exchange dates back to antiquity and was shared widely by diverse civilizations. Christopher Columbus once said, "Gold constitutes treasure, and he who possesses it has all he needs in this world." The first full-fledged **gold standard**, however, was not established until 1821 in Great Britain, when notes from the Bank of England were made fully redeemable for gold. As previously mentioned, France was effectively on the gold standard beginning in the 1850s and formally adopted the standard in 1878. The newly emergent German empire, which was to receive a sizable war indemnity from France, converted to the gold standard in 1875, discontinuing free coinage of silver. The United States adopted the gold standard in 1879, Russia and Japan in 1897.

---

[1]This does not imply that each individual country was on a bimetallic standard. In fact, many countries were on either a gold standard or a silver standard until the 1870s.

One can say roughly that the *international* gold standard existed as a historical reality during the period 1875–1914. The majority of countries got off gold in 1914 when World War I broke out. The classical gold standard as an international monetary system thus lasted for about 40 years. During this period, London became the center of the international financial system, reflecting Britain's advanced economy and its preeminent position in international trade.

An *international* gold standard can be said to exist when, in most major countries, (i) gold alone is assured of unrestricted coinage, (ii) there is two-way convertibility between gold and national currencies at a stable ratio, and (iii) gold may be freely exported or imported. In order to support unrestricted convertibility into gold, banknotes need to be backed by a gold reserve of a minimum stated ratio. In addition, the domestic money stock should rise and fall as gold flows in and out of the country. The above conditions were roughly met between 1875 and 1914.

Under the gold standard, the exchange rate between any two currencies will be determined by their gold content. For example, suppose that the pound is pegged to gold at six pounds per ounce, whereas one ounce of gold is worth 12 francs. The exchange rate between the pound and the franc should then be two francs per pound. To the extent that the pound and the franc remain pegged to gold at given prices, the exchange rate between the two currencies will remain stable. There were indeed no significant changes in exchange rates among the currencies of such major countries as Great Britain, France, Germany, and the United States during the entire period. For example, the dollar–sterling exchange rate remained within a narrow range of $4.84 and $4.90 per pound. Highly stable exchange rates under the classical gold standard provided an environment that was conducive to international trade and investment.

Under the gold standard, misalignment of the exchange rate will be automatically corrected by cross-border flows of gold. In the above example, suppose that one pound is trading for 1.80 francs at the moment. Since the pound is undervalued in the exchange market, people will buy pounds with francs, but not francs with pounds. For people who need francs, it would be cheaper first to buy gold from the Bank of England and ship it to France and sell it for francs. For example, suppose that you need to buy 1,000 francs using pounds. If you buy 1,000 francs in the exchange market, it will cost you £555.56 at the exchange rate of Fr1.80/£. Alternatively, you can buy 83.33 = 1,000/12 ounces of gold from the Bank of England for £500:

$$£500 = (1,000/12) \times 6$$

Then you could ship it to France and sell it to the Bank of France for 1,000 francs. This way, you can save about £55.56.[2] Since people only want to buy, not sell, pounds at the exchange rate of Fr1.80/£, the pound will eventually appreciate to its fair value, namely, Fr2.0/£.

Under the gold standard, international imbalances of payment will also be corrected automatically. Consider a situation where Great Britain exported more to France than the former imported from the latter. This kind of trade imbalance will not persist under the gold standard. Net export from Great Britain to France will be accompanied by a net flow of gold in the opposite direction. This international flow of gold from France to Great Britain will lead to a lower price level in France and, at the same time, a higher price level in Great Britain. (Recall that under the gold standard, the domestic money stock is supposed to rise or fall as the country experiences an inflow or outflow of gold.) The resultant change in the relative price level, in turn, will slow exports from Great Britain and encourage exports from France. As a result, the initial net export from Great Britain will eventually disappear. This adjustment mechanism is referred

---

[2]In this example, we ignored shipping costs. But as long as the shipping costs do not exceed £55.56, it is still advantageous to buy francs via "gold export" than via the foreign exchange market.

EXHIBIT 2.1

The Design of the
Gold-Exchange System

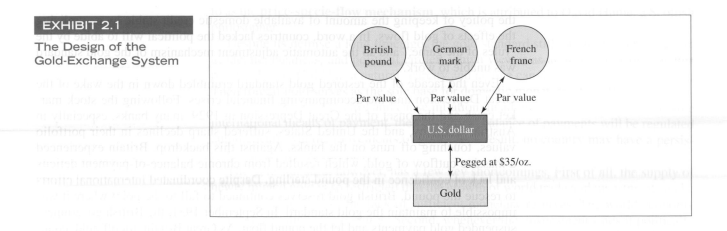

illustrated in Exhibit 2.1. Each country was responsible for maintaining its exchange rate within ±1 percent of the adopted par value by buying or selling foreign exchanges as necessary. However, a member country with a "fundamental disequilibrium" may be allowed to make a change in the par value of its currency. Under the Bretton Woods system, the U.S. dollar was the only currency that was fully convertible to gold; other currencies were not directly convertible to gold. Countries held U.S. dollars, as well as gold, for use as an international means of payment. Because of these arrangements, the Bretton Woods system can be described as a dollar-based **gold-exchange standard**. A country on the gold-exchange standard holds most of its reserves in the form of currency of a country that is *really* on the gold standard.

Advocates of the gold-exchange system argue that the system economizes on gold because countries can use not only gold but also foreign exchanges as an international means of payment. Foreign exchange reserves offset the deflationary effects of limited addition to the world's monetary gold stock. Another advantage of the gold-exchange system is that individual countries can earn interest on their foreign exchange holdings, whereas gold holdings yield no returns. In addition, countries can save transaction costs associated with transporting gold across countries under the gold-exchange system. An ample supply of international monetary reserves coupled with stable exchange rates provided an environment highly conducive to the growth of international trade and investment throughout the 1950s and 1960s.

Professor Robert Triffin warned, however, that the gold-exchange system was programmed to collapse in the long run. To satisfy the growing need for reserves, the United States had to run balance-of-payments deficits continuously, thereby supplying the dollar to the rest of the world. Yet if the United States ran perennial balance-of-payments deficits, it would eventually impair the public confidence in the dollar, triggering a run on the dollar. Under the gold-exchange system, the reserve-currency country should run balance-of-payments deficits to supply reserves, but if such deficits are large and persistent, they can lead to a crisis of confidence in the reserve currency itself, causing the downfall of the system. This dilemma, known as the **Triffin paradox**, was indeed responsible for the eventual collapse of the dollar-based gold-exchange system in the early 1970s.

The United States began to experience trade deficits with the rest of the world in the late 1950s, and the problem persisted into the 1960s. By the early 1960s the total value of the U.S. gold stock, when valued at $35 per ounce, fell short of foreign dollar holdings. This naturally created concern about the viability of the dollar-based system. Against this backdrop, President Charles de Gaulle prodded the Bank of France to buy gold from the U.S. Treasury, unloading its dollar holdings. Efforts to remedy the problem centered on (i) a series of dollar defense measures taken by the U.S. government and (ii) the creation of a new reserve asset, **special drawing rights (SDRs)**, by the IMF.

In 1963, President John Kennedy imposed the Interest Equalization Tax (IET) on U.S. purchases of foreign securities in order to stem the outflow of dollars. The IET was designed to increase the cost of foreign borrowing in the U.S. bond market. In 1965, the Federal Reserve introduced the U.S. voluntary Foreign Credit Restraint Program (FCRP), which regulated the amount of dollars U.S. banks could lend to U.S. multinational companies engaged in foreign direct investments. In 1968, these regulations became legally binding. Such measures as IET and FCRP lent a strong impetus to the rapid growth of the Eurodollar market, which is a transnational, unregulated fund market.

www.imf.org/external/fin.htm

Provides detailed information about the SDR, such as SDR exchange rates, interests, allocations, etc.

To partially alleviate the pressure on the dollar as the central reserve currency, the IMF created an artificial international reserve called the SDR in 1970. The SDR, which is a basket currency comprising major individual currencies, was allotted to the members of the IMF, who could then use it for transactions among themselves or with the IMF. In addition to gold and foreign exchanges, countries could use the SDR to make international payments.

Initially, the SDR was designed to be the weighted average of 16 currencies of those countries whose shares in world exports were more than 1 percent. The percentage share of each currency in the SDR was about the same as the country's share in world exports. In 1981, however, the SDR was greatly simplified to comprise only five major currencies: U.S. dollar, German mark, Japanese yen, British pound, and French franc. As Exhibit 2.2 shows, the weight for each currency is updated periodically, reflecting the relative importance of each country in the world trade of goods and services and the amount of the currencies held as reserves by the members of the IMF. Currently, the SDR is composed of four major currencies—the U.S. dollar (41.9 percent weight), euro (37.4 percent), British pound (11.3 percent), and Japanese yen (9.4 percent).

The SDR is used not only as a reserve asset but also as a denomination currency for international transactions. Since the SDR is a "portfolio" of currencies, its value tends to be more stable than the value of any individual currency included in the SDR. The portfolio nature of the SDR makes it an attractive denomination currency for international commercial and financial contracts under exchange rate uncertainty.

The efforts to support the dollar-based gold-exchange standard, however, turned out to be ineffective in the face of expansionary monetary policy and rising inflation in the United States, which were related to the financing of the Vietnam War and the Great Society program. In the early 1970s, it became clear that the dollar was over-valued, especially relative to the mark and the yen. As a result, the German and Japanese central banks had to make massive interventions in the foreign exchange market to maintain their par values. Given the unwillingness of the United States to control its monetary expansion, the repeated central bank interventions could not solve the underlying disparities. In August 1971, President Richard Nixon suspended the convertibility of the dollar into gold and imposed a 10 percent import surcharge. The foundation of the Bretton Woods system began to crack under the strain.

EXHIBIT 2.2		The Composition of the Special Drawing Right (SDR)[a]					
Currencies	1981–85	1986–90	1991–95	1996–2000	2001–2005	2006–2010	2011–
U.S. dollar	42%	42%	40%	39%	45%	44%	41.9%
Euro	—	—	—	—	29	34	37.4
German mark	19	19	21	21	—	—	—
Japanese yen	13	15	17	18	15	11	9.4
British pound	13	12	11	11	11	11	11.3
French franc	13	12	11	11	—	—	—

[a]The composition of the SDR changes every 5 years.

Source: The International Monetary Fund.

in small amounts at a fixed rate or in response to changes in selected quantitative indicators, such as past inflation differentials vis-à-vis major trading partners or differentials between the inflation target and expected inflation in major trading partners. Examples are Bolivia and Nicaragua.

Crawl-like arrangement: The exchange rate must remain within a narrow margin of 2 percent relative to a statistically identified trend for six months or more (with the exception of a specified number of outliers), and the exchange rate arrangement cannot be considered as floating. Usually, a minimum rate of change greater than allowed under a stabilized (peg-like) arrangement is required. Ethiopia, China, and Croatia are examples.

Pegged exchange rate within horizontal bands: The value of the currency is maintained within certain margins of fluctuation of at least ±1 percent around a fixed central rate, or the margin between the maximum and minimum value of the exchange rate exceeds 2 percent. Tonga is the only example.

Other managed arrangement: This category is a residual, and is used when the exchange rate arrangement does not meet the criteria for any of the other categories. Arrangements characterized by frequent shifts in policies may fall into this category. Examples are Costa Rica, Switzerland, and Russia.

Floating: A floating exchange rate is largely market determined, without an ascertainable or predictable path for the rate. In particular, an exchange rate that satisfies the statistical criteria for a stabilized or a crawl-like arrangement will be classified as such unless it is clear that the stability of the exchange rate is not the result of official actions. Foreign exchange market intervention may be either direct or indirect, and serves to moderate the rate of change and prevent undue fluctuations in the exchange rate, but policies targeting a specific level of the exchange rate are incompatible with floating. Examples include Brazil, Korea, Turkey, and India.

Free floating: A floating exchange rate can be classified as *free floating* if intervention occurs only exceptionally and aims to address disorderly market conditions and if the authorities have provided information or data confirming that intervention has been limited to at most three instances in the previous six months, each lasting no more than three business days. Examples are Canada, Mexico, Japan, Israel, U.K., United States, and euro zone.

As of April 2012, a large number of countries (31), including Australia, Canada, Japan, the United Kingdom, euro area, and the United States, allow their currencies to float freely against other currencies; the exchange rates of these countries are essentially determined by market forces. Thirty-five countries, including India, Brazil, and Korea, adopt floating exchange rates that are largely market determined. In contrast, 13 countries do not have their own national currencies. For example, Panama and Ecuador are using the U.S. dollar. Twelve countries, including Bulgaria, Hong Kong SAR, and Dominica, on the other hand, maintain national currencies, but they are permanently fixed to such hard currencies as the U.S. dollar or euro. The remaining countries adopt a mixture of fixed and floating exchange rate regimes. As is well known, the European Union has pursued Europe-wide monetary integration by first establishing the European Monetary System and then the European Monetary Union. These topics deserve a detailed discussion.

European Monetary System

According to the Smithsonian Agreement, which was signed in December 1971, the band of exchange rate movements was expanded from the original plus or minus 1 percent to plus or minus 2.25 percent. Members of the European Economic

Community (EEC), however, decided on a narrower band of ±1.125 percent for their currencies. This scaled-down, European version of the (quasi-) fixed exchange rate system that arose concurrently with the decline of the Bretton Woods system was called the **snake**. The name "snake" was derived from the way the EEC currencies moved closely together within the wider band allowed for other currencies like the dollar.

The EEC countries adopted the snake because they felt that stable exchange rates among the EEC countries were essential for promoting intra-EEC trade and deepening economic integration. The snake arrangement was replaced by the **European Monetary System (EMS)** in 1979. The EMS, which was originally proposed by German Chancellor Helmut Schmidt, was formally launched in March 1979. Among its chief objectives are:

1. To establish a "zone of monetary stability" in Europe.
2. To coordinate exchange rate policies vis-à-vis the non-EMS currencies.
3. To pave the way for the eventual European monetary union.

At the political level, the EMS represented a Franco-German initiative to speed up the movement toward European economic and political unification. All EEC member countries, except the United Kingdom and Greece, joined the EMS. The two main instruments of the EMS are the European Currency Unit and the Exchange Rate Mechanism.

The **European Currency Unit (ECU)** is a "basket" currency constructed as a weighted average of the currencies of member countries of the European Union (EU). The weights are based on each currency's relative GNP and share in intra-EU trade. The ECU serves as the accounting unit of the EMS and plays an important role in the workings of the exchange rate mechanism.

The **Exchange Rate Mechanism (ERM)** refers to the procedure by which EMS member countries collectively manage their exchange rates. The ERM is based on a "parity grid" system, which is a system of par values among ERM currencies. The par values in the parity grid are computed by first defining the par values of EMS currencies in terms of the ECU.

When the EMS was launched in 1979, a currency was allowed to deviate from the parities with other currencies by a maximum of plus or minus 2.25 percent, with the exception of the Italian lira, for which a maximum deviation of plus or minus 6 percent was allowed. In September 1993, however, the band was widened to a maximum of plus or minus 15 percent. When a currency is at the lower or upper bound, the central banks of both countries are required to intervene in the foreign exchange markets to keep the market exchange rate within the band. To intervene in the exchange markets, the central banks can borrow from a credit fund to which member countries contribute gold and foreign reserves.

Since the EMS members were less than fully committed to coordinating their economic policies, the EMS went through a series of realignments. The Italian lira, for instance, was devalued by 6 percent in July 1985 and again by 3.7 percent in January 1990. In September 1992, Italy and the U.K. pulled out of the ERM as high German interest rates were inducing massive capital flows into Germany. Following German reunification in October 1990, the German government experienced substantial budget deficits, which were not accommodated by the monetary policy. Germany would not lower its interest rates for fear of inflation, and the U.K. and Italy were not willing to raise their interest rates (which was necessary to maintain their exchange rates) for fear of higher unemployment. Italy, however, rejoined the ERM in December 1996 in an effort to participate in the European monetary union. However, the U.K. still remains outside the European monetary union.

Despite the recurrent turbulence in the EMS, European Union members met at Maastricht (Netherlands) in December 1991 and signed the **Maastricht Treaty**. According to the treaty, the EMS would irrevocably fix exchange rates among the member currencies by January 1, 1999, and subsequently introduce a common European currency, replacing individual national currencies. The European Central Bank, to be located in Frankfurt, Germany, would be solely responsible for the issuance of common currency and conducting monetary policy in the euro zone. National central banks of individual countries then would function pretty much like regional member banks of the U.S. Federal Reserve System. Exhibit 2.5 provides a chronology of the European Union.

To pave the way for the European Monetary Union (EMU), the member countries of the European Monetary System agreed to closely coordinate their fiscal, monetary, and exchange rate policies and achieve a convergence of their economies. Specifically, each member country shall strive to: (i) keep the ratio of government budget deficits to gross domestic product (GDP) below 3 percent, (ii) keep gross public debts below 60 percent of GDP, (iii) achieve a high degree of price stability, and (iv) maintain its currency within the prescribed exchange rate ranges of the ERM. Currently, "convergence" is the buzz word in such countries as the Czech Republic, Hungary, and Poland that may join the EMU in the future.

EXHIBIT 2.5 Chronology of the European Union	

1951	The treaty establishing the European Coal and Steel Community (ECSC), which was inspired by French Foreign Minister Robert Schuman, was signed in Paris by six countries: France, Germany, Italy, Netherlands, Belgium, and Luxembourg.
1957	The treaty establishing the European Economic Community (EEC) was signed in Rome.
1968	The Custom Union became fully operational; trade restrictions among the EEC member countries were abolished and a common external tariff system was established.
1973	The U.K., Ireland, and Denmark became EEC members.
1978	The EEC became the European Community (EC).
1979	The European Monetary System (EMS) was established for the purpose of promoting exchange rate stability among the EC member countries.
1980	Greece became an EC member.
1986	Portugal and Spain became EC members.
1987	The Single European Act was adopted to provide a framework within which the common internal market could be achieved by the end of 1992.
1991	The Maastricht Treaty was signed and subsequently ratified by 12 member states. The treaty establishes a timetable for fulfilling the European Monetary Union (EMU). The treaty also commits the EC to political union.
1994	The European Community was renamed the European Union (EU).
1995	Austria, Finland, and Sweden became EU members.
1999	A common European currency, the euro, was adopted by 11 EU member countries.
2001	Greece adopted the euro on January 1.
2002	Euro notes and coins were introduced; national currencies were withdrawn from circulation.
2004	EU expanded by admitting 10 new member countries: Cyprus, Czech Republic, Estonia, Hungary, Latvia, Lithuania, Malta, Poland, Slovak Republic, and Slovenia.
2007	Bulgaria and Romania were admitted to the EU. Slovenia adopted the euro.
2008	Cyprus and Malta adopted the euro.
2009	Slovakia adopted the euro.
2010	Europe's sovereign debt crisis.
2011	Estonia adopted the euro.
2013	Croatia joined the EU.
2014	Latvia adopted the euro.

The Euro and the European Monetary Union

On January 1, 1999, an epochal event took place in the arena of international finance: Eleven of 15 EU countries adopted a common currency called the euro, voluntarily giving up their monetary sovereignty. The original euro-11 includes Austria, Belgium, Finland, France, Germany, Ireland, Italy, Luxembourg, the Netherlands, Portugal, and Spain. Four member countries of the European Union—Denmark, Greece, Sweden, and the United Kingdom—did not join the first wave. Greece, however, joined the euro club in 2001 when it could satisfy the convergence criteria. Subsequently, Slovenia adopted the euro in 2007, and Cyprus and Malta did so in 2008. Slovakia adopted the euro in 2009 and Estonia did the same in 2011.

The advent of a European single currency, which may potentially rival the U.S. dollar as a global currency, has profound implications for various aspects of international finance. In this section, we are going to (i) describe briefly the historical background for the euro and its implementation process, (ii) discuss the potential benefits and costs of the euro from the perspective of the member countries, and (iii) investigate the broad impacts of the euro on international finance in general.

A Brief History of the Euro

Considering that no European currency has been in circulation since the fall of the Roman Empire, the advent of the euro in January 1999 indeed qualifies as an epochal event. The Roman emperor Gaius Diocletianus, A.D. 286–301, reformed the coinage and established a single currency throughout the realm. The advent of the euro also marks the first time that sovereign countries voluntarily have given up their monetary independence to foster economic integration. The euro thus represents a historically unprecedented experiment, the outcome of which will have far-reaching implications. If the experiment succeeds, for example, both the euro and the dollar will dominate the world of international finance. In addition, a successful euro may give a powerful impetus to the political unionization of Europe.

The euro should be viewed as a product of historical evolution toward an ever deepening integration of Europe, which began in earnest with the formation of the European Economic Community in 1958. As discussed previously, the European Monetary System (EMS) was created in 1979 to establish a European zone of monetary stability; members were required to restrict fluctuations of their currency exchange rates. In 1991, the Maastricht European Council reached agreement on a draft Treaty on the European Union, which called for the introduction of a single European currency by 1999. With the launching of the euro on January 1, 1999, the **European Monetary Union (EMU)** was created. The EMU is a logical extension of the EMS, and the European Currency Unit (ECU) was the precursor of the euro. Indeed, ECU contracts were required by EU law to be converted to euro contracts on a one-to-one basis.

As the euro was introduced, each national currency of the euro-11 countries was *irrevocably* fixed to the euro at a conversion rate as of January 1, 1999. The conversion rates are provided in Exhibit 2.6. On January 1, 2002, euro notes and coins were introduced to circulation while national bills and coins were being gradually withdrawn. Once the changeover was completed by July 1, 2002, the legal-tender status of national currencies was canceled, leaving the euro as the sole legal tender in the euro zone countries.

Monetary policy for the euro zone countries is now conducted by the **European Central Bank (ECB)** headquartered in Frankfurt, Germany, whose primary objective is to maintain price stability. The independence of the ECB is legally guaranteed so that in conducting its monetary policy, it will not be unduly subjected to political pressure from any member countries or institutions. By and large, the ECB is modeled after the German Bundesbank, which was highly successful in achieving price stability in Germany. Willem (Wim) Duisenberg, the first president of the ECB, who previously served as the president of the Dutch National Bank, defined "price stability" as an annual inflation rate of "less than but close to 2 percent."

www.ecb.int

Website of the European Central Bank offers a comprehensive coverage of the euro and links to EU central banks.

1 Euro Is Equal to	
Austrian schilling	13.7603
Belgian franc	40.3399
Dutch guilder	2.20371
Finnish markka	5.94573
French franc	6.55957
German mark	1.95583
Irish punt	0.78756
Italian lira	1936.27
Luxembourg franc	40.3399
Portuguese escudo	200.482
Spanish peseta	166.386

Source: *The Wall Street Journal.*

The national central banks of the euro zone countries will not disappear. Together with the European Central Bank, they form the **Eurosystem**, which is in a way similar to the Federal Reserve System of the United States. The tasks of the Eurosystem are threefold: (i) to define and implement the common monetary policy of the Union; (ii) to conduct foreign exchange operations; and (iii) to hold and manage the official foreign reserves of the euro member states. In addition, governors of national central banks will sit on the Governing Council of the ECB. Although national central banks will have to follow the policies of the ECB, they will continue to perform important functions in their jurisdiction such as distributing credit, collecting resources, and managing payment systems.

Before we proceed, let us briefly examine the behavior of exchange rate between the dollar and euro. Panel A of Exhibit 2.7 plots the daily dollar-euro exchange rate since the inception of the euro, whereas Panel B plots the rate of change of the exchange rate. As can be seen from Panel A, since its introduction at $1.18 per euro in January 1999, the euro was steadily depreciating against the dollar, reaching a low point of $0.83 per euro in October 2000. The depreciation of the euro during this period reflects the robust performance of the U.S. economy and massive European investments in the United States. From the start of 2002, however, the euro began to appreciate against the dollar, reaching a rough parity by July 2002. This, in turn, reflects a slowdown of the U.S. economy and lessening European investments in the United States. The euro continued to strengthen against the dollar, reaching $1.60 per euro in July 2008 before it started to fall as the global financial crisis spread. During a crisis period, the dollar tends to become stronger, reflecting investors' preference for the dollar as a safe haven. Although the euro began to rebound in early 2009, it started to fall again against the dollar as Europe's sovereign debt crisis hurt the euro's credibility. Panel B confirms that the dollar–euro exchange rate is highly volatile.

What Are the Benefits of Monetary Union?

The euro zone countries obviously decided to form a monetary union with a common currency because they believed the benefits from such a union would outweigh the associated costs—in contrast to those eligible countries that chose not to adopt the single currency. It is thus important to understand the potential benefits and costs of monetary union.

What are the main benefits from adopting a common currency? The most direct and immediate benefits are reduced transaction costs and the elimination of exchange rate uncertainty. There was a popular saying in Europe that if one travels through all EU countries, changing money in each country but not actually spending it, one returns home with only half the original amount. Once countries use the same currency, transactions costs will be reduced substantially. These savings will accrue to practically all economic agents, benefiting individuals, companies, and governments. Although it is difficult to estimate accurately the magnitude of foreign exchange transaction costs, a consensus estimation is around 0.4 percent of Europe's GDP.

EXHIBIT 2.7 The Daily Dollar-Euro Exchange Rate since the Euro's Inception

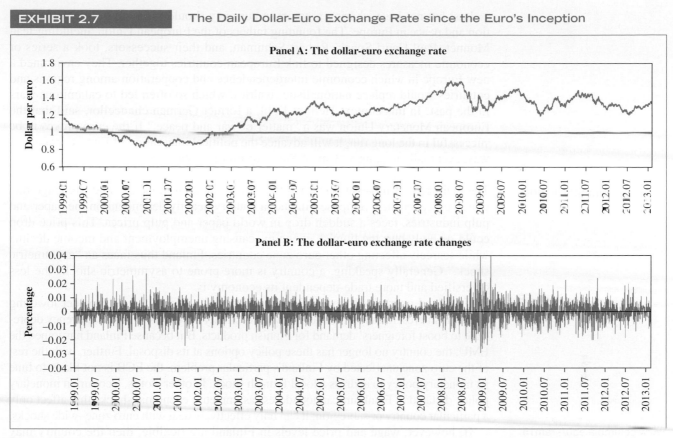

Panel A: The dollar-euro exchange rate

Panel B: The dollar-euro exchange rate changes

Source: IMF, *International Financial Statistics*, www.exchange-rates.org.

Economic agents should also benefit from the elimination of exchange rate uncertainty. Companies will not suffer currency loss anymore from intra–euro zone transactions. Companies that used to hedge exchange risk will save hedging costs. As price comparison becomes easier because of the common currency, consumers can benefit from comparison shopping. Increased price transparency will promote Europewide competition, exerting a downward pressure on prices. Reduced transaction costs and the elimination of currency risk together will have the net effect of promoting cross-border investment and trade within the euro zone. By furthering the economic integration of Europe, the single currency will promote corporate restructuring via mergers and acquisitions, encourage optimal business location decisions, and ultimately strengthen the international competitive position of European companies. Thus, the enhanced efficiency and competitiveness of the European economy can be regarded as the third major benefit of the monetary union.

The advent of the common European currency also helps create conditions conducive to the development of continental capital markets with depth and liquidity comparable to those of the United States. In the past, national currencies and a localized legal/regulatory framework resulted in largely illiquid, fragmented capital markets in Europe, which prevented European companies from raising capital on competitive terms. The common currency and the integration of European financial markets pave the way for a European capital market in which both European and non-European companies can raise money at favorable rates. A study by Bris, Koskinen, and Nilsson (2004) indeed documents that the adoption of the euro as the common European currency has lowered firms' cost of capital in the euro zone and enhanced the firm value by about 17 percent on average. The increases in firm valuation are larger for firms that were exposed to intra-European currency risks, that is, those firms that were expected to benefit more from the common currency.

Last but not least, sharing a common currency should promote political cooperation and peace in Europe. The founding fathers of the European Union, including Jean Monnet, Paul-Henri Spaak, Robert Schuman, and their successors, took a series of economic measures designed to link European countries together. They envisioned a new Europe in which economic interdependence and cooperation among regions and countries would replace nationalistic rivalries, which so often led to calamitous wars in the past. In this context Helmut Kohl, a former German chancellor, said that the European Monetary Union was a "matter of war and peace." If the euro proves to be successful in the long run, it will advance the political integration of Europe in a major way, eventually making a "United States of Europe" feasible.

Costs of Monetary Union

The main cost of monetary union is the loss of national monetary and exchange rate policy independence. Suppose Finland, a country heavily dependent on the paper and pulp industries, faces a sudden drop in world paper and pulp prices. This price drop could severely hurt the Finnish economy, causing unemployment and income decline while scarcely affecting other euro zone countries. Finland thus faces an "asymmetric shock." Generally speaking, a country is more prone to asymmetric shocks the less diversified and more trade-dependent its economy is.

If Finland maintained monetary independence, the country could consider lowering domestic interest rates to stimulate the weak economy as well as letting its currency depreciate to boost foreigners' demand for Finnish products. But because Finland has joined the EMU, the country no longer has these policy options at its disposal. Further, with the rest of the euro zone unaffected by Finland's particular problem, the ECB is not likely to tune its monetary policy to address a local Finnish shock. In other words, a common monetary policy dictated in Frankfurt cannot address asymmetric economic shocks that affect only a particular country or subregion; it can only effectively deal with euro zone–wide shocks.

If, however, wage and price levels in Finland are flexible, then the country may still be able to deal with an asymmetric shock; lower wage and price levels in Finland would have economic effects similar to those of a depreciation of the Finnish currency. Furthermore, if capital flows freely across the euro zone and workers are willing to relocate to where jobs are, then again much of the asymmetric shock can be absorbed without monetary adjustments. If these conditions are not met, however, the asymmetric shock can cause a severe and prolonged economic dislocation in the affected country. In this case, monetary union will become a costly venture. According to the theory of **optimum currency areas**, originally conceived by Professor Robert Mundell of Columbia University, the relevant criterion for identifying and designing a common currency zone is the degree of factor (i.e., capital and labor) mobility within the zone; a high degree of factor mobility would provide an adjustment mechanism, providing an alternative to country-specific monetary/currency adjustments.

Considering the high degree of capital and labor mobility in the United States, one might argue that the United States approximates an optimum currency area; it would be suboptimal for each of the 50 states to issue its own currency. In contrast, unemployed workers in Helsinki, for example, are not very likely to move to Amsterdam or Stuttgart for job opportunities because of cultural, religious, linguistic, and other barriers. The stability pact of EMU, designed to discourage irresponsible fiscal behavior in the post-EMU era, also constrains the Finnish government to restrict its budget deficit to 3 percent of GDP at most. At the same time, Finland cannot expect to receive a major transfer payment from Brussels, because of a rather low degree of fiscal integration among EU countries. These considerations taken together suggest that the European Monetary Union will involve significant economic costs. Due to the sluggish economic conditions, France and Germany often let the budget deficit exceed the 3 percent limit. This violation of the stability pact compromises the fiscal discipline necessary for supporting the euro.

An empirical study by von Hagen and Neumann (1994) identified Austria, Belgium, France, Luxembourg, the Netherlands, and Germany as nations that satisfy the conditions for an optimum currency area. However, Denmark, Italy, and the United

www.columbia.edu/~ram15

This homepage of Professor Robert Mundell provides a synopsis of his academic works, Nobel lecture, etc.

Kingdom do not. It is noted that Denmark and the United Kingdom actually chose to stay out of the EMU. Von Hagen and Neumann's study suggests that Italy joined the EMU prematurely. It is interesting to note that some politicians in Italy blame the country's economic woes on the adoption of the euro and argue for the restoration of Italian lira. The International Finance in Practice box, "Mundell Wins Nobel Prize in Economics," explains Professor Mundell's view on the monetary union.

Prospects of the Euro: Some Critical Questions

Will the euro survive and succeed in the long run? The first real test of the euro will come when the euro zone experiences major asymmetric shocks. A successful response to these shocks will require wage, price, and fiscal flexibility. A cautionary note is in order: Asymmetric shocks can occur even within a country. In the United States, for example, when oil prices jumped in the 1970s, oil-consuming regions such as New England suffered a severe recession, whereas Texas, a major oil-producing state, experienced a major boom. Likewise, in Italy, the highly industrialized Genoa–Milan region and the southern Mezzogiorno, an underdeveloped region, can be in very different phases of the business cycle. But these countries have managed their economies with a common national monetary policy. Although asymmetric shocks are no doubt more serious internationally, one should be careful not to exaggerate their significance as an impediment to monetary union. In addition, since the advent of the EMS in 1979, the EMU member countries have restricted their monetary policies in order to maintain exchange rate stability in Europe. Considering that intra–euro zone trade accounts for about 60 percent of foreign trade of the euro zone countries, benefits from the EMU may exceed the associated costs. Furthermore, leaders in political and business circles in Europe have invested substantial political capital in the success of the euro. So long as Europe can resolve internal frictions and imbalances as revealed in the Greek debt crisis, it seems safe to predict that the euro will survive. Despite the bailout funds and austerity programs, however, if southern European countries, i.e., Greece, Portugal, and Spain, fail to reduce debts and restart economic growth in the near future, they may reach the tipping point where people can no longer sustain job loss and other economic pains and demand the exit from euro zone. Thus, the future of the euro as the common currency critically depends on whether or not these countries can find a way of growing their economies while retaining the euro. At the moment, the jury is still out on this question.

Will the euro become a global currency rivaling the U.S. dollar? The U.S. dollar has been the dominant global currency since the end of the First World War, replacing the British pound as the currency of choice in international commercial and financial transactions. Even after the dollar got off the gold anchor in 1971, it retained its dominant position in the world economy. This dominance was possible because the dollar was backed by the sheer size of the U.S. economy and the relatively sound monetary policy of the Federal Reserve. Now, as can be seen from Exhibit 2.8, the euro zone is comparable to the United States in terms of population size, GDP, and international

EXHIBIT 2.8

Macroeconomic Data for Major Economies[a]

Economy	Population (Million)	GDP ($ Trillion)	Annual Inflation	World Trade Share	International Bonds Outstanding ($ Billion)
United States	314.8	15.6	2.4%	10.2%	7183.5
Euro zone	332.8	12.2	2.2%	14.1%	7636.7
Japan	127.5	5.9	−0.3%	4.6%	474.1
United Kingdom	63.2	2.4	2.9%	3.1%	1187.0

[a]The inflation rate is the annual average from 1999–2012. The international bonds outstanding refer to international bonds and notes outstanding by December 2012 by currency of issue. The remaining data are 2012 figures.

Source: IMF, *International Financial Statistics,* European Commission Economic and Financial Affairs.

Mundell Wins Nobel Prize in Economics

Robert A. Mundell, one of the intellectual fathers of both the new European common currency and Reagan-era supply-side economics, won the Nobel Memorial Prize in Economic Science.

Mr. Mundell conducted innovative research into common currencies when the idea of the euro, Europe's new currency, was still a fantasy. The 66-year-old Columbia University professor, a native of Canada, also examined the implications of cross-border capital flows and flexible foreign-exchange rates when capital flows were still restricted and currencies still fixed to each other.

"Mundell chose his problems with uncommon—almost prophetic—accuracy in terms of predicting the future development of international monetary arrangements and capital markets," the selection committee said in announcing the prize.

An eccentric, white-haired figure who once bought an abandoned Italian castle as a hedge against inflation, Mr. Mundell later became a hero of the economic Right with his dogged defense of the gold standard and early advocacy of the controversial tax-cutting, supply-side economics that became the hallmark of the Reagan administration.

While the Nobel committee sidestepped his political impact in awarding Mr. Mundell the $975,000 prize for his work in the 1960s, his conservative fans celebrated the award as an endorsement of supply-side thinking.

"I know it will take a little longer, but history eventually will note that it was Mundell who made it possible for Ronald Reagan to be elected president," by providing the intellectual backing for the Reagan tax cuts, wrote conservative economist Jude Wanniski on his website.

Mr. Mundell's advocacy of supply-side economics sprang from his work in the 1960s examining what fiscal

Mundell's View

Great currencies and great powers according to Robert Mundell:

Country	Period
Greece	7th–3rd C. B.C.
Persia	6th–4th C. B.C.
Macedonia	4th–2nd C. B.C.
Rome	2nd C. B.C.–4th C.
Byzantium	5th–13th C.
Franks	8th–11th C.
Italian city states	13th–16th C.
France	13th–18th C.
Holland	17th–18th C.
Germany (thaler)	14th–19th C.
France (franc)	1803–1870
Britain (pound)	1820–1914
U.S. (dollar)	1915–present
E.U. (euro)	1999

Source: The Euro and the Stability of the International Monetary System, Robert Mundell, Columbia University.

and monetary policies are appropriate if exchange rates are either fixed—as they were prior to the collapse of the gold-based Bretton Woods system in the early 1970s—or floating, as they are in the U.S. and many other countries today.

One major finding has since become conventional wisdom: When money can move freely across borders, policy makers must choose between exchange-rate stability and an independent monetary policy. They can't have both.

trade share. Exhibit 2.8 also shows that the euro is as important a denomination currency as the dollar in international bond markets. In contrast, the Japanese yen plays an insignificant role in international bond markets. As previously discussed, there is little doubt that the ECB will pursue a sound monetary policy. Reflecting both the size of the euro zone economy and the mandate of the ECB, the euro is emerging as the second global currency, challenging the dollar's sole dominance. The Japanese yen is likely to be a junior partner in the dollar–euro condominium. However, the emergence of the euro as another global currency may prompt Japan and other Asian countries to explore cooperative monetary arrangements for the region.

The Mexican Peso Crisis

On December 20, 1994, the Mexican government under new president Ernesto Zedillo announced its decision to devalue the peso against the dollar by 14 percent. This decision, however, touched off a stampede to sell pesos as well as Mexican stocks and

Mr. Mundell's work has long had an impact on policy makers. In 1962, he wrote a paper addressing the Kennedy administration's predicament of how to spur the economy while facing a balance-of-payments deficit. "The only correct way to do it was to have a tax cut and then protect the balance of payments by tight money," he recalled in a 1996 interview. The Kennedy administration eventually came around to the same way of thinking.

Mr. Mundell traces the supply-side movement to a 1971 meeting of distinguished economists, including Paul Volcker and Paul Samuelson, at the Treasury Department. At the time, most economists were stumped by the onset of stagflation—a combination of inflationary pressures, a troubled dollar, a worsening balance of payments and persistent unemployment. They thought any tightening of monetary or fiscal policy would bolster the dollar and improve the balance of payments, but worsen unemployment. An easing of monetary or fiscal policy might generate jobs, but weaken the dollar, lift prices and expand the balance-of-payments deficit.

Mr. Mundell suggested a heretical solution: Raise interest rates to protect the dollar, but cut taxes to spur the economy. Most others in the room were aghast at the idea, fearing tax cuts would lead to a swelling budget deficit—something many nonsupply-siders believe was exactly what happened during the Reagan years.

"I knew I was in the minority," he said in an 1988 interview. "But I thought my vote should count much more than the others because I understood the subject."

At the University of Chicago early in his career, Mr. Mundell befriended a student named Arthur Laffer, and together they were at the core of the supply-side movement. Even today, Mr. Mundell predicts similar policies will be necessary to keep the U.S. economic expansion going. "Monetary policy isn't going to be enough to stay up there and avoid a recession," he said in an interview yesterday. "We'll have to have tax reduction, too."

While in Chicago, he found himself constantly at odds with Milton Friedman, who advocated monetary rules and floating exchange rates. Mr. Mundell joined Columbia in 1974, two years before Mr. Friedman won the economics Nobel.

Ever the maverick, Mr. Mundell remains a fan of the gold standard and fixed exchange rates at a time when they're out of favor with most other economists. "You have fixed rates between New York and California, and it works perfectly," he said.

The Nobel committee also praised Mr. Mundell's research into common currency zones, which laid the intellectual foundation for the 11-country euro. In 1961, when European countries still clung to their national currencies, he described the circumstances in which nations could share a common currency.

"At the time, it just seemed like such a wacko thing to work on, and that's why it's so visionary," said Kenneth Rogoff, a Harvard economist.

In particular, Mr. Mundell argued that in any successful currency zone, workers must be able to move freely from areas that are slowing to areas that are booming. Some critics suggest the euro nations don't fit his description.

But Mr. Mundell believes the new currency will eventually challenge the dollar for global dominance. "The benefits will derive from transparency of pricing, stability of expectations and lower transactions costs, as well as a common monetary policy run by the best minds that Europe can muster," Mr. Mundell wrote last year. He began working on the euro project as a consultant to European monetary authorities in 1969.

Outside academia, Mr. Mundell has led a colorful life. Worried about the onset of inflation in the late 1960s, he bought and renovated a 16th century Italian castle originally built for Pandolfo Petrucci, the "Strong Man of Siena." Mr. Mundell has four children, who range in age from one to 40.

Source: Michael M. Phillips, *The Wall Street Journal*, October 14, 1999. p. A2. © 1999 Dow Jones & Company, Inc. All Rights Reserved Worldwide.

bonds. As Exhibit 2.9 shows, by early January 1995 the peso had fallen against the U.S. dollar by as much as 40 percent, forcing the Mexican government to float the peso. As concerned international investors reduced their holdings of emerging market securities, the peso crisis rapidly spilled over to other Latin American and Asian financial markets.

Faced with an impending default by the Mexican government and the possibility of a global financial meltdown, the Clinton administration, together with the International Monetary Fund (IMF) and the Bank for International Settlement (BIS), put together a $53 billion package to bail out Mexico.[8] As the bailout plan was put together and announced on January 31, the world's, as well as Mexico's, financial markets began to stabilize.

---

[8]The United States contributed $20 billion out of its Exchange Stabilization Fund, whereas IMF and BIS contributed, respectively, $17.8 billion and $10 billion. Canada, Latin American countries, and commercial banks collectively contributed $5 billion.

EXHIBIT 2.9

U.S. Dollar versus
Mexican Peso Exchange
Rate (November 1,
1994–January 31, 1995)

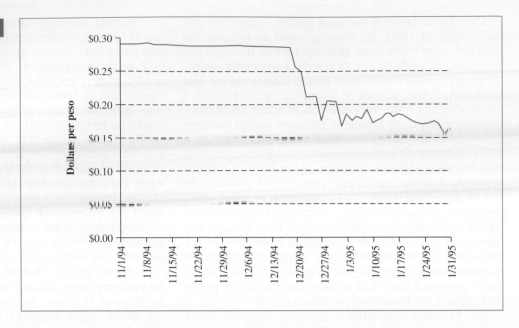

The Mexican peso crisis is significant in that it is perhaps the first serious international financial crisis touched off by cross-border flight of portfolio capital. International mutual funds are known to have invested more than $45 billion in Mexican securities during a three-year period prior to the peso crisis. As the peso fell, fund managers quickly liquidated their holdings of Mexican securities as well as other emerging market securities. This had a highly destabilizing, contagious effect on the world financial system.

As the world's financial markets are becoming more integrated, this type of contagious financial crisis is likely to occur more often. Two lessons emerge from the peso crisis. First, it is essential to have a multinational safety net in place to safeguard the world financial system from the peso-type crisis. No single country or institution can handle a potentially global crisis alone. In addition, the usually slow and parochial political processes cannot cope with rapidly changing market conditions. In fact, the Clinton administration faced stiff opposition in Congress and from foreign allies when it was working out a bailout package for Mexico. As a result, early containment of the crisis was not possible. Fortunately, the G-7 countries endorsed a $50 billion bailout fund for countries in financial distress, which would be administered by the IMF, and a series of increased disclosure requirements to be followed by all countries. The reluctance of the outgoing Salinas administration to disclose the true state of the Mexican economy, that is, the rapid depletion of foreign exchange reserves and serious trade deficits, contributed to the sudden collapse of the peso. Transparency always helps prevent financial crises.

Second, Mexico excessively depended on foreign portfolio capital to finance its economic development. In hindsight, the country should have saved more domestically and depended more on long-term rather than short-term foreign capital investments. As Professor Robert MacKinnon of Stanford University pointed out, a flood of foreign money had two undesirable effects. It led to an easy credit policy on domestic borrowings, which caused Mexicans to consume more and save less.[9] Foreign capital influx also caused a higher domestic inflation and an overvalued peso, which hurt Mexico's trade balances.

[9]See "Flood of Dollars, Sunken Pesos," *New York Times*, January 20, 1995, p. A2g.

The Asian Currency Crisis

On July 2, 1997, the Thai baht, which had been largely fixed to the U.S. dollar, was suddenly devalued. What at first appeared to be a local financial crisis in Thailand quickly escalated into a global financial crisis, first spreading to other Asian countries—Indonesia, Korea, Malaysia, and the Philippines—then far afield to Russia and Latin America, especially Brazil. As can be seen from Exhibit 2.10, at the height of the crisis the Korean won fell by about 50 percent in its dollar value from its precrisis level, whereas the Indonesian rupiah fell an incredible 80 percent.

The 1997 Asian crisis was the third major currency crisis of the 1990s, preceded by the crises of the European Monetary System (EMS) of 1992 and the Mexican peso in 1994–95. The Asian crisis, however, turned out to be far more serious than its two predecessors in terms of the extent of contagion and the severity of resultant economic and social costs. Following the massive depreciations of local currencies, financial institutions and corporations with foreign-currency debts in the afflicted countries were driven to extreme financial distress and many were forced to default. What's worse, the currency crisis led to an unprecedentedly deep, widespread, and long-lasting recession in East Asia, a region that, for the last few decades, has enjoyed the most rapidly growing economy in the world. At the same time, many lenders and investors from the developed countries also suffered large capital losses from their investments in emerging-market securities. For example, Long Term Capital Management (LTCM), one of the largest and, until then, profitable hedge funds, experienced a near bankruptcy due to its exposure to Russian bonds. In mid-August 1998, the Russian ruble fell sharply from 6.3 rubles per dollar to about 20 rubles per dollar. The prices of Russian stocks and bonds also fell sharply. The Federal Reserve System, which feared a domino-like systemic financial failure in the United States, orchestrated a $3.5 billion bailout of LTCM in September 1998.

Given the global effects of the Asian currency crisis and the challenges it poses for the world financial system, it would be useful to understand its origins and causes and discuss how similar crises might be prevented in the future.

EXHIBIT 2.10

Asian Currency Crisis

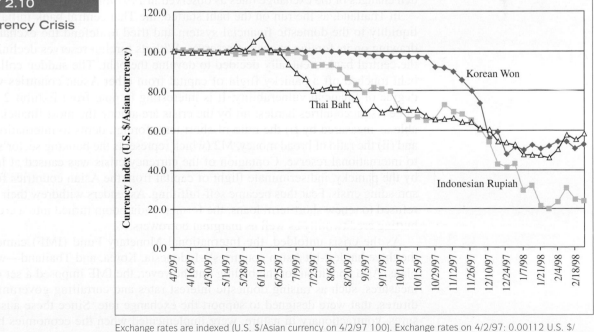

Exchange rates are indexed (U.S. $/Asian currency on 4/2/97 100). Exchange rates on 4/2/97: 0.00112 U.S. $/Korean won, 0.03856 U.S. $/Thai baht, and 0.00041 U.S. $/Indonesian rupiah.

Origins of the Asian Currency Crisis

Several factors are responsible for the onset of the Asian currency crisis: a weak domestic financial system, free international capital flows, the contagion effects of changing market sentiment, and inconsistent economic policies. In recent decades, both developing and developed countries were encouraged to liberalize their financial markets and allow free flows of capital across countries. As capital markets were liberalized, both firms and financial institutions in the Asian developing countries eagerly borrowed foreign currencies from U.S., Japanese, and European investors, who were attracted to these fast-growing emerging markets for extra returns for their portfolios. In 1996 alone, for example, five Asian countries—Indonesia, Korea, Malaysia, the Philippines, and Thailand—experienced an inflow of private capital worth $93 billion. In contrast, there was a net outflow of $12 billion from the five countries in 1997.

Large inflows of private capital resulted in a credit boom in the Asian countries in the early and mid-1990s. The credit boom was often directed to speculations in real estate and stock markets as well as to investments in marginal industrial projects. Fixed or stable exchange rates also encouraged unhedged financial transactions and excessive risk-taking by both lenders and borrowers, who were not much concerned with exchange risk. As asset prices declined (as happened in Thailand prior to the currency crisis) in part due to the government's effort to control the overheated economy, the quality of banks' loan portfolios also declined as the same assets were held as collateral for the loans. Clearly, banks and other financial institutions in the afflicted countries practiced poor risk management and were poorly supervised. In addition, their lending decisions were often influenced by political considerations, likely leading to suboptimal allocation of resources. However, the so-called crony capitalism was not a new condition, and the East Asian economies achieved an economic miracle under the same system.

Meanwhile, the booming economy with a fixed or stable nominal exchange rate inevitably brought about an appreciation of the real exchange rate. This, in turn, resulted in a marked slowdown in export growth in such Asian countries as Thailand and Korea. In addition, a long-lasting recession in Japan and the yen's depreciation against the dollar hurt Japan's neighbors, further worsening the trade balances of the Asian developing countries. If the Asian currencies had been allowed to depreciate in real terms, which was not possible because of the fixed nominal exchange rates, such catastrophic, sudden changes of the exchange rates as observed in 1997 might have been avoided.

In Thailand, as the run on the baht started, the Thai central bank initially injected liquidity to the domestic financial system and tried to defend the exchange rate by drawing on its foreign exchange reserves. With its foreign reserves declining rapidly, the central bank eventually decided to devalue the baht. The sudden collapse of the baht touched off a panicky flight of capital from other Asian countries with a high degree of financial vulnerability. It is interesting to note from Exhibit 2.11 that the three Asian countries hardest hit by the crisis are among the most financially vulnerable as measured by (i) the ratio of short-term foreign debts to international reserve and (ii) the ratio of broad money, M2 (which represents the banking sector's liabilities) to international reserve. Contagion of the currency crisis was caused at least in part by the panicky, indiscriminate flight of capital from the Asian countries for fear of a spreading crisis. Fear thus became self-fulfilling. As lenders withdrew their capital and refused to renew short-term loans, the former credit boom turned into a credit crunch, hurting creditworthy as well as marginal borrowers.

As the crisis unfolded, the International Monetary Fund (IMF) came to rescue the three hardest-hit Asian countries—Indonesia, Korea, and Thailand—with bailout plans. As a condition for the bailing out, however, the IMF imposed a set of austerity measures, such as raising domestic interest rates and curtailing government expenditures, that were designed to support the exchange rate. Since these austerity measures, contractionary in nature, were implemented when the economies had already been contracting because of a severe credit crunch, the Asian economies consequently

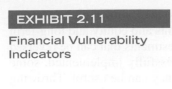

EXHIBIT 2.11

Financial Vulnerability
Indicators

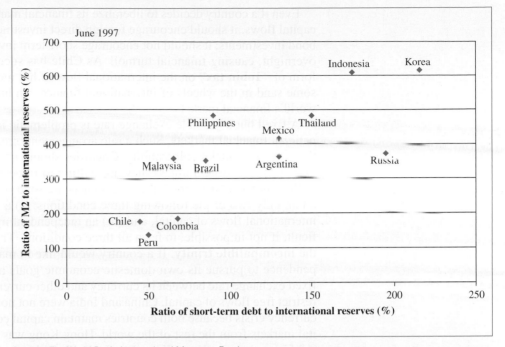

June 1997

Source: The World Bank, International Monetary Fund.

suffered a deep, long-lasting recession. According to a World Bank report (1999), one-year declines in industrial production of 20 percent or more in Thailand and Indonesia are comparable to those in the United States and Germany during the Great Depression. One can thus argue that the IMF initially prescribed the wrong medicine for the afflicted Asian economies. The IMF bailout plans were also criticized on another ground: moral hazard. IMF bailouts may breed dependency in developing countries and encourage risk-taking on the part of international lenders. There is a sentiment that taxpayers' money should not be used to bail out "fat-cat" investors. Former U.S. senator Lauch Faircloth was quoted as saying: "Through the IMF we have privatized profits and socialized losses." No bailout, however, can be compared with the proposal to get rid of the only fire department in town so that people will be more careful about fire.

Lessons from the Asian Currency Crisis

www.adb.org

Provides a broad coverage of Asian financial developments.

Generally speaking, liberalization of financial markets when combined with a weak, underdeveloped domestic financial system tends to create an environment susceptible to currency and financial crises. Interestingly, both Mexico and Korea experienced a major currency crisis within a few years after joining the OECD, which required a significant liberalization of financial markets. It seems safe to recommend that countries first strengthen their domestic financial system and then liberalize their financial markets.

A number of measures can and should be undertaken to strengthen a nation's domestic financial system. Among other things, the government should strengthen its system of financial-sector regulation and supervision. One way of doing so is to sign on to the "Core Principle of Effective Banking Supervision" drafted by the Basle Committee on Banking Supervision and to monitor its compliance with the principle. In addition, banks should be encouraged to base their lending decisions solely on economic merits rather than political considerations. Furthermore, firms, financial institutions, and the government should be required to provide the public with reliable financial data in a timely fashion. A higher level of disclosure of financial information and the resultant transparency about the state of the economy will make it easier for all the concerned parties to monitor the situation better and mitigate the destabilizing cycles of investor euphoria and panic accentuated by the lack of reliable information.

Even if a country decides to liberalize its financial markets by allowing cross-border capital flows, it should encourage foreign direct investments and equity and long-term bond investments; it should not encourage short-term investments that can be reversed overnight, causing financial turmoil. As Chile has successfully implemented, some form of **"Tobin tax"** on the international flow of hot money can be useful. Throwing some sand in the wheels of international finance can have a stabilizing effect on the world's financial markets.

A fixed but adjustable exchange rate is problematic in the face of integrated international financial markets. Such a rate arrangement often invites speculative attack at the time of financial vulnerability. Countries should not try to restore the same fixed exchange rate system unless they are willing to impose capital controls. According to the so-called "trilemma" that economists are fond of talking about, a country can attain only two of the following three conditions: (i) a fixed exchange rate, (ii) free international flows of capital, and (iii) an independent monetary policy. It is very difficult, if not impossible, to have all three conditions. This difficulty is also known as the **incompatible trinity**. If a country would like to maintain monetary policy independence to pursue its own domestic economic goals and still would like to keep a fixed exchange rate between its currency and other currencies, then the country should restrict free flows of capital. China and India were not noticeably affected by the Asian currency crisis because both countries maintain capital controls, segmenting their capital markets from the rest of the world. Hong Kong was less affected by the crisis for a different reason. Hong Kong has firmly fixed its exchange rate to the U.S. dollar via a currency board and allowed free flows of capital; in consequence, Hong Kong gave up its monetary independence. A currency board is an extreme form of the fixed exchange rate regime under which local currency is "fully" backed by the dollar (or another chosen standard currency). Hong Kong has essentially dollarized its economy.

As previously mentioned, China maintained a fixed exchange rate between its currency, renminbi (RMB), otherwise known as the yuan, and the U.S. dollar at 8.27 RMB per dollar for a long while. As can be seen from Exhibit 2.12, however, the RMB was allowed to appreciate from mid-July 2005 for about three years before it reverted back to a (quasi-) fixed rate at around 6.82RMB per dollar in mid-July 2008. This reversion is attributable to the heightened economic uncertainty associated with the global financial crisis. But from late June 2010, RMB began to float again. The latest floating decision is related to the mounting pressure from China's trading partners for a stronger RMB as a way of reducing their trade deficits vis-à-vis China. But it is also

EXHIBIT 2.12

Renminbi (RMB) versus
U.S. Dollar Exchange
Rate

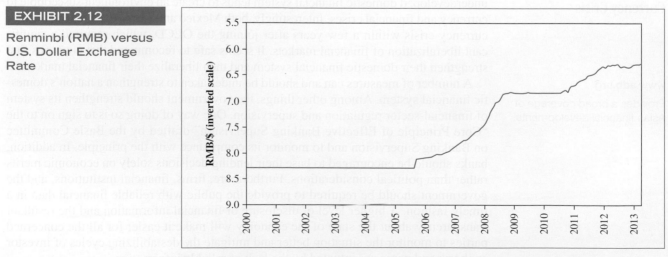

Source: Bloomberg.

related to China's own broad move toward liberalized capital markets. In recent years, China has been gradually lowering barriers to international capital flows. At the same time, China has been promoting a greater usage of the RMB in international transactions, with the long-term goal of establishing the RMB as a major global currency like the U.S. dollar. Considering the large transactions domain of the RMB, measured in terms of population, GDP, or international trade share, China's currency has the potential to become a global currency. However, for the RMB to become a full-fledged global currency, China will need to meet a few critical, related conditions, such as (i) full convertibility of its currency, (II) open capital markets with depth and liquidity, and (iii) the rule of law and protection of property rights. Note that the United States and euro zone satisfy these conditions.

The Argentine Peso Crisis

The 2002 crisis of the Argentine peso, however, shows that even a currency board arrangement cannot be completely safe from a possible collapse. Exhibit 2.13 shows how the peso–dollar exchange rate, fixed at parity throughout much of the 1990s, collapsed in January 2002. Short of a complete dollarization (as is the case with Panama, for example), a currency board arrangement can collapse unless the arrangement is backed by the political will and economic discipline to defend it.

When the peso was first linked to the U.S. dollar at parity in February 1991 under the Convertibility Law, initial economic effects were quite positive: Argentina's chronic inflation was curtailed dramatically and foreign investment began to pour in, leading to an economic boom. Over time, however, the peso appreciated against the majority of currencies as the U.S. dollar became increasingly stronger in the second half of the 1990s. A strong peso hurt exports from Argentina and caused a protracted economic downturn that eventually led to the abandonment of the peso–dollar parity in January 2002. This change, in turn, caused severe economic and political distress in the country. The unemployment rate rose above 20 percent and inflation reached a monthly rate of about 20 percent in April 2002. In contrast, Hong Kong was able to successfully defend its currency board arrangement during the Asian financial crisis, a major stress test for the arrangement.

Although there is no clear consensus on the causes of the Argentine crisis, there are at least three factors that are related to the collapse of the currency board system and ensuing economic crisis: (i) the lack of fiscal discipline, (ii) labor market inflexibility, and

EXHIBIT 2.13

Collapse of the Currency Board Arrangement in Argentina

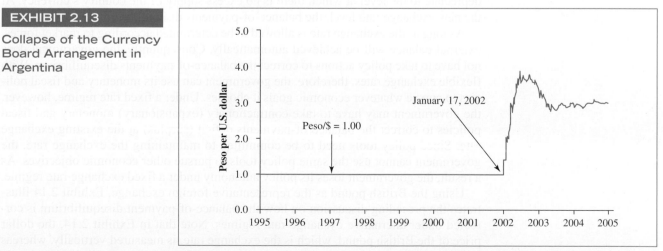

January 17, 2002

Peso/$ = 1.00

Source: Bloomberg.

(iii) contagion from the financial crises in Russia and Brazil. Reflecting the traditional sociopolitical divisions in the Argentine society, competing claims on economic resources by different groups were accommodated by increasing public sector indebtedness. Argentina is said to have a "European-style welfare system in a Third World economy." The federal government of Argentina borrowed heavily in dollars throughout the 1990s. As the economy entered a recession in the late 1990s, the government encountered increasing difficulty with rising debts, eventually defaulting on its internal and external debts. The hard fixed exchange rate that Argentina adopted under the currency board system made it impossible to restore competitiveness by a traditional currency depreciation. Further, a powerful labor union also made it difficult to lower wages and thus cut production costs that could have effectively achieved the same real currency depreciation with the fixed nominal exchange rate. The situation was exacerbated by a slowdown of international capital inflows following the financial crises in Russia and Brazil. Also, a sharp depreciation of the Brazil real in 1999 hampered exports from Argentina.

While the currency crisis is over, the debt problem has not been completely resolved. The government of Argentina ceased all debt payments in December 2001 in the wake of persistent recession and rising social and political unrest. It represents the largest sovereign default in history. Argentina faces a complex task of restructuring over $100 billion borrowed in seven different currencies and governed by the laws of eight legal jurisdictions. In June 2004, the Argentine government made a "final" offer amounting to a 75 percent reduction in the net present value of the debt. Foreign bondholders rejected this offer and asked for an improved offer. In early 2005, bondholders finally agreed to the restructuring, under which they took a cut of about 70 percent on the value of their bond holdings.

Fixed versus Flexible Exchange Rate Regimes

Since some countries, including the United States, the United Kingdom, and possibly Japan, prefer flexible exchange rates, while others, notably the members of the EMU and many developing countries, would like to maintain fixed exchange rates, it is worthwhile to examine some of the arguments advanced in favor of fixed versus flexible exchange rates.

The key arguments for flexible exchange rates rest on (i) easier external adjustments and (ii) national policy autonomy. Suppose a country is experiencing a balance-of-payments deficit at the moment. This means that there is an excess supply of the country's currency at the prevailing exchange rate in the foreign exchange market. Under a flexible exchange rate regime, the external value of the country's currency will simply depreciate to the level at which there is no excess supply of the country's currency. At the new exchange rate level, the balance-of-payments disequilibrium will disappear.

As long as the exchange rate is allowed to be determined according to market forces, external balance will be achieved automatically. Consequently, the government does not have to take policy actions to correct the balance-of-payments disequilibrium. With flexible exchange rates, therefore, the government can use its monetary and fiscal policies to pursue whatever economic goals it chooses. Under a fixed rate regime, however, the government may have to take contractionary (expansionary) monetary and fiscal policies to correct the balance-of-payments deficit (surplus) at the existing exchange rate. Since policy tools need to be committed to maintaining the exchange rate, the government cannot use the same policy tools to pursue other economic objectives. As a result, the government loses its policy autonomy under a fixed exchange rate regime.

Using the British pound as the representative foreign exchange, Exhibit 2.14 illustrates the preceding discussion on how the balance-of-payment disequilibrium is corrected under alternative exchange rate regimes. Note that in Exhibit 2.14, the dollar price of the British pound, which is the exchange rate, is measured vertically, whereas the quantity of British pounds demanded or supplied at different exchange rates is

External Adjustment
Mechanism: Fixed versus
Flexible Exchange Rates

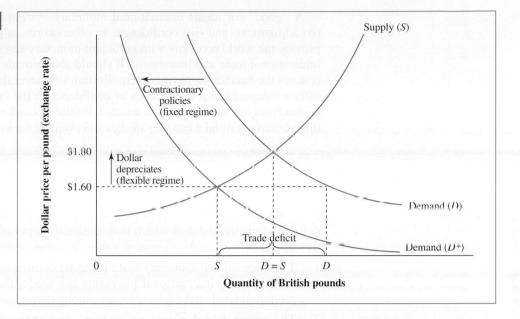

measured horizontally. As is the case with most other commodities, the demand for British pounds would be downward sloping, whereas the supply of British pounds would be upward sloping. Suppose that the exchange rate is $1.60/£ at the moment. As can be seen from the exhibit, the demand for British pounds far exceeds the supply (i.e., the supply of U.S. dollars far exceeds the demand) at this exchange rate. The United States experiences trade (or balance of payment) deficits. Under the flexible exchange rate regime, the dollar will simply depreciate to a new level of exchange rate, $1.80/£, at which the excess demand for British pounds (and thus the trade deficit) will disappear. Now, suppose that the exchange rate is "fixed" at $1.60/£, and thus the excess demand for British pounds cannot be eliminated by the exchange rate adjustment. Facing this situation, the U.S. Federal Reserve Bank may initially draw on its foreign exchange reserve holdings to satisfy the excess demand for British pounds. If the excess demand persists, however, the U.S. government may have to resort to contractionary monetary and fiscal policies so that the demand curve can shift to the left (from D to D^* in the exhibit) until the excess demand for British pounds can be eliminated at the fixed exchange rate, $1.60/£. In other words, it is necessary for the government to take policy actions to maintain the fixed exchange rate.

A possible drawback of the flexible exchange rate regime is that exchange rate uncertainty may hamper international trade and investment. Proponents of the fixed exchange rate regime argue that when future exchange rates are uncertain, businesses tend to shun foreign trade. Since countries cannot fully benefit from international trade under exchange rate uncertainty, resources will be allocated suboptimally on a global basis. Proponents of the fixed exchange rate regime argue that fixed exchange rates eliminate such uncertainty and thus promote international trade. However, to the extent that firms can hedge exchange risk by means of currency forward or options contracts, uncertain exchange rates do not necessarily hamper international trade.

As the preceding discussion suggests, the choice between the alternative exchange rate regimes is likely to involve a trade-off between national policy independence and international economic integration. If countries would like to pursue their respective domestic economic goals, they are likely to pursue divergent macroeconomic policies, rendering fixed exchange rates infeasible. On the other hand, if countries are committed to promoting international economic integration (as is the case with the core members of the European Union like France and Germany), the benefits of fixed exchange rates are likely to outweigh the associated costs.

A "good" (or ideal) international monetary system should provide (i) liquidity, (ii) adjustment, and (iii) confidence. In other words, a good IMS should be able to provide the world economy with sufficient monetary reserves to support the growth of international trade and investment. It should also provide an effective mechanism that restores the balance-of-payments equilibrium whenever it is disturbed. Lastly, it should offer a safeguard to prevent crises of confidence in the system that result in panicked flights from one reserve asset to another. Politicians and economists should keep these three criteria in mind when they design and evaluate the international monetary system.

SUMMARY

This chapter provides an overview of the international monetary system, which defines an environment in which multinational corporations and international investors operate.

1. The international monetary system can be defined as the institutional framework within which international payments are made, the movements of capital are accommodated, and exchange rates among currencies are determined.

2. The international monetary system went through five stages of evolution: (a) bimetallism, (b) classical gold standard, (c) interwar period, (d) Bretton Woods system, and (e) flexible exchange rate regime.

3. The classical gold standard spanned 1875 to 1914. Under the gold standard, the exchange rate between two currencies is determined by the gold contents of the currencies. Balance-of-payments disequilibrium is automatically corrected through the price-specie-flow mechanism. The gold standard still has ardent supporters who believe that it provides an effective hedge against price inflation. Under the gold standard, however, the world economy can be subject to deflationary pressure due to the limited supply of monetary gold.

4. To prevent the recurrence of economic nationalism with no clear "rules of the game" witnessed during the interwar period, representatives of 44 nations met at Bretton Woods, New Hampshire, in 1944 and adopted a new international monetary system. Under the Bretton Woods system, each country established a par value in relation to the U.S. dollar, which was fully convertible to gold. Countries used foreign exchanges, especially the U.S. dollar, as well as gold as international means of payments. The Bretton Woods system was designed to maintain stable exchange rates and economize on gold. The Bretton Woods system eventually collapsed in 1973 mainly because of U.S. domestic inflation and the persistent balance-of-payments deficits.

5. The flexible exchange rate regime that replaced the Bretton Woods system was ratified by the Jamaica Agreement. Following a spectacular rise and fall of the U.S. dollar in the 1980s, major industrial countries agreed to cooperate to achieve greater exchange rate stability. The Louvre Accord of 1987 marked the inception of the managed-float system under which the G-7 countries would jointly intervene in the foreign exchange market to correct over- or undervaluation of currencies.

6. In 1979, the EEC countries launched the European Monetary System (EMS) to establish a "zone of monetary stability" in Europe. The two main instruments of the EMS are the European Currency Unit (ECU) and the Exchange Rate Mechanism (ERM). The ECU is a basket currency comprising the currencies of the EMS members and serves as the accounting unit of the EMS. The ERM refers to the procedure by which EMS members collectively manage their exchange rates. The ERM is based on a parity grid that the member countries are required to maintain.

7. On January 1, 1999, 11 European countries, including France and Germany, adopted a common currency called the euro. Greece adopted the euro in 2001. Subsequently, five other countries—Cyprus, Malta, Slovakia, Slovenia, and Estonia—adopted the euro. The advent of a single European currency, which may eventually rival the U.S. dollar as a global vehicle currency, will have major implications for the European as well as world economy. Euro zone countries will benefit from reduced transaction costs and the elimination of exchange rate uncertainty. The advent of the euro will also help develop continentwide capital markets where companies can raise capital at favorable rates.

8. Under the European Monetary Union (EMU), the common monetary policy for the euro zone countries is formulated by the European Central Bank (ECB) located in Frankfurt. The ECB is legally mandated to maintain price stability in Europe. Together with the ECB, the national central banks of the euro zone countries form the Eurosystem, which is responsible for defining and implementing the common monetary policy for the EMU.

9. While the core EMU members, including France and Germany, apparently prefer the fixed exchange rate regime, other major countries such as the United States and Japan are willing to live with flexible exchange rates. Under the flexible exchange rate regime, governments can retain policy independence because the external balance will be achieved by the exchange rate adjustments rather than by policy intervention. Exchange rate uncertainty, however, can potentially hamper international trade and investment. The choice between the alternative exchange rate regimes is likely to involve a trade-off between national policy autonomy and international economic integration.

KEY WORDS

bimetallism, *28*	Eurosystem, *44*	par value, *31*
Bretton Woods system, *31*	gold-exchange standard, *32*	Plaza Accord, *35*
currency board, *36*	gold standard, *28*	price-specie-flow mechanism, *30*
euro, *27*	Gresham's law, *28*	Smithsonian Agreement, *34*
European Central Bank (ECB), *43*	incompatible trinity, *54*	snake, *41*
European Currency Unit (ECU), *41*	international monetary system, *27*	special drawing rights (SDRs), *32*
European Monetary System (EMS), *41*	Jamaica Agreement, *34*	sterilization of gold, *30*
European Monetary Union (EMU), *43*	Louvre Accord, *35*	"Tobin tax," *54*
Exchange Rate Mechanism (ERM), *41*	Maastricht Treaty, *41*	Triffin paradox, *32*
	managed-float system, *35*	
	optimum currency areas, *46*	

QUESTIONS

1. Explain Gresham's law.

2. Explain the mechanism that restores the balance-of-payments equilibrium when it is disturbed under the gold standard.

3. Suppose that the pound is pegged to gold at 6 pounds per ounce, whereas the franc is pegged to gold at 12 francs per ounce. This, of course, implies that the equilibrium exchange rate should be two francs per pound. If the current market exchange rate is 2.2 francs per pound, how would you take advantage of this situation? What would be the effect of shipping costs?

4. Discuss the advantages and disadvantages of the gold standard.

5. What were the main objectives of the Bretton Woods system?

6. Comment on the proposition that the Bretton Woods system was programmed to an eventual demise.

7. Explain how special drawing rights (SDRs) are constructed. Also, discuss the circumstances under which the SDRs were created.

8. Explain the arrangements and workings of the European Monetary System (EMS).

9. There are arguments for and against the alternative exchange rate regimes.

   a. List the advantages of the flexible exchange rate regime.

   b. Criticize the flexible exchange rate regime from the viewpoint of the proponents of the fixed exchange rate regime.

   c. Rebut the above criticism from the viewpoint of the proponents of the flexible exchange rate regime.

10. In an integrated world financial market, a financial crisis in a country can be quickly transmitted to other countries, causing a global crisis. What kind of measures would you propose to prevent the recurrence of an Asia-type crisis?

11. Discuss the criteria for a "good" international monetary system.

12. Once capital markets are integrated, it is difficult for a country to maintain a fixed exchange rate. Explain why this may be so.

13. Assess the possibility for the euro to become another global currency rivaling the U.S. dollar. If the euro really becomes a global currency, what impact will it have on the U.S. dollar and the world economy?

INTERNET EXERCISES

1. Using the data from http://federalreserve.gov/releases/h10/hist, first plot the monthly exchange rate between the euro and the U.S. dollar since January 2000, and try to explain why the exchange rate behaved the way it did.

MINI CASE

Will the United Kingdom Join the Euro Club?

When the euro was introduced in January 1999, the United Kingdom was conspicuously absent from the list of European countries adopting the common currency. Although the previous Labour government led by Prime Minister Tony Blair appeared to be in favor of joining the euro club, the current Tory goverment is not in favor of adopting the euro and thus giving up monetary sovereignty of the country. Public opinion is also divided on the issue.

Whether the United Kingdom will eventually join the euro club is a matter of considerable importance for the future of the European Union as well as that of the United Kingdom. If the United Kingdom, with its sophisticated finance industry, joins, it will most certainly propel the euro into a global currency status rivaling the U.S. dollar. The United Kingdom for its part will firmly join the process of economic and political unionization of Europe, abandoning its traditional balancing role.

Investigate the political, economic, and historical situations surrounding British participation in the European economic and monetary integration and write your own assessment of the prospect of Britain joining the euro club. In doing so, assess from the British perspective, among other things, (i) potential benefits and costs of adopting the euro, (ii) economic and political constraints facing the country, and (iii) the potential impact of British adoption of the euro on the international financial system, including the role of the U.S. dollar.

REFERENCES & SUGGESTED READINGS

Bris, Arturo, Yrjö Koskinen, and Mattias Nilsson. The Euro and Corporate Valuation. Working Paper (2004).

Chinn, Menzie, and Jeffrey Frankel. "Why the Euro Will Rival the Dollar," *International Finance* 11 (2008), pp. 49–73.

Cooper, Richard N. *The International Monetary System: Essays in World Economics*. Cambridge, Mass.: MIT Press, 1987.

Eichengreen, Barry. *The Gold Standard in Theory and History*. Methuen: London, 1985, pp. 39–48.

Eichengreen, Barry. *Exorbitant Privilege: The Rise and Fall of the Dollar and the Future of the International Monetary System*. Oxford University Press, 2011.

Friedman, Milton. *Essays in Positive Economics*. Chicago: University of Chicago Press, 1953.

Jorion, Philippe. "Properties of the ECU as a Currency Basket." *Journal of Multinational Financial Management* 1 (1991), pp. 1–24.

Machlup, Fritz. *Remaking the International Monetary System: The Rio Agreement and Beyond*. Baltimore: Johns Hopkins Press, 1968.

Mundell, Robert. "A Theory of Optimum Currency Areas." *American Economic Review* 51 (1961), pp. 657–65.

———. "Currency Areas, Volatility and Intervention," *Journal of Policy Modeling* 22 (2000), pp. 281–99.

Nurkse, Ragnar. *International Currency Experience: Lessons of the Interwar Period*. Geneva: League of Nations, 1944.

Obstfeld, Maurice, Jay Shambaugh, and Alan Taylor. "The Trilemma in History: Tradeoffs among Exchange Rates, Monetary Policies, and Capital Mobility." *Review of Economics and Statistics*. 87 (2005), pp. 423–38.

Solomon, Robert. *The International Monetary System, 1945–1981*. New York: Harper & Row, 1982.

Stiglitz, Joseph. "Reforming the Global Economic Architecture: Lessons from Recent Crisis." *Journal of Finance* 54 (1999), pp. 1508–21.

Tobin, James. "Financial Globalization," Unpublished manuscript presented at American Philosophical Society, 1998

Triffin, Robert. *Gold and the Dollar Crisis*. New Haven, Conn.: Yale University Press, 1960.

3 Balance of Payments

THE TERM balance of payments is often mentioned in the news media and continues to be a popular subject of economic and political discourse around the world. It is not always clear, however, exactly what is meant by the term when it is mentioned in various contexts. This ambiguity is often attributable to misunderstanding and misuse of the term. The balance of payments, which is a statistical record of a country's transactions with the rest of the world, is worth studying for a few reasons.

First, the balance of payments provides detailed information concerning the demand and supply of a country's currency. For example, if the United States imports more than it exports, then this means that the supply of dollars is likely to exceed the demand in the foreign exchange market, *ceteris paribus*. One can thus infer that the U.S. dollar would be under pressure to depreciate against other currencies. On the other hand, if the United States exports more than it imports, then the dollar would be likely to appreciate.

Second, a country's balance-of-payment data may signal its potential as a business partner for the rest of the world. If a country is grappling with a major balance-of-payment difficulty, it may not be able to expand imports from the outside world. Instead, the country may be tempted to impose measures to restrict imports and discourage capital outflows in order to improve the balance-of-payment situation. On the other hand, a country experiencing a significant balance-of-payment surplus would be more likely to expand imports, offering marketing opportunities for foreign enterprises, and less likely to impose foreign exchange restrictions.

Third, balance-of-payments data can be used to evaluate the performance of the country in international economic competition. Suppose a country is experiencing trade deficits year after year. This trade data may then signal that the country's domestic industries lack international competitiveness. To interpret balance-of-payments data properly, it is necessary to understand how the balance-of-payments account is constructed.

Balance-of-Payments Accounting

The balance of payments can be formally defined as *the statistical record of a country's international transactions over a certain period of time presented in the form of double-entry bookkeeping.* Examples of international transactions include import and export of goods and services and cross-border investments in businesses, bank accounts, bonds, stocks, and real estate. Since the balance of payments is recorded over a certain period of time (i.e., a quarter or a year), it has the same time dimension as national income accounting.[1]

---

[1]In fact, the current account balance, which is the difference between a country's exports and imports, is a component of the country's GNP. Other components of GNP include consumption and investment and government expenditure.

Generally speaking, any transaction that results in a receipt from foreigners will be recorded as a credit, with a positive sign, in the U.S. balance of payments, whereas any transaction that gives rise to a payment to foreigners will be recorded as a debit, with a negative sign. Credit entries in the U.S. balance of payments result from foreign sales of U.S. goods and services, goodwill, financial claims, and real assets. Debit entries, on the other hand, arise from U.S. purchases of foreign goods and services, goodwill, financial claims, and real assets. Further, credit entries give rise to the demand for dollars, whereas debit entries give rise to the supply of dollars. Note that the demand (supply) for dollars is associated with the supply (demand) of foreign exchange.

Since the balance of payments is presented as a system of double-entry bookkeeping, every credit in the account is balanced by a matching debit and vice versa.

EXAMPLE | 3.1

For example, suppose that Boeing Corporation exported a Boeing 747 aircraft to Japan Airlines for $50 million, and that Japan Airlines pays from its dollar bank account kept with Chase Manhattan Bank in New York City. Then, the receipt of $50 million by Boeing will be recorded as a credit (+), which will be matched by a debit (–) of the same amount representing a reduction of the U.S. bank's liabilities.

EXAMPLE | 3.2

Suppose, for another example, that Boeing imports jet engines produced by Rolls-Royce for $30 million, and that Boeing makes payment by transferring the funds to a New York bank account kept by Rolls-Royce. In this case, payment by Boeing will be recorded as a debit (–), whereas the deposit of the funds by Rolls-Royce will be recorded as a credit (+).

As shown by the preceding examples, every credit in the balance of payments is matched by a debit somewhere to conform to the principle of double-entry bookkeeping.

Not only international trade, that is, exports and imports, but also cross-border investments are recorded in the balance of payments.

EXAMPLE | 3.3

Suppose that Thomson Corporation, a U.S. information services company, acquires Reuters, a British news agency, for $750 million, and that Reuters deposits the money in Barclays Bank in London, which, in turn, uses the sum to purchase U.S. treasury notes. In this case, the payment of $750 million by Thomson will be recorded as a debit (–), whereas Barclays' purchase of the U.S. Treasury notes will be recorded as a credit (+).

The above examples can be summarized as follows:

Transactions	Credit	Debit
Boeing's export	+$50 million	
Withdrawal from U.S. bank		−$50 million
Boeing's import		−$30 million
Deposit at U.S. bank	+$30 million	
Thomson's acquisition of Reuters		−$750 million
Barclays' purchase of U.S. securities	+$750 million	

Balance-of-Payments Accounts

Since the balance of payments records all types of international transactions a country consummates over a certain period of time, it contains a wide variety of accounts. However, a country's international transactions can be grouped into the following three main types:

1. The current account.
2. The capital account.
3. The official reserve account.

The **current account** includes the export and import of goods and services, whereas the **capital account** includes all purchases and sales of assets such as stocks, bonds, bank accounts, real estate, and businesses. The **official reserve account**, on the other hand, covers all purchases and sales of international reserve assets such as dollars, foreign exchanges, gold, and special drawing rights (SDRs).

Let us now examine a detailed description of the balance-of-payments accounts. Exhibit 3.1 summarizes the U.S. balance-of-payments accounts for the year 2011 that we are going to use as an example.

The Current Account

Exhibit 3.1 shows that U.S. exports were $2,843.7 billion in 2011 while U.S. imports were $3,182.8 billion. The current account balance, which is defined as exports minus imports plus unilateral transfers, that is, (1) + (2) + (3) in Exhibit 3.1, was negative, −$473.6 billion. The United States thus had a balance-of-payments deficit on the current account in 2011. The current account deficit implies that the United States used

EXHIBIT 3.1		Credits	Debits
A Summary of the U.S. Balance of Payments for 2011 (in $ billion)	*Current Account*		
	(1)　Exports	2,843.7	
	(1.1) Merchandise	1,501.5	
	(1.2) Services	603.5	
	(1.3) Factor income	738.7	
	(2)　Imports		−3,182.8
	(2.1) Merchandise		−2,236.8
	(2.2) Services		−428.3
	(2.3) Factor income		−517.7
	(3)　Unilateral transfer	19.5	−154.0
	Balance on current account		−473.6
	[(1) + (2) + (3)]		
	Capital Account		
	(4)　Direct investment	227.9	−406.2
	(5)　Portfolio investment	166.9	−14.7
	(5.1) Equity securities	20.9	−87.8
	(5.2) Debt securities	139.2	73.1
	(5.3) Derivatives, net	6.8	
	(6)　Other investment	395.8	40.4
	Balance on capital account	410.1	
	[(4) + (5) + (6)]		
	(7)　Statistical discrepancies	79.4	
	Overall balance	15.9	
	Official Reserve Account		−15.9

Source: IMF, *International Financial Statistics Yearbook, 2012.*

Note: Liquidation and repatriation of foreign debt securities ($73.1 billion) and other investment ($40.4 billion) are recorded with a positive sign.

www.bea.gov

Website of the Bureau of Economic Analysis, U.S. Department of Commerce, provides data related to the U.S. balance of payments.

up more output than it produced.[2] Since a country must finance its current account deficit either by borrowing from foreigners or by drawing down on its previously accumulated foreign wealth, a current account deficit represents a reduction in the country's net foreign wealth. On the other hand, a country with a current account surplus acquires IOUs from foreigners, thereby increasing its net foreign wealth.

The current account is divided into four finer categories: merchandise trade, services, factor income, and unilateral transfers. **Merchandise trade** represents exports and imports of tangible goods, such as oil, wheat, clothes, automobiles, computers, and so on. As Exhibit 3.1 shows, U.S. merchandise exports were $1,501.5 billion in 2011 while imports were $2,236.8 billion. The United States thus had a deficit on the **trade balance** or a trade deficit. The trade balance represents the net merchandise export. As is well known, the United States has experienced persistent trade deficits since the early 1980s, whereas such key trading partners as China, Japan, and Germany have generally realized trade surpluses. This persistent trade imbalance between the United States and her key trading partners has been a source of international contention.

Services, the second category of the current account, include payments and receipts for legal, consulting, and engineering services, royalties for patents and intellectual properties, insurance premiums, shipping fees, and tourist expenditures. These trades in services are sometimes called **invisible trade**. In 2011, U.S. service exports were $603.5 billion and imports were $428.3 billion, realizing a surplus of $175.2 billion. Clearly, the United States performed better in services than in merchandise trade. It is noted that thanks to the rapid advancement of information technology (IT), many services that were previously nontradable are becoming tradable. For example, X-ray pictures taken at a local hospital in the United States may be transmitted overnight via the Internet to an IT outsourcing center in India. Then, doctors there would examine the digital images and data and e-mail their diagnosis back to the U.S. hospital for a fee. In this case, the U.S. effectively imported medical service from India.

Factor income, the third category of the current account, consists largely of payments and receipts of interest, dividends, and other income on foreign investments that were previously made. If United States investors receive interest on their holdings of foreign bonds, for instance, it will be recorded as a credit in the balance of payments. On the other hand, interest payments by U.S. borrowers to foreign creditors will be recorded as debits. In 2011, U.S. residents paid out $517.7 billion to foreigners as factor income and received $738.7 billion, realizing a $221 billion surplus. Considering, however, that the United States has heavily borrowed from foreigners in recent years, U.S. payments of interest and dividends to foreigners are likely to rise significantly. This can increase the U.S. current account deficit in the future, *ceteris paribus*.

Unilateral transfers, the fourth category of the current account, involve "unrequited" payments. Examples include foreign aid, reparations, official and private grants, and gifts. Unlike other accounts in the balance of payments, unilateral transfers have only one-directional flows, without offsetting flows. In the case of merchandise trade, for example, goods flow in one direction and payments flow in the opposite direction. For the purpose of preserving the double-entry bookkeeping rule, unilateral transfers are regarded as an act of buying *goodwill* from the recipients. So a country that gives foreign aid to another country can be viewed as importing goodwill from the latter. As can be expected, the United States made a net unilateral transfer of $134.5 billion, which is the receipt of transfer payments ($19.5 billion) minus transfer payments to foreign entities ($154.0 billion).

---

[2]The current account balance (BCA) can be written as the difference between national output (Y) and domestic absorption, which comprises consumption (C), investment (I), and government expenditures (G):

$$BCA = Y - (C + I + G)$$

If a country's domestic absorption falls short of its national output, the country's current account must be in surplus, for more detailed discussion, refer to Appendix 3A.

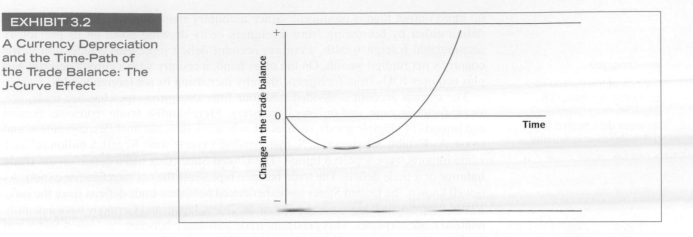

EXHIBIT 3.2

A Currency Depreciation
and the Time-Path of
the Trade Balance: The
J-Curve Effect

The current account balance, especially the trade balance, tends to be sensitive to exchange rate changes. When a country's currency depreciates against the currencies of major trading partners, the country's exports tend to rise and imports fall, improving the trade balance. For example, Mexico experienced continuous deficits in its trade balance of about $4.5 billion per quarter throughout 1994. Following the depreciation of the peso in December 1994, however, Mexico's trade balance began to improve immediately, realizing a surplus of about $7 billion for the year 1995.

The effect of currency depreciation on a country's trade balance can be more complicated than the case described above. Indeed, following a depreciation, the trade balance may at first deteriorate for a while. Eventually, however, the trade balance will tend to improve over time. This particular reaction pattern of the trade balance to a depreciation is referred to as the **J-curve effect**, which is illustrated in Exhibit 3.2. The curve shows the initial deterioration and the eventual improvement of the trade balance following a depreciation. The J-curve effect received wide attention when the British trade balance worsened after a devaluation of the pound in 1967. Sebastian Edwards (1989) examined various cases of devaluations carried out by developing countries from the 1960s through the 1980s, and confirmed the existence of the J-curve effect in about 40 percent of the cases.

A depreciation will begin to improve the trade balance immediately if imports and exports are *responsive* to the exchange rate changes. On the other hand, if imports and exports are inelastic, the trade balance will worsen following a depreciation. Following a depreciation of the domestic currency and the resultant rise in import prices, domestic residents may still continue to purchase imports because it is difficult to change their consumption habits in a short period of time. With higher import prices, the domestic country comes to spend more on imports. Even if domestic residents are willing to switch to less expensive domestic substitutes for foreign imports, it may take time for domestic producers to supply import substitutes. Likewise, foreigners' demand for domestic products, which become less expensive with a depreciation of the domestic currency, can be inelastic essentially for the same reasons. In the long run, however, both imports and exports tend to be responsive to exchange rate changes, exerting positive influences on the trade balance.

The Capital Account

The capital account balance measures the difference between U.S. sales of assets to foreigners and U.S. purchases of foreign assets. U.S. sales (or exports) of assets are recorded as credits, as they result in *capital inflow*. On the other hand, U.S. purchases (imports) of foreign assets are recorded as debits, as they lead to *capital outflow*. Unlike trades in goods and services, trades in financial assets affect future payments and receipts of factor income.

Exhibit 3.1 shows that the United States had a capital account surplus of $410.1 billion in 2011, implying that capital inflow to the United States far exceeded capital outflow.

Clearly, the current account deficit was substantially offset by the capital account surplus. As previously mentioned, a country's current account deficit must be paid for either by borrowing from foreigners or by selling off past foreign investments. In the absence of the government's reserve transactions, the current account balance must be equal to the capital account balance but with the opposite sign. When nothing is excluded, a country's balance of payments must necessarily balance.

The capital account can be divided into three categories: direct investment, portfolio investment, and other investment. Direct investment occurs when the investor acquires a measure of control of the foreign business. In the U.S. balance of payments, acquisition of 10 percent or more of the voting shares of a business is considered giving a measure of control to the investor.

When Honda, a Japanese automobile manufacturer, built an assembly factory in Ohio, it was engaged in **foreign direct investment (FDI)**. Another example of direct investment was provided by Nestlé Corporation, a Swiss multinational firm, when it *acquired* Carnation, a U.S. firm. Of course, U.S. firms also are engaged in direct investments in foreign countries. For instance, Coca-Cola built bottling facilities all over the world. In recent years, many U.S. corporations moved their production facilities to Mexico and China, in part, to take advantage of lower costs of production. Generally speaking, foreign direct investments take place as firms attempt to take advantage of various market imperfections, such as underpriced labor services and protected markets. In 2011, U.S. direct investment overseas was $406.2 billion, whereas foreign direct investment in the United States was $227.9 billion.

Firms undertake foreign direct investments when the expected returns from foreign investments exceed the cost of capital, allowing for foreign exchange and political risks. The expected returns from foreign projects can be higher than those from domestic projects because of lower wage rates and material costs, subsidized financing, preferential tax treatment, exclusive access to local markets, and the like. The volume and direction of FDI can also be sensitive to exchange rate changes. For instance, Japanese FDI in the United States soared in the latter half of the 1980s, partly because of the sharp appreciation of the yen against the dollar. With a stronger yen, Japanese firms could better afford to acquire U.S. assets that became less expensive in terms of the yen. The same exchange rate movement discouraged U.S. firms from making FDI in Japan because Japanese assets became more expensive in terms of the dollar.

Portfolio investment, the second category of the capital account, mostly represents sales and purchases of foreign financial assets such as stocks and bonds that do not involve a transfer of control. International portfolio investments have boomed in recent years, partly due to the general relaxation of capital controls and regulations in many countries, and partly due to investors' desire to diversify risk globally. Portfolio investment comprises equity, debt, and derivative securities. Exhibit 3.1 shows that in 2011, foreigners invested $166.9 billion in U.S. financial securities, whereas Americans invested $14.7 billion in foreign securities, realizing a surplus, $152.2 billion, for the United States. Much of the surplus represents foreigners' investment in U.S. debt securities and U.S. liquidation and repatriation of foreign debt securities. Exhibit 3.1 shows that foreigners invested $139.2 billion in U.S. debt securities in 2011, whereas U.S. investors divested $73.1 billion in foreign debt securities.

Investors typically diversify their investment portfolios to reduce risk. Since security returns tend to have relatively low correlations among countries, investors can reduce risk more effectively if they diversify their portfolio holdings internationally rather than purely domestically. In addition, investors may be able to benefit from higher expected returns from some foreign markets.[3]

---

[3]Refer to Chapter 15 for a detailed discussion of international portfolio investment.

In recent years, government-controlled investment funds, known as *sovereign wealth funds* (SWFs), are playing an increasingly visible role in international investments. SWFs are mostly domiciled in Asian and Middle Eastern countries and usually are responsible for recycling foreign exchange reserves of these countries swelled by trade surpluses and oil revenues. It is noted that SWFs invested large sums of money in many western banks that were severely affected by subprime mortgage–related losses (i.e., housing loans made to borrowers with marginal creditworthiness). For example, Abu Dhabi Investment Authority invested $7.5 billion in Citigroup, which needed to replenish its capital base in the wake of subprime losses, whereas Temasek Holdings, Singapore's state-owned investment company, injected $5.0 billion into Merrill Lynch, one of the largest investment banks in the United States. Although SWFs play a positive role in stabilizing the global banking system and help the balance-of-payment situations of the host countries, they are increasingly under close scrutiny due to their sheer size and the lack of transparency about the way these funds are operating.

The third category of the capital account is **other investment**, which includes transactions in currency, bank deposits, trade credits, and so forth. These investments are quite sensitive to both changes in relative interest rates between countries and the anticipated change in the exchange rate. If the interest rate rises in the United States while other variables remain constant, the United States will experience capital inflows, as investors would like to deposit or invest in the United States to take advantage of the higher interest rate. On the other hand, if a higher U.S. interest rate is more or less offset by an expected depreciation of the U.S. dollar, capital inflows to the United States will not materialize.[4] Since both interest rates and exchange rate expectations are volatile, these capital flows are highly reversible. In 2011, the United States experienced a major inflow of $395.8 billion in this category. At the same time, U.S. investors divested $40.4 billion in their holdings of foreign assets in this category.

Statistical Discrepancy

Exhibit 3.1 shows that there was a statistical discrepancy of $79.4 billion in 2011, representing omitted and misrecorded transactions. Recordings of payments and receipts arising from international transactions are done at different times and places, possibly using different methods. As a result, these recordings, upon which the balance-of-payments statistics are constructed, are bound to be imperfect. While merchandise trade can be recorded with a certain degree of accuracy at the customs houses, provisions of invisible services like consulting can escape detection. Cross-border financial transactions, a bulk of which might have been conducted electronically, are far more difficult to keep track of. For this reason, the balance of payments always presents a "balancing" debit or credit as a statistical discrepancy.[5] It is interesting to note that the sum of the balance on capital account and the statistical discrepancy more than offset the balance of current account in magnitude, –$473.6 billion. This suggests that financial transactions may be mainly responsible for the discrepancy.

When we compute the *cumulative* balance of payments including the current account, capital account, and the statistical discrepancies, we obtain the so-called **overall balance** or **official settlement balance**. All the transactions comprising the overall balance take place *autonomously* for their own sake.[6] The overall balance is

---

[4]We will discuss the relationship between the relative interest rates and the expected exchange rate change in Chapter 6.

[5]Readers might wonder how to compute the statistical discrepancies in the balance of payments. Statistical discrepancies, which represent errors and omissions, by definition, cannot be known. Since, however, the balance of payments must balance to zero when every item is included, one can determine the statistical discrepancies in the "residual" manner.

[6]Autonomous transactions refer to those transactions that occur without regard to the goal of achieving the balance-of-payments equilibrium.

significant because it indicates a country's international payment gap that must be *accommodated* with the government's official reserve transactions.

It is also indicative of the pressure that a country's currency faces for depreciation or appreciation. If, for example, a country continuously realizes deficits on the overall balance, the country will eventually run out of reserve holdings and its currency may have to depreciate against foreign currencies. In 2011, the United States had a $15.9 billion surplus on the overall balance. This means that the United States received a net payment equal to that amount from the rest of the world. If the United States had realized a deficit on the overall balance, the United States would have made a net payment to the rest of the world.

Official Reserve Account

When a country must make a net payment to foreigners because of a balance-of-payments deficit, the central bank of the country (the Federal Reserve System in the United States) should either run down its **official reserve assets**, such as gold, foreign exchanges, and SDRs, or borrow anew from foreign central banks. On the other hand, if a country has a balance-of-payments surplus, its central bank will either retire some of its foreign debts or acquire additional reserve assets from foreigners. Exhibit 3.1 shows that to accommodate a $15.9 billion balance-of-payment surplus, the U.S. increased its external reserve holdings by the same amount. When the United States increases its reserve holdings by either adding to its reserve holdings or retiring debts, it will spend funds, which will be recorded under debits.

The official reserve account includes transactions undertaken by the authorities to finance the overall balance and intervene in foreign exchange markets. When the United States and foreign governments wish to support the value of the dollar in the foreign exchange markets, they sell foreign exchanges, SDRs, or gold to "buy" dollars. These transactions, which give rise to the demand for dollars, will be recorded as a positive entry under official reserves. On the other hand, if governments would like to see a weaker dollar, they "sell" dollars and buy gold, foreign exchanges, and so forth. These transactions, which give rise to the supply of dollars, will be recorded as a negative entry under official reserves. The more actively governments intervene in the foreign exchange markets, the greater the official reserve changes.

On September 6, 2011, the Swiss National Bank (SNB), the central bank of Switzerland, surprised financial markets by announcing that it will intervene in currency markets "without limit" in order to keep the Swiss franc from appreciating beyond SFr1.20/€, which is equivalent to about €0.833/SFr. The central bank announced that "with immediate effect, the bank will no longer tolerate an exchange rate in the euro against the Swiss franc below the minimum rate of SFr1.20. The SNB will enforce this minimum rate with the utmost determination and is prepared to buy foreign currency in unlimited quantities." As Switzerland was receiving safe-haven investment flows from the eurozone uncertainties, the Swiss franc has been steadily appreciating from €0.61 per Swiss franc in early 2008 to a near-parity with the euro in August 2011, hurting the export-driven economy of Switzerland. To prevent the appreciation of the Swiss franc, the SNB has been buying up euros by printing and selling francs. The intervention was focused on the euro because the euro zone is by far the largest export market for the Swiss products. As can be seen in Exhibit 3.3, the official reserve assets of Switzerland were essentially constant in 2008, implying non-intervention, but began to rise fast since 2009, reflecting the SNB intervention. Despite the intervention, the Swiss franc continued to appreciate against the euro, pushing the Swiss economy toward recession. Against this backdrop, the SNB announced the drastic measure to intervene in currency markets without limit in order to keep the minimum exchange rate of SFr1.20 against the euro. Exhibit 3.3 shows that the Swiss franc fell sharply upon the announcement and the SNB was successful in keeping the Swiss franc at the minimum rate. As a result of the central bank interventions over the years, the official reserve assets of Switzerland have increased from under $50 billion in 2008 to nearly

Swiss Intervention
in Foreign Exchange
Markets

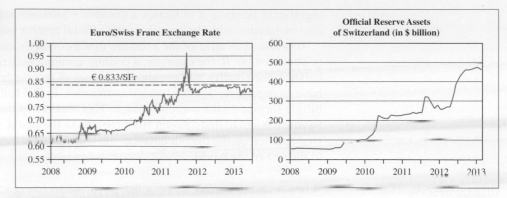

Source: Datastream and International Financial Statistics.

$500 billion in 2013. The Swiss episode shows that the negative effect of the so-called "market-determined exchange rate" on the real economy can force the government to tie up the "invisible hands" of the market.

Until the advent of the Bretton Woods System in 1945, gold was the predominant international reserve asset. After 1945, however, international reserve assets comprise:

1. Gold.
2. Foreign exchanges.
3. Special drawing rights (SDRs).
4. Reserve positions in the International Monetary Fund (IMF).

As can be seen from Exhibit 3.4, the relative importance of gold as an international means of payment has steadily declined, whereas the importance of foreign exchanges has grown substantially. As of 2012, foreign exchanges account for about 94 percent

Composition of Total
Official Reserves
(in Percent)

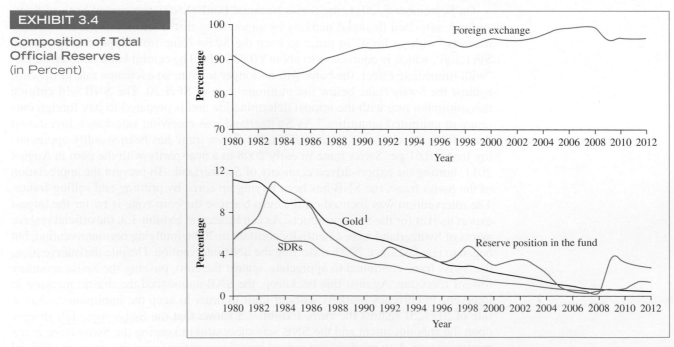

[1]Values at SDR 35 per ounce.

Source: IMF, International Financial Statistics.

of the total reserve assets held by IMF member countries, with gold accounting for less than 1 percent of the total reserves. Similar to gold, the relative importance of SDRs and reserve positions in the IMF have steadily declined. However, due to the IMF's issuance of $250 billion in new SDRs, SDRs' share in global reserves rose to about 4 percent in 2009. The new issuance of SDRs was based on the recommendation of the G-20 summit meeting held in London in April 2009. The objective of the new issuance was to boost global liquidity.

As can be seen from Exhibit 3.5, the U.S. dollar's share in the world's foreign exchange reserves was 50.9 percent in 1991, followed by the German mark (15.7 percent), ECU (10.0 percent), Japanese yen (8.7 percent), British pound (3.4 percent), French franc (2.8 percent), Swiss franc (1.2 percent), and Dutch guilder (1.1 percent). The "predecessor" currencies of the euro, including the German mark, French franc, Dutch guilder, and ECU, collectively received a substantial weight, about 30 percent, in the world's foreign exchange reserves. For comparison, in 1997, the world's reserves comprised the U.S. dollar (59.1 percent), German mark (13.7 percent), Japanese yen (5.1 percent), British pound (3.3 percent), French franc (1.5 percent), ECU (5.0 percent), Swiss franc (0.5 percent), Dutch guilder (0.5 percent), and miscellaneous currencies (11.3 percent). In other words, the U.S. dollar's share increased substantially throughout the 1990s at the expense of other currencies. This change could be attributed to a strong performance of the dollar in the 1990s and the uncertainty associated with the introduction of the new currency, that is, the euro. In 2011, the world reserves comprised the U.S. dollar (62.1 percent), euro (24.9 percent), Japanese yen (3.6 percent), British pound (3.8 percent), Swiss franc (0.3 percent), and miscellaneous currencies (5.3 percent). The dollar's dominant position in the world's reserve holdings may decline to a certain extent as the euro becomes a better "known quantity" and central banks wish to diversify their reserve holdings. In fact, the euro's share has increased from 13.5 percent in 1999 to 27.4 percent in 2009. In 2011, however, it declined somewhat to 24.9 percent due to the euro-zone debt crisis.

In addition to the emergence of the euro as a credible reserve currency, continued U.S. trade deficits and foreigners' desire to diversify their currency holdings away from U.S. dollars could further diminish the position of the U.S. dollar as the dominant reserve currency. Particularly, the value of the U.S. dollar would also be very much affected by the currency diversification decisions of Asian central banks. These banks collectively hold an enormous amount of foreign currency reserves, mostly in dollars, arising from trade surpluses. Asian central banks also purchase U.S. dollars in foreign exchange markets in order to limit appreciation of their local currencies against the dollar.

Currency Composition of the World's Foreign Exchange Reserves
(Percent of Total)

EXHIBIT 3.5 Currency	1989	1991	1993	1995	1997	1999	2001	2003	2005	2007	2009	2011
U.S. dollar	51.9	50.9	56.2	53.4	59.1	64.9	66.9	63.8	66.9	64.1	62.1	62.1
Japanese yen	7.3	8.7	8.0	6.7	5.1	5.4	5.5	4.8	3.6	2.9	3.0	3.6
Pound sterling	2.6	3.4	3.1	2.8	3.3	3.6	4.0	4.4	3.6	4.7	4.3	3.8
Swiss franc	1.4	1.2	1.2	0.5	0.5	0.4	0.5	0.4	0.1	0.2	0.1	0.3
Euro	—	—	—	—	—	13.5	16.7	19.7	24.0	26.3	27.4	24.9
Deutsche mark	18.0	15.7	14.1	14.7	13.7	—	—	—	—	—	—	—
French franc	1.4	2.8	2.2	2.4	1.5	—	—	—	—	—	—	—
Dutch guilder	1.1	1.1	0.6	0.5	0.5	—	—	—	—	—	—	—
ECU	10.5	10.0	8.3	6.8	5.0	—	—	—	—	—	—	—
Other currencies	5.7	6.2	6.2	12.1	11.3	12.1	6.4	6.8	1.7	1.8	3.1	5.3

Source: IMF, *Annual Report of the Executive Board,* various issues.

The Balance-of-Payments Identity

When the balance-of-payments accounts are recorded correctly, the combined balance of the current account, the capital account, and the reserves account must be zero, that is,

$$BCA + BKA + BRA = 0 \qquad (3.1)$$

where:

BCA = balance on the current account
BKA = balance on the capital account
BRA = balance on the reserve account

The balance on the reserves account, BRA, represents the change in the official reserves.

Equation 3.1 is the **balance-of-payments identity (BOPI)** that must necessarily hold. The BOPI equation indicates that a country can run a balance-of-payments surplus or deficit by increasing or decreasing its official reserves. Under the fixed exchange rate regime, countries maintain official reserves that allow them to have balance-of-payments disequilibrium, that is, BCA + BKA is nonzero, without adjusting the exchange rate. Under the fixed exchange rate regime, the combined balance on the current and capital accounts will be equal in size, but opposite in sign, to the change in the official reserves:

$$BCA + BKA = -BRA \qquad (3.2)$$

For example, if a country runs a deficit on the overall balance, that is, BCA + BKA is negative, the central bank of the country can supply foreign exchanges out of its reserve holdings. But if the deficit persists, the central bank will eventually run out of its reserves, and the country may be forced to devalue its currency. This is roughly what happened to the Mexican peso in December 1994.

Under the *pure* flexible exchange rate regime, central banks will not intervene in the foreign exchange markets. In fact, central banks do not need to maintain official reserves. Under this regime, the overall balance thus must necessarily balance, that is,

$$BCA = -BKA \qquad (3.3)$$

In other words, a current account surplus or deficit must be matched by a capital account deficit or surplus, and vice versa. In a *dirty* floating exchange rate system under which the central banks discreetly buy and sell foreign exchanges, Equation 3.3 will not hold tightly.

Being an identity, Equation 3.3 does not imply a causality by itself. A current account deficit (surplus) may cause a capital account surplus (deficit), or the opposite may hold. It has often been suggested that the persistent U.S. current account deficits made it necessary for the United States to run matching capital account surpluses, implying that the former *causes* the latter. One can argue, with equal justification, that the persistent U.S. capital account surpluses, which may have been caused by high U.S. interest rates, have caused the persistent current account deficits by strengthening the value of the dollar. The issue can be settled only by careful empirical studies.

Balance-of-Payments Trends in Major Countries

Considering the significant attention that balance-of-payments data receive in the news media, it is useful to closely examine balance-of-payments trends in some of the major countries. Exhibit 3.6 provides the balance on the current account (BCA) as well as the balance on the capital account (BKA) for each of the five key

EXHIBIT 3.6 Balances on the Current (BCA) and Capital (BKA) Accounts of Five Major Countries: 1982–2011 ($ billion)[a]

Year	China BCA	China BKA	Japan BCA	Japan BKA	Germany BCA	Germany BKA	United Kingdom BCA	United Kingdom BKA	United States BCA	United States BKA
1982	5.7	0.6	6.9	−11.6	4.9	−2.0	8.0	−10.6	−11.6	16.6
1983	4.2	−0.1	20.8	−19.3	4.6	−6.6	5.3	−7.1	−44.2	45.4
1984	2.0	−1.9	35.0	−32.9	9.6	−9.9	1.8	−2.8	−99.0	102.1
1985	−11.4	9.0	51.1	−51.6	17.6	−15.4	3.3	0.7	124.5	128.3
1986	−7.0	5.0	85.9	70.7	40.9	−36.5	−1.3	5.0	−150.5	150.2
1987	0.3	4.5	84.4	−46.3	46.4	−24.9	−8.1	28.2	−166.5	157.3
1988	−3.8	6.2	79.2	−61.7	50.4	−66.0	−29.3	33.9	−127.7	131.6
1989	−4.3	3.8	63.2	−76.3	57.0	−54.1	−36.7	28.6	−104.3	129.5
1990	12.0	0.1	44.1	−53.2	48.3	−41.1	−32.5	32.5	94.3	96.5
1991	13.3	1.3	68.2	−76.6	−17.7	11.5	−14.3	19.0	−9.3	3.5
1992	6.4	−8.5	112.6	−112.0	−19.1	56.3	−18.4	11.7	−61.4	57.4
1993	−11.6	13.4	131.6	104.2	13.9	0.3	15.5	21.0	−90.6	91.9
1994	6.9	23.5	130.3	−105.0	−20.9	18.9	−2.3	3.8	−132.9	127.6
1995	1.6	20.9	111.0	−52.4	−22.6	29.8	−5.9	5.0	−129.2	138.9
1996	7.2	24.5	65.9	−30.7	−13.8	12.6	−3.7	3.2	−148.7	142.1
1997	29.7	6.1	94.4	−87.8	−1.2	2.6	6.8	−11.0	−166.8	167.8
1998	31.5	−6.3	120.7	−116.8	−6.4	17.6	−8.0	0.2	−217.4	151.6
1999	21.1	5.2	106.9	−31.1	−18.0	−40.5	−31.9	31.0	−324.4	367.9
2000	20.5	2.0	116.9	−75.5	−18.7	13.2	−28.8	26.2	−444.7	443.6
2001	17.4	34.8	87.8	−51.0	1.7	−24.1	−32.1	31.5	−385.7	419.9
2002	35.4	32.3	112.4	−66.7	43.4	−70.4	−26.2	17.3	−473.9	572.7
2003	45.9	52.7	136.2	67.9	54.9	−79.3	−30.5	24.8	−530.7	541.2
2004	68.7	110.7	172.1	22.5	120.3	−146.9	−35.2	10.4	−640.2	553.9
2005	160.8	58.9	165.8	−122.7	131.8	−151.2	−55.0	73.8	−754.9	763.3
2006	249.9	6.0	170.5	−102.3	150.8	−179.8	−77.6	49.0	−811.5	830.8
2007	371.8	70.4	210.5	−187.2	263.1	−325.3	−74.7	66.2	−726.6	663.7
2008	426.1	18.9	156.6	−172.6	243.9	−300.8	−39.9	21.5	−706.1	509.9
2009	297.1	144.8	142.2	−130.2	168.0	−185.9	−28.7	38.1	−419.8	474.9
2010	237.8	229.2	203.9	−155.1	200.7	−194.8	−75.2	79.5	−470.9	472.9
2011	201.7	180.6	119.1	57.1	204.3	−201.2	−46.0	51.2	−473.4	489.5

[a]The balance on the capital account (BKA) in this table includes statistical discrepancies. Most discrepancies occur in the capital account.
Source: IMF, *International Financial Statistics Yearbook*, various issues.

countries, China, Japan, Germany, the United Kingdom, and the United States, during the period 1982–2011.

Exhibit 3.6 shows first that the United States has experienced continuous deficits on the current account since 1982 and continuous surpluses on the capital account. Clearly, the magnitude of U.S. current account deficits is far greater than any that other countries ever experienced during the 30-year sample period. In 2006, the U.S. current account deficit reached $812 billion before it started to decline due to the recession. The U.S. balance-of-payments trend is illustrated in Exhibit 3.7. The exhibit shows that the U.S. current account deficit has increased sharply since 1997. This situation has led some politicians and commentators to lament that Americans are living far beyond their means. As a matter of fact, the net international investment position of the United States turned negative in 1987 for the first time in decades and continued to deteriorate. The overseas debt burden of the United States—the difference between the value of foreign-owned assets in the United States and the value of U.S.-owned assets abroad—reached about $2,540 billion at the end of 2006, when valued by the replacement cost of the investments made abroad and at home. As recently as 1986, the United States was considered a net creditor nation, with about $35 billion more in assets overseas than foreigners owned in the United States. Since 2006, however, the current account deficit has declined for the U.S., reflecting the effect of the "Great Recession." The

A New Global Reserve?

"Network effects make the US Dollar very difficult to replace as the main international reserve currency, even if other currencies could in principle play the same role."

Every three months the IMF publishes data on the composition of official foreign exchange reserves. There are two things predictable about this release. One, the level of reserves continues to rise and two, renewed speculation about the role of the dollar as a global reserve currency.

This time round was no different. Total worldwide reserves stood at $8.3 trillion in the first quarter of 2010, up from $7.2 trillion during the same period last year. As a share of allocated reserves, the dollar's weight has fallen from 73% in 2001 to 61%. Even China, which makes up the bulk of the $3.7 trillion unallocated reserves, is thought to be diversifying away from the dollar.

But adding weight to the numbers are two reports, one from the Asian Development Bank and the other from the UN, calling for a new global reserve system. Both reports correctly point out that as a store of value, the dollar is too volatile. The dollar-dominated regime probably worsened the crisis due to a liquidity shortage, before the Fed opened swap lines with other banks. Rising deficits and slow growth in America are also making central bankers weary of holding additional US debt.

These are all valid points, but it could be said that they overlook an important aspect of a reserve currency—ease of transaction. Central bank reserve managers are not like traditional asset managers who need to trade in and out of currencies. Nonetheless, a reserve currency must have a deep and liquid market. This is where the dollar scores over other currencies. Even the euro, which was a viable alternative before the current crisis, has not been able to displace the dollar's dominant position as an international medium of exchange. One explanation is obviously inertia. Banks are used to dealing with

International Finance in Practice box "A New Global Reserve?" looks at issues associated to international currency reserve.

Second, Exhibit 3.6 reveals that Japan has had an unbroken string of current account surpluses since 1982 despite the fact that the value of the yen rose steadily until the mid-1990s. The same point can be seen clearly from Exhibit 3.7. As can be expected, during this period Japan realized capital account deficits in most years; Japan invested heavily in foreign stocks and bonds, businesses, real estates, art objects, and the like to recycle its huge, persistent current account surpluses. Consequently, Japan emerged as the world's largest creditor nation, whereas the United States became the largest debtor nation. Japan had a capital account surplus in 2003, 2004 and 2011, reflecting increased foreign investments in Japanese securities and businesses. The persistent current account disequilibrium was a major source of friction between Japan and its key trading partners, especially the United States. In fact, Japan has often been criticized for pursuing **mercantilism** to ensure continuous trade surpluses.[7] In more recent years, however, China replaced Japan as the trading partner, realizing the largest trade surplus with the U.S. As a result, China has been under pressure to let its currency appreciate against the dollar.

[7]Mercantilism, which originated in Europe during the period of absolute monarchies, holds that precious metals like gold and silver are the key components of national wealth, and that a continuing trade surplus should be a major policy goal as it ensures a continuing inflow of precious metals and thus continuous increases in national wealth. Mercantilists, therefore, abhor trade deficits and argue for imposing various restrictions on imports. Mercantilist ideas were criticized by such British thinkers as David Hume and Adam Smith. Both argued that the main source of wealth of a country is its productive capacity, not precious metals.

a set of bilateral exchange rates and will continue to do so. But these attitudes can change, particularly with a crisis. What is more difficult to get over is network externalities—if dollars can be exchanged easily against other foreign currencies, then any domestic currency can be exchanged against dollars.

To understand how difficult it is to break this network, consider the natural experiment that is highlighted in the BIS annual report.[8] In Hungary, the forint had a well-developed swap market for exchanging the domestic currency into both the dollar and the euro. Before the crisis the currency of choice for swaps was the dollar. But after the collapse of Lehman Brothers in September 2008, dollar shortage was acute. Consequently the price of a dollar swap rose over that of the euro swap, and traders switched to the euro.

Once the Fed provided dollar funding to the European banks, the yields on the dollar went down and traders switched back to the dollar. Why not stay with the euro once you have made the switch? The report concludes that in Hungary, as in other eastern European countries, loans are denominated in Swiss francs.

So banks that were looking to hedge, ultimately needed to convert domestic currency into francs. And since the Swiss franc/dollar swap market overwhelms the Swiss franc/euro market, traders reverted to swapping the domestic currency against the dollar in the aftermath of the crisis.

Arguably, that highlights the biggest challenge in designing a new global reserve system. Beyond just a store of value, the currency must be at the center of international banking and cross-border lending. Introducing a new currency into this network will be hard, even if it's the right thing to do. Like Facebook, the dollar may not be the best system around, but it's what everyone else uses, hence it's hard to displace.

www.ecb.int/stats

This website provides balance-of-payment data on the euro zone countries.

Third, like the United States, the United Kingdom recently experienced continuous current account deficits, coupled with capital account surpluses. The magnitude, however, is far less than that of the United States. Germany, on the other hand, traditionally had current account surpluses. Since 1991, however, Germany has been experiencing current account deficits. This is largely due to German reunification and the resultant need to absorb more output domestically to rebuild the East German region. This has left less output available for exports. Since 2001, however, Germany began to realize current account surpluses and capital account deficits, returning to the earlier pattern.

Fourth, like Japan, China tends to have a balance-of-payment surplus on the current account. Unlike Japan, however, China tends to realize a surplus on the capital account as well. In 2011, for instance, China had a $201.7 billion surplus on the current account and, at the same time, a $180.6 billion surplus on the capital account. This implies that China's official reserve holdings must have gone up for the year. In fact, China's official reserves have increased sharply in recent years, reaching $3.30 trillion as of the end of 2012.

It is clear from Exhibit 3.6 that the United States and United Kingdom tend to realize current account deficits, whereas China, Japan, and Germany tend to realize current account surpluses. This "global imbalance" implies that the United States and United Kingdom generally use up more outputs than they produce, whereas the opposite holds for China, Japan, and Germany. Thus, if the global imbalance is to be reduced, it would be desirable for deficit countries to consume less and save more and for surplus countries to consume more and save less.[9]

---

[8]The reference is to the 80th Annual Report, covering the period 1 April 2009-31 March 2010, published on 28 June 2010, page 57.

[9]The current account balance (BCA) is equal to national output (Y) minus domestic absorption (which comprises consumption, investment, and government expenditure), i.e., $BCA = Y - (C + I + G)$.

EXHIBIT 3.7   Balance-of-Payments Trends: 1982–2011

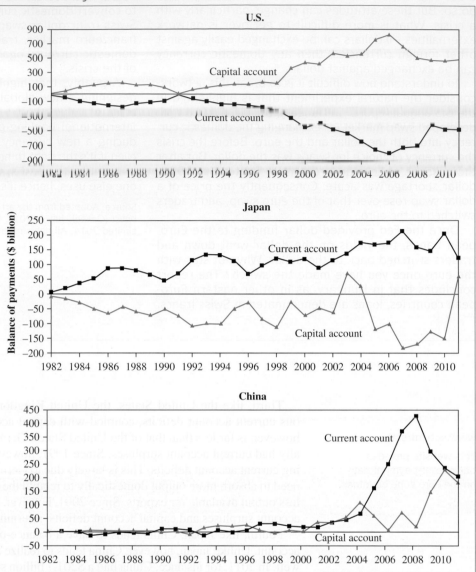

Source: IMF, *International Financial Statistics.*

While perennial balance-of-payments deficits or surpluses can be a problem, each country need not achieve balance-of-payments equilibrium every year. Suppose a country is currently experiencing a trade deficit because of the import demand for capital goods that are necessary for economic development projects. In this case, the trade deficit can be self-correcting in the long run because once the projects are completed, the country may be able to export more or import less by substituting domestic products for foreign imports. In contrast, if the trade deficit is the result of importing consumption goods, the situation may not correct itself. Thus, what matters is the nature and causes of the disequilibrium.

Lastly, let us briefly examine which countries the United States trades with most actively. Exhibit 3.8 provides the list of top 15 trading partners of the United States in terms of merchandise imports and exports. As can be expected, the United States trades most with Canada, its northern neighbor and a member of NAFTA, importing $324.2 billion and exporting $292.4 billion in 2012. China is the second most

EXHIBIT 3.8

Top U.S. Trading Partners, 2012 (in billions of dollars)

Rank	Country	Imports	Exports	Trade Balance	Total Trade
1	Canada	324.2	292.4	−31.8	616.7
2	China	425.6	110.6	−315.0	536.2
3	Mexico	277.7	216.3	−61.4	494.0
4	Japan	146.4	70.0	−76.4	216.4
5	Germany	108.5	48.8	−59.7	157.3
6	United Kingdom	54.9	54.8	0.1	109.8
7	Korea, South	50.9	42.3	−16.6	101.2
8	Brazil	32.1	43.7	11.6	75.8
9	Saudi Arabia	55.7	18.1	−37.6	73.8
10	France	41.6	30.8	−10.8	72.4
11	Taiwan	38.9	24.4	14.5	63.2
12	Netherlands	22.3	40.7	18.4	63.0
13	India	40.5	22.3	−18.2	62.9
14	Venezuela	38.7	17.6	−21.1	56.4
15	Italy	36.9	16.0	−20.9	52.9

Source: Census Bureau.

important trading partner for the United States, importing $425.6 billion and exporting $110.6 billion in 2012. Clearly, imports from China far exceed exports to China, resulting in a bilateral trade deficit of $315 billion for the United States in 2012. This large trade surplus for China (and deficit for the United States) is a major factor driving appreciation of Chinese renminbi (RMB) against the United States dollar in recent years. Mexico, a southern neighbor of the United States and another member of NAFTA, is the third most important trading partner of the United States, followed by Japan and Germany. It is noted that the United States had trade deficits with most of its trading partners in 2012.

SUMMARY

1. The balance of payments can be defined as the statistical record of a country's international transactions over a certain period of time presented in the form of double-entry bookkeeping.

2. In the balance of payments, any transaction resulting in a receipt from foreigners is recorded as a credit, with a positive sign, whereas any transaction resulting in a payment to foreigners is recorded as a debit, with a minus sign.

3. A country's international transactions can be grouped into three main categories: the current account, the capital account, and the official reserve account. The current account includes exports and imports of goods and services, whereas the capital account includes all purchases and sales of assets such as stocks, bonds, bank accounts, real estate, and businesses. The official reserve account covers all purchases and sales of international reserve assets, such as dollars, foreign exchanges, gold, and SDRs.

4. The current account is divided into four subcategories: merchandise trade, services, factor income, and unilateral transfers. Merchandise trade represents exports and imports of tangible goods, whereas trade in services includes payments and receipts for legal, engineering, consulting, and other performed services and tourist expenditures. Factor income consists of payments and receipts of interest, dividends, and other income on previously made foreign investments. Lastly, unilateral transfer involves unrequited payments such as gifts, foreign aid, and reparations.

www.mcgraw-hill.co.uk/textbooks/eun

5. The capital account is divided into three subcategories: direct investment, portfolio investment, and other investment. Direct investment involves acquisitions of controlling interests in foreign businesses. Portfolio investment represents investments in foreign stocks and bonds that do not involve acquisitions of control. Other investment includes bank deposits, currency investment, trade credit, and the like.

6. When we compute the cumulative balance of payments including the current account, capital account, and the statistical discrepancies, we obtain the overall balance or official settlement balance. The overall balance is indicative of a country's balance-of-payments gap that must be accommodated by official reserve transactions. If a country must make a net payment to foreigners because of a balance-of-payments deficit, the country should either run down its official reserve assets, such as gold, foreign exchanges, and SDRs, or borrow anew from foreigners.

7. A country can run a balance-of-payments surplus or deficit by increasing or decreasing its official reserves. Under the fixed exchange rate regime, the combined balance on the current and capital accounts will be equal in size, but opposite in sign, to the change in the official reserves. Under the pure flexible exchange rate regime where the central bank does not maintain any official reserves, a current account surplus or deficit must be matched by a capital account deficit or surplus.

KEY WORDS

balance of payments, *62*
balance-of-payments
  identity (BOPI), *72*
capital account, *64*
current account, *64*
factor income, *65*
foreign direct investment
  (FDI), *67*

invisible trade, *65*
J-curve effect, *66*
mercantilism, *74*
merchandise trade, *65*
official reserve account, *64*
official reserve assets, *69*
official settlement
  balance, *68*

other investment, *68*
overall balance, *68*
portfolio investment, *67*
services, *65*
trade balance, *65*
unilateral transfers, *65*

QUESTIONS

1. Define *balance of payments*.

2. Why would it be useful to examine a country's balance-of-payments data?

3. The United States has experienced continuous current account deficits since the early 1980s. What do you think are the main causes for the deficits? What would be the consequences of continuous U.S. current account deficits?

4. In contrast to the United States, Japan has realized continuous current account surpluses. What could be the main causes for these surpluses? Is it desirable to have continuous current account surpluses?

5. Comment on the following statement: "Since the United States imports more than it exports, it is necessary for the United States to import capital from foreign countries to finance its current account deficits."

6. Explain how a country can run an overall balance-of-payments deficit or surplus.

7. Explain *official reserve assets* and its major components.

8. Explain how to compute the overall balance and discuss its significance.

9. Since the early 1980s, foreign portfolio investors have purchased a significant portion of U.S. Treasury bond issues. Discuss the short-term and long-term effects of foreigners' portfolio investment on the U.S. balance of payments.

10. Describe the *balance-of-payments identity* and discuss its implications under the fixed and flexible exchange rate regimes.

11. Exhibit 3.6 indicates that in 1999, Germany had a current account deficit and at the same time a capital account deficit. Explain how this can happen.

12. Explain how each of the following transactions will be classified and recorded in the debit and credit of the U.S. balance of payments:

   a. A Japanese insurance company purchases U.S. Treasury bonds and pays out of its bank account kept in New York City.

   b. A U.S. citizen consumes a meal at a restaurant in Paris and pays with her American Express card.

   c. An Indian immigrant living in Los Angeles sends a check drawn on his LA bank account as a gift to his parents living in Mumbai.

   d. A U.S. computer programmer is hired by a British company for consulting and gets paid from the U.S. bank account maintained by the British company.

13. Construct a balance-of-payments table for Germany for the year 2010 which is comparable in format to Exhibit 3.1, and interpret the numerical data. You may consult *International Financial Statistics* published by IMF or search for useful websites for the data yourself.

14. Discuss the possible strengths and weaknesses of SDRs versus the dollar as the main reserve currency. Do you think the SDR should or could replace the U.S. dollar as the main global reserve currency?

PROBLEMS

1. Examine the following summary of the U.S. balance of payments for 2000 (in $ billion) and fill in the blank entries.

	Credits	Debits
Current Account		
(1) Exports	1,418.64	
(1.1) Merchandise	774.86	
(1.2) Services	290.88	
(1.3) Factor income	352.90	
(2) Imports		−1,809.18
(2.1) Merchandise		☐
(2.2) Services		−217.07
(2.3) Factor income		−367.68
(3) Unilateral transfer	10.24	−64.39
Balance on current account		☐
Capital Account		
(4) Direct investment	287.68	−152.44
(5) Portfolio investment	474.59	−124.94
(5.1) Equity securities	193.85	−99.74
(5.2) Debt securities	280.74	−25.20
(6) Other investment	262.64	−303.27
Balance on capital account	☐	
(7) Statistical discrepancies	☐	
Overall balance	0.30	
Official Reserve Account		−0.30

Source: IMF, *International Financial Statistics Yearbook, 2001.*

1. Study the website of the International Monetary Fund (IMF), www.imf.org, and discuss the role of the IMF in dealing with balance-of-payment and currency crises.

MINI CASE

Mexico's Balance-of-Payments Problem

Mexico experienced large-scale trade deficits, depletion of foreign reserve holdings, and a major currency devaluation in December 1994, followed by the decision to freely float the peso. These events also brought about a severe recession and higher unemployment in Mexico. Since the devaluation, however, the trade balance has improved.

Investigate the Mexican experiences in detail and write a report on the subject. In the report, you may:

1. Document the trend in Mexico's key economic indicators, such as the balance of payments, the exchange rate, and foreign reserve holdings, during the period 1994.1 through 1995.1?

2. Investigate the causes of Mexico's balance-of-payments difficulties prior to the peso devaluation.

3. Discuss what policy actions might have prevented or mitigated the balance-of-payments problem and the subsequent collapse of the peso.

4. Derive lessons from the Mexican experience that may be useful for other developing countries.

In your report, you may identify and address any other relevant issues concerning Mexico's balance-of-payments problem. *International Financial Statistics* published by the IMF provides basic macroeconomic data on Mexico.

REFERENCES & SUGGESTED READINGS

Edwards, Sebastian. *Real Exchange Rates, Devaluation and Adjustment: Exchange Rate Policy in Developing Countries.* Cambridge, Mass.: MIT Press, 1989.

Grabbe, Orlin. *International Financial Markets.* New York: Elsevier, 1991.

Kemp, Donald. "Balance of Payments Concepts—What Do They Really Mean?" *Federal Reserve Bank of St. Louis Review*, July 1975, pp. 14–23.

Ohmae, Kenichi. "Lies, Damned Lies and Statistics: Why the Trade Deficit Doesn't Matter in a Borderless World." *Journal of Applied Corporate World*, Winter, 1991, pp. 98–106.

Salop, Joan, and Erich Spitaller. "Why Does the Current Account Matter?" International Monetary Fund, *Staff Papers*, March 1980, pp. 101–34.

U.S. Department of Commerce. "Report of the Advisory Committee on the Presentation of the Balance of Payments Statistics." *Survey of Current Business*, June, 1991, pp. 18–25.

Yeager, Leland. *International Monetary Relations.* New York: Harper & Row, 1965.

3A The Relationship Between Balance of Payments and National Income Accounting

This section is designed to explore the mathematical relationship between balance-of-payments accounting and national income accounting and to discuss the implications of this relationship. National income (Y), or gross domestic product (GDP), is identically equal to the sum of nominal consumption (C) of goods and services, private investment expenditures (I), government expenditures (G), and the difference between exports (X) and imports (M) of goods and services:

$$GDP \equiv Y \equiv C + I + G + X - M. \tag{3A.1}$$

Private savings (S) is defined as the amount left from national income after consumption and taxes (T) are paid:

$$S \equiv Y - C - T, \text{ or} \tag{3A.2}$$

$$S \equiv C + I + G + X - M - C - T. \tag{3A.3}$$

Noting that the BCA $\equiv$ X $-$ M, equation (3A.3) can be rearranged as:

$$(S - I) + (T - G) = X - M \equiv BCA \tag{3A.4}$$

Equation (3A.4) shows that there is an intimate relationship between a country's BCA and how the country finances its domestic investment and pays for government expenditures. In equation (3A.4), (S − I) is the difference between a country's savings and investment. If (S − I) is negative, it implies that a country's domestic savings is insufficient to finance domestic investment. Similarly, (T − G) is the difference between tax revenue and government expenditures. If (T − G) is negative, it implies that tax revenue is insufficient to cover government spending and a government budget deficit exists. This deficit must be financed by the government issuing debt securities.

Equation (3A.4) also shows that when a country imports more than it exports, its BCA will be negative because through trade foreigners obtain a larger claim to domestic assets than the claim the country's citizens obtain to foreign assets. Consequently, when BCA is negative, it implies that government budget deficits and/or part of domestic investment are being financed with foreign-controlled capital. In order for a country to reduce a BCA deficit, one of the following must occur:

1. For a given level of S and I, the government budget deficit (T − G) must be reduced.
2. For a given level of I and (T − G), S must be increased.
3. For a given level S and (T − G), I must fall.

4 Corporate Governance Around the World

IN CHAPTER 1, we argue that the key goal of financial management should be shareholder wealth maximization. In reality, however, there is no guarantee that managers would run the company to maximize the welfare of shareholders. In fact, the recent spate of corporate scandals and failures, including Enron, WorldCom, and Global Crossing in the United States, Daewoo Group (a major *chaebol*) in Korea, Parmalat in Italy, and HIH (a major insurance group) in Australia, has raised serious questions about the way public corporations are governed around the world. When "self-interested" managers take control of the company, they sometimes engage in actions that are profoundly detrimental to the interests of shareholders and other stakeholders. For example, such managers may give themselves excessive salaries and indulge perquisites, squander resources for corporate empire building, divert the company's cash and assets for private benefits, engage in cronyism, and steal business opportunities from the company. A recent report in the *Harvard Business Review* (January 2003) describes how American executives "treat their companies like ATMs, awarding themselves millions of dollars in corporate perks." In many less developed and transitional countries, corporate governance mechanisms are either very weak or virtually nonexistent. In Russia, for example, a weak corporate governance system allows managers to divert assets from newly privatized companies on a large scale.

When managerial self-dealings are excessive and left unchecked, they can have serious negative effects on corporate values and the proper functions of capital markets. In fact, there is a growing consensus around the world that it is vitally important to strengthen **corporate governance** to protect **shareholder rights**, curb managerial excesses, and restore confidence in capital markets. *Corporate governance* can be defined as *the economic, legal, and institutional framework in which corporate control and cash flow rights are distributed among shareholders, managers, and other stakeholders of the company*. Other stakeholders may include workers, creditors, banks, institutional investors, and even the government. As we will see later, corporate governance structure varies a great deal across countries, reflecting divergent cultural, economic, political, and legal environments. It is thus essential for international investors and multinational corporations to have a solid understanding of the corporate governance environments around the world. An example of governance risk is provided by Citigroup's dealings with Parmalat. According to BBC News (March 18, 2005), William Mills of Citigroup said, "Citigroup is a victim of Parmalat's fraud and lost more than 500 million euros as a result…. If Citigroup had known the truth, it would not have done business with Parmalat."

Governance of the Public Corporation: Key Issues

The **public corporation**, which is jointly owned by a multitude of shareholders protected by limited liability, is a major organizational innovation with powerful economic consequences. The majority of global corporations that drive economic growth and innovations worldwide, such as Apple, Google, General Electric (GE), IBM, Toyota, Samsung Electronics, British Petroleum (BP), and BMW, are chartered as public corporations rather than as private companies. The genius of public corporations stems from their capacity to allow efficient sharing or spreading of risk among many investors, who can buy and sell their ownership shares on liquid stock exchanges and let professional managers run the company on behalf of shareholders. This efficient risk-sharing mechanism enables public corporations to raise large amounts of capital at relatively low costs and undertake many investment projects that individual entrepreneurs or private investors might eschew because of the costs and/or risks. Public corporations have played a pivotal role in spreading economic growth and capitalism worldwide for the last few centuries.

However, the public corporation has a key weakness—namely, the conflicts of interest between managers and shareholders. The separation of the company's ownership and control, which is especially prevalent in such countries as the United States and the United Kingdom, where corporate ownership is highly diffused, gives rise to possible conflicts between shareholders and managers. In principle, shareholders elect the board of directors of the company, which in turn hires managers to run the company for the interests of shareholders. In the United States, managers are legally bound by the "duty of loyalty" to shareholders. Managers are thus supposed to be agents working for their principals, that is, shareholders, who are the real owners of the company. In a public company with diffused ownership, the board of directors is entrusted with the vital tasks of monitoring the management and safeguarding the interests of shareholders.

In reality, however, management-friendly insiders often dominate the board of directors, with relatively few outside directors who can independently monitor the management. In the case of Enron and similarly dysfunctional companies, the boards of directors grossly failed to safeguard shareholder interests. Furthermore, with diffused ownership, few shareholders have strong enough incentive to incur the costs of monitoring management themselves when the benefits from such monitoring accrue to all shareholders alike. The benefits are shared, but not the costs. When company ownership is highly diffused, this "free-rider" problem discourages shareholder activism. As a result, the interests of managers and shareholders are often allowed to diverge. With an ineffective and unmotivated board of directors, shareholders are basically left without effective recourse to control managerial self-dealings. Recognition of this key weakness of the public corporation can be traced at least as far back as Adam Smith's *Wealth of Nations* (1776), which stated:

> The directors of such joint-stocks companies, however, being the managers rather of other people's money than of their own, it cannot well be expected that they should watch over it with the same anxious vigilance with which the partners of a private copartnery frequently watch over their own. . . . Negligence and profusion, therefore, must always prevail, more or less, in the management of the affairs of such a company.

Two hundred years later, Jensen and Meckling (1976) provided a formal analysis of the "agency problem" of the public corporation in their celebrated paper "Theory of the Firm: Managerial Behavior, Agency Costs, and Ownership Structure." The Jensen-Meckling agency theory drew attention to this vitally important corporate finance problem.

It is suggested, however, that outside the United States and the United Kingdom, diffused ownership of the company is more the exception than the rule. In Italy, for instance, the three largest shareholders control, on average, about 60 percent of the shares of a public company. The average comparable ownership by the three largest shareholders is 54 percent in Hong Kong, 64 percent in Mexico, 48 percent in Germany, 40 percent in India, and 51 percent in Israel.[1] These large shareholders (often including founding families of the company) effectively control managers and may run the company for their own interests, expropriating outside shareholders in one way or another. In many countries with concentrated corporate ownership, conflicts of interest are greater between large controlling shareholders and small outside shareholders than between managers and shareholders.

In a series of influential studies, La Porta, Lopez-de-Silanes, Shleifer, and Vishny (LLSV, hereafter) document sharp differences among countries with regard to (i) corporate ownership structure, (ii) depth and breadth of capital markets, (iii) access of firms to external financing, and (iv) dividend policies. LLSV argue that these differences among countries can be explained largely by how well investors are protected by law from expropriation by the managers and controlling shareholders of firms. LLSV also argue that the degree of legal protection of investors significantly depends on the "legal origin" of countries. Specifically, English common law countries, such as Canada, the United States, and the United Kingdom, provide the strongest protection for investors, whereas French civil law countries, such as Belgium, Italy, and Mexico, provide the weakest. We will revisit the issue of law and corporate governance later in the chapter.

Shareholders in different countries may indeed face divergent corporate governance systems. However, the central problem in corporate governance remains the same everywhere: *how to best protect outside investors from expropriation by the controlling insiders so that the investors can receive fair returns on their investments.* How to deal with this problem has enormous practical implications for shareholder welfare, corporate allocation of resources, corporate financing and valuation, development of capital markets, and economic growth. In the rest of this chapter, we will discuss the following issues in detail:[2]

- Agency problem
- Remedies for the agency problem
- Law and corporate governance
- Consequences of law
- Corporate governance reform

The Agency Problem

Suppose that the manager (or entrepreneur) and the investors sign a contract that specifies how the manager will use the funds and also how the investment returns will be divided between the manager and the investors. If the two sides can write a **complete contract** that specifies exactly what the manager will do under each of all possible future contingencies, there will be no room for any conflicts of interest or managerial discretion. Thus, under a complete contract, there will be no **agency problem**. However, it is practically impossible to foresee all future contingencies and write a complete contract. This means that the manager and the investors will have to allocate the rights (control) to make decisions under those contingencies that are not specifically covered by the contract. Because the outside investors may be neither qualified

---

[1]Source: R. La Porta, F. Lopez-de-Silanes, A. Shleifer, and R. Vishny, "Law and Finance," *Journal of Political Economy* 106 (1998), pp. 1113–55.

[2]Our discussion here draws on the contributions of Jensen and Meckling (1976), Jensen (1989), La Porta, Lopez-de-Silanes, Shleifer, and Vishny (1997–2002), and Denis and McConnell (2002).

nor interested in making business decisions, the manager often ends up acquiring most of this **residual control right**. The investors supply funds to the company but are not involved in the company's daily decision making. As a result, many public companies come to have "strong managers and weak shareholders." The agency problem refers to the possible conflicts of interest between self-interested managers as agents and shareholders of the firm who are the principals.

Having captured residual control rights, the manager can exercise substantial discretion over the disposition and allocation of investors' capital. Under this situation, the investors are no longer assured of receiving fair returns on their funds. In the contractual view of the firm described above, the agency problem arises from the difficulty that outside investors face in assuring that they actually receive fair returns on their capital.[3]

With the control rights, the manager may allow himself or herself to consume exorbitant perquisites. For example, Steve Jobs, the former CEO of Apple Inc., reportedly had a $90 million company jet at his disposal.[4] Sometimes, the manager simply steals investors' funds. Alternatively, the manager may use a more sophisticated scheme, setting up an independent company that he owns and diverting to it the main company's cash and assets through *transfer pricing*. For example, the manager can sell the main company's output to the company he owns at below market prices, or buy the output of the company he owns at above market prices. Some Russian oil companies are known to sell oil to manager-owned trading companies at below market prices and not always bother to collect the bills.[5]

Self-interested managers may also waste funds by undertaking unprofitable projects that benefit themselves but not investors. For example, managers may misallocate funds to take over other companies and overpay for the targets if it serves their private interests. Needless to say, this type of investment will destroy shareholder value. What is more, the same managers may adopt antitakeover measures for their own company in order to ensure their personal job security and perpetuate private benefits. In the same vein, managers may resist any attempts to be replaced even if shareholders' interests will be better served by their dismissal. These **managerial entrenchment** efforts are clear signs of the agency problem.

As pointed out by Jensen (1989), the agency problem tends to be more serious in companies with "free cash flows." **Free cash flows** represent a firm's internally generated funds in excess of the amount needed to undertake all profitable investment projects, that is, those with positive net present values (NPVs). Free cash flows tend to be high in mature industries with low future growth prospects, such as the steel, chemical, tobacco, paper, and textile industries. It is the *fiduciary duty* of managers to return free cash flows to shareholders as dividends. However, managers in these cash-rich and mature industries will be most tempted to waste cash flows to undertake unprofitable projects, destroying shareholders' wealth but possibly benefiting themselves.

There are a few important incentives for managers to retain cash flows. First, cash reserves provide corporate managers with a measure of independence from the capital markets, insulating them from external scrutiny and discipline. This will make life easier for managers. Second, growing the size of the company via retention of cash tends to have the effect of raising managerial compensation. As is well known, executive compensation depends as much on the size of the company as on its profitability, if not more. Third, senior executives can boost their social and political power and prestige by increasing the size of their company. Executives presiding over large companies are likely to enjoy greater social prominence and visibility than those running small companies. Also, the company's size itself can be a way of satisfying the executive ego.

[3]The contractual view of the firm was developed by Coase (1937) and Jensen and Meckling (1976).
[4]Source: *Financial Times*, November 27, 2002, p. 15.
[5]Source: A. Shleifer and R. Vishny, "A Survey of Corporate Governance," *Journal of Finance* (1997).

In the face of strong managerial incentives for retaining cash, few effective mechanisms exist that can compel the managers to disgorge cash flows to shareholders. Jensen cites a revealing example of this widespread problem (1989, p. 66):

> A vivid example is the senior management of Ford Motor Company, which sits on nearly $15 billion in cash and marketable securities in an industry with excess capacity. Ford's management has been deliberating about acquiring financial service companies, aerospace companies, or making some other multibillion-dollar diversification move— rather than deliberating about effectively distributing Ford's excess cash to its owners so they can decide how to reinvest it.

He also points out that in the 1980s, many Japanese public companies retained enormous amounts of free cash flow, far exceeding what they needed to finance profitable internal projects. For example, Toyota Motor Company, with a cash hoard of more than $10 billion, was known as the "Toyota Bank." Lacking effective internal control and external monitoring mechanisms, these companies went on an overinvestment binge in the 1980s, engaging in unprofitable acquisitions and diversification moves. This wasteful corporate spending is, at least in part, responsible for the economic slump that Japan has experienced since the early 1990s.

The preceding examples show that the heart of the agency problem is the conflicts of interest between managers and the outside investors over the disposition of free cash flows. However, in high-growth industries, such as biotechnology, financial services, and pharmaceuticals, where companies' internally generated funds fall short of profitable investment opportunities, managers are less likely to waste funds in unprofitable projects. After all, managers in these industries need to have a "good reputation," as they must repeatedly come back to capital markets for funding. Once the managers of a company are known for wasting funds for private benefits, external funding for the company may dry up quickly. The managers in these industries thus have an incentive to serve the interests of outside investors and build a reputation so that they can raise the funds needed for undertaking their "good" investment projects.

Remedies for the Agency Problem

Obviously, it is a matter of vital importance for shareholders to control the agency problem; otherwise, they may not be able to get their money back. It is also important for society as a whole to solve the agency problem, since the agency problem leads to waste of scarce resources, hampers capital market functions, and retards economic growth. Several governance mechanisms exist to alleviate or remedy the agency problem:

1. Independent board of directors
2. Incentive contracts
3. Concentrated ownership
4. Accounting transparency
5. Debt
6. Overseas stock listings
7. Market for corporate control

In the following sections, we discuss the corporate governance role of each of these mechanisms.

Board of Directors

In the United States, shareholders have the right to elect the board of directors, which is legally charged with representing the interests of shareholders. If the board of directors remains independent of management, it can serve as an effective mechanism for curbing the agency problem. For example, studies show that the appointment of outside directors is associated with a higher turnover rate of CEOs following poor firm performances, thus curbing managerial entrenchment. In the same vein, in a study of corporate governance in the United Kingdom, Dahya, McConnell, and Travlos (2002) report that the board of directors is more likely to appoint an outside CEO after an increase in outsiders' representation on the board. But due to the diffused ownership structure of the public company, management often gets to choose board members who are likely to be friendly to management. The International Finance in Practice box "The Satyam Scandal," highlights the issue of an insider-dominated board and the poor governance mechanisms that can result.

The structure and legal charge of corporate boards vary greatly across countries. In Germany, for instance, the corporate board is not legally charged with representing the interests of shareholders. Rather, it is charged with looking after the interests of stakeholders (e.g., workers, creditors) in general, not just shareholders. In Germany, there are two-tier boards consisting of supervisory and management boards. Based on the German *codetermination* system, the law requires that workers be represented on the supervisory board. Likewise, some U.S. companies have labor union representatives on their boards, although it is not legally mandated. In the United Kingdom, the majority of public companies voluntarily abide by the *Code of Best Practice* on corporate governance recommended by the *Cadbury Committee*. The code recommends that there should be at least three outside directors and that the board chairman and the CEO should be different individuals. Apart from outside directors, separation of the chairman and CEO positions can further enhance the independence of the board of directors. In Japan, most corporate boards are insider-dominated and are primarily concerned with the welfare of the *keiretsu* to which the company belongs.

Incentive Contracts

As previously discussed, managers capture residual control rights and thus have enormous discretion over how to run the company. But they own relatively little of the equity of the company they manage. To the extent that managers do not own equity shares, they do not have cash flow rights. Although managers run the company at their own discretion, they may not significantly benefit from the profit generated from their efforts and expertise. Jensen and Murphy (1990) show that the pay of American executives changes only by about $3 per every $1,000 change of shareholder wealth; executive pay is nearly insensitive to changes in shareholder wealth. This situation implies that managers may not be very interested in the maximization of shareholder wealth. This "wedge" between managerial control rights and cash flow rights may exacerbate the agency problem. *When professional managers have small equity positions of their own in a company with diffused ownership, they have both power and a motive to engage in self-dealings.*

Aware of this situation, many companies provide managers with **incentive contracts**, such as stocks and stock options, in order to reduce this wedge and better align the interests of managers with those of investors. With the grant of stocks or stock options, managers can be given an incentive to run the company in such a way that enhances shareholder wealth as well as their own. Against this backdrop, incentive contracts for senior executives have become common among public companies in the United States. As we have seen lately, however, senior executives can abuse incentive contracts by artificially manipulating accounting numbers, sometimes with the connivance of auditors (for example, Arthur Andersen's involvements with the Enron debacle), or by altering investment policies so that they can reap enormous personal benefits. It is thus important for the board of directors to set up an independent compensation committee that can carefully design incentive contracts for executives and diligently monitor their actions.

Concentrated Ownership

An effective way to alleviate the agency problem is to concentrate shareholdings. If one or a few large investors own significant portions of the company, they will have a strong incentive to monitor management. For example, if an investor owns 51 percent

The Satyam Scandal

The issue of agency costs is one of considerable importance to investors and arises through the separation of ownership and control of a firm. One way to limit managerial self-dealing and promote investor protection through accountability and integrity is to have independent directors on a board. Typically investors rely on corporate governance and audit procedures to monitor firms. However, sometimes this proves ineffective, as evidenced by recent corporate scandals across the globe.

Take India's fourth largest IT company, Satyam Computer Services, as an example. A scandal began to unfold when Satyam made a $1.66 billion offer, approved by the board on December 16 2008, to buy two property companies owned largely by the family of the Chief Executive Officer of Satyam, Ramlinga Raju. When news of the bid was announced, analysts immediately signalled that it was far too high, investors responded by dumping the stock, and the share price of Satyam fell sharply. As a result, the bid was withdrawn within a matter of hours. Investors were seething that the board had approved the investment in the first instance but it would soon become apparent that this was only the

tip of the iceberg. Following the incident, several of the independent board members resigned. The CEO himself resigned in January and in his letter of resignation, he admitted that the company accounts had been falsified for years, an act for which he assumed full responsibility. It transpired that the company had been overstating revenues and exaggerating profits by $1 billion. The revelations were all the more surprising because Satyam had listed its ADRs (American Depository Receipts) on the New York Stock Exchange. Firms that are based in emerging markets often find it difficult to raise funds and in some cases list on the stock exchanges of developed markets in an attempt to reduce their cost of capital. The trade-off for the emerging market firm is they will be subject to higher standards of corporate governance as the accounting and disclosure requirements tend to be more rigorous and more costly to comply with than those of emerging markets. The very fact that Satyam listed in the U.S. sent a signal to investors that corporate governance quality was high. Ironically, Satyam had been lauded for its corporate governance standards, being previously awarded a Golden Peacock award for

of the company, he or she can definitely control the management (he can easily hire or fire managers) and will make sure that shareholders' rights are respected in the conduct of the company's affairs. With **concentrated ownership** and high stakes, the free-rider problem afflicting small, atomistic shareholders dissipates.

In the United States and the United Kingdom, concentrated ownership of a public company is relatively rare. Elsewhere in the world, however, concentrated ownership is the norm. In Germany, for example, commercial banks, insurance companies, other companies, and families often own significant blocks of company stock. Similarly, extensive cross-holdings of equities among *keiretsu* member companies and main banks are commonplace in Japan. Also in France, cross-holdings and "core" investors are common. In Asia and Latin America, many companies are controlled by founders or their family members. In China, the government is often the controlling shareholder for public companies. Previous studies indicate that concentrated ownership has a positive effect on a company's performance and value. For example, Kang and Shivdasani (1995) report such positive effects for Japan, and Gorton and Schmid (2000) for Germany. This suggests that large shareholders indeed play a significant governance role.

Of particular interest here is the effect of managerial equity holdings. Previous studies suggest that there can be a nonlinear relationship between managerial ownership share and firm value and performance. Specifically, as the managerial ownership share increases, firm value may initially increase, since the interests of managers and outside investors become better aligned (thus reducing agency costs). But if the managerial ownership share exceeds a certain point, firm value may actually start to decline as managers become more entrenched. With larger shareholdings, for example, managers may be able to more effectively resist takeover bids and extract larger private benefits at the expense of outside investors. If the managerial ownership share continues to rise, however, the alignment effect may become dominant again. When managers are large shareholders, they do not want to rob themselves. To summarize, there can be an "interim range" of managerial ownership share over which the entrenchment effect is dominant.

excellence in corporate governance. The award was subsequently withdrawn as the scandal came to light.

Observers raised many questions about the extent of the scandal and the role of the independent directors. Each of the board members were there at the personal invitation of the CEO and that can diminish their monitoring role. Whether crucial information was being withheld from the directors or not, there were warning signs that should have warranted further investigation including the rationale behind Satyam deciding to invest $1.6 billion in real estate. Even if the directors believed this would be an appropriate diversification strategy, the fact that the property companies were operated by family members of the CEO of Satyam should have prompted queries regarding the obvious conflict of interest. Instead, the decision was made to approve the investment without putting it to a shareholder vote. The role of the auditor is to ensure transparency and that the financial statements provide an accurate picture of the financial position of the company. The failure of the auditors to uncover the financial malpractice raised serious concerns especially after it was revealed that Satyam was paying PricewaterhouseCoopers almost twice the rate that rival companies were paying to their audit firms. Eventually, PWC admitted that its audit report was wrong but argued that it was due to incorrect financial statements provided by Satyam's management.

There was concern that the scandal could do unprecedented damage to "Brand India". Regulators reacted swiftly in an attempt to minimise the damage. The board of Satyam was replaced and a criminal investigation was launched. The investigation led to the arrest of Ramlinga Raju, several high-ranking members of Satyam, and two members of PWC. Following a tendering process by the Indian government, the company was acquired by Tech Mahindra just four months after the scandal emerged and renamed Mahindra Satyam. A new board was established, new auditors appointed, and by the first quarter of 2011, the company had recorded a profit. However, the entire saga raised questions as to the strength of the corporate governance system in India.

Sources: Compiled from various sources, including:

Scandal at Satyam: Truth, Lies and Corporate Governance: https://knowledge.wharton.upenn.edu/article/scandal-at-satyam-truth-lies-and-corporate-governance/
The Satyam Scandal. Forbes: http://www.forbes.com/2009/01/07/satyam-raju-governance-oped-cx_sb_0107balachandran.html
Satyam Chief Admits Huge Fraud: New York Times: http://www.nytimes.com/2009/01/08/business/worldbusiness/08satyam.html?_r = 0
The Satyam scandal: Offshore inmates: The Economist: http://www.economist.com/node/12943984

This situation is illustrated in Exhibit 4.1, depicting a possible relationship between managerial ownership share and firm value. According to Morck, Shleifer, and Vishny (1988), who studied the relationship for *Fortune* 500 U.S. companies, the first turning point (x) is reached at about 5 percent and the second (y) at about 25 percent. This means that the "entrenchment effect" is roughly dominant over the range of managerial ownership between 5 percent and 25 percent, whereas the "alignment effect" is dominant for the ownership shares less than 5 percent and exceeding 25 percent.[6] The relationship between managerial ownership and firm value is likely to vary across countries. For instance, Short and Keasey (1999) indicate that the inflection point (x) is reached at 12 percent in the United Kingdom, a much higher level of managerial ownership than in the United States. They attribute this difference to more effective monitoring by U.K. institutional investors and the lesser ability of U.K. managers to resist takeover.

Accounting Transparency

Considering that major corporate scandals, such as Enron and Parmalat, are associated with massive accounting frauds, strengthening accounting standards can be an effective way of alleviating the agency problem. Self-interested managers or corporate insiders can have an incentive to "cook the books" (for example, inflating earnings and hiding debts) to extract private benefits from the company. The managers need a veil of opaque accounting numbers to pursue their own interests at the expense of shareholders. Therefore, if companies are required to release more accurate accounting information in a timely fashion, managers may be less tempted to take actions that are detrimental to the interests of shareholders. Basically, a greater accounting transparency will reduce the information asymmetry between corporate insiders and the public and discourage managerial self-dealings.

To achieve a greater transparency, however, it is important for (i) countries to reform the accounting rules and (ii) companies to have an active and qualified audit committee.

---

[6]It is noted that the authors actually used "Tobin's q" to measure firm value. Tobin's q is the ratio of the market value of company assets to the replacement costs of the assets.

EXHIBIT 4.1

The Alignment versus
Entrenchment Effects of
Managerial Ownership

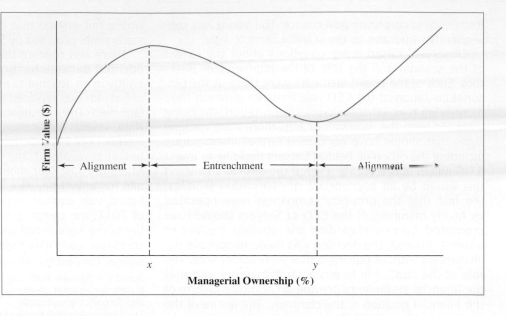

As we will discuss later in this chapter, the Sarbanes-Oxley Act of 2002 aims, among other things, to promote a greater accounting transparency in the United States.

Debt

Although managers have discretion over how much of a dividend to pay to shareholders, debt does not allow such managerial discretion. If managers fail to pay interest and principal to creditors, the company can be forced into bankruptcy and its managers may lose their jobs. Borrowing and the subsequent obligation to make interest payments on time can have a major disciplinary effect on managers, motivating them to curb private perks and wasteful investments and trim bloated organizations. In fact, debt can serve as a substitute for dividends by forcing managers to disgorge free cash flow to outside investors rather than wasting it. For firms with free cash flows, debt can be a stronger mechanism than stocks for credibly bonding managers to release cash flows to investors.[7]

Excessive debt, however, can create its own problem. In turbulent economic conditions, equities can buffer the company against adversity. Managers can pare down or skip dividend payments until the situation improves. With debt, however, managers do not have such flexibility and the company's survival can be threatened. Excessive debt may also induce the risk-averse managers to forgo profitable but risky investment projects, causing an underinvestment problem. For this reason, debt may not be such a desirable governance mechanism for young companies with few cash reserves or tangible assets. In addition, companies can misuse debt to finance corporate empire building. Daewoo, a Korean *chaebol*, borrowed excessively to finance global expansion until it went into bankruptcy; its debt-to-equity ratio reached 600 percent before bankruptcy.

Overseas Stock Listings

Companies domiciled in countries with weak investor protection, such as Italy, Korea, and Russia, can bond themselves credibly to better investor protection by listing their stocks in countries with strong investor protection, such as the United States and the

---

[7]Leveraged buyouts (LBOs) can also be viewed as a remedy for the agency problem. LBOs involve managers or buyout partners acquiring controlling interests in public companies, usually financed by heavy borrowing. Concentrated ownership and high level of debt associated with LBOs can be effective in solving the agency problem.

United Kingdom. In other words, foreign firms with weak governance mechanisms can opt to outsource a superior corporate governance regime available in the United States via cross-listings. Suppose that Fiat, an Italian automobile company, announces its decision to list its stock on the New York Stock Exchange (NYSE).[8] Since the level of shareholder protection afforded by the U.S. Securities and Exchange Commission (SEC) and the NYSE is much higher than that provided in Italy, the action will be interpreted as signaling the company's commitment to shareholder rights. Then, investors both in Italy and abroad will be more willing to provide capital to the company and value the company shares more. Generally speaking, the beneficial effects from U.S. listings will be greater for firms from countries with weaker governance mechanisms.

Studies confirm the effects of cross-border listings. Specifically, Doidge, Karolyi, and Stulz (2002) report that foreign firms listed in the United States are valued more than those from the same countries that are not listed in the United States. They argue that firms listed in the United States can take better advantage of growth opportunities and that controlling shareholders cannot extract as many private benefits. It is pointed out, however, that foreign firms in mature industries with limited growth opportunities are not very likely to seek U.S. listings, even though these firms face more serious agency problems than firms with growth opportunities that are more likely to seek U.S. listings. In other words, firms with more serious problems are less likely to seek the remedies.

Emerging stock markets, such as China, India, Russia, and Vietnam, are highly imperfect, reflecting inadequate disclosure and regulation, opaque legal and governance framework, and ownership restrictions. In the case of China, for example, stock markets are dominated by a multitude of small individual investors who are neither well informed nor protected. So far, institutional investors, such as mutual funds, pension funds, and insurance companies, who can produce high-quality information about listed companies and effectively protect shareholders' rights, play a relatively minor role in China. However, public Chinese companies can offer the so-called "B-shares" to foreign investors that are listed on domestic stock exchanges alongside A-shares for local investors, or directly list their shares on the Hong Kong Stock Exchange as "H-shares" or on other foreign stock exchanges, including the New York Stock Exchange. Eun and Huang (2007) found that domestic Chinese investors pay higher prices for local A-shares of those Chinese companies that offer B- or H-shares to international investors. This is in recognition of the facts that (i) the issuance of international shares, that is, B-shares and H-shares, is subject to much more stringent disclosure and listing standards, making more information available to shareholders; and (ii) that foreign shareholders, especially institutional investors, may provide more rigorous monitoring of the management, thereby benefiting Chinese local shareholders as well. The Eun and Huang study also found that *ceteris paribus*, Chinese investors pay a premium for dividend-paying stocks as dividends convincingly signal the management's willingness to return cash flows to outside shareholders, rather than expropriating them.

Market for Corporate Control

Suppose a company continually performs poorly and all of its internal governance mechanisms fail to correct the problem. This situation may prompt an outsider (another company or investor) to mount a takeover bid. In a hostile takeover attempt, the bidder typically makes a tender offer to the target shareholders at a price substantially exceeding the prevailing share price. The target shareholders thus have an opportunity to sell their shares at a substantial premium. If the bid is successful, the bidder will acquire the control rights of the target and restructure the company. Following a successful takeover, the bidder often replaces the management team, divests some assets or divisions, and trims employment in an effort to enhance efficiency. If these efforts are successful, the combined market value of the acquirer and target companies will

---

[8]Fiat is actually listed on the New York Stock Exchange.

become higher than the sum of stand-alone values of the two companies, reflecting the synergies created. The market for corporate control, if it exists, can have a disciplinary effect on managers and enhance company efficiency.

In the United States and the United Kingdom, hostile takeovers can serve as a drastic governance mechanism of the last resort. Under the potential threat of takeover, managers cannot take their control of the company for granted. In many other countries, however, hostile takeovers are relatively rare. This is so partly because of concentrated ownership in these countries and partly because of cultural values and political environments disapproving hostile corporate takeovers. But even in these countries, the incidence of corporate takeovers has been gradually increasing. This can be due, in part, to the spreading of equity culture and the opening and deregulation of capital markets. In Germany, for instance, takeovers are carried out through transfer of block holdings. In Japan, as in Germany, interfirm cross-holdings of equities are loosening, creating capital market conditions that are more conducive to takeover activities. To the extent, however, that companies with poor investment opportunities and excess cash initiate takeovers, it may be a symptom, rather than a cure, of the agency problem.

Law and Corporate Governance

When outside investors entrust funds to the company, they receive certain rights that are legally protected. Among these are the rights to elect the board of directors, receive dividends on a pro-rata basis, participate in shareholders' meetings, and sue the company for expropriation. These rights empower investors to extract from management fair returns on their funds. However, the content of law protecting investors' rights and the quality of law enforcement vary a great deal across countries. According to the studies of La Porta, Lopez-de-Silanes, Shleifer, and Vishny (LLSV), many of the observed differences in international corporate governance systems arise from the differences in how well outside investors are protected by law from expropriation by managers and other corporate insiders. LLSV argue that the legal protection of investor rights systematically varies, depending on the historical origins of national legal systems.

Legal scholars show that the commercial legal systems (for example, company, security, bankruptcy, and contract laws) of most countries derive from relatively few **legal origins**:

- English common law
- French civil law
- German civil law
- Scandinavian civil law

The French and German civil laws derived from the Roman law, whereas the Scandinavian countries developed their own civil law tradition that is less derivative of Roman law. The civil law tradition, which is the most influential and widely spread, is based on the comprehensive *codification of legal rules*. In contrast, English common law is formed by the *discrete rulings* of independent judges on specific disputes and *judicial precedent.*

These distinct legal systems, especially **English common law** and **French civil law**, spread around the world through conquest, colonization, voluntary adoption, and subtle imitation. The United Kingdom and its former colonies, including Australia, Canada, India, Malaysia, Singapore, South Africa, New Zealand, and the United States, have the English common law system. France and the parts of Europe conquered by Napoleon, such as Belgium, the Netherlands, Italy, Portugal, and Spain, ended up with the French civil law tradition. Further, many former overseas colonies of France, the Netherlands, Portugal, and Spain, such as Algeria, Argentina, Brazil, Chile, Indonesia, Mexico, and the Philippines, also ended up with the French civil law system. The German civil law family comprises Germany and the Germanic countries of Europe, such as Austria and Switzerland, and a few East Asian countries such as Japan and Korea. The Scandinavian civil law family includes four Nordic countries: Denmark, Finland, Norway, and Sweden. Thus, in most countries, the national legal system did not indigenously develop but rather was transplanted from one of several legal origins. Although national legal systems have evolved and adapted to local conditions, it is still possible to classify them into a few distinct families. Such a classification is provided in Exhibit 4.2. The exhibit also provides the indexes for shareholder rights and rule of law for each country as computed by LLSV (1998).

Exhibit 4.2 shows that the average shareholder rights index is 4.00 for English common law countries, 2.33 for both French and German civil law countries, and 3.00 for Scandinavian civil law countries. Thus, English common law countries tend to offer the strongest protection for investors, French and German civil law countries offer the weakest, and Scandinavian civil law countries fall in the middle. The quality of law enforcement, as measured by the rule of law index, is the highest in Scandinavian and German civil law countries, followed by English common law countries; it is lowest in French civil law countries.

Clearly, there is a marked difference in the legal protection of investors between the two most influential legal systems, namely, English common law and French civil law. A logical question is: Why is the English common law system more protective of investors than the French civil law system? According to the prevailing view, the state historically has played a more active role in regulating economic activities and has been less protective of property rights in civil law countries than in common law countries. In England, control of the court passed from the crown to Parliament and property owners in the seventeenth century. English common law thus became more protective of property owners, and this protection was extended to investors over time. This legal tradition in England allows the court to exercise its discretionary judgment or "smell test" over which managerial self-dealings are *unfair* to investors. In France as well as in Germany, parliamentary power was weak and commercial laws were codified by the state, with the role of the court confined to simply determining whether the codified rules were violated or not. Since managers can be creative enough to expropriate investors without obviously violating the codified rules, investors receive low protection in civil law countries.

Glaesser and Shleifer (2002) offer an intriguing explanation of the English and French legal origins based on the divergent political situations prevailing in the Middle Ages. In France, local feudal lords were powerful and there were incessant wars. Under this turbulent situation, there was a need for the protection of adjudicators from local powers, which can only be provided by the king. France came to adopt a royal judge-inquisitor model based on the *Justinian code* of the Roman Empire in the thirteenth century. According to this model, judges appointed by the king collect evidence, prepare written records, and determine the outcome of the case. Understandably, royal judges were mindful of the preferences of the king. The French legal tradition was formalized by the *Code Napoleon*. Napoleon extensively codified legal rules, *bright line rules* in legal terms, and required state-appointed judges to merely apply these rules. In England, in contrast, local lords were less powerful and war was less frequent. In a more peaceful England, which partly reflects the country's geographical isolation, local magnates were mainly afraid of royal power and preferred adjudication by a local jury that was not beholden to the preferences of the crown and was more knowledgeable about local facts and preferences. Initially, the jury consisted of 12 armed knights who were less likely to be intimidated by local bullies or special pressure groups. After the adoption of *Magna Carta* in 1215, local magnates basically paid the crown for the privilege of local, independent adjudication and other rights. The divergent legal developments in England and France came to have lasting effects on the legal systems of many countries.

EXHIBIT 4.2

Classification of
Countries by Legal
Origins

Legal Origin	Country	Shareholder Rights Index	Rule of Law Index
1. English common law	Australia	4	10.00
	Canada	5	10.00
	Hong Kong	5	8.22
	India	5	4.17
	Ireland	4	7.80
	Israel	3	4.82
	Kenya	3	5.42
	Malaysia	4	6.78
	New Zealand	4	10.00
	Nigeria	3	2.73
	Pakistan	5	3.03
	Singapore	4	8.57
	South Africa	5	4.42
	Sri Lanka	3	1.90
	Thailand	2	6.25
	United Kingdom	5	8.57
	United States	5	10.00
	Zimbabwe	3	3.68
	English-origin average	**4.00**	**6.46**
2. French civil law	Argentina	4	5.35
	Belgium	0	10.00
	Brazil	3	6.32
	Chile	5	7.02
	Colombia	3	2.08
	Ecuador	2	6.67
	Egypt	2	4.17
	France	3	8.98
	Greece	2	6.18
	Indonesia	2	3.98
	Italy	1	8.33
	Jordan	1	4.35
	Mexico	1	5.35
	Netherlands	2	10.00
	Peru	3	2.50
	Philippines	3	2.73
	Portugal	3	8.68
	Spain	4	7.80
	Turkey	2	5.18
	Uruguay	2	5.00
	Venezuela	1	6.37
	French-origin average	**2.33**	**6.05**
3. German civil law	Austria	2	10.00
	Germany	1	9.23
	Japan	4	8.98
	South Korea	2	5.35
	Switzerland	2	10.00
	Taiwan	3	8.52
	German-origin average	**2.33**	**8.68**
4. Scandinavian civil law	Denmark	2	10.00
	Finland	3	10.00
	Norway	4	10.00
	Sweden	3	10.00
	Scandinavian-origin average	**3.00**	**10.00**

Note: Shareholder rights index scales from 0 (lowest) to 6 (highest). Rule of law index scales from 0 (lowest) to 10 (highest).

Source: Rafael La Porta, Florencio Lopez-de-Silanes, Andrei Shleifer, Robert W. Vishny, "Law and Finance," *Journal of Political Economy* 106 (1998), pp. 1113–55.

Consequences of Law

Protection of investors' rights not only has interesting legal origins, but the concept is shown to have major economic consequences on the pattern of corporate ownership and valuation, the development of capital markets, economic growth, and others. To illustrate, let us consider two European countries, Italy and the United Kingdom. As shown in Exhibit 4.3, Italy has a French civil law tradition with weak shareholder protection, whereas the United Kingdom, with its common law tradition, provides strong investor protection. In Italy (U.K.), the three largest shareholders own 58 percent (19 percent) of the company, on average. Company ownership is thus highly concentrated in Italy and more diffuse in the United Kingdom. In addition, as of 1999, only 247 companies were listed on the stock exchange in Italy, whereas 2,292 companies were listed in the United Kingdom. In the same year, the stock market capitalization as a proportion of the annual GDP was 71 percent in Italy but 248 percent in the United Kingdom. The stark contrast between the two countries suggests that protection of investors can have significant economic consequences. Concentrated ownership can be viewed as a rational response to weak investor protection, but it may create different conflicts of interest between large controlling shareholders and small outside shareholders. We now discuss some of the issues in detail.

Ownership and Control Pattern

Companies domiciled in countries with weak investor protection may need to have concentrated ownership as a substitute for legal protection. With concentrated ownership, large shareholders can control and monitor managers effectively and solve the agency problem. LLSV (1998) indeed found that corporate ownership tends to be more concentrated in countries with weaker investor protection. As can be seen from Exhibit 4.4, the three largest shareholders own 43 percent of companies on average in English common law countries, and 54 percent of companies on average in French civil law countries.

If large shareholders benefit only from pro-rata cash flows, there will be no conflicts between large shareholders and small shareholders. What is good for large shareholders should be good for small shareholders as well. Since investors may be able to derive private benefits from control, however, they may seek to acquire control rights exceeding cash flow rights. Dominant investors may acquire control through various schemes, such as:

1. Shares with superior voting rights
2. Pyramidal ownership structure
3. Interfirm cross-holdings

Many companies issue shares with differential voting rights, deviating from the one-share one-vote principle. By accumulating superior voting shares, investors can acquire control rights exceeding cash flow rights. In addition, large shareholders, who

<table>
<tr><td>EXHIBIT 4.3</td><td></td><td>Italy</td><td>U.K.</td></tr>
<tr><td rowspan="5">Does Law Matter?: Italy versus the U.K.</td><td>Legal origin</td><td>French civil law</td><td>English common law</td></tr>
<tr><td>Shareholder rights</td><td>1 (low)</td><td>5 (high)</td></tr>
<tr><td>Ownership by three largest shareholders</td><td>58%</td><td>19%</td></tr>
<tr><td>Market cap/GDP</td><td>71%</td><td>248%</td></tr>
<tr><td>Listed stocks</td><td>247</td><td>2,292</td></tr>
</table>

Note: Shareholder rights refer to the antidirector rights index as computed by La Porta, Lopez-de-Silanes, Shleifer, and Vishny (1998). Both the ratio of stock market capitalization to GDP and the number of listed stocks are as of 1999.

Source: Various studies of LLSV and the CIA's *World Factbook*.

EXHIBIT 4.4 Consequences of Law: Ownership and Capital Markets

Legal Origin	Country	Ownership Concentration	External Cap/GNP	Domestic Firms/Population
1. English common law	Australia	0.28	0.49	63.55
	Canada	0.40	0.39	40.86
	Hong Kong	0.54	1.18	88.16
	India	0.40	0.31	7.79
	Ireland	0.39	0.27	20.00
	Israel	0.51	0.25	127.60
	Kenya	na	na	2.24
	Malaysia	0.54	1.48	25.15
	New Zealand	0.48	0.28	69.00
	Nigeria	0.40	0.27	1.68
	Pakistan	0.37	0.18	5.88
	Singapore	0.49	1.18	80.00
	South Africa	0.52	1.45	16.00
	Sri Lanka	0.60	0.11	11.94
	Thailand	0.47	0.56	6.70
	United Kingdom	0.19	1.00	35.68
	United States	0.20	0.58	30.11
	Zimbabwe	0.55	0.18	5.81
	English-origin average	**0.43**	**0.60**	**35.45**
2. French civil law	Argentina	0.53	0.07	4.58
	Belgium	0.54	0.17	15.50
	Brazil	0.57	0.18	3.48
	Chile	0.45	0.80	19.92
	Colombia	0.63	0.14	3.13
	Ecuador	na	na	13.18
	Egypt	0.62	0.08	3.48
	France	0.34	0.23	8.05
	Greece	0.67	0.07	21.60
	Indonesia	0.58	0.15	1.15
	Italy	0.58	0.08	3.91
	Jordan	na	na	23.75
	Mexico	0.64	0.22	2.28
	Netherlands	0.39	0.52	21.13
	Peru	0.56	0.40	9.47
	Philippines	0.57	0.10	2.90
	Portugal	0.52	0.08	19.50
	Spain	0.51	0.17	9.71
	Turkey	0.59	0.18	2.93
	Uruguay	na	na	7.00
	Venezuela	0.51	0.08	4.28
	French-origin average	**0.54**	**0.21**	**10.00**
3. German civil law	Austria	0.58	0.06	13.87
	Germany	0.48	0.13	5.14
	Japan	0.18	0.62	17.78
	South Korea	0.23	0.44	15.88
	Switzerland	0.41	0.62	33.85
	Taiwan	0.18	0.86	14.22
	German-origin average	**0.34**	**0.46**	**16.79**
4. Scandinavian civil law	Denmark	0.45	0.21	50.40
	Finland	0.37	0.25	13.00
	Norway	0.36	0.22	33.00
	Sweden	0.28	0.51	12.66
	Scandinavian-origin average	**0.37**	**0.30**	**27.26**

Note: Ownership concentration measures the average share ownership by three largest shareholders. External Cap/GNP is the ratio of the stock market capitalization held by minority shareholders (other than three shareholders) to the gross national product for 1994. Domestic Firms/Population is the ratio of the number of domestic firms listed in a given country to its population (million) in 1994.

Source: Various studies of LLSV.

EXHIBIT 4.5

Hutchison Whampoa: The
Chain of Control

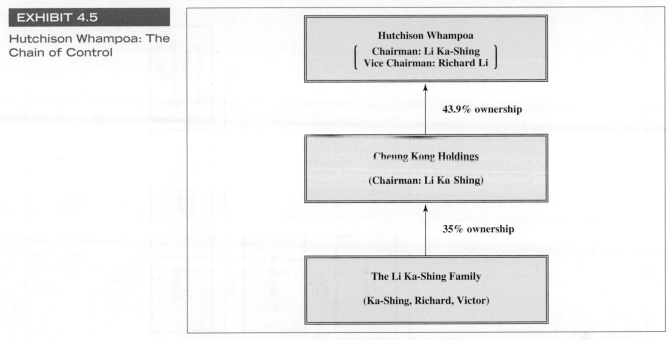

Source: R. La Porta, F. Lopez-de-Silanes, A. Shleifer, and R. Vishny, "Corporate Ownership around the World," *Journal of Finance* 54 (1999), p. 483.

are often founders and their families, can use a **pyramidal ownership** structure in which they control a holding company that owns a controlling block of another company, which in turn owns controlling interests in yet another company, and so on. Also, **equity cross-holdings** among a group of companies, such as *keiretsu* and *chaebols*, can be used to concentrate and leverage voting rights to acquire control. Obviously, a combination of these schemes may also be used to acquire control.

Hutchison Whampoa, the third most valuable public company in Hong Kong, provides an interesting example of pyramidal control structure. The company is 43.9 percent controlled by another public company, Cheung Kong Holdings, which is the fifth-largest publicly traded company in Hong Kong. Cheung Kong Holdings, in turn, is 35 percent controlled by the Li Ka-Shing family. The cash flow rights of the Li family in Hutchison Whampoa are thus 15.4 percent (.35 × .439 = .154), but the family's control rights in Hutchson Whampoa is 43.9 percent. The chain of control of Hutchison Whampoa is illustrated in Exhibit 4.5. In Korea, the ownership structure can be more complicated. Take Samsung Electronics, Korea's most valuable company. Lee Keun-Hee, the chairman of the Samsung *chaebol* and the son of Samsung's founder, controls 8.3 percent of Samsung Electronics directly. In addition, Lee controls 15 percent of Samsung Life, which controls 8.7 percent of Samsung Electronics and 14.1 percent of Cheil Chedang, which controls 3.2 percent of Samsung Electronics and 11.5 percent of Samsung Life. This byzantine web of cross-holdings enables Lee to exercise an effective control of Samsung Electronics.[9]

As in Asia, concentrated ownership and a significant wedge between control and cash flow rights are widespread in continental Europe. Exhibit 4.6 illustrates the pyramidal ownership structure for Daimler-Benz, a German company, at the beginning of the 1990s.[10] The company has three major block holders: Deutsche Bank

[9]Examples here are from R. La Porta, F. Lopez-de-Silanes, A. Shleifer, and R. Vishny, "Corporate Ownership around the World," *Journal of Finance* 54 (1999), pp. 471–517.

[10]This example is from Julian Franks and Colin Mayer, "Ownership and Control of German Corporations," *Review of Financial Studies* 14 (2001), pp. 943–77. Note that the ownership structure of Daimler-Benz has been significantly altered since 1990.

EXHIBIT 4.6 Ownership Structure of Daimler-Benz AG, 1990

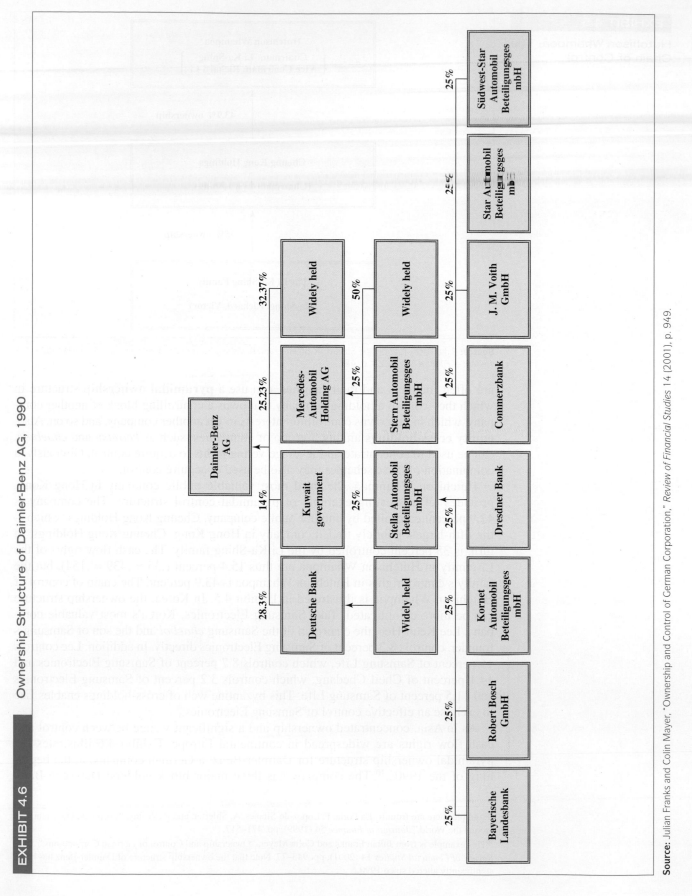

Source: Julian Franks and Colin Mayer, "Ownership and Control of German Corporation," *Review of Financial Studies* 14 (2001). p. 949.

(28.3 percent), Mercedes-Automobil Holding AG (25.23 percent), and the Kuwait government (14 percent). The remaining 32.37 percent of shares are widely held. The pyramidal ownership structure illustrated in Exhibit 4.6 makes it possible for large investors to acquire significant control rights with relatively small investments. For example, Robert Bosch GmbH controls 25 percent of Stella Automobil, which in turn owns 25 percent of Mercedes-Automobil Holding, which controls 25 percent of Daimler-Benz AG. Robert Bosch can possibly control up to 25 percent of the voting rights of Daimler-Benz AG with only 1.56 percent cash flow rights in the company

Private Benefits of Control

Once large shareholders acquire control rights exceeding cash flow rights, they may extract **private benefits of control** that are not shared by other shareholders on a pro-rata basis. A few studies document the existence and magnitude of private benefits. Nenova (2001) computed the premium for voting shares relative to nonvoting shares in different countries. The voting premium, defined as the total vote value (value of a vote times the number of votes) as a proportion of the firm's equity market value, is only about 2 percent in the United States and 2.8 percent in Canada. This implies that private benefits of control are not very significant in both countries. In contrast, the voting premium is 23 percent in Brazil, 9.5 percent in Germany, 29 percent in both Italy and Korea, and 36 percent in Mexico, suggesting that in these countries, dominant shareholders extract substantial private benefits of control. Unless investors can derive significant private benefits of control, they will not pay substantial premiums for voting shares over nonvoting shares.

Dyck and Zingales (2004), on the other hand, computed "block premium," that is, the difference between the price per share paid for the control block and the exchange price after the announcement of the control transaction, divided by the exchange price after the control transaction. Obviously, control blocks will command premiums only if block holders can extract private benefits of control. Similar to Nenova's findings, Dyck and Zingales report that during the period 1990–2000, the average block premium was only 1 percent in Canada, the United Kingdom, and the United States, and 2 percent in Australia and Finland. However, the average block premium was much higher in other countries—65 percent in Brazil, 58 percent in the Czech Republic, 27 percent in Israel, 37 percent in Italy, 16 percent in Korea, and 34 percent in Mexico. Clearly, large shareholders extract significant private benefits of control in those countries where the rights of minority shareholders are not well protected.

Capital Markets and Valuation

The legal analysis of corporate governance predicts that investor protection promotes the development of external capital markets. When investors are assured of receiving fair returns on their funds, they will be willing to pay more for securities. To the extent that this induces companies to seek more funds from outside investors, strong investor protection will be conducive to large capital markets. LLSV (1997) empirically document that countries with strong shareholder protection tend to have more valuable stock markets and more companies listed on stock exchanges per capita than countries with weak protection. Also, a few studies report that higher insider cash flow rights are associated with higher valuation of corporate assets, whereas greater insider control rights are associated with lower valuation of corporate assets. Exhibit 4.4 shows that the stock market capitalization held by minority shareholders (excluding the three largest shareholders) as a proportion to the GNP for the year 1994 is 0.60 in English common law countries and 0.21 in French civil law countries. The exhibit also shows that the number of domestic firms listed on stock exchanges per population (million) is about 35 in English common law countries, compared with only 10 in French civil law countries.

Weak investor protection can also be a contributing factor to sharp market declines during a financial crisis. In countries with weak investor protection, insiders may treat outside investors reasonably well as long as business prospects warrant continued

www.gcgf.org
This site is for the Global Corporate Governance Forum, founded by the World Bank and the OECD to improve the institutional framework and practices of corporate governance.

external financing. However, once future prospects dim, insiders may start to expropriate the outside investors as the need for external funding dissipates. The accelerated expropriation can induce sharp declines in security prices. Johnson, Boon, Breach, and Friedman (2000) provide evidence that during the Asian financial crisis of 1997–98, stock markets actually declined more in countries with weaker investor protection.

The existence of well-developed financial markets, promoted by strong investor protection, may stimulate economic growth by making funds readily available for investment at low cost. Earlier, Schumpeter (1934) argued that financial development promotes economic growth. Several studies now document the empirical link between financial development and economic growth, supporting the Schumpeter hypothesis.[11] According to Beck et al. (2000), financial development can contribute to economic growth in three major ways: (i) It enhances savings; (ii) it channels savings toward real investments in productive capacities, thereby fostering capital accumulation; and (iii) it enhances the efficiency of investment allocation through the monitoring and signaling functions of capital markets.

Corporate Governance Reform

In the wake of the Asian financial crisis of 1997–98 and the spectacular failure of several major companies like Daewoo, Enron, WorldCom, and Parmalat, scandal-weary investors around the world are demanding corporate governance reform. The failure of these companies hurts shareholders as well as other stakeholders, including workers, customers, and suppliers. Many employees who invested heavily in company stock for their retirement were dealt severe financial blows. It is not just the companies' internal governance mechanisms that failed; auditors, regulators, banks, and institutional investors also failed in their respective roles. Failure to reform corporate governance will damage investor confidence, stunt the development of capital markets, raise the cost of capital, distort capital allocation, and even shake confidence in capitalism itself.

Objectives of Reform

During the 1980s, when the economies of Germany and Japan were strong performers, the governance systems of the two countries received much attention and admiration. In both Germany and Japan, banks and a few permanent large shareholders play the central role in corporate governance. This "bank-centered" governance system was seen as guiding corporate managers to pursue long-term performance goals and also as effectively supporting companies when they were in financial distress. In contrast, the "market-centered" governance system of the United States was viewed as inducing short-term-oriented corporate decisions and being ineffectual in many ways. However, as the U.S. economy and its stock market surged ahead in the 1990s, with Germany and Japan lagging behind, the U.S.-style market-centered governance system replaced the German-Japanese system as a subject of admiration. The American market-oriented system seemed the wave of the future. But then, the subsequent slowdown of the U.S. economy and stock market and the shocking corporate scandals again dethroned the U.S. system. It seems fair to say that no country has a perfect system for other countries to emulate.

There is a growing consensus that corporate governance reform should be a matter of global concern. Although some countries face more serious problems than others, existing governance mechanisms have failed to effectively protect outside investors in many countries. What should be the objective of reform? Our discussion in this chapter suggests a simple answer: *Strengthen the protection of outside investors from expropriation by managers and controlling insiders.* Among other things, reform requires: (i) strengthening the independence of boards of directors with more outsiders, (ii) enhancing the transparency and disclosure standard of financial statements, and

---

[11] Examples include King and Levine (1993), Rajan and Zingales (1998), and Beck, Levine, and Loayza (2000).

(iii) energizing the regulatory and monitoring functions of the SEC (in the United States) and stock exchanges. In many developing and transition countries, it may be necessary to first modernize the legal framework.

Political Dynamics

However, as we have seen from the experiences of many countries, governance reform is easier said than done. First of all, the existing governance system is a product of the historical evolution of the country's economic, legal, and political infrastructure. It is not easy to change historical legacies. Second, many parties have vested interests in the current system, and they will resist any attempt to change the status quo. For example, Arthur Levitt, chairman of the SEC during much of the 1990s, attempted to reform the accounting industry, but it successfully resisted the attempt through the use of lobbyists and advertising. In Levitt's words (*The Wall Street Journal*, June 17, 2002, p. C7): "The ferocity of the accounting profession's opposition to our attempt to reform the industry a few years ago is no secret. . . . They will do everything possible to protect their franchise, and will do so with little regard for the public interest." This earlier failure to reform the accounting industry contributed to the breakout of corporate scandals in the United States. It is noted that the former executives of World-Com were indicted for allegedly orchestrating the largest accounting fraud in history, with the help of conniving auditors.[12] In another example, following the Asian financial crisis, the Korean government led efforts to reform the country's *chaebol* system but met with stiff resistance from the founding families, which were basically afraid of losing their private benefits of control. Nevertheless, reform efforts in Korea were partially successful, partly because the weight and prestige of the government were behind them and partly because public opinion was generally in favor of reform.

http://leadership.wharton.
upenn.edu/governance/index.
shtml

This site offers online resources and academic readings concerning corporate governance.

To be successful, reformers should understand the political dynamics surrounding governance issues and seek help from the media, public opinion, and nongovernmental organizations (NGOs). The role of NGOs and the media can be illustrated by the success of the People's Solidarity for Participatory Democracy (PSPD) in Korea, organized by Hasung Jang of Korea University. The PSPD and Professor Jang have utilized legal pressure and media exposure to create public opinion and to shame corporate executives into changing their practices. For example, PSPD successfully challenged the transfer pricing of SK Telecom. Specifically, SK Telecom transferred huge profits to two subsidiaries, Sunkyung Distribution, which is 94.6 percent owned by SK Group Chairman Choi Jong-Hyun, and Daehan Telecom, fully owned by Choi's son and his son-in-law, thereby expropriating outside shareholders of SK Telecom. The PSPD exposed this practice to the media, and the episode was reported in the *Financial Times* as well as local newspapers and television. Facing unfavorable public opinion, SK Telecom finally agreed to stop the practice.[13]

The Sarbanes-Oxley Act

Facing public uproar following the U.S. corporate scandals, politicians took actions to remedy the problem. The U.S. Congress passed the **Sarbanes-Oxley Act** in July 2002. The key objective of the Act is to protect investors by improving the accuracy and reliability of corporate disclosure, thereby restoring the public's confidence in the integrity of corporate financial reporting. The major components of the Sarbanes-Oxley Act are:

- Accounting regulation—The creation of a public accounting oversight board charged with overseeing the auditing of public companies, and restricting the consulting services that auditors can provide to clients.
- Audit committee—The company should appoint independent "financial experts" to its audit committee.

---

[12]*New York Times*, September 2, 2002, p. A16.

[13]Alexander Dyck and Luigi Zingales, "The Corporate Governance Role of the Media," working paper (2002).

- Internal control assessment—Public companies and their auditors should assess the effectiveness of internal control of financial record keeping and fraud prevention.
- Executive responsibility—Chief executive and finance officers (CEO and CFO) must sign off on the company's quarterly and annual financial statements. If fraud causes an overstatement of earnings, these officers must return any bonuses.

The Sarbanes-Oxley Act represents one of the most important securities legislations since the original securities laws of the 1930s. As mandated by the Act, the NYSE and the NASDAQ also strengthened the listing standards by adopting various measures to protect investors. These measures call for, among other things: (i) listed companies to have boards of directors with a majority of independents; (ii) the compensation, nominating, and audit committees to be entirely composed of independent directors; and (iii) the publication of corporate governance guidelines and reporting of annual evaluation of the board and CEO. These measures, if properly implemented, should improve the corporate governance regime in the United States.

Evidences regarding the effect of the Sarbanes-Oxley Act on the corporate disclosure and governance standards are generally positive. For example, Lobo and Zhou (2006) found a marked increase in "conservatism" in financial reporting following the enactment. Specifically, firms began to report lower discretionary accruals (meaning less active earnings management) and recognize losses more quickly than gains when they report income in the post-Act period. It is noted that Enron managed earnings very aggressively by prematurely recognizing revenue and hiding or shifting losses and liabilities to many non-consolidated special purpose entities. These dubious accounting practices, which eventually led to Enron's implosion, declined partly because of the harsh penalties on CEO and CFO imposed by the Sarbanes-Oxley Act (up to a $5 million fine and 20 years in prison) for falsely certifying financial statements that do not satisfy the requirements of the Act. Another study by Linck, Netter, and Yang (2009) found substantial changes in the company boards and directors as well following the Sarbanes-Oxley enactment. Specifically, the study noted that (i) board committees meet more often, (ii) boards become larger and more independent, and (iii) board members are more likely to be lawyers, consultants, or financial experts and less likely to be corporate insiders. These findings indicate that the boards of directors became more proactive for fulfilling their responsibilities and also better qualified for doing their duties.

The implementation of the Sarbanes-Oxley Act, however, was not free from frictions. Many companies find the compliance with a particular provision of the act, Section 404, onerous, costing millions of dollars. Section 404 requires public companies and their auditors to assess the effectiveness of internal control of financial record keeping and fraud prevention and file reports with the Securities and Exchange Commission (SEC). Clearly, the cost of compliance disproportionately affects smaller companies. In addition, many U.S.-listed foreign firms that have different governance structures at home also find it costly to comply with the Sarbanes-Oxley Act. Since the passage of the act, some foreign firms have chosen to list their shares on the London Stock Exchange and other European exchanges, instead of U.S. exchanges, to avoid the costly compliance.

The Cadbury Code of Best Practice

Like the United States, the United Kingdom was hit by a spate of corporate scandals in the 1980s and early 1990s, resulting in the bankruptcy of such high-profile companies as Ferranti, Colorol Group, BCCI, and Maxwell Group. The "scandalous" collapse of these prominent British companies was popularly attributed to their complete corporate control by a single top executive, weak governance mechanisms, and the failure of their boards of directors. Against this backdrop, the British government appointed the *Cadbury Committee* in 1991 with the broad mandate of addressing corporate governance problems in the United Kingdom. Sir Adrian Cadbury, CEO of Cadbury Company, chaired the committee.[14] The work of the committee led to successful governance reform in the United Kingdom.

In December 1992, the Cadbury Committee issued its report, including the *Code of Best Practice* in corporate governance. The code recommends that (i) boards of directors of public companies include at least three outside (nonexecutive) directors, and that (ii) the positions of chief executive officer (CEO) and chairman of the board (COB) of these companies be held by two different individuals; boards of directors of most British companies were dominated by insiders, with the positions of CEO and COB often held by the same individuals. Specifically, the code prescribed that:

> The board should meet regularly, retain full and effective control over the company and monitor the executive management. There should be a clearly accepted division of responsibilities at the head of a company, which will ensure a balance of power and authority, such that no one individual has unfettered power of decisions. Where the chairman is also the chief executive, it is essential that there should be a strong and independent element on the board, with a recognized senior member. The board should include non-executive directors of significant calibre and number for their views to carry significant weight in the board's decisions.

The **Cadbury Code** has not been legislated into law, and compliance with the code is voluntary. However, the London Stock Exchange (LSE) currently requires that each listed company show whether the company is in compliance with the code and explain why if it is not. This "comply or explain" approach has apparently persuaded many companies to comply rather than explain; currently, 90 percent of all LSE-listed companies have adopted the Cadbury Code. According to a study by Dahya, McConnell, and Travlos (2002), the proportion of outside directors rose from 26 percent before the adoption to 47 percent afterwards among those companies newly complying with the code. On the other hand, joint CEO/COB positions declined from 37 percent of the companies before the adoption to 15 percent afterwards. This means that even though the compliance is voluntary, the Cadbury Code has made a significant impact on the internal governance mechanisms of U.K. companies. The Dahya et al. study further shows that the "negative" relationship between CEO turnover and company performance became stronger after the introduction of the Cadbury Code. This means that the job security of chief executives has become more sensitive to company performance, strengthening managerial accountability and weakening its entrenchment.

The Dodd-Frank Act

Following the subprime mortgage crisis and the bailout of large financial institutions with taxpayers' money, the U.S. government passed the Dodd-Frank Wall Street Reform and Consumer Protection Act in July 2010. Among other things, the act aims at strengthening government regulation of banking firms and their internal governance mechanisms, thereby preventing similar financial crises in the future. The act represents the most comprehensive overhaul of the rules of finance since the Great Depression and is likely to have a major impact on the way decisions are made within financial firms. The key features of the **Dodd-Frank Act** include:

- Volker rule—Deposit-taking banks will be banned from proprietary trading and from owning more than a small fraction of hedge funds and private equity firms. The rule is named after Paul Volker, former Federal Reserve chairman, who argued that banks should not be allowed to engage in casino-like activities that endanger the safety of depositors' money.

---

[14]For a detailed discussion of the Cadbury Committee and its effect on corporate governance in the U.K., refer to Dahya, McConnell, and Travlos (2002).

- Resolution authority—The government can seize and dismantle a large bank in an orderly manner if the bank faces impending failure and poses a systemic risk to the broader financial system. This authority aims, in part, to reduce the cost and risk associated with the bailing out of banks that are "too big to fail." Banks that are deemed too big to fail can have skewed incentives for excessive risk-taking. Shareholders at big firms get nonbinding votes on executive pay and golden parachutes, to control skewed executive incentives.

- Derivative securities—Derivatives trading in over-the-counter markets will be transferred to electronic exchanges, with contracts settled through central clearing houses, to increase transparency and reduce counter-party risk.

- Systemic risk regulation—A Financial Stability Oversight Council of government regulators chaired by the Treasury secretary will identify systemically important financial firms and monitor their activities and financial conditions. These firms must draw up a "living will" to describe how they would be liquidated if they fail.

- Consumer protection—A new, independent Consumer Financial Protection Bureau will monitor predatory mortgage loans and other loan products.

The Dodd-Frank Act is focused on controlling banks' excessive risk-taking and mitigating the systemic risk in the financial system. If the act is successfully implemented, it would strengthen bank governance and help reduce the probability and cost of financial crises in the future.

Lastly, it is noted that corporate governance reforms would not only strengthen shareholders' cash flow rights but also enhance corporate performance. For instance, in their study of U.S. firms, Gompers, Ishii, and Metrick (2003) found that firms with stronger corporate governance have higher firm value, higher profits, higher sales growth, and lower capital expenditure, and make fewer corporate acquisitions. They also found that an investment strategy based on buying firms with the strongest corporate governance and selling firms with the weakest corporate governance would have earned a large "abnormal return" during their study period. Their study shows that enhancement of corporate governance would improve firm performance, boost firm value, and raise stock returns. In a comparative study of corporate valuation around the world, Chua, Eun, and Lai (2007) found that despite international financial integration in recent years, corporate valuation varies a great deal across countries. Specifically, corporate valuation is directly related to the quality of corporate governance, as well as the economic growth options and the degree of financial openness.

SUMMARY

In the wake of recurrent financial crises and high-profile corporate scandals and failures in the United States and abroad, corporate governance has attracted a lot of attention worldwide. This chapter provides an overview of corporate governance issues, with the emphasis on intercountry differences in the governance mechanisms.

1. The public corporation, which is jointly owned by many shareholders with limited liability, is a major organizational innovation with significant economic consequences. The efficient risk-sharing mechanism allows the public corporation to raise large amounts of capital at low cost and profitably undertake many investment projects, boosting economic growth.

2. The public corporation has a major weakness: the agency problem associated with the conflicts of interest between shareholders and managers. Self-interested managers can take actions to promote their own interests at the expense of shareholders. The agency problem tends to be more serious for firms with excessive free cash flows but without growth opportunities.

3. To protect shareholder rights, curb managerial excesses, and restore confidence in capital markets, it is important to strengthen corporate governance, defined as the economic, legal, and institutional framework in which corporate control and cash flow rights are distributed among shareholders, managers, and other stakeholders of the company.

4. The central issue in corporate governance is: how to best protect outside investors from expropriation by managers and controlling insiders so that investors can receive fair returns on their funds.

5. The agency problem can be alleviated by various methods, including (a) strengthening the independence of boards of directors; (b) providing managers with incentive contracts, such as stocks and stock options, to better align the interests of managers with those of shareholders; (c) concentrated ownership so that large shareholders can control managers; (d) using debt to induce managers to disgorge free cash flows to investors; (e) listing stocks on the London or New York stock exchange where shareholders are better protected; and (f) inviting hostile takeover bids if the managers waste funds and expropriate shareholders.

6. Legal protection of investor rights systematically varies across countries, depending on the historical origin of the national legal system. English common law countries tend to provide the strongest protection, French civil law countries the weakest. The civil law tradition is based on the comprehensive codification of legal rules, whereas the common law tradition is based on discrete rulings by independent judges on specific disputes and on judicial precedent. The English common law tradition, based on independent judges and local juries, evolved to be more protective of property rights, which were extended to the rights of investors.

7. Protecting the rights of investors has major economic consequences in terms of corporate ownership patterns, the development of capital markets, economic growth, and more. Poor investor protection results in concentrated ownership, excessive private benefits of control, underdeveloped capital markets, and slower economic growth.

8. Outside the United States and the United Kingdom, large shareholders, often founding families, tend to control managers and expropriate small outside shareholders. In other words, large, dominant shareholders tend to extract substantial private benefits of control.

9. Corporate governance reform efforts should be focused on how to better protect outside investors from expropriation by controlling insiders. Often, controlling insiders resist reform efforts, as they do not like to lose their private benefits of control. Reformers should understand political dynamics and mobilize public opinion to their cause.

KEY WORDS

agency problem, 84	equity cross-holdings, 97	private benefits of control, 99
Cadbury Code, *103*	Free cash flows, 85	
complete contract, 84	French civil law, 92	public corporation, 83
concentrated ownership, 88	incentive contracts, 87	pyramidal ownership, 97
corporate governance, 82	legal origins, 92	residual control rights, 85
Dodd-Frank Act, *103*	managerial entrenchment, 85	Sarbanes-Oxley Act, *101*
English common law, 92		shareholder rights, 82

QUESTIONS

1. The majority of major corporations are franchised as public corporations. Discuss the key strength and weakness of the "public corporation." When do you think the public corporation as an organizational form is unsuitable?

2. The public corporation is owned by a multitude of shareholders but run by professional managers. Managers can take self-interested actions at the expense of shareholders. Discuss the conditions under which the so-called agency problem arises.

3. Following corporate scandals and failures in the United States and abroad, there has been a growing demand for corporate governance reform. What should be the key objectives of corporate governance reform? What kinds of obstacles can thwart reform efforts?

4. Studies show that the legal protection of shareholder rights varies a great deal across countries. Discuss the possible reasons why the English common law tradition provides the strongest protection of investors and the French civil law tradition the weakest.

5. Explain "the wedge" between control and cash flow rights and discuss its implications for corporate governance.

6. Discuss different ways that dominant investors may establish and maintain control of a company with relatively small investments.

7. The *Cadbury Code of Best Practice*, adopted in the United Kingdom, led to a successful reform of corporate governance in the country. Explain the key requirements of the code and discuss how it contributed to the success of reform.

8. Many companies grant stock or stock options to managers. Discuss the benefits and possible costs of using this kind of incentive compensation scheme.

9. It has been shown that foreign companies listed on U.S. stock exchanges are valued more than those from the same countries that are not listed in the United States. Explain why U.S.-listed foreign firms are valued more than those that are not. Also explain why not every foreign firm wants to list stocks in the United States.

10. Explain "free cash flows." Why do managers like to retain free cash flows instead of distributing it to shareholders? Discuss what mechanisms may be used to solve this problem.

INTERNET EXERCISES

It is often mentioned that the United States has a "market-centered" corporate governance system, whereas Germany has a "bank-centered" system. Review the website of the OECD, www.oecd.org, or any other relevant websites and answer the following questions:

(a) Compare and contrast the corporate governance systems of the two countries.

(b) How did the two countries come to have the particular governance systems?

(c) What are the consequences of the different governance systems in the two countries?

MINI CASE

Parmalat: Europe's Enron

Following such high-profile corporate scandals as Enron and WorldCom in the United States, European business executives smugly proclaimed that the same could not happen on their side of the Atlantic as Europe does not share America's laissez-faire capitalism. Unfortunately, however, they were proved wrong quickly when Parmalat, a jewel of Italian capitalism, collapsed spectacularly as a result of massive accounting frauds.

Parmalat was founded in 1961 as a dairy company. Calisto Tanzi, the founder, transformed Parmalat into a national player by embarking on an aggressive acquisition program in the 1980s when local governments of Italy privatized their municipal dairies. While solidifying its dominant position in the Italian home market, Parmalat aggressively ventured into international markets during the 1990s, establishing operations in 30 countries throughout the Americas, Asia/Pacific, and Southern Africa. To finance its rapid expansion, the company borrowed heavily from international banks and investors.

Worldwide sales of Parmalat reached €7.6 billion in 2002 and its aspiration to become the Coca-Cola of milk seemed within reach. However, things began to unravel in 2003.

Parmalat's Stock Price

Data Source: DataStream.

Parmalat first defaulted on a $185 million debt payment in November 2003, which prompted a scrutiny of the firm's finances. Auditors and regulators soon found out that a $4.9 billion cash reserve supposedly held in a Bank of America account of the Cayman Island subsidiary of Parmalat actually did not exist, and that the total debt of the company was around €16 billion—more than double the amount (€7.2 billion) shown on the balance sheet. Italian investigators subsequently discovered that Parmalat managers simply "invented assets" to cover the company's debts and falsified accounts over a 15-year period. Following the discovery of massive frauds, Parmalat was forced into bankruptcy in December 2003. Calisto Tanzi, founder and former CEO, was arrested on suspicion of fraud, embezzlement, false accounting, and misleading investors. The Parmalat saga represents the largest and most brazen corporate fraud case in European history and is widely dubbed Europe's Enron.

Enrico Bondi, a new CEO of Parmalat, filed a $10 billion lawsuit against Citigroup, Bank of America, and former auditors Grant Thornton and Deloitte Touche Tohmatsu, for sharing responsibility for the company's collapse. He also filed legal actions against UBS of Switzerland and Deutsche Bank for the transactions that allegedly contributed to the collapse of Parmalat. Bondi has alleged that Parmalat's foreign "enablers," including international banks and auditors, were complicit in the frauds. He maintained that they knew about Parmalat's fraudulent finances and helped the company to disguise them in exchange for fat fees. Bondi effectively declared a war on Parmalat's international bankers and creditors.

The following graph illustrates Parmalat's share price behavior. Following a sharp drop in share price, trading of the company's shares was suspended on December 22, 2003.

Discussion Points

1. How was it possible for Parmalat managers to "cook the books" and hide it for so long?

2. Investigate and discuss the role that international banks and auditors might have played in Parmalat's collapse.

3. Study and discuss Italy's corporate governance regime and its role in the failure of Parmalat.

www.mcgraw-hill.co.uk/textbooks/eun

www.mcgraw-hill.co.uk/textbooks/eun

REFERENCES & SUGGESTED READINGS

Beck, T., R. Levine, and N. Loayza. "Finance and the Sources of Growth." *Journal of Financial Economics* 58 (2000), pp. 261–300.

Chua, Choong, C. Eun, and S. Lai. "Corporate Valuation around the World: The Effects of Governance, Growth, and Openness." *Journal of Banking and Finance* 3 (2007), pp. 35–56.

Claessens, S., S. Djankov, and L. H. P. Lang. "The Separation of Ownership and Control in East Asian Corporations." *Journal of Financial Economics* 58 (2000), pp. 81–112.

Coase, Ronald. "The Nature of the Firm." *Economica* 4 (1937), pp. 386–405.

Dahya, Jay, John McConnell, and Nickolaos Travlos. "The Cadbury Committee, Corporate Performance, and Top Management Turnover." *Journal of Finance* 57 (2002), pp. 461–83.

Demsetz, H., and K. Lehn. "The Structure of Corporate Ownership: Causes and Consequences." *Journal of Political Economy* 93 (1985), pp. 1155–77.

Denis, D., and J. McConnell. "International Corporate Governance." Working Paper (2002).

Doidge, C., A. Karolyi, and R. Stulz. "Why Are Foreign Firms Listed in the U.S. Worth More?" Working Paper, NBER (2002).

Dyck, A., and L. Zingales. "The Corporate Governance Role of the Media." Working Paper (2002).

Dyck, A., and L. Zingales. "Private Benefits of Control: An International Comparison." *Journal of Finance* 59 (2004), pp. 537–600.

Eun, C., and Victor Haung. "Asset Pricing in Chinese Domestic Stock Markets: Is There a Logic?" *Pacific-Basin Finance Journal* (2007), pp. 452–80.

Franks, J. R., and C. Mayer. "Ownership and Control of German Corporations." *Review of Financial Studies* 14 (2001), pp. 943–77.

Glaesser, E., and A. Shleifer. "Legal Origin." *Quarterly Journal of Economics* 117 (2002), pp. 1193–1229.

Gompers, Paul, Joy Ishii, and Andrew Metrick. "Corporate Governance and Equity Prices." *Quarterly Journal of Economics* 118 (2003), pp. 107–55.

Gorton, G., and F. A. Schmid. "Universal Banking and the Performance of German Firms." *Journal of Financial Economics* 58 (2000), pp. 28–80.

Holstrom, B., and S. N. Kaplan. "Corporate Governance and Merger Activity in the U.S.: Making Sense of the 1980s and 1990s." Working Paper, NBER (2001).

Jensen, M. "Eclipse of the Public Corporation." *Harvard Business Review* (1989), pp. 61–74.

Jensen, M., and W. Meckling. "Theory of the Firm: Managerial Behavior, Agency Cost, and Ownership Structure." *Journal of Financial Economics* 3 (1976), pp. 305–60.

Jensen, M., and K. Murphy. "Performance Pay and Top Management Incentives." *Journal of Political Economy* 98 (1990), pp. 225–63.

Johnson, S., P. Boon, A. Breach, and E. Friedman. "Corporate Governance in the Asian Financial Crisis." *Journal of Financial Economics* 58 (2000), pp. 141–86.

Johnson, S., R. La Porta, F. Lopez-de-Silanes, and A. Shleifer. "Tunneling." *American Economic Review* 90 (2000), pp. 22–27.

Kang, J., and A. Shivdasani. "Firm Performance, Corporate Governance, and Top Executive Turnover in Japan." *Journal of Financial Economics* 38 (1995), pp. 29–58.

King, R., and R. Levine. "Finance and Growth: Schumpeter Might Be Right." *Quarterly Journal of Economics* 108 (1993), pp. 717–38.

La Porta, R., F. Lopez-de-Silanes, A. Shleifer, and R. Vishny. "Legal Determinants of External Finance." *Journal of Finance* 52 (1997), pp. 1131–50.

———. "Law and Finance." *Journal of Political Economy* 106 (1998), pp. 1113–55.

———. "Corporate Ownership around the World." *Journal of Finance* 54 (1999), pp. 471–517.

———. "Investor Protection and Corporate Governance." *Journal of Financial Economics* 58 (2000), pp. 3–27.

———. "Investor Protection and Corporate Valuation." *Journal of Finance* 57 (2002), pp. 1147–69.

Lemmon, M. L., and K. V. Lins. "Ownership Structure, Corporate Governance, and Firm Value: Evidence from the East Asian Financial Crisis." Working Paper (2001).

Linck, J., J. Netter, and T. Yang. "The Effects and Unintended Consequences of the Sarbanes-Oxley Act on the Supply and Demand for Directors," *Review of Financial Studies* 22(2009), pp. 3287–3328.

Lobo, G. and J. Zhou. "Did Conservatism in Financial Reporting Increase after the Sarbanes-Oxley Act? Initial Evidence," *Accounting Horizons* 20 (2006), pp. 57–73.

Morck, R., A. Shleifer, and R. Vishny. "Management Ownership and Market Valuation: An Empirical Analysis." *Journal of Financial Economics* 20 (1988), pp. 293–315.

Nenova, T., "The Value of Corporate Votes and Control Benefits: A Cross-Country Analysis." Working Paper (2001).

Rajan, R., and L. Zingales. "Financial Dependence and Growth." *American Economic Review* 88 (1998), pp. 559–86.

Reese, W. A., Jr., and M. S. Weisbach. "Protection of Minority Shareholder Interests, Cross-listings in the United States, and Subsequent Equity Offerings." Working Paper, NBER (2001).

Schumpeter, J. *The Theory of Economic Development*. Translated by R. Opie. Cambridge, MA: Harvard University Press, 1934.

Shleifer, A., and R. Vishny. "A Survey of Corporate Governance," *Journal of Finance* 52 (1997), pp. 737–83.

Short, H., and K. Keasey "Managerial Ownership and the Performance of Firms: Evidence from the UK." *Journal of Corporate Finance* 5 (1999), pp. 79–101.

Smith, Adam. *An Inquiry Into the Nature and Causes of the Wealth of Nations*. (1776).

Stulz, R., and R. Williamson. "Culture, Openness, and Finance." *Journal of Financial Economics* 10 (2003), pp. 313–49.

Zingales, L. "The Value of the Voting Right: A Study of the Milan Stock Exchange Experience." *Review of Financial Studies* 7 (1994), pp. 125–48.www.ecgi.org

The Foreign Exchange Market, Exchange Rate Determination, and Currency Derivatives

PART TWO begins with a discussion of the organization of the market for foreign exchange. Both spot and forward transactions are studied. The next chapter examines exchange rate determination. The discussion focuses on how changes in the exchange rate between two countries' currencies depend on the relative difference between the nominal interest rates and inflation rates between the two countries. The final chapter of this section introduces currency derivative contracts useful for managing foreign currency exposure.

CHAPTER 5 provides an introduction to the organization and operation of the spot and forward foreign exchange market. This chapter describes institutional arrangements of the foreign exchange market and details of how foreign exchange is quoted and traded worldwide.

CHAPTER 6 presents the fundamental international parity relationships among exchange rates, interest rates, and inflation rates. An understanding of these parity relationships is essential for practicing financial management in a global setting.

CHAPTER 7 provides an extensive treatment of exchange-traded currency futures and options contracts. Basic valuation models are developed.

5 The Market for Foreign Exchange

www.bis.org

This is the website of the Bank for International Settlements. Many interesting reports and statistics can be obtained here. The report titled *Triennial Central Bank Survey* can be downloaded for study.

MONEY REPRESENTS PURCHASING power. Possessing money from your country gives you the power to purchase goods and services produced (or assets held) by other residents of your country. However, to purchase goods and services produced by the residents of another country generally requires first purchasing the other country's currency. This is done by selling one's own currency for the currency of the country with whose residents you desire to transact. More formally, one's own currency has been used to buy *foreign exchange*, and in doing so the buyer has converted his purchasing power into the purchasing power of the seller's country.

The market for foreign exchange is the largest financial market in the world by virtually any standard. It is open somewhere in the world 365 days a year, 24 hours a day. The 2013 triennial central bank survey compiled by the Bank for International Settlements (BIS) places worldwide daily trading of spot and forward foreign exchange at $4.95 trillion. This is equivalent to $700 in daily transactions for every person on earth. This represents a 33 percent increase over 2010 at current exchange rates. The increase in turnover can be attributed to an increase in trading activity by financial institutions other than reporting dealers, i.e., smaller banks, pension funds, insurance companies, and hedge funds. London remains the world's largest foreign exchange trading center. According to the 2013 triennial survey, daily trading volume in the U.K. is estimated at $2.33 trillion, a 44 percent increase from 2010. The U.S. daily turnover was $1.19 trillion, which represents a 45 percent increase from 2010. Exhibit 5.1 presents a pie chart showing the shares of global foreign exchange turnover.

Broadly defined, the **foreign exchange (FX) market** encompasses the conversion of purchasing power from one currency into another, bank deposits of foreign currency, the extension of credit denominated in a foreign currency, foreign trade financing, trading in foreign currency options and futures contracts, and currency swaps. Obviously, one chapter cannot adequately cover all these topics. Consequently, we confine the discussion in this chapter to the spot and forward market for foreign exchange. In Chapter 7, we examine currency futures and options contracts, and in Chapter 14, currency swaps are discussed.

This chapter begins with an overview of the function and structure of the foreign exchange market and the major market participants that trade currencies in this market. Following is a discussion of the spot market for foreign exchange. This section covers how to read spot market quotations, derives cross-rate quotations, and develops the concept of triangular arbitrage as a means of ensuring market efficiency. The chapter concludes with a discussion of the forward market for foreign exchange.

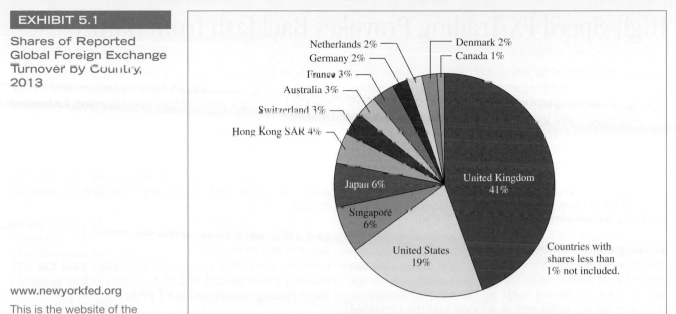

Netherlands 2%
Germany 2%
France 3%
Australia 3%
Switzerland 3%
Hong Kong SAR 4%
Japan 6%
Singapore 6%
United States 19%
Denmark 2%
Canada 1%
United Kingdom 41%
Countries with shares less than 1% not included.

Note: Percent of total reporting foreign exchange turnover, adjusted for local inter-dealer double-counting.

Source: Tabulated from data in Table 6 in the *Triennial Central Bank Survey, Preliminary Results.* Bank for International Settlements, Basle, September 2013.

Forward market quotations are presented, the purpose of the market is discussed, and the purpose of swap rate quotations is explained.

This chapter lays the foundation for much of the discussion throughout the remainder of the text. Without a solid understanding of how the foreign exchange market works, international finance cannot be studied in an intelligent manner. As authors, we urge you to read this chapter carefully and thoughtfully.

Function and Structure of the FX Market

The structure of the foreign exchange market is an outgrowth of one of the primary functions of a commercial banker: to assist clients in the conduct of international commerce. For example, a corporate client desiring to import merchandise from abroad would need a source of foreign exchange if the import was invoiced in the exporter's home currency. Alternatively, the exporter might need a way to dispose of foreign exchange if payment for the export was invoiced and received in the importer's home currency. Assisting in foreign exchange transactions of this type is one of the services that commercial banks provide for their clients, and one of the services that bank customers expect from their bank.

The spot and forward foreign exchange markets are **over-the-counter (OTC) markets**; that is, trading does not take place in a central marketplace where buyers and sellers congregate. Rather, the foreign exchange market is a worldwide linkage of bank currency traders, nonbank dealers, and FX brokers, who assist in trades, connected to one another via a network of telephones, computer terminals, and automated dealing systems. Thomson Reuters and ICAP are the largest vendors of quote screen monitors used in trading currencies. The communications system of the foreign exchange market is second to none, including industry, government, the military, and national security and intelligence operations. The International Finance in Practice box "High-speed FX Trading Provokes Backlash from Banks" describes the electronic nature of today's FX trading environment.

Twenty-four-hour-a-day currency trading follows the sun around the globe. Three major market segments can be identified: Australasia, Europe, and North America.

High-Speed FX Trading Provokes Backlash from Banks

Traders' frustration at being outpaced by high-speed computer algorithms operating on foreign exchange dealing platforms is contributing to a fall in spot volumes on the market's two biggest trading venues and prompting some to look elsewhere.

The two primary providers of interbank platforms dealing—Thomson Reuters and EBS, owned by ICAP Plc—both saw year on year spot trading volumes decline in June 2012. The drop came even as the average daily value of FX settled topped the $5 trillion mark, according to data from settlement service CLS Bank.

Traders said the fall was partly due to other factors including the rise of liquidity aggregators—computer programs, separate from algorithms, that split orders between a number of platforms to find the best price—and single dealer bank platforms such as Citigroup's Velocity or Deutsche Bank's Autobahn. But many said the perceived technological advantage that "algos", also known as high-frequency traders (HFTs), enjoyed on the platforms was also deterring some traditional bank clients.

Thanks to faster connections and superior technological firepower, HFTs can often hit quoted prices before manual traders even if their order is not put in first. "Thomson Reuters and EBS were basically building their business with HFTs, and HFTs were modeling voice traders' behavior and front-running all the big orders," said one global head of spot trading at a European bank. "It was creating a business but making it more difficult and expensive for manual traders."

Other HFT practices include creating a false illusion of liquidity through "quote stuffing", whereby models enter and withdraw large orders within milliseconds, and "statistical arbitrage" in which models profit from discrepancies in the market that change too fast for humans to spot.

Analysts from Boston-based consultancy Aite Group said HFTs were more active on EBS than Thomson Reuters but both platforms were popular because they have the deepest liquidity. Many traders said the fifth decimal place quoted in EBS currency prices provided more trading opportunities for HFTs.

Technological arms race

Traders said smaller platforms such as Currenex, Hotspot and FXall, which Thomson Reuters recently announced plans to buy, could be poised to pick up business from their bigger rivals. There is also appetite for new platforms in the increasingly fragmented FX market to address concerns that speedy computer networks are becoming more important than trading acumen.

---

www.Fxall.com

This is the website for the Internet FX trading platform discussed in the article "The Mouse Takes Over the Floor." It is a Thomson Reuters Company.

Australasia includes the trading centers of Sydney, Tokyo, Hong Kong, Singapore, and Bahrain; Europe includes Zurich, Frankfurt, Paris, Brussels, Amsterdam, and London; and North America includes New York, Montreal, Toronto, Chicago, San Francisco, and Los Angeles. Most trading rooms operate over a 9- to 12-hour working day, although some banks have experimented with operating three eight-hour shifts in order to trade around the clock. Especially active trading takes place when the trading hours of the Australasia centers and the European centers overlap and when the hours of the European and the North American centers overlap. More than half of the trading in the United States occurs between 8:00 A.M. and noon eastern standard time (1:00 P.M. and 5:00 P.M. Greenwich Mean Time [London]), when the European markets are still open. Certain trading centers have a more dominant effect on the market than others. For example, trading diminishes dramatically in the Australasian market segment when the Tokyo traders are taking their lunch break! Exhibit 5.2 provides a general indication of the participation level in the global FX market by showing average electronic conversations per hour. All conversations do not result in a completed trade.

FX Market Participants

The market for foreign exchange can be viewed as a two-tier market. One tier is the **wholesale** or **interbank market** and the other tier is the **retail** or **client market**. FX market participants can be categorized into five groups: international banks, bank customers, nonbank dealers, FX brokers, and central banks.

Interdealer broker Tradition Ltd is launching new platform traFXpure in co-operation with banks including Barclays, BNP Paribas, Deutsche Bank, RBC and UBS. "The majority of participants are happy to compete in the FX market but they are not happy to compete in a technological arms race," said Campbell Adams, managing director of traFXpure.

Although HFTs will still be allowed access to traFXpure when it launches later this year, Tradition said there will be no advantage in having faster technology and participants will be able to see who they are trading with. Traders said EBS seemed to be taking notice of what one London-based head of trading described as "the common moan" that manual traders cannot compete with HFTs.

In July 2012, as part of a series of planned enhancements, ICAP announced updated dealing rules containing a new artificial intelligence policy aimed at preventing algorithms from distorting genuine price discovery.

EBS is also considering scrapping the fifth decimal place. "It's certainly conceivable we are going to end up changing it, and we are unlikely to added a sixth," said Gil Mandelzis, chief executive officer of EBS.

Jas Singh, managing director of Marketplaces at Thomson Reuters, said Thomson Reuters platforms already enforced a minimum price quote life, intended to prevent quote stuffing, and a mixture of participants were needed to ensure liquidity. He attributed the fall in spot volumes to low volatility in the euro/dollar trading pair and a rise in FX swaps transactions as banks sought short-term dollar funding.

Short-lived fightback?

Some market players have suggested HFTs and high speed algorithms are facing a backlash. Once touted as the future of trading and expected to dominate FX markets in the same way they dominate equities, they are also being increasingly scrutinised by regulators.

But one veteran FX trader said although support for HFTs appeared to be wavering, the future of the market was still tilted in favor of computers as trading desk numbers are trimmed at even the biggest banks. "These things indicate some sort of fightback but I think it will be short-lived," he said. "Young people coming in should be looking at e-commerce. If a box of tricks will be taking the jobs, you want to make sure you are programming that box."

Source: Adapted from 'High-speed FX trading provokes backlash from banks', edited by Nigel Stephenson, Reuters, July 19, 2012 @2014 Thomson Reuters. All rights reserved.

EXHIBIT 5.2

Average Electronic FX Conversations per Hour (Monday–Friday, 2001)

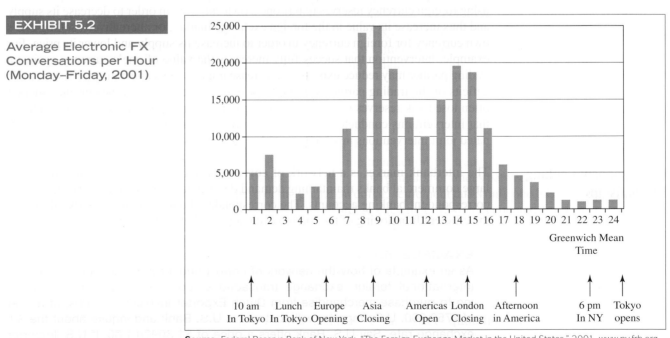

Source: Federal Reserve Bank of New York, "The Foreign Exchange Market in the United States," 2001, www.ny.frb.org. .

Where Money Talks Very Loudly

Foreign exchange is the largest, most dynamic market in the world. About $4.95 trillion worth of currency is traded daily in a market that literally does not sleep. Centered in Tokyo, London and New York, traders deal smoothly across borders and time zones, often in multiples of $1bn, in transactions that take less than a second.

The market's development into its current form has left it virtually unrecognizable from 10 years ago.

Then, banks dealt currencies on behalf of their clients via traders holding multiple telephone conversations or perhaps using the relatively new electronic systems offered by Thomson Reuters and Electronic Broking Services (EBS). Today, clients can deal alongside banks on a number of platforms and the quiet hum of computers has done much to reduce the noise level on trading floors.

Old timers complain that a lot of the "personality" has been drained from trading by the rise of faceless systems. But the marketplace itself is, if anything, more vigorous now than then. Many banks and trading platforms are reporting stiff rises in recent volumes traded and, allowing for some growth in market share, most believe overall trading activity has risen as the transparency of the market, and access to it, has improved.

EBS recently said that half of its top 35 busiest trading days since the launch of the company 10 years ago had been in the first two months of 2004. Thomson Reuters said it saw growth of 35 percent year-on-year in 2003 in spot market transactions and that year-to-date,

it estimated spot volumes to be 50 percent higher from a year ago.

"FX has come of age as an asset class over the last five years," says Nick Beecroft, head of foreign exchange trading at Standard Chartered. "There is much more activity, from active hedgers and from asset managers in other classes who tend to worry about FX much more than they did five, let alone 10 years ago."

Then, the market largely consisted of deals between banks and the technologies being introduced were designed to replicate that. Roughly 50 percent of foreign exchange deals were conducted by conversations between two counterparties and a further 35 percent were conducted through voice brokers, who "matched" bids and offers without either side knowing who the counterparty was.

Thomson Reuters had launched its first screen-based system in 1982, and in 1989 followed it up with a conversational platform designed to mimic dealers' telephone trades. In 1992 it went live with a matching system aimed at reproducing the role played by voice brokers. EBS's matching platform was launched in 1993 in a bid by banks to curb Thomson Reuters' development of a monopoly position. [EBS was acquired by ICAP in 2006.]

The advent of electronic broking for the interbank market gave smaller banks, which previously had little access to the best prices, the opportunity to deal alongside the bigger banks on an even basis because of the transparency afforded by electronic price provision.

Foreign Exchange Survey 2012

Overall		Nonfinancial Corporations		Banks	
Company	Market Share %	Company	Market Share %	Company	Market Share %
Deutsche Bank	14.57	Citi	15.27	Deutsche Bank	17.28
Citi	12.26	HSBC	9.49	UBS	14.01
Barclays	10.95	Deutsche Bank	8.86	Barclays	13.02
UBS	10.48	RBS	7.09	Citi	11.93
HSBC	6.72	JPMorgan	5.68	HSBC	7.67
JPMorgan	6.60	Societé Générale	5.48	RBS	5.65
RBS	5.86	Barclays	5.01	JPMorgan	5.16
Credit Suisse	4.68	BNP Paribas	4.04	Credit Suisse	4.72
Morgan Stanley	3.52	UBS	3.98	Commerzbank	2.14
Goldman Sachs	3.12	Bank of America Merrill Lynch	3.47	BNP Paribas	2.10

Source: *Euromoney*, May 2012.

Today, only a few specialist voice-broking firms still operate and the bulk of interbank business flows over Thomson Reuters and EBS's platforms.

Since then however, there has been another seismic shift in the foreign exchange (FX) marketplace: the extension of price transparency to clients outside the banking world.

Through an array of web-based platforms fund managers and hedge funds, for example, can rapidly view a series of quotes for a particular currency pair, and conduct the deal themselves. On some platforms, the counterparty could as easily be another fund manager as a bank.

"The market has changed more in the last three years than the previous seven," says John Nelson, global head of FX markets at ABN Amro. "One stroke of a key will send a trade from the back office of one counterparty and settle in the back of the other almost instantly."

Rapid price dissemination has, to a great extent, now leveled the playing field and extended the reach of FX trading well beyond the core investment bank market.

"What differentiated banks from customers then was that banks could see the real market prices and customers couldn't. Fast-forward to now, and I can see real-time market prices streaming over my desktop," says Justyn Trenner, chief executive of ClientKnowledge, an independent research firm. "This greatly facilitates the more sophisticated fund managers in actively trading FX as an asset class." The near instant dissemination of news, data and price information has led to what market theorists call "efficiency"—an accurate price at any given time. But it has affected the way in which currency pairs move.

"You get more zigs and zags within a trend than you used to see because everybody reacts to every piece of news at the same time," says Chris Furness, senior currencies strategist at 4Cast economic consultancy, who likened today's behaviour to a school of fish that all change direction at the same time. The upshot of more dramatic intraday price movement, particularly over the past two years, is greater overall volatility.

"Having absorbed the uncertainties around the launch of the euro and despite a contraction in the number of traders, this is a very healthy time for the market," says Mark Robson, head of treasury and fixed income at Thomson Reuters.

But although there are new direct players as a result of new trading opportunities and as the price playing field has been leveled, many of the smaller banks have been relegated to the sidelines.

Once more they may specialise in their regional currency but they are more usually clients of the bigger banks because of the expense of the new wave of trading technology.

The few banks with the deepest pockets have developed and operate successful e-trading platforms of their own that add to the volumes they trade and their profits. In turn, they can afford to offer clients the tailormade products that are becoming the norm.

"The intense competition in this space means everyone is trying to distinguish themselves through customisation," says Joe Novlello, chief information officer at e-speed, Cantor Fitzgerald's online platform, which expanded to offer FX trading last year.

Source: Excerpted from Jennifer Hughes, *Financial Times,* Special Report: Foreign Exchange, May 27, 2004, p. 2.

Leveraged Funds		E-Trading, Proprietary Platforms		E-Trading, Multibank and Independent Platforms	
Company	Market Share %	Company	Market Share %	Company	Market Share %
Deutsche Bank	15.76	Deutsche Bank	16.84	FXall	21.70
Barclays	13.42	Citi	14.81	FX Connect	18.71
UBS	10.62	Barclays	13.69	Reuters Dealing 3000 Direct	18.53
JPMorgan	8.21	UBS	11.42	360 Treasury Systems	15.09
Citi	7.82	JPMorgan	5.47	Currenex	8.31
Morgan Stanley	7.24	RBS	5.32	FX Trading on Bloomberg	7.74
HSBC	6.06	Credit Suisse	4.92	Integral – FX Inside	4.85
RBS	5.96	HSBC	4.62	Hotspot FXI	3.34
Credit Suisse	5.83	Morgan Stanley	3.65	Gain GTX	0.79
Bank of America Merrill Lynch	4.07	Goldman Sachs	3.53	SaxoTrader	0.45

EXAMPLE | 5.2: Calculating the Cross-Exchange Rate Bid-Ask Spread.
Let's assume (as we did earlier) that the $/£ bid-ask prices are $1.5400–$1.5405 and the £/$ bid-ask prices are £0.6491–£0.6494. Let's also assume the $/€ bid-ask prices are $1.3087–$1.3092 and the €/$ bid-ask prices are €0.7638–€0.7641. These bid and ask prices and Equation 5.12 imply that $S^b(€/£) = 1.5400 \times .7638 = 1.1763$. The reciprocal of $S^b(€/£)$ implies that $S^a(£/€) = .8501$. Analogously, Equation 5.13 suggests that $S^a(€/£) = 1.5405 \times .7641 = 1.1771$, and its reciprocal implies that $S^b(£/€) = .8495$. That is, the €/£ bid-ask prices are €1.1763–€1.1771 and the £/€ bid-ask prices are £0.8495–£0.8501. Note that the cross-rate bid-ask spreads are much larger than the American or European bid-ask spreads. For example, the €/£ bid-ask spread is €0.0008 versus a €/$ spread of €0.0003. The £/€ bid-ask spread is £0.0006 versus the $/€ spread of $0.0005, which is a sizable difference since a British pound is priced at more than 1.5 dollars. The implication is that cross-exchange rates *implicitly* incorporate the bid-ask spreads of the two transactions that are necessary for trading out of one nondollar currency and into another. Hence, even when a bank makes a direct market in one nondollar currency versus another, the trade is *effectively* going through the dollar because the "currency against currency" exchange rate is consistent with a cross-exchange rate calculated from the dollar exchange rates of the two currencies. Exhibit 5.7 provides a more detailed presentation of cross-rate foreign exchange transactions.

Taking reciprocals of Equation 5.12 yields

$$S^a(£/SF) = S^a(£/\$) \times S^a(\$/SF) \tag{5.13}$$

which is analogous to Equation 5.9. In terms of our example, Equation 5.13 says the bank could alternatively quote its customer an offer (ask) price for Swiss francs in terms of British pounds determined by multiplying its European term ask price (for U.S. dollars) stated in British pounds by its American term ask price for Swiss francs.

EXHIBIT 5.7

Cross-Rate Foreign
Exchange Transactions

	American Terms		European Terms	
Bank Quotations	**Bid**	**Ask**	**Bid**	**Ask**
British pounds	1.5400	1.5405	.6491	.6494
Euros	1.3087	1.3092	.7638	.7641

a. Bank Customer wants to sell £1,000,000 for euros. The Bank will sell U.S. dollars (buy British pounds) for $1.5400. The sale yields Bank Customer:
   £1,000,000 × 1.5400 = $1,540,000.
   The Bank will buy dollars (sell euros) for €0.7638. The sale of dollars yields Bank Customer:
   $1,540,000 × €0.7638 = €1,176,252.
   Bank Customer has effectively sold British pounds at a €/£ bid price of €1,176,252/£1,000,000 = €1.1763/£1.00.
b. Bank Customer wants to sell €1,000,000 for British pounds. The Bank will sell U.S. dollars (buy euros) for €0.7641. The sale yields Bank Customer:
   €1,000,000 ÷ .7641 = $1,308,729.
   The Bank will buy dollars (sell British pounds) for $1.5405. The sale of dollars yields Bank Customer:
   $1,308,729 ÷ 1.5405 = £849,548.
   Bank Customer has effectively bought British pounds at a €/£ ask price of €1,000,000/£849,548 = €1.1771/£1.00.
   From parts (a) and (b), we see the currency against currency bid-ask spread for British pounds is €1.1763 − €1.1771.

Triangular Arbitrage

Certain banks specialize in making a direct market between nondollar currencies, pricing at a narrower bid-ask spread than the cross-rate spread. Nevertheless, the implied cross-rate bid-ask quotations impose a discipline on the nondollar market makers. If their direct quotes are not consistent with cross-exchange rates, a triangular arbitrage profit is possible.[3] **Triangular arbitrage** is the process of trading out of the U.S. dollar into a second currency, then trading it for a third currency, which is in turn traded for U.S. dollars. The purpose is to earn an arbitrage profit via trading from the second to the third currency when the direct exchange rate between the two is not in alignment with the cross-exchange rate.

EXAMPLE | 5.3: Taking Advantage of a Triangular Arbitrage Opportunity

To illustrate a triangular arbitrage, assume the cross-rate trader at Deutsche Bank notices that Crédit Lyonnais is buying dollars at $S^b(€/\$) = .7638$, the same as Deutsche Bank's bid price. Similarly, he observes that Barclays is buying British pounds at $S^b(\$/£) = 1.5400$, also the same as Deutsche Bank. He next finds that Crédit Agricole is making a direct market between the euro and the pound, with a current ask price of $S^a(€/£) = 1.1705$. Cross-rate Equation 5.12 implies that the €/£ bid price should be no lower than $S^b(€/£) = 1.5400 \times .7638 = 1.1763$. Yet Crédit Agricole is offering to sell British pounds at a rate of only 1.1705!

A triangular arbitrage profit is available if the Deutsche Bank traders are quick enough. A sale of $5,000,000 to Crédit Lyonnais for euros will yield €3,819,000 = $5,000,000 × .7638. The €3,819,000 will be resold to Crédit Agricole for £3,262,708 = €3,819,000/1.1705. Likewise, the British pounds will be resold to Barclays for $5,024,570 = £3,262,708 × 1.5400, yielding an arbitrage profit of $24,570. Exhibit 5.8 presents a diagram and a summary of this triangular arbitrage example.

Obviously, Crédit Agricole must raise its asking price above €1.1705/£1.00. The cross-exchange rates (from Exhibit 5.7) gave €/£ bid-ask prices of €1.1763 − €1.1771. These prices imply that Crédit Agricole can deal inside the spread and sell for less than €1.1771, but not less than €1.1763. An ask price of €1.1767, for example, would eliminate the arbitrage profit. At that price, the €3,819,000 would be resold for £3,245,517 = €3,819,000/1.1767, which in turn would yield only $4,998,096 = £3,245,517 × 1.5400, or a loss of $1,904. In today's "high-tech" FX market, many FX trading rooms around the world have developed in-house software that receives a digital feed of real-time FX prices from the EBS Spot electronic broking system to explore for triangular arbitrage opportunities. Just a few years ago, prior to the development of computerized dealing systems, the FX market was considered too efficient to yield triangular arbitrage profits!

Spot Foreign Exchange Market Microstructure

Market microstructure refers to the basic mechanics of how a marketplace operates. Five empirical studies on FX market microstructure shed light on the operation of the spot FX marketplace. Huang and Masulis (1999) studied spot FX rates on DM/$ trades over the period from October 1, 1992 to September 29, 1993. They found that bid-ask spreads in the spot FX market increased with FX exchange rate volatility and decreased with dealer competition. These results are consistent with models of market microstructure. They also found that the bid-ask spread decreased when the percentage of large dealers in the marketplace increased. They concluded that dealer competition is a fundamental determinant of the spot FX bid-ask spread.

Lyons (1998) tracked the trading activity of a DM/$ trader at a large New York bank over a period of five trading days. The dealer he tracked was extremely profitable over the study period, averaging profits of $100,000 per day on volume of $1 billion.

---

[3]An arbitrage is a zero-risk, zero-investment strategy from which a profit is guaranteed.

are:

$$S(SF/\$) = .9421$$
$$F_1(SF/\$) = .9418$$
$$F_3(SF/\$) = .9412$$
$$F_6(SF/\$) = .9402$$

From these quotations, we can see that in European terms the dollar is trading at a *discount* to the Swiss franc and that the discount increases out to six months, the further the forward maturity date is from June 5. Thus, according to the forward rate, when the dollar is trading at a discount to the Swiss franc in European terms, we can say the market expects the Swiss franc to **appreciate**, or become more valuable, relative to the dollar. Consequently, it costs fewer Swiss francs to buy a dollar forward. This is exactly what we should expect, since the European term quotes are the reciprocals of the corresponding American term quotations.

Long and Short Forward Positions

One can buy (take a long position) or sell (take a short position) foreign exchange forward. Bank customers can contract with their international bank to buy or sell a specific sum of freely traded FX for delivery on a certain date. Likewise, interbank traders can establish a long or short position by dealing with a trader from a competing bank. Exhibit 5.9 graphs both the long and short positions for the three-month Swiss franc contract, using the American quote for June 5, 2013, from Exhibit 5.4. The graph measures profits or losses on the vertical axis. The horizontal axis shows the spot price of foreign exchange on the maturity date of the forward contract, $S_3(\$/SF)$. If one uses the forward contract, he has "locked in" the forward price for forward purchase or sale of foreign exchange. Regardless of what the spot price is on the maturity date of the forward contract, the trader buys (if he is long) or sells (if he is short) at $F_3(\$/SF) = 1.0624$ per unit of FX. Forward contracts can also be used for speculative purposes, as Example 5.4 demonstrates.

Non-Deliverable Forward Contracts

Because of government-instituted capital controls, the currencies of some emerging market countries are not freely traded and thus it is not possible to obtain these currencies offshore in the spot market to settle a forward position. For many of these currencies (such as the Chinese yuan and Russian ruble), trading in *non-deliverable forward (NDF)* contracts exists. A non-deliverable forward contract is settled in cash, usually U.S. dollars, at the difference between the spot exchange on the maturity date of the contract and the NDF rate times the notional amount of the contract. For example, a long position in a NDF contract on CNY12,000,000 with a forward price of $F(\$/CNY) = .1653$ would be settled by the long receiving $6,000 = (.1658 - .1653) \times$ CNY12,000,000 from the short if the spot rate at the maturity date of the NDF contract is $S(\$/CNY) = .1658$. This cash settlement is in lieu of the long receiving CNY12,000,000, with a spot dollar value of $1,989,600 = (CNY12,000,000 \times $0.1658)$, for payment of the forward price $1,983,600 = (CNY12,000,000 \times $0.1653)$, a $6,000 difference in sums.

Forward Cross-Exchange Rates

Forward cross-exchange rate quotations are calculated in an analogous manner to spot cross-rates, so it is not necessary to provide detailed examples. In generic terms,

$$F_N(j/k) = \frac{F_N(\$/k)}{F_N(\$/j)} \tag{5.14}$$

or

$$F_N(j/k) = \frac{F_N(j/\$)}{F_N(k/\$)} \tag{5.15}$$

and

$$F_N(k/j) = \frac{F_N(\$/j)}{F_N(\$/k)} \tag{5.16}$$

or

$$F_N(k/j) = \frac{F_N(k/\$)}{F_N(j/\$)} \qquad (5.17)$$

For example, using the forward quotations in Exhibit 5.4, the three-month AD/SF cross-exchange forward rate using American term quotes (Equation 5.14) is:

$$F_3(AD/SF) = \frac{F_3(\$/SF)}{F_3(\$/AD)} = \frac{1.0624}{.9482} = 1.1204$$

and using European term quotes (Equation 5.15) is:

$$F_3(AD/SF) = \frac{F_3(AD/\$)}{F_3(SF/\$)} = \frac{1.0546}{.9412} = 1.1205.$$

where the difference from 1.1204 is due to rounding.

EXAMPLE | 5.4: A Speculative Forward Position

It is June 5, 2013. Suppose the $/SF trader has just heard an economic forecast from the bank's head economist that causes him to believe that the dollar will likely appreciate in value against the Swiss franc over the next three months. If he decides to act on this information, the trader will short the three-month $/SF contract. We will assume that he sells SF5,000,000 forward against dollars. Suppose the forecast has proven correct, and on September 5, 2013, spot $/SF is trading at $1.0554. The trader can buy Swiss franc spot at $1.0554 and deliver it under the forward contract at a price of $1.0624. The trader has made a speculative profit of ($1.0624 − $1.0554) = $0.0070 per unit, as Exhibit 5.9 shows. The total profit from the trade is $35,000 = (SF5,000,000 × $0.0070). If the dollar depreciated and S_3 was $1.0654, the speculator would have lost ($1.0624 − $1.0654) = −$0.0030 per unit, for a total loss of −$15,000 = (SF5,000,000)(−$0.0030).

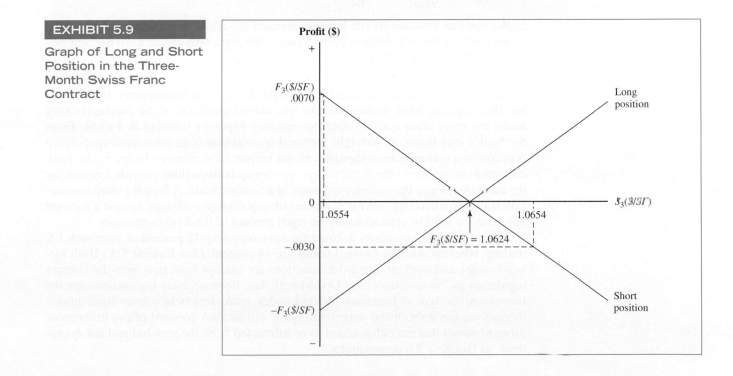

EXHIBIT 5.9

Graph of Long and Short Position in the Three-Month Swiss Franc Contract

Forward Premium

It is common to express the premium or discount of a forward rate as an annualized percentage deviation from the spot rate. The forward premium (or discount) is useful for comparing against the interest rate differential between two countries, as we will see more clearly in Chapter 6 on international parity relationships. The **forward premium** or **discount** can be calculated using American or European term quotations, as Example 5.5 demonstrates.

EXAMPLE | 5.5: Calculating the Forward Premium/Discount

The formula for calculating the forward premium or discount for currency j in American terms is:

$$f_{N,j} = \frac{F_N(\$/j) - S(\$/j)}{S(\$/j)} \times 360/\text{days} \tag{5.18}$$

When the context is clear, the forward premium will simply be stated as f.

As an example of calculating the forward premium, let's use the June 5 quotes from Exhibit 5.4 to calculate the three-month forward premium or discount for the Japanese yen versus the U.S. dollar. The calculation is:

$$f_{3,¥} = \frac{.010099 - .010094}{.010094} \times \frac{360}{94} = .0019$$

We see that the three-month forward premium is .0019, or .19 percent. In words, we say that the Japanese yen is trading at a .19 percent premium versus the U.S. dollar for delivery in 94 days.

In European terms the forward premium or discount for the U.S. dollar is calculated as:

$$f_{N,\$} = \frac{F_N(j/\$) - S(j/\$)}{S(j/\$)} \times 360/\text{days} \tag{5.19}$$

Using the June 5 three-month European term quotations for the Japanese yen from Exhibit 5.4 yields:

$$f_{3,\$} = \frac{99.02 - 99.07}{99.07} \times \frac{360}{94} = -.0019$$

We see that the three-month forward discount is −.0019, or −.19 percent. In words, we say that the U.S. dollar is trading versus the Japanese yen at a .19 percent discount for delivery in 94 days.

Swap Transactions

Forward swap trades can be classified as outright or swap transactions. In conducting their trading, bank dealers do take speculative positions in the currencies they trade, but more often traders offset the currency exposure inherent in a trade. From the bank's standpoint, an **outright forward transaction** is an uncovered speculative position in a currency, even though it might be part of a currency hedge to the bank customer on the other side of the transaction. **Swap transactions** provide a means for the bank to mitigate the currency exposure in a forward trade. A forward swap transaction is the simultaneous sale (or purchase) of spot foreign exchange against a forward purchase (or sale) of approximately an equal amount of the foreign currency.

Forward swap transactions account for approximately 45 percent of interbank FX trading, whereas outright forward trades are 14 percent. (See Exhibit 5.3.) Both forward swaps and outright forward transactions are exempt from new over-the-counter regulation as "swaps" under the Dodd-Frank Act. Because swap transactions are the more common type of interbank forward trades, bank dealers in conversation among themselves use a shorthand notation to quote bid and ask forward prices in terms of *forward points* that are either added to or subtracted from the spot bid and ask quotations, as Example 5.6 demonstrates.

EXAMPLE | 5.6: Forward Point Quotations

Assume the Swiss franc/U.S. dollar (*SF*/$) bid-ask rates are SF0.9421–SF0.9424. With reference to these rates, forward prices might be displayed as:

Spot	.9421–.9424
One-Month	3–1
Three Month	9–5
Six-Month	19–13

When the second number in a forward point "pair" is smaller than the first, the dealer "knows" the forward points are subtracted from the spot bid and ask prices to obtain the outright forward rates. For example, the spot bid price of SF0.9421 minus .0003 (or 3 points) equals SF0.9418, the one month forward bid price. The spot ask price of SF0.9424 minus .0001 (or 1 point) equals SF0.9423, the one-month ask price. Analogously, the three-month outright forward bid-ask rates are SF0.9412–SF0.9419 and the six-month outright forward bid-ask rates are SF0.9402–SF0.9411.[5] The following table summarizes the calculations.

Spot		.9421–.9424
	Forward Point Quotations	Outright Forward Quotations
One-Month	3–1	.9418–.9423
Three-Month	9–5	.9412–.9419
Six-Month	19–13	.9402–.9411

Three things are notable about the outright prices. First, the dollar is trading at a forward discount to the Swiss franc. Second, all bid prices are less than the corresponding ask prices, as they must be for a trader to be willing to make a market. Third, the bid-ask spread increases in time to maturity, as is typical. These three conditions prevail only *because* the forward points were subtracted from the spot prices. As a check, note that in points the spot bid-ask spread is 3 points, the one-month forward bid-ask spread is 5 points, the three-month spread is 7 points, and the six-month spread is 9 points.

If the forward prices were trading at a premium to the spot price, the second number in a forward point pair would be larger than the first, and the trader would know to add the points to the spot bid and ask prices to obtain the outright forward bid and ask rates. For example, if the three-month and six-month swap points were 5–9 and 13–19, the corresponding three-month and six-month bid-ask rates would be SF0.9426–SF0.9433 and SF0.9434–SF0.9443. In points, the three- and six-month bid-ask spreads would be 7 and 9, that is, increasing in term to maturity.

Exhibit 5.10 presents spot and forward point quotations for the euro on June 17, 2013. Forward point quotations are for maturities of one week to 18 months. Note that for each pair the ask number of points is larger than the bid; therefore, they are to be added to the spot quotes. The 18 months forward points are 43.5 (bid) and 53.84 (ask). Since the spot quotes are 1.3331 – 1.3332, the 18-month outright forward quotes are 1.337450 – 1.338584.

Quoting forward rates in terms of forward points is convenient for two reasons. First, forward points may remain constant for long periods of time, even if the spot rates fluctuate frequently. Second, in swap transactions where the trader is attempting to minimize currency exposure, the actual spot and outright forward rates are often of no consequence. What is important is the premium or discount differential, measured in forward points.

---

[5]If the one-month forward points quotation were, say, 12–12, further elaboration from the market maker would be needed to determine if the forward points would be added to or subtracted from the spot prices. An electronic dealing system would state forward points as −12−−12 if they were to be subtracted.

EXHIBIT 5.10

Spot and Forward Point
Quotations for the Euro
in American Terms

	Bid	**Ask**
Spot	1.3331	1.3332
Term	Forward	Points
1W FWD	0.37	0.47
2W FWD	0.79	0.92
3W FWD	1.04	1.56
1M FWD	1.67	2.01
2M FWD	3.84	5.00
3M FWD	5.84	6.39
4M FWD	8.08	8.71
5M FWD	10.11	10.95
6M FWD	12.32	13.45
7M FWD	15.27	17.14
8M FWD	17.72	19.47
9M FWD	20.20	21.82
10M FWD	23.04	25.93
11M FWD	25.42	28.60
12M FWD	28.33	30.77
18M FWD	43.50	53.84

Source: www.fxstreet.com, June 17, 2013.

To illustrate, suppose a bank customer wants to sell dollars three months forward against Swiss francs. The bank can handle this trade for its customer and simultaneously neutralize the exchange rate risk in the trade by selling (borrowed) dollars spot against Swiss francs. The bank will lend francs for three months until they are needed to deliver against the dollars it has purchased forward. The dollars received will be used to liquidate the dollar loan. Implicit in this transaction is the interest rate differential between the dollar borrowing rate and the Swiss franc lending rate. The interest rate differential is captured by the forward premium or discount measured in forward points. As a rule, when the interest rate of the quoted (indirect) currency is less than the interest rate of the quoting (direct) currency, the outright forward rate is greater than the spot exchange rate, and vice versa. This will become clear in Chapter 6 on international parity relationships, where in American terms it is shown that the forward premium $(F - S)/S \approx i_\$ - i_f$, the difference between the U.S. dollar and foreign currency interest rates.

As in the spot market, the bid-ask spread in the forward retail market is wider than the interbank spread. In addition to the bid-ask spread, banks will typically require their retail clients to maintain a compensating balance to cover the cost of the bank's advisory services in assisting with forward foreign exchange transactions and for other bank services. During the depths of the global financial crisis, banks, fearing that some of their cash-strapped customers might default, started asking customers to post collateral of as much as 2 percent of the value of the deal to cover the credit risk that the banks assume when writing forward contracts—as when a customer's long (short) forward position becomes unfavorable because the spot price falls below (rises above) the contractual forward price. From the customer's perspective, this represented a massive withdrawal of credit.

Exchange-Traded Currency Funds

An **exchange-traded fund (ETF)** is a portfolio of financial assets in which shares representing fractional ownership of the fund trade on an organized exchange. In recent years, ETFs have been created representing investment in a number of stock market indices. Like mutual funds, ETFs allow small investors the opportunity to invest in portfolios of financial assets that they would find difficult to construct individually. In 2005, a firm associated with Guggenheim Investments first offered an ETF on the euro common currency named the CurrencyShares Euro Trust. The fund is designed for both institutional and retail investors who desire to take a position in a financial asset that will track the performance of the euro with respect to the U.S. dollar. Upon obtaining dollars from investors, the trust purchases euros that are held in two deposit accounts, one of which earns interest. Guggenheim issues baskets of 50,000 shares for trading, with each share representing 100 euros. Individual shares are denominated in the U.S. dollar and trade on the New York Stock Exchange. The net asset value (NAV) of one share at any point in time will reflect the spot dollar value of 100 euros plus accumulated interest minus expenses. Guggenheim has since created eight additional currency trusts on the Australian dollar, British pound sterling, Canadian dollar, Chinese yuan, Japanese yen, Singapore dollar, Swedish krona, and the Swiss franc. The total NAV of all nine currency trusts stood at $1.7 billion in June 2013. Currency is now recognized as a distinct asset class, like stocks and bonds. Guggenheim currency trusts facilitate investing in these nine currencies.

SUMMARY

This chapter presents an introduction to the market for foreign exchange. Broadly defined, the foreign exchange market encompasses the conversion of purchasing power from one currency into another, bank deposits of foreign currency, the extension of credit denominated in a foreign currency, foreign trade financing, and trading in foreign currency options and futures contracts. This chapter limits the discussion to the spot and forward markets for foreign exchange. The other topics are covered in later chapters.

1. The FX market is the largest and most active financial market in the world. It is open somewhere in the world 24 hours a day, 365 days a year. In 2013, average daily trading in spot and forward foreign exchange was $4.95 trillion.

2. The FX market is divided into two tiers: the retail or client market and the wholesale or interbank market. The retail market is where international banks service their customers who need foreign exchange to conduct international commerce or trade in international financial assets. The great majority of FX trading takes place in the interbank market among international banks that are adjusting inventory positions or conducting speculative and arbitrage trades.

3. The FX market participants include international banks, bank customers, nonbank FX dealers, FX brokers, and central banks.

4. In the spot market for FX, nearly immediate purchase and sale of currencies take place. In the chapter, notation for defining a spot rate quotation was developed. Additionally, the concept of a cross-exchange rate was developed. It was determined that nondollar currency transactions must satisfy the bid-ask spread determined from the cross-rate formula or a triangular arbitrage opportunity exists.

5. In the forward market, buyers and sellers can transact today at the forward price for the future purchase and sale of foreign exchange. Notation for forward exchange rate quotations was developed. The use of forward points as a shorthand method for expressing forward quotes from spot rate quotations was presented. Additionally, the concept of a forward premium was developed.

6. Exchange-traded currency funds were discussed as a means for both institutional and retail traders to easily take positions in nine key currencies.

KEY WORDS

American terms, *120*	correspondent banking	depreciate, *129*
appreciate, *130*	relationships, *116*	direct quotation, *117*
ask price, *123*	cross-exchange rate, *122*	European terms, *120*
bid price, *123*	currency against	exchange-traded fund
client market, *114*	currency, *125*	(ETF), *134*

foreign exchange (FX) market, *112*	interbank market, *114*	spot market, *117*
	offer price, *123*	spot rate, *117*
forward market, *129*	outright forward	swap transactions, *132*
forward premium/	transaction, *132*	triangular arbitrage, *127*
discount, *132*	over-the-counter (OTC)	wholesale market, *114*
forward rate, *129*	market, *113*	
indirect quotation, *120*	retail market, *114*	

QUESTIONS

1. Give a full definition of the market for foreign exchange.

2. What is the difference between the retail or client market and the wholesale or interbank market for foreign exchange?

3. Who are the market participants in the foreign exchange market?

4. How are foreign exchange transactions between international banks settled?

5. What is meant by a currency trading at a discount or at a premium in the forward market?

6. Why does most interbank currency trading worldwide involve the U.S. dollar?

7. Banks find it necessary to accommodate their clients' needs to buy or sell FX forward, in many instances for hedging purposes. How can the bank eliminate the currency exposure it has created for itself by accommodating a client's forward transaction?

8. A CAD/$ bank trader is currently quoting a *small figure* bid-ask of 35–40, when the rest of the market is trading at CAD1.3436–CAD1.3441. What is implied about the trader's beliefs by his prices?

9. What is triangular arbitrage? What is a condition that will give rise to a triangular arbitrage opportunity?

10. Over the past five years, the exchange rate between the British pound and the U.S. dollar, $/£, has changed from about 1.90 to about 1.45. Would you agree that over this five-year period, British goods have become cheaper for buyers in the United States?

PROBLEMS

1. Using the American term quotes from Exhibit 5.4, calculate a cross-rate matrix for the euro, Swiss franc, Japanese yen, and British pound so that the resulting triangular matrix is similar to the portion above the diagonal in Exhibit 5.6.

2. Using the American term quotes from Exhibit 5.4, calculate the one-, three-, and six-month forward cross-exchange rates between the Australian dollar and the Swiss franc. State the forward cross-rates in "Australian" terms.

3. A foreign exchange trader with a U.S. bank took a short position of £5,000,000 when the $/£ exchange rate was 1.55. Subsequently, the exchange rate has changed to 1.61. Is this movement in the exchange rate good from the point of view of the position taken by the trader? By how much has the bank's liability changed because of the change in exchange rate?

4. Restate the following one-, three-, and six-month outright forward European term bid-ask quotes in forward points.

Spot	1.3431–1.3436
One-Month	1.3432–1.3442
Three-Month	1.3448–1.3463
Six-Month	1.3488–1.3508

5. Using the spot and outright forward quotes in problem 4, determine the corresponding bid-ask spreads in points.

6. Using Exhibit 5.4, calculate the one-, three-, and six-month forward premium or discount for the Canadian dollar versus the U.S. dollar using American term quotations. For simplicity, assume each month has 30 days. What is the interpretation of your results?

7. Using Exhibit 5.4, calculate the one-, three-, and six-month forward premium or discount for the U.S. dollar versus the British pound using European term quotations. For simplicity, assume each month has 30 days. What is the interpretation of your results?

8. Indirect currency conversions can be illustrated by using arrows to represent each conversion of a currency into a different currency. The arrow should point from the former to the latter currency; the price per unit of the currency being purchased should be written on the arrow. If we form a path from the currency to be delivered to the one to be ultimately purchased, we then obtain the cross exchange rate by multiplying the numbers next to all arrows.

TABLE 1

A set of bid and ask spot exchange rates.

	Bid	Ask
BRL/€	3.2174	3.2254
€/NZD	0.6072	0.6076
QAR/€	5.0126	5.0206

For example, if we want to calculate the bid and the ask BRL/NZD cross rates based on the information in Table 1, we can write

$$NZD \xrightarrow{1/0.6072} € \xrightarrow{1/3.2174} BRL \qquad BRL \xrightarrow{3.2254} € \xrightarrow{0.6076} NZD$$

The bid and ask cross rates are thus NZD $1/0.6072 \times 1/3.2174$ per BRL1, namely BRL1/($1/0.6072 \times 1/3.2174$) = 1.9536 per NZD1, and BRL3.2254 $\times$ 0.6076 = 1.9597 per NZD1, respectively. Calculate the bid and ask cross exchange rates BRL/QAR and NZD/QAR.

9. Doug Bernard specializes in cross-rate arbitrage. He notices the following quotes:

Swiss franc/dollar = SFr1.5971/$

Australian dollar/U.S. dollar = A$1.8215/$

Australian dollar/Swiss franc = A$1.1440/SFr

Ignoring transaction costs, does Doug Bernard have an arbitrage opportunity based on these quotes? If there is an arbitrage opportunity, what steps would he take to make an arbitrage profit, and how much would he profit if he has $1,000,000 available for this purpose?

10. Assume you are a trader with Deutsche Bank. From the quote screen on your computer terminal, you notice that Dresdner Bank is quoting €0.7627/$1.00 and Credit Suisse is offering SF1.1806/$1.00. You learn that UBS is making a direct market between the Swiss franc and the euro, with a current €/SF quote of .6395. Show how you can make a triangular arbitrage profit by trading at these prices. (Ignore bid-ask spreads for this problem.) Assume you have $5,000,000 with which to conduct the arbitrage. What happens if you initially sell dollars for Swiss francs? What €/SF price will eliminate triangular arbitrage?

11. The current spot exchange rate is $1.95/£ and the three-month forward rate is $1.90/£. On the basis of your analysis of the exchange rate, you are pretty confident that the spot exchange rate will be $1.92/£ in three months. Assume that you would like to buy or sell £1,000,000.

  a. What actions do you need to take to speculate in the forward market? What is the expected dollar profit from speculation?

  b. What would be your speculative profit in dollar terms if the spot exchange rate actually turns out to be $1.86/£?

12. Omni Advisors, an international pension fund manager, plans to sell equities denominated in Swiss francs (CHF) and purchase an equivalent amount of equities denominated in South African rands (ZAR).

Omni will realize net proceeds of 3 million CHF at the end of 30 days and wants to eliminate the risk that the ZAR will appreciate relative to the CHF during this 30-day period. The following exhibit shows current exchange rates between the ZAR, CHF, and the U.S. dollar (USD).

Currency Exchange Rates

Maturity	ZAR/USD		CHF/USD	
	Bid	Ask	Bid	Ask
Spot	6.2681	6.2789	1.5282	1.5343
30-day	6.2538	6.2641	1.5226	1.5285
90-day	6.2104	6.2200	1.5058	1.5115

a. Describe the currency transaction that Omni should undertake to eliminate currency risk over the 30-day period.

b. Calculate the following:
   - The CHF/ZAR cross-currency rate Omni would use in valuing the Swiss equity portfolio.
   - The current value of Omni's Swiss equity portfolio in ZAR.
   - The annualized forward premium or discount at which the ZAR is trading versus the CHF.

INTERNET EXERCISES

1. A currency trader makes a market in a currency and attempts to generate speculative profits from dealing against other currency traders. Today electronic dealing systems are frequently used by currency traders. The most widely used spot trading system is EBS Spot. Go to their website, www.icap.com/spotdemo. Click on the EBS Spot and EBS Prime demo indicator to receive a demonstration of the EBS Spot trading platform.

2. In addition to the historic currency symbols, such as, $, ¥, £, and €, there is an official three-letter symbol for each currency that is recognized worldwide. These symbols can be found at the Full Universal Currency Converter website: www.xe.com/currencyconverter/full. Go to this site. What is the currency symbol for the Costa Ricon colon? The Guyanese dollar?

MINI CASE

Shrewsbury Herbal Products, Ltd.

Shrewsbury Herbal Products, located in central England close to the Welsh border, is an old-line producer of herbal teas, seasonings, and medicines. Its products are marketed all over the United Kingdom and in many parts of continental Europe as well.

Shrewsbury Herbal generally invoices in British pound sterling when it sells to foreign customers in order to guard against adverse exchange rate changes. Nevertheless, it has just received an order from a large wholesaler in central France for £320,000 of its products, conditional upon delivery being made in three months' time and the order invoiced in euros.

Shrewsbury's controller, Elton Peters, is concerned with whether the pound will appreciate versus the euro over the next three months, thus eliminating all or most of the profit when the euro receivable is paid. He thinks this an unlikely possibility, but he decides to contact the firm's banker for suggestions about hedging the exchange rate exposure.

Mr. Peters learns from the banker that the current spot exchange rate in €/£ is €1.4537; thus the invoice amount should be €465,184. Mr. Peters also learns that the three-month forward rates for the pound and the euro versus the U.S. dollar are $1.8990/£1.00 and $1.3154/€1.00, respectively. The banker offers to set up a forward hedge for selling the euro receivable for pound sterling based on the €/£ forward cross-exchange rate implicit in the forward rates against the dollar.

What would you do if you were Mr. Peters?

REFERENCES & SUGGESTED READINGS

Bank for International Settlements. *Triennial Central Bank Survey, 2010, Preliminary Results*. Basle, Switzerland: Bank for International Settlements, September 2010.

Cheung, Yin-Wong, and Menzie David Chinn. "Currency Traders and Exchange Rate Dynamics: A Survey of the US Market." *Journal of International Money and Finance* 20 (2001), pp. 439–71.

Dominguez, Kathryn M. "Central Bank Intervention and Exchange Rate Volatility." *Journal of International Money and Finance* 17 (1998), pp. 161–90.

Federal Reserve Bank of New York. *The Foreign Exchange and Interest Rate Derivatives Markets: Turnover in the United States.* New York: Federal Reserve Bank of New York, April 2007.

Grabbe, J. Orlin. *International Financial Markets*, 3rd ed. Upper Saddle River, N.J.: Prentice Hall, 1996.

Huang, Roger D., and Ronald W. Masulis. "FX Spreads and Dealer Competition across the 24-Hour Trading Day." *Review of Financial Studies* 12 (1999), pp. 61–93.

International Monetary Fund. *International Capital Markets: Part I. Exchange Rate Management and International Capital Flows*. Washington, D.C.: International Monetary Fund, 1993.

Ito, Takatoshi, Richard K. Lyons, and Michael T. Melvin. "Is There Private Information in the FX Market? The Tokyo Experiment." *Journal of Finance* 53 (1998), pp. 1111–30.

Lyons, Richard K. "Profits and Position Control: A Week of FX Dealing." *Journal of International Money and Finance* 17 (1998), pp. 97–115.

UBS Investment Bank. *Foreign Exchange and Money Market Transactions*. This book can be found and downloaded at www.ibb.ubs.com/Individuals/files/brochure/booken.pdf.

International Parity Relationships and Forecasting Foreign Exchange Rates

FOR COMPANIES AND investors alike, it is important to have a firm understanding of the forces driving exchange rate changes as these changes would affect investment and financing opportunities. To that end, this chapter examines several key international parity relationships, such as interest rate parity and purchasing power parity, that have profound implications for international financial management. Some of these are, in fact, manifestations of the *law of one price* that must hold in *arbitrage equilibrium*.[1] An understanding of these parity relationships provides insights into (i) how foreign exchange rates are determined, and (ii) how to forecast foreign exchange rates.

Since **arbitrage** plays a critical role in the ensuing discussion, we should define it upfront. The term *arbitrage* can be defined as *the act of simultaneously buying and selling the same or equivalent assets or commodities for the purpose of making certain, guaranteed profits*. As long as there are profitable arbitrage opportunities, the market cannot be in equilibrium. The market can be said to be in equilibrium when no profitable arbitrage opportunities exist. Such well-known parity relationships as interest rate parity and purchasing power parity, in fact, represent arbitrage equilibrium conditions. Let us begin our discussion with interest rate parity.

Interest Rate Parity

Interest rate parity (IRP) is an arbitrage condition that must hold when international financial markets are in equilibrium. Suppose that you have $1 to invest over, say, a one-year period. Consider two alternative ways of investing your fund: (i) invest domestically at the U.S. interest rate, or, alternatively, (ii) invest in a foreign country, say, the U.K., at the foreign interest rate and hedge the exchange risk by selling the maturity value of the foreign investment forward. It is assumed here that you want to consider only default-free investments.

If you invest $1 domestically at the U.S. interest rate ($i_\$$), the maturity value will be

$$\$1(1 + i_\$)$$

Since you are assumed to invest in a default-free instrument like a U.S. Treasury note, there is no uncertainty about the future maturity value of your investment in dollar terms.

---

[1]The law of one price prevails when the same or equivalent things are trading at the same price across different locations or markets, precluding profitable arbitrage opportunities. As we will see, many equilibrium pricing relationships in finance are obtained from imposing the law of one price, i.e., the two things that are equal to each other must be selling for the same price.

To invest in the U.K., on the other hand, you carry out the following sequence of transactions:

1. Exchange $1 for a pound amount, that is, £$(1/S)$, at the prevailing spot exchange rate (S).[2]

2. Invest the pound amount at the U.K. interest rate $(i_£)$, with the maturity value of £$(1/S)(1 + i_£)$.

3. Sell the maturity value of the U.K. investment forward in exchange for a *predetermined dollar amount*, that is, $\$[(1/S)(1 + i_£)]F$, where F denotes the forward exchange rate.

Note that the exchange rate, S or F, represents the dollar price of one unit of foreign currency, i.e., British pound in the above example. When your British investment matures in one year, you will receive the full maturity value, £$(1/S)(1 + i_£)$. But since you have to deliver exactly the same amount of pounds to the counterparty of the forward contract, your net pound position is reduced to zero. In other words, the exchange risk is completely hedged. Since, as with the U.S. investment, you are assured of receiving a predetermined dollar amount, your U.K. investment coupled with forward hedging is a perfect substitute for the domestic U.S. investment. Because you've hedged the exchange risk by a forward contract, you've effectively *redenominated* the U.K. investment in dollar terms. The "effective" dollar interest rate from the U.K. investment alternative is given by

$$\frac{F}{S}(1 + i_£) - 1$$

Arbitrage equilibrium then would dictate that the future dollar proceeds (or, equivalently, the dollar interest rates) from investing in the two equivalent investments must be the same, implying that

$$(1 + i_\$) = \frac{F}{S}(1 + i_£), \text{ or alternatively}$$

$$F = S\left[\frac{1 + i_\$}{1 + i_£}\right] \tag{6.1}$$

which is a formal statement of IRP. It should be clear from the way we arrived at Equation 6.1 that IRP is a manifestation of the **law of one price (LOP)** applied to international money market instruments. The IRP relationship has been known among currency traders since the late 19th century. But it was only during the 1920s that the relationship became widely known to the public from the writings of John M. Keynes and other economists.[3]

Alternatively, IRP can be derived by constructing an **arbitrage portfolio**, which involves (i) no net investment, as well as (ii) no risk, and then requiring that such a portfolio should not generate any net cash flow in equilibrium. Consider an arbitrage portfolio consisting of three separate positions:

1. Borrowing $\$S$ in the United States, which is just enough to buy £1 at the prevailing spot exchange rate (S).

2. Lending £1 in the U.K. at the U.K. interest rate.

3. Selling the maturity value of the U.K. investment forward.

Exhibit 6.1 summarizes the present and future (maturity date) cash flows, CF_0 and CF_1, from investing in the arbitrage portfolio.

Two things are noteworthy in Exhibit 6.1. First, the net cash flow at the time of investment is zero. This, of course, implies that the arbitrage portfolio is indeed

---

[2]For notational simplicity, we delete the currency subscripts for the exchange rate notations, S and F. If the exchange rate, S or F, is expressed as the amount of foreign currency per dollar, the IRP formula will become as follows: $(1 + i_\$) = (S/F)(1 + i_£)$.

[3]A systematic exposition of the interest rate parity is generally attributed to Keynes's *Monetary Reform* (1924).

EXHIBIT 6.1	Transactions	CF_0	CF_1
	1. Borrow in the U.S.	$\$S$	$-S(1 + i_\$)$
Dollar Cash Flows to an Arbitrage Portfolio	2. Lend in the U.K.	$-\$S$	$S_1(1 + i_£)$
	3. Sell the £ receivable forward*	0	$(1 + i_£)(F - S_1)$
	Net cash flow	0	$(1 + i_£)F - (1 + i_\$)S$

*Selling the £ receivable "forward" will not result in any cash flow at the present time, that is, $CF_0 = 0$. But at the maturity, the seller will receive $\$(F - S_1)$ for each pound sold forward. S_1 denotes the future spot exchange rate

fully self-financing; it doesn't cost any money to hold this portfolio. Second, the net cash flow on the maturity date is known with certainty. That is so because none of the variables involved in the net cash flow, that is, S, F, $i_\$$, and $i_£$, is uncertain. Since no one should be able to make certain profits by holding this arbitrage portfolio, market equilibrium requires that the net cash flow on the maturity date be zero for this portfolio:

$$(1 + i_£)F - (1 + i_\$)S = 0 \tag{6.2}$$

which, upon simple rearrangement, is the same result as Equation 6.1.

The IRP relationship is sometimes approximated as follows:

$$(i_\$ - i_£) = \left[\frac{F - S}{S}\right](1 + i_£) \cong \left[\frac{F - S}{S}\right] \tag{6.3}$$

As can be seen clearly from Equation 6.1, IRP provides a linkage between interest rates in two different countries. Specifically, the interest rate will be higher in the United States than in the U.K. when the dollar is at a forward discount, that is, $F > S$. Recall that the exchange rates, S and F, represent the dollar prices of one unit of foreign currency. When the dollar is at a forward discount, this implies that the dollar is expected to depreciate against the pound. If so, the U.S. interest rate should be higher than the U.K. interest rate to compensate for the expected depreciation of the dollar. Otherwise, nobody would hold dollar-denominated securities. On the other hand, the U.S. interest rate will be lower than the U.K. interest rate when the dollar is at a forward premium, that is, $F < S$. Equation 6.1 indicates that the forward exchange rate will deviate from the spot rate as long as the interest rates of the two countries are not the same.[4]

When IRP holds, you will be indifferent between investing your money in the United States and investing in the U.K. with forward hedging. However, if IRP is violated, you will prefer one to another. You will be better off by investing in the United States (U.K.) if $(1 + i_\$)$ is greater (less) than $(F/S)(1 + i_£)$. When you need to borrow, on the other hand, you will choose to borrow where the dollar interest is lower. When IRP doesn't hold, the situation also gives rise to **covered interest arbitrage** opportunities.

Covered Interest Arbitrage

To understand the covered interest arbitrage (CIA) process, it is best to work with a numerical example.

> **EXAMPLE | 6.1:** Suppose that the annual interest rate is 5 percent in the United States and 8 percent in the U.K., and that the spot exchange rate is \$1.80/£ and the forward exchange rate, with one-year maturity, is \$1.78/£. In terms of our notation, $i_\$ = 5\%$, $i_£ = 8\%$, $S = \$1.80$, and $F = \$1.78$. Assume that the arbitrager can borrow up to \$1,000,000 or £555,556, which is equivalent to \$1,000,000 at the current spot exchange rate.
>
> Let us first check if IRP is holding under current market conditions. Substituting the given data, we find,
>
> $$\left[\frac{F}{S}\right](1 + i_£) = \left[\frac{1.78}{1.80}\right](1.08) = 1.068$$

continued

---

[4]To determine if an arbitrage opportunity exists, one should use the exact version of IRP, not the approximate version.

EXAMPLE | 6.1: continued

which is not exactly equal to $(1 + i_\$) = 1.05$. Specifically, we find that the current market condition is characterized by

$$(1 + i_\$) < \left[\frac{F}{S}\right](1 + i_£). \tag{6.4}$$

Clearly, IRP is not holding, implying that a profitable arbitrage opportunity exists. Since the interest rate is lower in the United States than in the U.K. after adjusting for the exchange rates (F/S), an arbitrage transaction should involve borrowing in the United States and lending in the U.K.

The arbitrager can carry out the following transactions:

1. In the United States, borrow $1,000,000. Repayment in one year will be $1,050,000 = $1,000,000 × 1.05.
2. Buy £555,556 spot using $1,000,000.
3. Invest £555,556 in the U.K. The maturity value will be £600,000 = £555,556 × 1.08.
4. Sell £600,000 forward in exchange for $1,068,000 = (£600,000)($1.78/£).

In one year when everything matures, the arbitrager will receive the full maturity value of his U.K. investment, that is, £600,000. The arbitrager then will deliver this pound amount to the counterparty of the forward contract and receive $1,068,000 in return. Out of this dollar amount, the maturity value of the dollar loan, $1,050,000, will be paid. The arbitrager still has $18,000 (= $1,068,000 − $1,050,000) left in his account, which is his arbitrage profit. In making this *certain profit,* the arbitrager neither invested any money out of his pocket nor bore any risk. He indeed carried out "covered interest arbitrage," which means that he borrowed at one interest rate and simultaneously lent at another interest rate, with exchange risk fully covered via forward hedging.[5] Exhibit 6.2 provides a summary of CIA transactions.

How long will this arbitrage opportunity last? A simple answer is: only for a short while. As soon as deviations from IRP are detected, informed traders will immediately carry out CIA transactions. As a result of these arbitrage activities, IRP will be restored quite quickly. To see this, let's get back to our numerical example, which induced covered interest arbitrage activities. Since every trader will (i) borrow in the United States as much as possible, (ii) lend in the U.K., (iii) buy the pound spot, and, at the same time, (iv) sell the pound forward, the following adjustments will occur to the initial market condition described in Equation 6.4:

1. The interest rate will rise in the United States ($i_\$\uparrow$).
2. The interest rate will fall in the U.K. ($i_£\downarrow$).
3. The pound will appreciate in the spot market ($S\uparrow$).
4. The pound will depreciate in the forward market ($F\downarrow$).

These adjustments will raise the left-hand side of Equation 6.4 and, at the same time, lower the right-hand side until both sides are equalized, restoring IRP.

The adjustment process is depicted in Exhibit 6.3. The initial market condition described by Equation 6.4 is represented by point A in the exhibit, substantially off the IRP line.[6] CIA activities will increase the interest rate differential (as indicated by the horizontal arrow) and, at the same time, lower the forward premium/discount (as indicated by the vertical arrow). Since the foreign exchange and money markets

---

[5]The arbitrage profit is, in fact, equal to the effective interest rate differential times the amount borrowed, i.e., $18,000 = (1.068 − 1.05)($1,000,000).

[6]Note that at point A, the interest rate differential is −3%, i.e., $i_\$ − i_£ = 5\% − 8\% = −3\%$, and the forward premium is −1.11%, i.e., $(F − S)/S = (1.78 − 1.80)/1.80 = − 0.0111$, or −1.11%.

EXHIBIT 6.2	Transactions	CF_0	CF_1
Covered Interest Arbitrage: Cash Flow Analysis	1. Borrow $1,000,000	$1,000,000	−$1,050,000
	2. Buy £ spot	−$1,000,000 £555,556	
	3. Lend £555,556	−£555,556	£600,000
	4. Sell £600,000 forward		−£600,000 $1,068,000
	Net cash flow	0	$18,000

EXHIBIT 6.3

The Interest Rate Parity Diagram

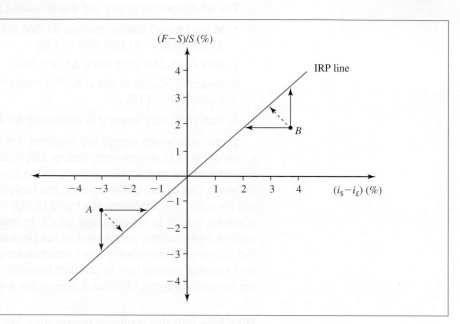

share the burden of adjustments, the actual path of adjustment to IRP can be depicted by the dotted arrow. When the initial market condition is located at point B, IRP will be restored partly by an increase in the forward premium, $(F - S)/S$, and partly by a decrease in the interest rate differential, $i_\$ - i_£$.

> **EXAMPLE | 6.2:** Before we move on, it would be useful to consider another CIA example. Suppose that the market condition is summarized as follows:
>
> Three-month interest rate in the United States: 8.0% per annum.
>
> Three-month interest rate in Germany: 5.0% per annum.
>
> Current spot exchange rate: €0.800/$.
>
> Three-month forward exchange rate: €0.7994/$.
>
> The current example differs from the previous example in that the transaction horizon is three months rather than a year, and the exchange rates are quoted in *European* rather than American terms.
>
> If we would like to apply IRP as defined in Equation 6.1, we should convert the exchange rates into American terms and use three-month interest rates, not annualized rates. In other words, we should use the following numerical values to check if IRP is holding:
>
> $i_\$ = 8.0/4 = 2.0\%$ $\qquad\qquad$ $i_€ = 5.0/4 = 1.25\%$
>
> $S = 1/0.800 = \$1.250/€$ $\qquad\qquad$ $F = 1/0.7994 = \$1.2510/€$

continued

EXAMPLE | 6.2: continued

It is important to make sure that both the interest rates and the forward exchange rate have the same maturity.

Now, we can compute the right-hand side of Equation 6.1:

$$\left[\frac{F}{S}\right](1 + i_\epsilon) - \left[\frac{1.2510}{1.2500}\right](1.0125) - 1.0133,$$

which is less than $(1 + i_\$) = 1.02$. Clearly, IRP is not holding and an arbitrage opportunity thus exists. Since the interest rate is lower in Germany after allowing for exchange rates than in the United States, the arbitrage transaction should involve borrowing in Germany and lending in the United States. Again, we assume that the arbitrager can borrow up to $1,000,000 or the equivalent € amount, €800,000.

The arbitrager can carry out the following transactions:

1. Borrow €800,000 in Germany. Repayment in three months will be €810,000 = €800,000 × 1.0125.
2. Buy $1,000,000 spot using €800,000.
3. Invest $1,000,000 in the United States. The maturity value will be $1,020,000 in three months.
4. Buy €810,000 forward in exchange for $1,013,310 = €810,000($1.2510/€).

In three months, the arbitrager will receive the full maturity value of the U.S. investment, $1,020,000. But then, the arbitrager should deliver $1,013,310 to the counter-party of the forward contract and receive €810,000 in return, which will be used to repay the euro loan. The arbitrage profit will thus be $6,690 (= $1,020,000 − $1,013,310).[7]

Interest Rate Parity and Exchange Rate Determination

Being an arbitrage equilibrium condition involving the (spot) exchange rate, IRP has an immediate implication for exchange rate determination. To see why, let us reformulate the IRP relationship in terms of the spot exchange rate:

$$S = \left[\frac{1 + i_\pounds}{1 + i_\$}\right]F \tag{6.5}$$

Equation 6.5 indicates that given the forward exchange rate, the spot exchange rate depends on relative interest rates. All else equal, an increase in the U.S. interest rate will lead to a higher foreign exchange value of the dollar.[8] This is so because a higher U.S. interest rate will attract capital to the United States, increasing the demand for dollars. In contrast, a decrease in the U.S. interest rate will lower the foreign exchange value of the dollar.

In addition to relative interest rates, the forward exchange rate is an important factor in spot exchange rate determination. Under certain conditions the forward exchange rate can be viewed as the expected future spot exchange rate conditional on all relevant information being available now, that is,

$$F = E(S_{t+1}|I_t) \tag{6.6}$$

where S_{t+1} is the future spot rate when the forward contract matures, and I_t denotes the set of information currently available.[9] When Equations 6.5 and 6.6 are combined, we obtain

$$S = \left[\frac{1 + i_\pounds}{1 + i_\$}\right]E(S_{t+1}|I_t) \tag{6.7}$$

---

[7]It is left to the readers to figure out how IRP may be restored in this example.

[8]A higher U.S. interest rate $(i_\$\uparrow)$ will lead to a lower spot exchange rate $(S\downarrow)$, which means a stronger dollar. Note that the variable S represents the number of U.S. dollars per pound.

[9]The set of relevant information should include money supplies, interest rates, trade balances, and so on that would influence the exchange rates.

Two things are noteworthy from Equation 6.7. First, "expectation" plays a key role in exchange rate determination. Specifically, the expected future exchange rate is shown to be a major determinant of the current exchange rate; when people "expect" the exchange rate to go up in the future, it goes up now. People's expectations thus become self-fulfilling. Second, exchange rate behavior will be driven by news events. People form their expectations based on the set of information (I_t) they possess. As they receive news continuously, they are going to update their expectations continuously. As a result, the exchange rate will tend to exhibit a *dynamic* and *volatile* short-term behavior, responding to various news events. By definition, news events are unpredictable, making forecasting future exchange rates an arduous task.

When the forward exchange rate F is replaced by the expected future spot exchange rate, $E(S_{t+1})$ in Equation 6.3, we obtain:

$$(i_\$ - i_£) \approx E(e) \tag{6.8}$$

where $E(e)$ is the expected rate of change in the exchange rate, that is, $[E(S_{t+1}) - S_t]/S_t$. Equation 6.8 states that the interest rate differential between a pair of countries is (approximately) equal to the expected rate of change in the exchange rate. This relationship is known as the **uncovered interest rate parity**.[10] If, for instance, the annual interest rate is 5 percent in the United States and 8 percent in the U.K., as assumed in our numerical example, the uncovered IRP suggests that the pound is expected to depreciate against the dollar by about 3 percent, that is, $E(e) \approx -3\%$.

Currency Carry Trade

Unlike IRP, the uncovered interest rate parity often doesn't hold, giving rise to uncovered interest arbitrage opportunities. A popular example of such trade is provided by **currency carry trade**. Currency carry trade involves buying a high-yielding currency and funding it with a low-yielding currency, without any hedging. Since the interest rate in Japan has been near zero since the mid-1990s, the yen has been the most popular funding currency for carry trade, followed by the Swiss franc. Due to the low-interest-rate policy of the Federal Reserve to combat the Great Recession, the U.S. dollar has also become a popular funding currency in recent years. Popular investment currencies, on the other hand, include the Australian dollar, New Zealand dollar, and British pound, due to relatively high interest rates prevalent in these countries. Suppose you borrow in Japanese yen and invest in the Australian dollar. Your carry trade then will be profitable as long as the interest rate spread between the Australian dollar and Japanese yen, $i_{A\$} - i_¥$, is greater than the rate of appreciation ($e_{A\$,¥}$) of the yen against the Australian dollar during the carry period, i.e., $i_{A\$} - i_¥ > e_{A\$,¥}$.

If many investors carry out the preceding trade on a massive scale, the yen may even depreciate, at least in the short run, against the Australian dollar, which is contrary to the prediction of the uncovered interest rate parity. The yen may depreciate in the short run as investors are selling the yen for the Australian dollar. If the yen depreciates against the Australian dollar by more than the Japanese interest rate, the funding cost for this carry trade would be effectively negative, making the carry trade more profitable.[11] However, if the Japanese yen appreciates against the Australian dollar by more than the interest rate spread, you would lose money from the carry trade. Clearly, currency carry trade is a risky investment, especially when the exchange rate is volatile.

Exhibit 6.4 plots the six-month interest rate spread between the yen and Australian dollar, $i_{A\$} - i_¥$, and the rate of change in the exchange rate between the two currencies, $e_{A\$,¥}$, during the same six-month period. The exhibit shows that for (nonoverlapping)

---

[10]As we will discuss shortly, the same relationship is also known as the international Fisher effect.

[11]Suppose you borrowed in Japanese yen at a 0.50% interest rate and the yen depreciated by 1.25% during the carry period. Then, the effective funding cost for the carry trade would become negative, -0.75% ($= 0.50\% - 1.25\%$).

Interest Rate Spreads
and Exchange Rate
Changes: Six-Month
Carry Periods for
Australian Dollar
Japanese Yen Pair

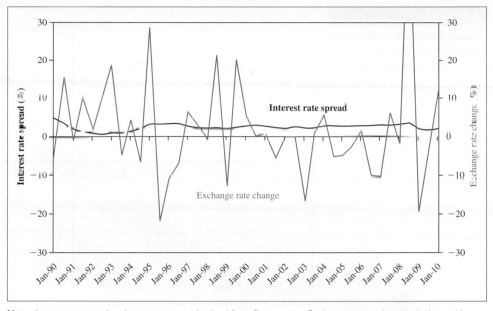

Note: Interest rates and exchange rates are obtained from Datastream. For interest rates, interbank six-month rates are used for both countries. The interest rate spread and the rate of change in the exchange rate are plotted at the start of each six-month carry period.

six-month periods examined, this carry trade was mostly profitable during the period 2000–2007, when the yen often depreciated against the Australian dollar. At other times, the carry trade was often unprofitable due to intermittent, sharp appreciations of the yen. Note that the yen appreciated very sharply in the second half of 2008, reflecting the surging demand for Japanese yen as a safe-haven asset during the recent global financial crisis, generating significant loss for the carry trade.

Reasons for Deviations from Interest Rate Parity

Although IRP tends to hold quite well, it may not hold precisely all the time for at least two reasons: transaction costs and capital controls.

In our previous examples of CIA transactions, we implicitly assumed, among other things, that no transaction costs existed. As a result, in our first CIA example, for each dollar borrowed at the U.S. interest rate ($i_\$$), the arbitrager could realize the following amount of positive profit:

$$(F/S)(1 + i_£) - (1 + i_\$) > 0 \tag{6.9}$$

In reality, transaction costs do exist. The interest rate at which the arbitrager borrows, i^a, tends to be higher than the rate at which he lends, i^b, reflecting the bid-ask spread. Likewise, there exist bid-ask spreads in the foreign exchange market as well. The arbitrager has to buy foreign exchanges at the higher ask price and sell them at the lower bid price. Each of the four variables in Equation 6.9 can be regarded as representing the midpoint of the spread.

Because of spreads, arbitrage profit from each dollar borrowed may become nonpositive:

$$(F^b/S^a)(1 + i_£^b) - (1 + i_\$^a) \leq 0 \tag{6.10}$$

where the superscripts a and b to the exchange rates and interest rates denote the ask and bid prices, respectively. This is so because

$$(F^b/S^a) < (F/S)$$
$$(1 + i_£^b) < (1 + i_£)$$
$$(1 + i_£^a) > (1 + i_\$)$$

EXHIBIT 6.5

Interest Rate Parity with
Transaction Costs

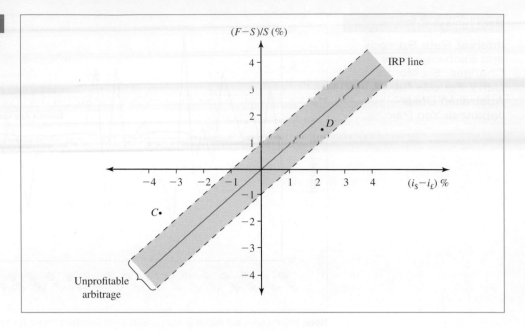

If the arbitrage profit turns negative because of transaction costs, the current deviation from IRP does not represent a profitable arbitrage opportunity. Thus, the IRP
line in Exhibit 6.5 can be viewed as included within a band around it, and only IRP
deviations outside the band, such as point C, represent profitable arbitrage opportunities. IRP deviations within the band, such as point D, would not represent profitable arbitrage opportunities. The width of this band will depend on the size of
transaction costs.

Another major reason for deviations from IRP is capital controls imposed by governments. For various macroeconomic reasons, governments sometimes restrict capital flows, inbound and/or outbound.[12] Governments achieve this objective by means of
jawboning, imposing taxes, or even outright bans on cross-border capital movements.
These control measures imposed by governments can effectively impair the arbitrage
process, and, as a result, deviations from IRP may persist.

An interesting historical example is provided by Japan, where capital controls were
imposed on and off until December 1980, when the Japanese government liberalized
international capital flows. Otani and Tiwari (1981) investigated the effect of capital controls on IRP deviations during the period 1978–81. They computed deviations
from interest rate parity (DIRP) as follows:[13]

$$\text{DIRP} = \left[\frac{(1 + i_¥)S}{(1 + i_\$)F}\right] - 1 \qquad (6.11)$$

where:

$i_¥$ = interest rate on three-month Gensaki bonds.[14]
$i_\$$ = interest rate on three-month Euro-dollar deposits.
S = yen/dollar spot exchange rate in Tokyo.
F = yen/dollar three-month forward exchange rate in Tokyo.

---

[12]Capital controls were often imposed by governments in an effort to improve the balance-of-payments
situations and to keep the exchange rate at a desirable level.

[13]Readers can convince themselves that DIRP in Equation 6.11 will be zero if IRP holds exactly.

[14]Gensaki bonds, issued in the Tokyo money market, are sold with a repurchase agreement. While interest rates
on Gensaki bonds are determined by market forces, they can still be affected by various market imperfections.

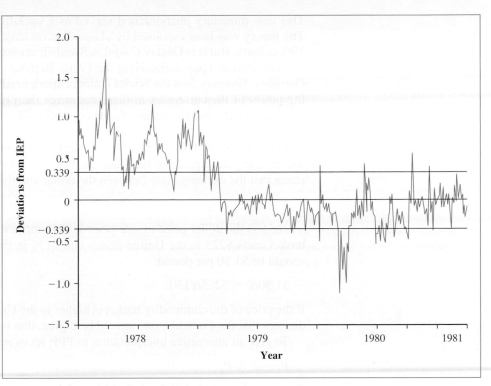

EXHIBIT 6.6

Deviations from Interest
Rate Parity: Japan,
1978–81 (in percent)

Note: Daily data were used in computing the deviations. The zone bounded by +0.339 and −0.339 represents the average width of the band around the IRP for the sample period.

Source: I. Otani and S. Tiwari, "Capital Controls and Interest Rate Parity: The Japanese Experience, 1978–81" *IMF Staff Papers* 28 (1981), pp. 793–816.

Deviations from IRP computed as above are plotted in Exhibit 6.6. If IRP holds strictly, deviations from it would be randomly distributed, with the expected value of zero.

Exhibit 6.6, however, shows that deviations from IRP hardly hover around zero. The deviations were quite significant at times until near the end of 1980. They were the greatest during 1978. This can be attributed to various measures the Japanese government took to discourage capital inflows, which was done to keep the yen from appreciating. As these measures were removed in 1979, the deviations were reduced. They increased again considerably in 1980, however, reflecting an introduction of capital control; Japanese financial institutions were asked to discourage foreign currency deposits.

In December 1980, Japan adopted the new *Foreign Exchange and Foreign Trade Control Law,* which generally liberalized foreign exchange transactions. Not surprisingly, the deviations hover around zero in the first quarter of 1981. The empirical evidence presented in Exhibit 6.6 closely reflects changes in capital controls during the study period. This implies that deviations from IRP, especially in 1978 and 1980, do not represent unexploited profit opportunities; rather, they reflect the existence of significant barriers to cross-border arbitrage.

Purchasing Power Parity

When the law of one price is applied internationally to a *standard consumption basket,* we obtain the theory of **purchasing power parity** (PPP). This theory states that the exchange rate between currencies of two countries should be equal to the ratio of the countries' price levels. The basic idea of PPP originated with scholars at the University of Salamanca, the oldest University in Spain, in the 16th century. Following the conquest of the Americas, Spain experienced a major influx of gold, which resulted in domestic inflation and the depreciation of the Spanish escudo against foreign currencies.

This new monetary phenomenon served as a backdrop for the birth of PPP theory. The theory was later espoused by classical economists such as David Ricardo in the 19th century. But it is Gustav Cassel, a Swedish economist, who formulated PPP in its modern form and popularized it in the 1920s. In those years, many countries, including Germany, Hungary, and the Soviet Union, experienced hyperinflation. As the purchasing power of the currencies in these countries sharply declined, the same currencies also depreciated sharply against stable currencies like the U.S. dollar. The PPP became popular against this historical backdrop.

Let $P_{\$}$ be the dollar price of the standard consumption basket in the United States and $P_{£}$ the pound price of the same basket in the United Kingdom. Formally, PPP states that the exchange rate between the dollar and the pound should be

$$S = P_{\$}/P_{£} \tag{6.12}$$

where S is the dollar price of one pound. PPP implies that if the standard commodity basket costs \$225 in the United States and £150 in the U.K., then the exchange rate should be \$1.50 per pound:

$$\$1.50/£ = \$225/£150$$

If the price of the commodity basket is higher in the United States, say, \$300, then PPP dictates that the exchange rate should be higher, that is, \$2.00/£.

To give an alternative interpretation to PPP, let us rewrite Equation 6.12 as follows:

$$P_{\$} = S \times P_{£}$$

This equation states that the dollar price of the commodity basket in the United States, $P_{\$}$, must be the same as the dollar price of the basket in the U.K., that is, $P_{£}$ multiplied by S. In other words, PPP requires that the price of the standard consumption basket be the same across countries when measured in a common currency. Clearly, PPP is the manifestation of the law of one price applied to the standard consumption basket. As discussed in the International Finance in Practice box "McCurrencies," PPP is a way of defining the equilibrium exchange rate.

www.economist.com/markets/
bigmac/index.cfm

Offers a discussion of
exchange rate theory using the
Big Mac Index.

As a light-hearted guide to the "correct" level of exchange rate, *The Economist* each year compiles local prices of Big Macs around the world and computes the so-called "Big Mac PPP," the exchange rate that would equalize the hamburger prices between America and elsewhere. Comparing this PPP and the actual exchange rate, a currency may be judged to be either undervalued or overvalued. In July 2012, a Big Mac cost (on average) \$4.33 in America and 15.65 yuan in China. Thus, the Big Mac PPP would be about 3.62 yuan per dollar. The actual exchange rate, however, is 6.39 yuan per dollar, implying that the yuan is substantially undervalued. In contrast, the Big Mac PPP for Switzerland is 1.52 Swiss francs per dollar, compared with the actual exchange rate of 0.99 francs per dollar. This implies that the Swiss franc is very much overvalued.

The PPP relationship of Equation 6.12 is called the *absolute* version of PPP. When the PPP relationship is presented in the "rate of change" form, we obtain the *relative* version:

$$e = \left[\frac{\pi_{\$} - \pi_{£}}{1 + \pi_{£}}\right] \approx \pi_{\$} - \pi_{£} \tag{6.13}$$

where e is the rate of change in the exchange rate and $\pi_{\$}$ and $\pi_{£}$ are the inflation rates in the United States and U.K., respectively. For example, if the inflation rate is 6 percent per year in the United States and 4 percent in the U.K., then the pound should appreciate against the dollar by about 2 percent, that is, $e \approx 2$ percent, per year. It is noted that even if absolute PPP does not hold, relative PPP may hold.[15]

---

[15]From Equation 6.12 we obtain $(1 + e) = (1 + \pi_{\$})/(1 + \pi_{£})$. Rearranging the above expression we obtain $e = (\pi_{\$} - \pi_{£})/(1 + \pi_{£})$, which is approximated by $e = \pi_{\$} - \pi_{£}$ as in Equation 6.13.

PPP Deviations and the Real Exchange Rate

Whether PPP holds or not has important implications for international trade. If PPP holds and thus the differential inflation rates between countries are exactly offset by exchange rate changes, countries' competitive positions in world export markets will not be systematically affected by exchange rate changes. However, if there are deviations from PPP, changes in nominal exchange rates cause changes in the **real exchange rates**, affecting the international competitive positions of countries. This, in turn, would affect countries' trade balances.

The real exchange rate, q, which measures deviations from PPP, can be defined as follows:[16]

$$q = \frac{1 + \pi_\$}{(1 + e)(1 + \pi_£)} \tag{6.14}$$

First note that if PPP holds, that is, $(1 + e) = (1 + \pi_\$)/(1 + \pi_£)$, the real exchange rate will be unity, $q = 1$. When PPP is violated, however, the real exchange rate will deviate from unity. Suppose, for example, the annual inflation rate is 5 percent in the United States and 3.5 percent in the U.K., and the pound appreciated against the dollar by 4.5 percent. Then the real exchange rate is .97:

$$q = (1.05)/(1.045)(1.035) = .97$$

In the above example, the dollar depreciated by more than is warranted by PPP, strengthening the competitiveness of U.S. industries in the world market. If the dollar depreciates by less than the inflation rate differential, the real exchange rate will be greater than unity, weakening the competitiveness of U.S. industries. To summarize,

$q = 1$: Competitiveness of the domestic country unaltered.
$q < 1$: Competitiveness of the domestic country improves.
$q > 1$: Competitiveness of the domestic country deteriorates.

Exhibit 6.7 plots the real "effective" exchange rates for the U.S. dollar, Japanese yen, Canadian dollar, Germany (euro), Chinese yuan, and British pound since 1980. The rates plotted in Exhibit 6.7 are, however, the real effective exchange rate "indices" computed using 2005 rates as the base, that is, $2005 = 100$. The real effective exchange rate is a weighted average of bilateral real exchange rates, with the weight for each foreign currency determined by the country's share in the domestic country's international trade. The real effective exchange rate rises if domestic inflation exceeds inflation abroad and the nominal exchange rate fails to depreciate to compensate for the higher domestic inflation rate. Thus, if the real effective exchange rate rises (falls), the domestic country's competitiveness declines (improves). It is noted that the real effective exchange rate of the Chinese yuan fell sharply in the first half of the 1980s and stayed at a low level until 2006 when it began to rise slowly. Similarly, the real effective exchange rate for Germany generally fell until 2000. On the other hand, the British pound appreciated in real terms from the mid-1990s until 2007, hurting the competitiveness of British companies, but it fell significantly since then.

Evidence on Purchasing Power Parity

As is clear from the above discussions, whether PPP holds in reality is a question of considerable importance. In view of the fact that PPP is the manifestation of the law of one price applied to a standard commodity basket, it will hold only if the prices of constituent commodities are equalized across countries in a given currency and if the composition of the consumption basket is the same across countries.

The PPP has been the subject of a series of tests, yielding generally negative results. For example, in his study of disaggregated commodity arbitrage between the United States and Canada, Richardson (1978) was unable to detect commodity arbitrage for

[16]The real exchange rate measures the degree of deviations from PPP over a certain period of time, assuming that PPP held roughly at a starting point. If PPP holds continuously, the real exchange rate will remain unity.

McCurrencies

When our economics editor invented the Big Mac index in 1986 as a light-hearted introduction to exchange-rate theory, little did she think that 26 years later she would still be munching her way, a little less sylph-like, around the world. As burgernomics enters its third decade, the Big Mac index is widely used and abused around the globe. It is time to take stock of what burgers do and do not tell you about exchange rates.

The Economist's Big Mac index is based on one of the oldest concepts in international economics: the theory of purchasing-power parity (PPP), which argues that in the long run, exchange rates should move towards levels that would equalise the prices of an identical basket of goods and services in any two countries. Our "basket" is a McDonald's Big Mac, produced in around 120 countries. The Big Mac PPP is the exchange rate that would leave burgers costing the same in America as elsewhere. Thus a Big Mac in China costs 15.65 yuan, against an average price in four American cities of $4.33. To make the two prices equal would require an exchange rate of 3.62 yuan to the dollar, compared with a market rate of 6.39. In other words, the yuan is 43% "undervalued" against the dollar. To put it another way, converted into dollars at market rates the Chinese burger is among the cheapest in the table.

Using the same method, the Japanese yen and sterling are somewhat undervalued, by 5% and 4% respectively; the Polish zloty and Russian ruble are much more undervalued. Note that most emerging market currencies also look too cheap. On the other hand, the Swedish and Swiss currencies are substantially overvalued, while the euro is correctly valued.

The index was never intended to be a precise predictor of currency movements, simply a take-away guide to whether currencies are at their "correct" long-run level. Curiously, however, burgernomics has an impressive record in predicting exchange rates: currencies that show up as overvalued often tend to weaken in later years. But you must always remember the Big Mac's limitations. Burgers cannot sensibly be traded across borders and prices are distorted by differences in taxes and the cost of non-tradable inputs, such as rents.

Despite our frequent health warnings, some American politicians are fond of citing the Big Mac index rather too freely when it suits their cause—most notably in their demands for a big appreciation of the Chinese currency in order to reduce America's huge trade deficit. But the cheapness of a Big Mac in China does not really prove that the yuan is being held far below its fair market value. Purchasing-power parity is a long-run concept. It signals where exchange rates are eventually heading, but it says little about today's market-equilibrium exchange rate that would make the prices of tradable goods equal. A burger is a product of both traded and non-traded inputs.

It is quite natural for average prices to be lower in poorer countries than in developed ones. Although the prices of tradable things should be similar, non-tradable services will be cheaper because of lower wages. PPPs are therefore a more reliable way to convert GDP per head into dollars than market exchange rates, because cheaper prices mean that money goes further. This is also why every poor country has an implied PPP exchange rate that is higher than today's market rate, making them all appear undervalued. Both theory and practice show that as countries get richer and their productivity rises, their real exchange rates appreciate. But this does not mean that a currency needs to rise massively today. Jonathan Anderson, chief economist at UBS in Hong Kong, reckons that the yuan is now only 10–15% below its fair-market value.

Even over the long run, adjustment towards PPP need not come from a shift in exchange rates; relative prices can change instead. For example, since 1995, when the yen was overvalued by 100% according to the Big Mac index, the local price of Japanese burgers has dropped by one-third. In the same period, American burgers have become one-third dearer. Similarly, the yuan's future real appreciation could come through faster inflation in China than in the United States.

The Big Mac index is most useful for assessing the exchange rates of countries with similar incomes per head. Thus, among emerging markets, the yuan does indeed look undervalued, while the currencies of Brazil and Turkey look overvalued. Economists would be unwise to exclude Big Macs from their diet, but Super Size servings would equally be a mistake.

Source: "McCurrencies," *The Economist*, updated.

a majority of commodity classes. Richardson reported: "The presence of commodity arbitrage could be rejected with 95 percent confidence for at least 13 out of the 22 commodity groups" (p. 346). Although Richardson did not directly test PPP, his findings can be viewed as highly negative news for PPP. If commodity arbitrage is imperfect between neighboring countries like the United States and Canada that have relatively few trade restrictions, PPP is not likely to hold much better for other pairs of countries.

The hamburger standard

	Big Mac prices		Implied PPP[a] of the dollar	Actual dollar exchange rate 7/25/2012	Under (−)/over (+) valuation against the dollar, %
	In local currency	In dollars			
United States[b]	$4.33	4.33	—	1.00	
Argentina	Peso 19	4.16	4.39	4.57	−4
Australia	A$ 4.56	4.68	1.05	0.97	8
Brazil	Real 10.08	4.94	2.33	2.04	14
Britain	£ 2.69	4.16	1.61[c]	1.55[c]	−4
Canada	C$ 3.89	3.82	0.90	1.02	−12
Chile	Peso 2050	4.16	473.71	493.05	−4
China	Yuan 15.65	2.45	3.62	6.39	−43
Czech Republic	Koruna 70.33	4.77	16.25	21.05	−23
Denmark	DK 28.5	4.65	6.59	6.14	7
Egypt	Pound 16	2.64	3.70	6.07	−39
Euro area[d]	€ 3.58	4.34	1.21[e]	1.21[e]	0
Hong Kong	HK$ 16.5	2.13	3.81	7.76	−51
Hungary	Forint 830	3.48	191.69	238.22	−19
Indonesia	Rupiah 24200	2.55	5592.00	9482.50	−41
Japan	Yen 320	4.09	73.95	78.22	−5
Malaysia	Ringgit 7.4	2.33	1.71	3.17	−46
Mexico	Peso 37	2.70	8.55	13.69	−38
New Zealand	NZ$ 5.1	4.02	1.18	1.27	−7
Peru	New Sol 8.932	3.15	2.75	3.45	−30
Philippines	Peso 118	2.80	27.27	42.20	−35
Poland	Zloty 9.1	2.63	2.10	3.46	−39
Russia	Ruble 75	2.29	17.33	32.77	−47
Singapore	S$ 4.4	3.49	1.02	1.26	−19
South Africa	Rand 19.95	2.36	4.61	8.47	−46
South Korea	Won 3700	3.21	855.00	1151.00	−26
Sweden	SKr 48.4	6.94	11.18	6.98	60
Switzerland	SFr 6.5	6.56	1.52	0.99	52
Taiwan	NT$ 75	2.48	17.33	30.20	−43
Thailand	Baht 82	2.59	18.95	31.70	−40
Turkey	Lire 8.25	4.52	1.91	1.83	4

[a]Purchasing power parity: local price divided by price in United States.
[b]Average of New York, Chicago, Atlanta, and San Francisco
[c]Dollars per pound
[d]Weighted average of prices in euro area
[e]Dollars per euro

Source: McDonald's; *The Economist,* August 3, 2012.

Exhibit 6.8, "A Guide to World Prices," also provides evidence against commodity price parity. The price of aspirin (20 units) ranges from $0.91 in Mexico City to $8.24 in Tokyo. In general, production and distribution of drugs are tightly regulated by the governments in most countries. These regulations make it difficult to carry out cross-border arbitrage, resulting in a wide price disparity for these products. Likewise, the cost of a man's haircut ranges widely from $17.25 in Munich to $80.13 in Hong Kong. It costs 365 percent (!) more to have a haircut in Hong Kong than in Munich. The price

EXHIBIT 6.7

Real Effective Exchange Rates for Selected Currencies (Index, 2005 = 100)

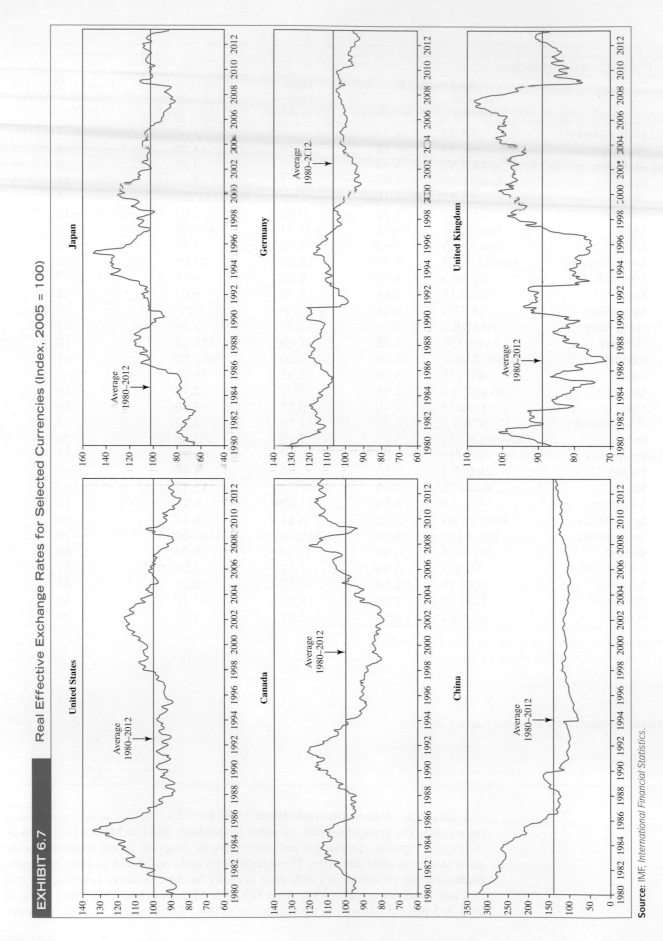

Source: IMF, *International Financial Statistics.*

EXHIBIT 6.8

A Guide to World Prices:
March 2013[a]

Location	Hamburger (1 unit)	Aspirin (20 units)	Man's Haircut (1 unit)	Movie Ticket (1 unit)
Athens	$3.81	$2.09	$58.72	$13.24
Copenhagen	$7.00	$4.86	$55.50	$13.82
Hong Kong	$2.82	$2.39	$80.13	$9.62
London	$5.71	$1.39	$56.60	$20.69
Los Angeles	$3.57	$2.72	$27.33	$11.90
Madrid	$5.40	$5.76	$20.43	$9.87
Mexico City	$4.02	$0.91	$21.72	$4.72
Munich	$4.71	$5.01	$17.25	$10.70
Paris	$5.97	$3.70	$68.49	$12.63
Rio de Janeiro	$5.56	$5.63	$44.70	$10.64
Rome	$5.14	$7.99	$42.19	$9.64
Sydney	$5.38	$4.34	$53.77	$16.29
Tokyo	$3.29	$8.24	$77.00	$18.91
Toronto	$5.32	$2.20	$40.28	$12.20
Vienna	$4.62	$5.04	$39.28	$12.52
Average	$4.82	$4.15	$46.89	$12.48
Standard Deviation	1.13	2.23	19.92	3.90
Coefficient of Variation[b]	0.24	0.54	0.42	0.31

[a]Prices include sales tax and value added tax except in the United States location.
[b]The coefficient of variation is obtained from dividing the standard deviation by the average. It thus provides a measure of dispersion adjusted for the magnitude of the variable.
Source: AIRINC.

differential, however, is likely to persist because haircuts are simply not tradable. In comparison, the price disparity for a hamburger is substantially less. For example, it costs $5.71 in London, $5.38 in Sydney, and $5.32 in Toronto. The lower price disparity may be attributable to the fact that multinational firms like McDonald's set the prices across countries on a comparable basis.

Kravis and Lipsey (1978) examined the relationship between inflation rates and exchange rates and found that price levels can move far apart without rapid correction via arbitrage, thus rejecting the notion of integrated international commodity price structure. In a similar vein, Adler and Lehman (1983) found that deviations from PPP follow a random walk, without exhibiting any tendency to revert to PPP.

Frenkel (1981) reported that while PPP did very poorly in explaining the behavior of exchange rates between the U.S. dollar and major European currencies, it performed somewhat better in explaining the exchange rates between a pair of European currencies, such as the British pound versus the German mark, and the French franc versus the German mark. Frenkel's finding may be attributable to the fact that, in addition to the geographical proximity of the European countries, these countries belonged to the European Common Market, with low internal trade barriers and low transportation costs. Even among these European currencies, however, Frenkel found that relative price levels are only one of the many potential factors influencing exchange rates. If PPP holds strictly, relative price levels should be sufficient in explaining the behavior of exchange rates.

Generally unfavorable evidence about PPP suggests that substantial barriers to international commodity arbitrage exist. Obviously, commodity prices can diverge between countries up to the transportation costs without triggering arbitrage. If it costs $50 to ship a ton of rice from Thailand to Korea, the price of rice can diverge by up to $50 in either direction between the two countries. Likewise, deviations from PPP can result from tariffs and quotas imposed on international trade.

As is well recognized, some commodities never enter into international trade. Examples of such **nontradables** include haircuts, housing, and the like. These items are either immovable or inseparable from the providers of these services. Suppose a quality haircut costs $35 in New York City, but the comparable haircut costs only $10 in Mexico City. Obviously, you cannot import haircuts from Mexico. Either you have to travel to Mexico or a Mexican barber must travel to New York City, both of which, of course, are impractical in view of the travel costs and the immigration laws. Consequently, a large price differential for haircuts will persist. As long as there are nontradables, PPP will not hold in its absolute version. If PPP holds for tradables and the relative prices between tradables and nontradables are maintained, then PPP can hold in its relative version. These conditions, however, are not very likely to hold.

Even if PPP may not hold in reality, it can still play a useful role in economic analysis. First, one can use the PPP-determined exchange rate as a benchmark in deciding if a country's currency is undervalued or overvalued against other currencies. Second, one can often make more meaningful international comparisons of economic data using PPP-determined rather than market-determined exchange rates. This point is highlighted in Exhibit 6.9, "How Large Is India's Economy?"

Suppose you want to rank countries in terms of gross domestic product (GDP). If you use market exchange rates, you can either underestimate or overestimate the true GDP values. Exhibit 6.9 provides the GDP values of the major countries in 2011 computed using both PPP and market exchange rates. A country's ranking in terms of GDP value can be quite sensitive to which exchange rate is used. India provides a striking example. When the market exchange rate is used, India ranks 10th, lagging behind such countries as Brazil, the U.K., and Italy. However, when the PPP exchange rate is used, India moves up to the third place after China, but ahead of Japan, Germany, France, and the U.K. China ranks second only after the United States whether the PPP or market exchange rates are used. In contrast, countries like Canada, France, and Brazil move down in the GDP ranking when PPP exchange rates are used.

Fisher Effects

Another parity condition we often encounter in the literature is the **Fisher effect**. The Fisher effect holds that *an increase (decrease) in the expected inflation rate in a country will cause a proportionate increase (decrease) in the interest rate in the country.* Formally, the Fisher effect can be written for the United States as follows:

$$i_\$ = \rho_\$ + E(\pi_\$) + \rho_\$ E(\pi_\$) \approx \rho_\$ + E(\pi_\$) \tag{6.15}$$

where $\rho_\$$ denotes the equilibrium expected "real" interest rate in the United States.[17]

For example, suppose the expected real interest rate is 2 percent per year in the United States. Given this, the U.S. (nominal) interest rate will be entirely determined by the expected inflation in the United States. If, for instance, the expected inflation rate is 4.0 percent per year, the interest rate will then be set at about 6 percent. With a 6 percent interest rate, the lender will be fully compensated for the expected erosion of the purchasing power of money while still expecting to realize a 2 percent real return. Of course, the Fisher effect should hold in each country as long as the bond market is efficient.

The Fisher effect implies that the expected inflation rate is the difference between the nominal and real interest rates in each country, that is,

$$E(\pi_\$) = (i_\$ - \rho_\$)/(1 + \rho_\$) \approx i_\$ - \rho_\$$$
$$E(\pi_£) = (i_£ - \rho_£)/(1 + \rho_£) \approx i_£ - \rho_£$$

Now, let us assume that the real interest rate is the same between countries, that is, $\rho_\$ = \rho_£$, because of unrestricted capital flows. When we substitute the above results into the relative PPP in its expectational form in Equation 6.13, i.e., $E(e) \approx E(\pi_\$) - E(\pi_£)$, we obtain

$$E(e) \approx i_\$ - i_£ \tag{6.16}$$

[17]It is noted that Equation 6.15 obtains from the relationship: $(1 + i_\$) = (1 + \rho_\$)(1 + E(\pi_\$))$.

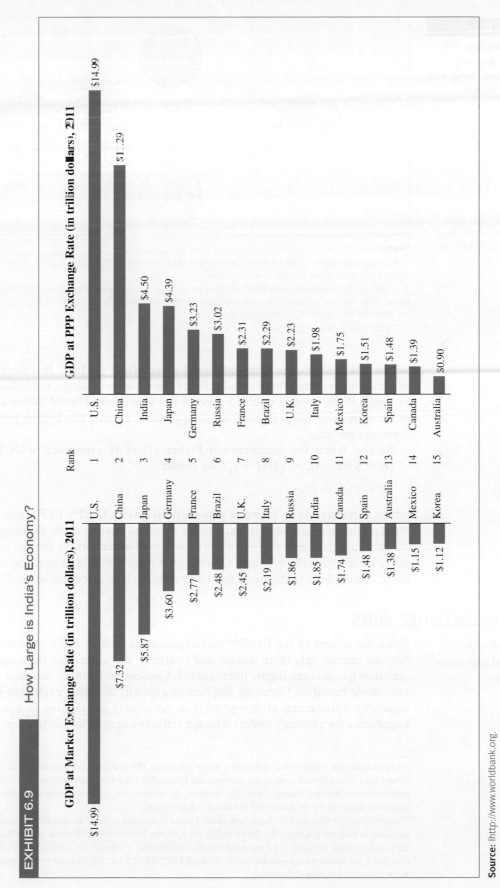

EXHIBIT 6.9   How Large is India's Economy?

GDP at Market Exchange Rate (in trillion dollars), 2011

U.S.	$14.99
China	$7.32
Japan	$5.87
Germany	$3.60
France	$2.77
Brazil	$2.48
U.K.	$2.45
Italy	$2.19
Russia	$1.86
India	$1.85
Canada	$1.74
Spain	$1.48
Australia	$1.38
Mexico	$1.15
Korea	$1.12

GDP at PPP Exchange Rate (in trillion dollars), 2011

Rank		
1	U.S.	$14.99
2	China	$11.29
3	India	$4.50
4	Japan	$4.39
5	Germany	$3.23
6	Russia	$3.02
7	France	$2.31
8	Brazil	$2.29
9	U.K.	$2.23
10	Italy	$1.98
11	Mexico	$1.75
12	Korea	$1.51
13	Spain	$1.48
14	Canada	$1.39
15	Australia	$0.90

Source: lhttp://www.worldbank.org.

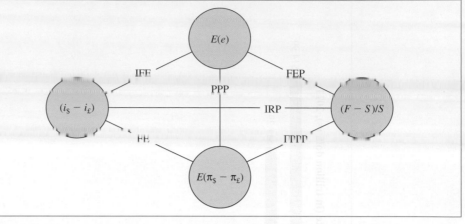

Notes:

1. With the assumption of the same real interest rate, the Fisher effect (FE) implies that the interest rate differential is equal to the expected inflation rate differential.

2. If both purchasing power parity (PPP) and forward expectations parity (FEP) hold, then the forward exchange premium or discount will be equal to the expected inflation rate differential. The latter relationship is denoted by the forward-PPP, i.e., FPPP in the exhibit.

3. IFE stands for the international Fisher effect.

which is known as the **international Fisher effect (IFE)**.[18] IFE suggests that the nominal interest rate differential reflects the expected change in exchange rate. For instance, if the interest rate is 5 percent per year in the United States and 7 percent in the U.K., the dollar is expected to appreciate against the British pound by about 2 percent per year.

Lastly, when the international Fisher effect is combined with IRP, that is, $(F - S)/S = (i_\$ - i_£)/(1 + i_£)$, we obtain

$$(F - S)/S = E(e) \qquad (6.17)$$

which is referred to as **forward expectations parity (FEP)**. FEP states that any forward premium or discount is equal to the expected change in the exchange rate. When investors are risk-neutral, forward parity will hold as long as the foreign exchange market is informationally efficient. Otherwise, it need not hold even if the market is efficient. Exhibit 6.10 summarizes the parity relationships discussed so far.[19]

Forecasting Exchange Rates

Since the advent of the flexible exchange rate system in 1973, exchange rates have become increasingly more volatile and erratic. At the same time, the scope of business activities has become highly international. Consequently, many business decisions are now made based on forecasts, implicit or explicit, of future exchange rates. Understandably, forecasting exchange rates as accurately as possible is a matter of vital importance for currency traders who are actively engaged in speculating, hedging, and

---

[18]The international Fisher effect is the same as the uncovered IRP previously discussed. While the Fisher effect should hold in an efficient market, the international Fisher effect need not hold even in an efficient market unless investors are risk-neutral. Generally speaking, the interest rate differential may reflect not only the expected change in the exchange rate but also a risk premium.

[19]Suppose that the Fisher effect holds both in the United States and in the U.K., and that the real interest rate is the same in both the countries. As shown in Exhibit 6.10, the Fisher effect (FE) then implies that the interest rate differential should be equal to the expected inflation differential. Furthermore, when forward parity and PPP are combined, we obtain what might be called "forward-PPP" (FPPP), i.e., the forward premium/discount is equal to the expected inflation differential.

arbitrage in the foreign exchange markets. It is also a vital concern for multinational corporations that are formulating international sourcing, production, financing, and marketing strategies. The quality of these corporate decisions will critically depend on the accuracy of exchange rate forecasts.

Some corporations generate their own forecasts, while others subscribe to outside services for a fee. While forecasters use a wide variety of forecasting techniques, most can be classified into three distinct approaches:

* Efficient market approach
* Fundamental approach
* Technical approach

Let us briefly examine each of these approaches.

Efficient Market Approach

Financial markets are said to be efficient if the current asset prices fully reflect all the available and relevant information. The **efficient market hypothesis** (EMH), which is largely attributable to Professor Eugene Fama of the University of Chicago, has strong implications for forecasting.[20]

Suppose that foreign exchange markets are efficient. This means that the current exchange rate has already reflected all relevant information, such as money supplies, inflation rates, trade balances, and output growth. The exchange rate will then change only when the market receives new information. Since news by definition is unpredictable, the exchange rate will change randomly over time. In a word, incremental changes in the exchange rate will be independent of the past history of the exchange rate. If the exchange rate indeed follows a random walk, the future exchange rate is expected to be the same as the current exchange rate, that is,

$$S_t = E(S_{t+1})$$

In a sense, the **random walk hypothesis** suggests that today's exchange rate is the best predictor of tomorrow's exchange rate.

While researchers found it difficult to reject the random walk hypothesis for exchange rates on empirical grounds, there is no theoretical reason why exchange rates should follow a pure random walk. The parity relationships we discussed previously indicate that the current forward exchange rate can be viewed as the market's consensus forecast of the future exchange rate based on the available information (I_t) if the foreign exchange markets are efficient, that is,

$$F_t = E(S_{t+1} | I_t)$$

To the extent that interest rates are different between two countries, the forward exchange rate will be different from the current spot exchange rate. This means that the future exchange rate should be expected to be different from the current spot exchange rate.

Those who subscribe to the efficient market hypothesis may predict the future exchange rate using either the current spot exchange rate or the current forward exchange rate. But which one is better? Researchers like Agmon and Amihud (1981) compared the performance of the forward exchange rate with that of the random walk model as a predictor of the future spot exchange rate. Their empirical findings indicate that the forward exchange rate failed to outperform the random walk model in predicting the future exchange rate; the two prediction models that are based on the efficient market hypothesis registered largely comparable performances.[21]

---

[20]For a detailed discussion of the efficient market hypothesis, refer to Eugene Fama, "Efficient Capital Markets II," *Journal of Finance* 26 (1991), pp. 1575–1617.

[21]For a detailed discussion, refer to Tamir Agmon and Yakov Amihud, "The Forward Exchange Rate and the Prediction of the Future Spot Rate," *Journal of Banking and Finance* 5 (1981), pp. 425–37.

Predicting the exchange rates using the efficient market approach has two advantages. First, since the efficient market approach is based on market-determined prices, it is costless to generate forecasts. Both the current spot and forward exchange rates are public information. As such, everyone has free access to it. Second, given the efficiency of foreign exchange markets, it is difficult to outperform the market-based forecasts unless the forecaster has access to private information that is not yet reflected in the current exchange rate.

Fundamental Approach

The fundamental approach to exchange rate forecasting uses various models. For example, the monetary approach to exchange rate determination suggests that the exchange rate is determined by three independent (explanatory) variables: (i) relative money supplies, (ii) relative velocity of monies, and (iii) relative national outputs.[22] One can thus formulate the monetary approach in the following empirical form:[23]

$$s = \alpha + \beta_1(m - m^*) + \beta_2(v - v^*) + \beta_3(y^* - y) + u \qquad (6.18)$$

where:

www.oecd.org/statsportal

Provides macroeconomic data useful for fundamental analysis.

s = natural logarithm of the spot exchange rate.
$m - m^*$ = natural logarithm of domestic/foreign money supply.
$v - v^*$ = natural logarithm of domestic/foreign velocity of money.
$y^* - y$ = natural logarithm of foreign/domestic output.
u = random error term, with mean zero.
α, β's = model parameters.

Generating forecasts using the fundamental approach would involve three steps:

Step 1: Estimation of the structural model like Equation 6.18 to determine the numerical values for the parameters such as α and β's.

Step 2: Estimation of future values of the independent variables like $(m - m^*)$, $(v - v^*)$, and $(y^* - y)$.

Step 3: Substituting the estimated values of the independent variables into the estimated structural model to generate the exchange rate forecasts.

If, for example, the forecaster would like to predict the exchange rate one year into the future, he or she has to estimate the values that the independent variables will assume in one year. These values will then be substituted in the structural model that was fitted to historical data.

The fundamental approach to exchange rate forecasting has three main difficulties. First, one has to forecast a set of independent variables to forecast the exchange rates. Forecasting the former will certainly be subject to errors and may not be necessarily easier than forecasting the latter. Second, the parameter values, that is, α and β's, that are estimated using historical data may change over time because of changes in government policies and/or the underlying structure of the economy. Either difficulty can diminish the accuracy of forecasts even if the model is correct. Third, the model itself can be wrong. For example, the model described by Equation 6.18 may be wrong. The forecast generated by a wrong model cannot be very accurate.

Not surprisingly, researchers found that the fundamental models failed to more accurately forecast exchange rates than either the forward rate model or the random walk model. Meese and Rogoff (1983), for example, found that the fundamental models developed based on the monetary approach did worse than the random walk model even if realized (true) values were used for the independent variables. They also

---

[22]For a detailed discussion of the monetary approach, see Appendix 6A.
[23]For notational simplicity, we omit the time subscripts in the following equation.

EXHIBIT 6.11

Moving Average
Crossover Rule: Golden
Cross vs. Death Cross

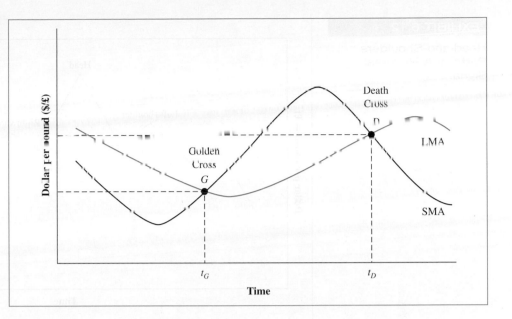

confirmed that the forward rate did not do better than the random walk model. In the words of Meese and Rogoff:

> Ignoring for the present the fact that the spot rate does no worse than the forward rate, the striking feature . . . is that none of the models achieves lower, much less significantly lower, RMSE than the random walk model at any horizon. . . . The structural models in particular fail to improve on the random walk model in spite of the fact that their forecasts are based on realized values of the explanatory variables.[24] (p. 12)

Technical Approach

The technical approach first analyzes the past behavior of exchange rates for the purpose of identifying "patterns" and then projects them into the future to generate forecasts. Clearly, the technical approach is based on the premise that *history repeats itself* (or at least rhymes with itself). The technical approach thus is at odds with the efficient market approach. At the same time, it differs from the fundamental approach in that it does not use the key economic variables such as money supplies or trade balances for the purpose of forecasting. However, technical analysts sometimes consider various transaction data like trading volume, outstanding interests, and bid-ask spreads to aid their analyses. Below, we discuss two examples of technical analysis—the moving average crossover rule and the head-and-shoulders pattern—that are among the most popular tools used by technical analysts.

First, the moving average crossover rule is illustrated in Exhibit 6.11. Many technical analysts or chartists compute moving averages as a way of separating short- and long-term trends from the vicissitudes of daily exchange rates. Exhibit 6.11 illustrates how exchange rates may be forecast based on the movements of short- and long-term moving averages. Since the short-term (such as 50-day) moving average (SMA) weighs recent exchange rate changes more heavily than the long-term (such as 200-day) moving average (LMA), the SMA will lie below (above) the LMA when the British pound is falling (rising) against the dollar. This implies that one may forecast exchange rate movements based on the crossover of the moving averages. According to this rule,

---

[24]RMSE, which stands for the root mean squared error, is the criterion that Meese and Rogoff used in evaluating the accuracy of forecasts.

Head-and-Shoulders
Pattern: A Reversal
Signal

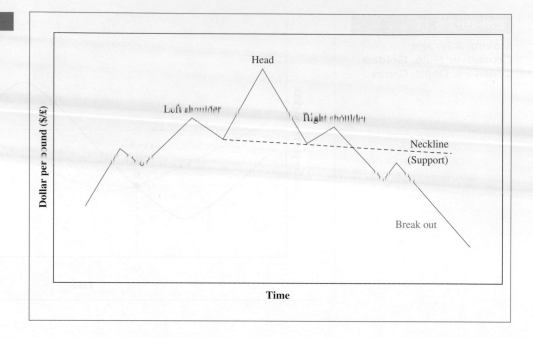

a crossover of the SMA above the LMA at point *G* signals that the British pound may continue to appreciate. On the other hand, a crossover of the SMA below the LMA at point *D* signals that the British pound may depreciate for a while. For traders, crossover *G*, called the "golden cross," is a signal to buy, whereas crossover *D*, known as the "death cross," is a signal to sell.

Next, the head-and-shoulders pattern is illustrated in Exhibit 6.12. The head-and-shoulders (HAS) pattern signals a reversal in an upward trending market. The HAS pattern consists of a head, two shoulders, left and right, and the neckline (support level). This pattern is typically viewed as signaling that the British pound is topping out and a major reversal is forthcoming. As the exhibit shows schematically, the left shoulder occurs as the British pound reaches a local high point in a rising market and then falls back to the neckline. The British pound then appreciates to an even higher level, the head, before it falls back again to the neckline. The right shoulder occurs when the British pound appreciates again but to a local high point lower than the head. The HAS pattern is completed when the neckline or the support level is broken. This occurs when the British pound depreciates through the neckline. The completion of the HAS pattern signals that the British pound will depreciate significantly.

While academic studies tend to discredit the validity of **technical analysis**, many traders depend on technical analyses for their trading strategies. If a trader knows that other traders use technical analysis, it can be rational for the trader to use technical analysis too. If enough traders use technical analysis, the predictions based on it can become self-fulfilling to some extent, at least in the short run.

Performance of the Forecasters

Because predicting exchange rates is difficult, many firms and investors subscribe to professional forecasting services for a fee. Since an alternative to subscribing to professional forecasting services is to use a market-determined price such as the forward exchange rate, it is relevant to ask: *Can professional forecasters outperform the market?*

An answer to the above question was provided by Professor Richard Levich of New York University, who evaluated the performances of 13 forecasting services using

| EXHIBIT 6.13 | Performance of Exchange Rate Forecasting Services | | | | | | | | | | | |

	Forecasting Services												
Currency	1	2	3	4	5	6	7	8	9	10	11	12	13
Canadian dollar	1.29	1.13	1.00	1.59	0.99	1.08	n.a.	1.47	1.17	1.03	1.47	1.74	0.80
British pound	1.11	1.24	0.91	1.44	1.09	0.90	1.05	1.09	1.27	1.89	1.05	1.22	1.01
Belgian franc	0.95	1.07	n.a.	1.33	1.17	n.a.	n.a.	0.99	1.21	n.a.	1.06	1.01	0.77
French franc	0.91	0.98	1.02	1.45	1.27	n.a.	0.98	0.92	1.00	0.96	1.03	1.16	0.70
German mark	1.08	1.13	1.07	1.28	1.19	1.35	1.06	0.83	1.19	1.07	1.13	1.04	0.76
Italian lira	1.07	0.91	1.09	1.45	1.14	n.a.	1.12	1.12	1.00	1.17	1.64	1.54	0.93
Dutch guilder	0.80	1.10	n.a.	1.41	1.06	n.a.	n.a.	0.91	1.26	1.26	1.10	1.01	0.81
Swiss franc	1.01	n.a.	1.08	1.21	1.32	n.a.	n.a.	0.86	1.06	1.04	1.04	0.94	0.63
Japanese yen	1.42	1.05	1.02	1.23	1.08	1.45	1.09	1.24	0.94	0.47	1.31	1.30	1.79

Note: Each entry represents the R ratio defined in Equation 6.19. If a forecasting service outperforms (underperforms) the forward exchange rate, the R ratio will be less (greater) than unity.

Source: Richard Levich, "Evaluating the Performance of the Forecasters," in Richard Ensor, ed., *The Management of Foreign Exchange Risk,* 2nd ed. (Euromoney Publications, 1982).

the forward exchange rate as a benchmark. Under certain conditions, the forward exchange rate can be viewed as the market's consensus forecast of the future exchange rate.[25] These services use different methods of forecasting, such as econometric, technical, and judgmental. In evaluating the performance of forecasters, Levich computed the following ratio:

$$R = \frac{\text{MAE(S)}}{\text{MAE(F)}} \qquad (6.19)$$

where:

MAE(S) = mean absolute forecast error of a forecasting service.

MAE(F) = mean absolute forecast error of the forward exchange rate as a predictor.[26]

If a professional forecasting service provides more accurate forecasts than the forward exchange rate, that is, MAE(S) < MAE(F), then the ratio R will be less than unity for the service. If the service fails to outperform the forward exchange rate, the ratio R will be greater than unity.

Exhibit 6.13 provides the R ratios for each service for the U.S. dollar exchange rates of nine major foreign currencies for a three-month forecasting horizon. The most striking finding presented in the exhibit is that only 24 percent of the entries, 25 out of 104, are less than unity. This, of course, means that the professional services as a whole clearly failed to outperform the forward exchange rate.[27] In other words, they failed to beat the market.

However, there are substantial variations in the performance records across individual services. In the cases of services 4 and 11, for instance, every entry is greater

[25]These conditions are: (a) the foreign exchange markets are efficient, and (b) the forward exchange rate does not contain a significant risk premium.

[26]The mean absolute forecast error (MAE) is computed as follows:

$$\text{MAE} = (1/N) \sum_i |P_i - A_i|$$

where P is the predicted exchange rate, A is the actual (realized) exchange rate, and N is the number of forecasts made. The MAE criterion penalizes the over- and underestimation equally. If a forecaster has perfect foresight so that $P = A$ always, then MAE will be zero.

[27]Levich found that the same qualitative result holds for different horizons like 1 month, 6 months, and 12 months.

than unity. In contrast, for service 13, which is Wharton Econometric Forecasting Associates, the majority of entries, seven out of nine, are less than unity. It is also clear from the exhibit that the performance record of each service varies substantially across currencies. The R ratio for Wharton, for example, ranges from 0.63 for the Swiss franc to 1.79 for the Japanese yen. Wharton Associates clearly has difficulty in forecasting the dollar/yen exchange rate. Service 10, on the other hand, convincingly beat the market in forecasting the yen exchange rate, with an R ratio of 0.47! This suggests that consumers need to discriminate among forecasting services depending on what currencies they are interested in. Lastly, note that service 12, which is known to use technical analysis, outperformed neither the forward rate nor other services. This result certainly does not add credence to the technical approach to exchange rate forecasting.

In a more recent study, Eun and Sabherwal (2002) evaluated the forecasting performances of 10 major commercial banks from around the world. They used the data from *Risk*, a London-based monthly publication dealing with practical issues related to derivative securities and risk management. During the period April 1989 to February 1993, *Risk* published forecasts provided by the banks for exchange rates 3, 6, 9, and 12 months ahead. These forecasts were made for the U.S. dollar exchange rates of the British pound, German mark, Swiss franc, and Japanese yen on the same day of the month by all the banks. This is a rare case where banks' exchange rate forecasts were made available to the public. Since commercial banks are the market makers as well as key players in foreign exchange markets, they should be in a position to observe the order flows and the market sentiments closely. It is thus interesting to check how these banks perform.

In evaluating the performance of the banks, Eun and Sabherwal used the spot exchange rate as the benchmark. Recall that if you believe the exchange rate follows a random walk, today's spot exchange rate can be taken as the prediction of the future spot exchange rate. They thus computed the forecasting accuracy of each bank and compared it with that of the current spot exchange rate, that is, the rate prevailing on the day the forecast is made. In evaluating the performance of banks, they computed the following ratio:

$$R = \frac{MSE(B)}{MSE(S)}$$

where:

MSE(B) = mean squared forecast error of a bank.
MSE(S) = mean squared forecast error of the spot exchange rate.

If a bank provides more accurate forecasts than the spot exchange rate, that is, MSE(B) < MSE(S), then the ratio R will be less than unity, that is, $R < 1$.

Exhibit 6.14 provides the computed R ratios for each of the 10 sample banks as well as the forward exchange rate. Overall, the majority of entries in the exhibit exceed unity, implying that these banks as a whole could not outperform the random walk model. However, some banks significantly outperformed the random walk model, especially in the longer run. For example, in forecasting the British pound exchange rate 12 months into the future, Barclays Bank ($R = 0.60$), Commerzbank ($R = 0.72$), and Industrial Bank of Japan ($R = 0.68$) provided more accurate forecasts, on average, than the random walk model. Likewise, Commerzbank outperformed the random walk model in forecasting the German mark and Swiss franc rates 12 months into the future. But these are more exceptional cases. It is noted that no bank, including the Japanese bank, could beat the random walk model in forecasting the Japanese yen rate at any lead. The last column of Exhibit 6.14 shows that the R-ratio for the forward exchange rate is about unity, implying that the performance of the forward rate is comparable to that of the spot rate.

EXHIBIT 6.14 Forecasting Exchange Rates: Do Banks Know Better?

Currency	Forecast Lead (months)	ANZ Bank (Australia)	Banque-Paribas (France)	Barclays Bank (U.K.)	Chemical Bank (U.S.)	Commerz Bank (Germany)	Generale Bank (France)	Harris Bank (U.S.)	Ind.Bank of Japan (Japan)	Midland-Montagu (U.K.)	Union Bank (Switzerland)	Forward Rate
British Pound	3	2.09	1.31	1.08	1.33	1.31	1.41	1.95	1.10	1.10	0.98	1.02
	6	1.60	1.12	0.92	0.96	1.01	1.17	1.97	0.94	1.11	0.96	1.04
	9	1.42	1.04	0.81	0.88	0.78	0.97	1.65	0.81	0.59	-.09	0.83
	12	1.06	0.84	0.60	1.07	0.72	0.77	1.69	0.68	0.55	-.16	1.02
German Mark	3	1.98	1.39	1.09	1.19	1.59	1.39	1.95	1.14	1.26	1.00	1.01
	6	1.15	1.53	1.16	1.03	1.21	1.21	1.97	1.07	1.27	1.05	1.00
	9	0.92	1.45	1.33	0.99	0.85	0.96	1.71	1.00	1.09	0.93	1.06
	12	0.80	1.19	1.14	1.16	0.62	0.97	1.51	1.00	0.87	1.16	0.96
Swiss Franc	3	2.15	1.47	1.13	1.26	1.66	1.32	1.98	1.05	1.19	1.03	1.02
	6	1.18	1.58	1.30	0.98	1.29	1.35	1.88	1.04	1.24	1.05	1.00
	9	0.88	1.46	1.38	0.84	0.96	1.10	1.66	0.96	1.13	0.87	0.99
	12	0.67	1.16	1.15	0.88	0.74	1.01	1.40	0.91	0.98	1.01	0.94
Japanese Yen	3	3.52	2.31	1.46	1.44	1.73	2.19	2.51	1.52	2.16	1.80	1.08
	6	2.32	2.43	1.55	1.39	1.59	1.62	2.31	1.62	1.68	1.70	1.06
	9	2.54	2.73	1.80	1.57	1.60	1.85	2.22	1.90	1.74	1.97	0.99
	12	2.70	2.61	1.83	1.79	1.44	1.97	1.89	1.93	1.68	2.00	1.10

Source: Cheol Eun and Sanjiv Sabherwal, "Forecasting Exchange Rates: Do Banks Know Better?" *Global Finance Journal*, 2002, pp. 195–215.

SUMMARY

This chapter provides a systematic discussion of the key international parity relationships and two related issues, exchange rate determination and prediction. A thorough understanding of parity relationships is essential for astute financial management.

1. Interest rate parity (IRP) holds that the forward premium or discount should be equal to the interest rate differential between two countries. IRP represents an arbitrage equilibrium condition that should hold in the absence of barriers to international capital flows.

2. If IRP is violated, one can lock in guaranteed profit by borrowing in one currency and lending in another, with exchange risk hedged via forward contract. As a result of this covered interest arbitrage, IRP will be restored.

3. IRP implies that in the short run, the exchange rate depends on (a) the relative interest rates between two countries, and (b) the expected future exchange rate. Other things being equal, a higher (lower) domestic interest rate will lead to appreciation (depreciation) of the domestic currency. People's expectations concerning future exchange rates are self-fulfilling.

4. Purchasing power parity (PPP) states that the exchange rate between two countries' currencies should be equal to the ratio of their price levels. PPP is a manifestation of the law of one price applied internationally to a standard commodity basket. The relative version of PPP states that the rate of change in the exchange rate should be equal to the inflation rate differential between countries. The existing empirical evidence, however, is generally negative on PPP. This implies that substantial barriers to international commodity arbitrage exist.

5. There are three distinct approaches to exchange rate forecasting: (a) the efficient market approach, (b) the fundamental approach, and (c) the technical approach. The efficient market approach uses such market-determined prices as the current exchange rate or the forward exchange rate to forecast the future exchange rate. The fundamental approach uses various formal models of exchange rate determination for forecasting purposes. The technical approach, on the other hand, identifies patterns from the past history of the exchange rate and projects it into the future. The existing empirical evidence indicates that neither the fundamental nor the technical approach outperforms the efficient market approach.

KEY WORDS

arbitrage, *140*
arbitrage portfolio, *141*
covered interest
  arbitrage, *142*
currency carry trade, *146*
efficient market
  hypothesis, *159*
Fisher effect, *156*
forward expectations
  parity (FEP), *158*

interest rate parity, *140*
international Fisher effect
  (IFE), *158*
law of one price
  (LOP), *141*
monetary approach, *172*
nontradables, *155*
purchasing power
  parity, *149*

quantity theory of
  money, *172*
random walk
  hypothesis, *159*
real exchange rates, *151*
technical analysis, *162*
uncovered interest rate
  parity, *146*

QUESTIONS

1. Give a full definition of *arbitrage*.

2. Discuss the implications of interest rate parity for exchange rate determination.

3. Explain the conditions under which the forward exchange rate will be an unbiased predictor of the future spot exchange rate.

4. Explain purchasing power parity, both the absolute and relative versions. What causes deviations from purchasing power parity?

5. Discuss the implications of the deviations from purchasing power parity for countries' competitive positions in the world market.

6. Explain and derive the international Fisher effect.

7. Researchers found that it is very difficult to forecast future exchange rates more accurately than the forward exchange rate or the current spot exchange rate. How would you interpret this finding?

8. Explain the random walk model for exchange rate forecasting. Can it be consistent with technical analysis?

9. Derive and explain the monetary approach to exchange rate determination.

10. Explain the following three concepts of purchasing power parity (PPP):

    a. The law of one price.

    b. Absolute PPP.

    c. Relative PPP.

11. Evaluate the usefulness of relative PPP in predicting movements in foreign exchange rates on:

    a. Short-term basis (for example, three months).

    b. Long-term basis (for example, six years).

PROBLEMS

1. Suppose that the treasurer of IBM has an extra cash reserve of $100,000,000 to invest for six months. The six-month interest rate is 8 percent per annum in the United States and 7 percent per annum in Germany. Currently, the spot exchange rate is €1.01 per dollar and the six-month forward exchange rate is €0.99 per dollar. The treasurer of IBM does not wish to bear any exchange risk. Where should he or she invest to maximize the return?

2. While you were visiting London, you purchased a Jaguar for £35,000, payable in three months. You have enough cash at your bank in New York City, which pays 0.35 percent interest per month, compounding monthly, to pay for the car. Currently, the spot exchange rate is $1.45/£ and the three-month forward exchange rate is $1.40/£. In London, the money market interest rate is 2.0 percent for a three-month investment. There are two alternative ways of paying for your Jaguar.

    a. Keep the funds at your bank in the United States and buy a £35,000 forward.

    b. Buy a certain pound amount spot today and invest the amount in the U.K. for three months so that the maturity value becomes equal to £35,000. Evaluate each payment method. Which method would you prefer? Why?

3. Consider the £/€ spot and forward exchange rates in the table below. The risk-free one-year interest rates on the euro and the pound are respectively equal to 0.25% and to 1.25%. Which investment strategy would be chosen by an investor with funds denominated i) in pounds, ii) in euros? Suppose, in both cases, that the investor wishes to realize the revenue from the investment in the currency initially invested, with no exchange risk.

	Bid	Ask
Spot rate	0.8362	0.8364
One year forward rate	0.8388	0.8391

4. Consider again the spot and forward €/£ exchange rates in the table in Problem 3, and the risk-free rates of interest of 0.25% and 1.25%, respectively paid on one year-investments denominated in euros and in pounds. Could an arbitrageur facing the borrowing rates of 1.1% and 2% for loans denominated in euros and in pounds implement any profitable risk-free strategies, in this scenario?

a. Show how to realize a certain profit via covered interest arbitrage, assuming that you want to realize profit in terms of U.S. dollars. Also determine the size of your arbitrage profit.

b. Assume that you want to realize profit in terms of euros. Show the covered arbitrage process and determine the arbitrage profit in euros.

5. In the October 23, 1999, issue, *The Economist* reports that the interest rate per annum is 5.93 percent in the United States and 70.0 percent in Turkey. Why do you think the interest rate is so high in Turkey? On the basis of the reported interest rates, how would you predict the change of the exchange rate between the U.S. dollar and the Turkish lira?

6. As of November 1, 1999, the exchange rate between the Brazilian real and U.S. dollar was R$1.95/$. The consensus forecast for the U.S. and Brazil inflation rates for the next one-year period was 2.6 percent and 20.0 percent, respectively. What would you have forecast the exchange rate to be at around November 1, 2000?

7. Omni Advisors, an international pension fund manager, uses the concepts of purchasing power parity (PPP) and the International Fisher Effect (IFE) to forecast spot exchange rates. Omni gathers the financial information as follows:

Base price level	100
Current U.S. price level	105
Current South African price level	111
Base rand spot exchange rate	$0.175
Current rand spot exchange rate	$0.158
Expected annual U.S. inflation	7%
Expected annual South African inflation	5%
Expected U.S. one-year interest rate	10%
Expected South African one-year interest rate	8%

Calculate the following exchange rates (ZAR and USD refer to the South African rand and U.S. dollar, respectively):

a. The current ZAR spot rate in USD that would have been forecast by PPP.

b. Using the IFE, the expected ZAR spot rate in USD one year from now.

c. Using PPP, the expected ZAR spot rate in USD four years from now.

8. Suppose that the current spot exchange rate is €1.50/£ and the one-year forward exchange rate is €1.60/£. The one-year interest rate is 5.4 percent in euros and 5.2 percent in pounds. You can borrow at most €1,000,000 or the equivalent pound amount, that is, £666,667, at the current spot exchange rate.

a. Show how you can realize a guaranteed profit from covered interest arbitrage. Assume that you are a euro-based investor. Also determine the size of the arbitrage profit.

b. Discuss how the interest rate parity may be restored as a result of the above transactions.

c. Suppose you are a pound-based investor. Show the covered arbitrage process and determine the pound profit amount.

9. Due to the integrated nature of their capital markets, investors in both the United States and the U.K. require the same real interest rate, 2.5 percent, on their lending. There is a consensus in capital markets that the annual inflation rate is likely to be 3.5 percent in the United States and 1.5 percent in the U.K. for the next three years. The spot exchange rate is currently $1.50/£.

a. Compute the nominal interest rate per annum in both the United States and the U.K., assuming that the Fisher effect holds.

b. What is your expected future spot dollar-pound exchange rate in three years from now?

c. Can you infer the forward dollar-pound exchange rate for one-year maturity?

CFA® PROBLEMS

10. After studying Iris Hamson's credit analysis, George Davies is considering whether he can increase the holding period return on Yucatán Resort's excess cash holdings (which are held in pesos) by investing those cash holdings in the Mexican bond market. Although Davies would be investing in a peso-denominated bond, the investment goal is to achieve the highest holding period return, measured in U.S. dollars, on the investment.

Davies finds the higher yield on the Mexican one-year bond, which is considered to be free of credit risk, to be attractive but he is concerned that depreciation of the peso will reduce the holding period return, measured in U.S. dollars. Hamson has prepared selected economic and financial data to help Davies make the decision.

Selected Economic and Financial Data for U.S. and Mexico

Expected U.S. Inflation Rate	2.0% per year
Expected Mexican Inflation Rate	6.0% per year
U.S. One-year Treasury Bond Yield	2.5%
Mexican One-year Bond Yield	6.5%

Nominal Exchange Rates

Spot	9.5000 Pesos = U.S. $1.00
One-year Forward	9.8707 Pesos = U.S. $1.00

Hamson recommends buying the Mexican one-year bond and hedging the foreign currency exposure using the one-year forward exchange rate. She concludes: "This transaction will result in a U.S. dollar holding period return that is equal to the holding period return of the U.S. one-year bond."

a. Calculate the U.S. dollar holding period return that would result from the transaction recommended by Hamson. Show your calculations. State whether Hamson's conclusion about the U.S. dollar holding period return resulting from the transaction is correct or incorrect.

After conducting his own analysis of the U.S. and Mexican economies, Davies expects that both the U.S. inflation rate and the real exchange rate will remain constant over the coming year. Because of favorable political developments in Mexico, however, he expects that the Mexican inflation rate (in annual terms) will fall from 6.0 percent to 3.0 percent before the end of the year. As a result, Davies decides to invest Yucatan Resort's cash holdings in the Mexican one-year bond but not to hedge the currency exposure.

b. Calculate the expected exchange rate (pesos per dollar) one year from now. Show your calculations. Note: Your calculations should assume that Davies is correct in his expectations about the real exchange rate and the Mexican and U.S. inflation rates.

c. Calculate the expected U.S. dollar holding period return on the Mexican one-year bond. Show your calculations. Note: Your calculations should assume that Davies is correct in his expectations about the real exchange rate and the Mexican and U.S. inflation rates.

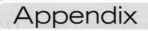
6A Purchasing Power Parity and Exchange Rate Determination

Although PPP itself can be viewed as a theory of exchange rate determination, it also serves as a foundation for a more complete theory, namely, the **monetary approach**. The monetary approach, associated with the Chicago School of Economics, is based on two basic tenets: purchasing power parity and the quantity theory of money.

From the **quantity theory of money**, we obtain the following identity that must hold in each country:

$$P_\$ = M_\$ \, V_\$/y_\$ \tag{6A.1A}$$

$$P_£ = M_£ \, V_£/y_£ \tag{6A.1B}$$

where M denotes the money supply, V the velocity of money, measuring the speed at which money is being circulated in the economy, y the national aggregate output, and P the general price level; the subscripts denote countries. When the above equations are substituted for the price levels in the PPP Equation 6.12, we obtain the following expression for the exchange rate:

$$S = (M_\$/M_£)(V_\$/V_£)(y_£/y_\$) \tag{6A.2}$$

According to the monetary approach, what matters in the exchange rate determination are

1. The relative money supplies.
2. The relative velocities of money.
3. The relative national outputs.

All else equal, an increase in the U.S. money supply will result in a proportionate depreciation of the dollar against the pound. So will an increase in the velocity of the dollar, which has the same effect as an increased supply of dollars. But an increase in U.S. output will result in a proportionate appreciation of the dollar.

The monetary approach, which is based on PPP, can be viewed as a long-run theory, not a short-run theory, of exchange rate determination. This is so because the monetary approach does not allow for price rigidities. It assumes that prices adjust fully and completely, which is unrealistic in the short run. Prices of many commodities and services are often fixed over a certain period of time. A good example of short-term price rigidity is the wage rate set by a labor contract. Despite this apparent shortcoming, the monetary approach remains an influential theory and serves as a benchmark in modern exchange rate economics.

7 Futures and Options on Foreign Exchange

ON JANUARY 24, 2008 it was disclosed by Société Générale, France's second largest bank, that a 31-year-old rogue trader had taken unauthorized positions in European stock index futures contracts totaling $73 billion that resulted in trading losses of $7.2 billion when the stock market turned downward against the trader's positions. The trader was able to hide his positions for months by concealing his bets with a series of offsetting transactions with fictional counterparties. The loss forced Société Générale to raise $8 billion in emergency capital. Similarly, in 1995, another rogue trader brought down Barings PLC by losing $1.3 billion from an unhedged $27 billion position in various exchanged-traded futures and options contracts, primarily the Nikkei 225 stock index futures contract traded on the Singapore International Monetary Exchange. The losses occurred when the market moved unfavorably against the trader's speculative positions. Barings was taken over by ING Group, the Dutch banking and insurance conglomerate. The trader served three years in prison in Singapore for fraudulent trading.

As these stories imply, futures and options contracts can be very risky investments, indeed, when used for speculative purposes. Nevertheless, they are also important risk-management tools. In this chapter, we introduce exchange-traded currency futures contracts, options contracts, and options on currency futures that are useful for both speculating on foreign exchange price movements and hedging exchange rate uncertainty. These contracts make up part of the foreign exchange market that was introduced in Chapter 5, where we discussed spot and forward exchange rates.

The discussion begins by comparing forward and futures contracts, noting similarities and differences between the two. We discuss the markets where futures are traded, the currencies on which contracts are written, and contract specifications for the various currency contracts.

Next, options contracts on foreign exchange are introduced, comparing and contrasting the options and the futures markets. The exchanges where options are traded are identified and contract terms are specified. The over-the-counter options market is also discussed. Basic option-pricing boundary relationships are illustrated using actual market prices. Additionally, illustrations of how a speculator might use currency options are also provided. The chapter closes with the development of a currency option-pricing model. This chapter and the knowledge gained about forward contracts in Chapters 5 and 6 set the stage for Chapters 8, 9, and 10, which explain how these vehicles can be used for hedging foreign exchange risk.

Futures Contracts: Some Preliminaries

In Chapter 5, a *forward contract* was defined as a vehicle for buying or selling a stated amount of foreign exchange at a stated price per unit at a specified time in the future. Both forward and futures contracts are classified as **derivative** or **contingent claim securities** because their values are derived from or contingent upon the value of the underlying security. But while a **futures** contract is similar to a forward contract, there are many distinctions between the two. A forward contract is tailor-made for a client by his international bank. In contrast, a futures contract has **standardized features** and is **exchange-traded**, that is, traded on organized exchanges rather than over the counter. A client desiring a position in futures contracts contacts his broker, who transmits the order to the exchange floor where it is transferred to the trading pit. In the trading pit, the price for the order is negotiated by open outcry between floor brokers or traders.

The main standardized features are the **contract size** specifying the amount of the underlying foreign currency for future purchase or sale and the **maturity date** of the contract. A futures contract is written for a specific amount of foreign currency rather than for a tailor-made sum. Hence, a position in multiple contracts may be necessary to establish a sizable hedge or speculative position. Futures contracts have specific **delivery months** during the year in which contracts mature on a specified day of the month.

An **initial performance bond** (formerly called *margin*) must be deposited into a collateral account to establish a futures position. The initial performance bond is generally equal to about 2 percent of the contract value. Either cash or Treasury bills may be used to meet the performance bond requirement. The account balance will fluctuate through daily settlement, as illustrated by the following discussion. The performance bond put up by the contract holder can be viewed as "good-faith" money that he will fulfill his side of the financial obligation.

The major difference between a forward contract and a futures contract is the way the underlying asset is priced for future purchase or sale. A forward contract states a price for the future transaction. By contrast, a futures contract is **settled-up**, or **marked-to-market**, daily at the settlement price. The **settlement price** is a price representative of futures transaction prices at the close of daily trading on the exchange. It is determined by a settlement committee for the commodity, and it may be somewhat arbitrary if trading volume for the contract has been light for the day. A buyer of a futures contract (one who holds a **long** position) in which the settlement price is higher (lower) than the previous day's settlement price has a positive (negative) settlement for the day. Since a long position entitles the owner to purchase the underlying asset, a higher (lower) settlement price means the futures price of the underlying asset has increased (decreased). Consequently, a long position in the contract is worth more (less). The change in settlement prices from one day to the next determines the settlement amount. That is, the change in settlement prices per unit of the underlying asset, multiplied by the size of the contract, equals the size of the daily settlement to be added to (or subtracted from) the long's performance bond account. Analogously, the seller of the futures contract (**short** position) will have his performance bond account increased (or decreased) by the amount the long's performance bond account is decreased (or increased). Thus, futures trading between the long and the short is a **zero-sum game**; that is, the sum of the long and short's daily settlement is zero. If the investor's performance bond account falls below a **maintenance performance bond** level (roughly equal to 90 percent of the initial performance bond), additional funds must be deposited into the account to bring it back to the initial performance bond level in order to keep the position open. An investor who suffers a liquidity crunch and cannot deposit additional funds will have his position liquidated by his broker.

EXHIBIT 7.1

Differences between
Futures and Forward
Contracts

Trading Location
Futures: Traded competitively on organized exchanges.
Forward: Traded by bank dealers via a network of telephones and computerized dealing systems.

Contractual Size
Futures: Standardized amount of the underlying asset.
Forward: Tailor-made to the needs of the participant.

Settlement
Futures: Daily settlement, or marking-to-market, done by the futures clearinghouse through the participant's performance bond account.
Forward: Participant buys or sells the contractual amount of the underlying asset from the bank at maturity at the forward (contractual) price.

Expiration Date
Futures: Standardized delivery dates.
Forward: Tailor-made delivery date that meets the needs of the investor.

Delivery
Futures: Delivery of the underlying asset is seldom made. Usually a reversing trade is transacted to exit the market.
Forward: Delivery of the underlying asset is commonly made.

Trading Costs
Futures: Bid-ask spread plus broker's commission.
Forward: Bid-ask spread plus indirect bank charges via compensating balance requirements.

The marking-to-market feature of futures markets means that market participants realize their profits or suffer their losses on a day-to-day basis rather than all at once at maturity as with a forward contract. At the end of daily trading, a futures contract is analogous to a new forward contract on the underlying asset at the new settlement price with a one-day-shorter maturity. Because of the daily marking-to-market, the futures price will converge through time to the spot price on the last day of trading in the contract. That is, the final settlement price at which any transaction in the underlying asset will transpire is the spot price on the last day of trading. The effective price is, nevertheless, the original futures contract price, once the profit or loss in the performance bond account is included. Exhibit 7.1 summarizes the differences between forward and futures contracts.

Two types of market participants are necessary for a derivatives market to operate most efficiently: **speculators** and **hedgers**. A speculator attempts to profit from a change in the futures price. To do this, the speculator will take a long or short position in a futures contract depending upon his expectations of future price movement. A hedger, on the other hand, wants to avoid price variation by locking in a purchase price of the underlying asset through a long position in the futures contract or a sales price through a short position. In effect, the hedger passes off the risk of price variation to the speculator, who is better able, or at least more willing, to bear this risk.

Both forward and futures markets for foreign exchange are very liquid. A **reversing trade** can be made in either market that will close out, or neutralize, a position.[1] In forward markets, approximately 90 percent of all contracts result in the short making delivery of the underlying asset to the long. This is natural given the tailor-made terms of forward contracts. By contrast, only about 1 percent of currency futures contracts

---

[1]In the forward market, the investor holds offsetting positions after a reversing trade; in the futures market the investor actually exits the marketplace.

result in delivery. While futures contracts are useful for speculation and hedging, their standardized delivery dates are unlikely to correspond to the actual future dates when foreign exchange transactions will transpire. Thus, they are generally closed out in a reversing trade. The **commission** that buyers and sellers pay to transact in the futures market is a single amount paid up front that covers the *round-trip* transactions of initiating and closing out the position. These days, through a discount broker, the commission charge can be as little as $15 per currency futures contract.

In futures markets, a **clearinghouse** serves as the third party to all transactions. That is, the buyer of a futures contract effectively buys from the clearinghouse and the seller sells to the clearinghouse. This feature of futures markets facilitates active secondary market trading because the buyer and the seller do not have to evaluate one another's creditworthiness. The clearinghouse is made up of *clearing members*. Individual brokers who are not clearing members must deal through a clearing member to clear a customer's trade. In the event of default of one side of a futures trade, the clearing member stands in for the defaulting party, and then seeks restitution from that party. The clearinghouse's liability is limited because a contractholder's position is marked-to-market daily. Given the organizational structure, it is only logical that the clearinghouse maintains the futures performance bond accounts for the clearing members.

Frequently, a futures exchange may have a **daily price limit** on the futures price, that is, a limit as to how much the settlement price can increase or decrease from the previous day's settlement price. Forward markets do not have this. Obviously, when the price limit is hit, trading will halt as a new market-clearing equilibrium price cannot be obtained. Exchange rules exist for expanding the daily price limit in an orderly fashion until a market-clearing price can be established.

Currency Futures Markets

On May 16, 1972, trading in currency futures contracts began at the Chicago Mercantile Exchange (CME). Trading activity in currency futures has expanded rapidly at the CME. In 1978, only 2 million contracts were traded; this figure stood at over 200 million contracts in 2012. In 2007, the CME Group was formed through a merger between the CME and the Chicago Board of Trade (CBOT). The following year, the CME Group acquired the New York Mercantile Exchange (NYMEX). Most CME currency futures trade in a March, June, September, and December expiration cycle, with the delivery date being the third Wednesday of the expiration month. The last day of trading for most contracts is the second business day prior to the delivery date. Regular trading in CME currency futures contracts takes place each business day from 7:20 A.M. to 2:00 P.M. Chicago time. Additional CME currency futures trading takes place Sunday through Thursday on the GLOBEX trading system from 5:00 P.M. to 4:00 P.M. Chicago time the next day. GLOBEX is a worldwide automated order-entry and matching system for futures and options that facilitates nearly 24-hour trading after the close of regular exchange trading. Exhibit 7.2 summarizes the basic CME Group currency contract specifications. The International Finance in Practice box "FX Market Volumes Surge" details the popularity of CME Group currency products and the GLOBEX trading platform.

In addition to the CME, currency futures trading takes place on the Intercontinental Exchange (ICE) Futures U.S. (formerly the New York Board of Trade), the Mexican Derivatives Exchange, the BM&F Exchange in Brazil, the Budapest Commodity Exchange, and the Derivatives Market Division of the Korea Exchange.

FX Market Volumes Surge

The FX market is growing at record levels, according to figures released by the CME Group, the largest regulated foreign exchange market in the world.

Last month, the CME Group reported average daily notional volume at a record level of $121 billion, up 82 percent compared to a year earlier.

With a number of indicators at play, like the news of Greece's credit concerns and the continued appetite for high-yielding currencies like the Australian dollar and the Canadian dollar, the CME saw record volumes and notional values in the euro and Australian and Canadian dollars. Euro FX futures and options saw total average daily volume of 362,000 contracts with total notional ADV of slightly over $62 billion.

Australian dollar futures and options climbed to nearly 119,000 contracts in average daily volume with almost $11 billion in total notional ADV, and Canadian dollar futures and options surpassed 88,000 contracts in ADV and $8 billion in total notional ADV.

With foreign currency futures going from strength to strength, the CME Group recently published a white paper outlining the benefits of FX futures.

"These contracts provide an ideal tool to manage currency or FX risks in an uncertain world," it said, "Product innovation, liquidity, and financial surety are the three pillars upon which the CME Group has built its world-class derivatives market. The CME Group provides products based on a wide range of frequently transacted currencies, liquidity offered on the state-of-the-art CME Globex electronic trading platform, and financial sureties afforded by its centralized clearing system."

Source: *Global Investor*, March 2010.

EXHIBIT 7.2

CME Group Currency Futures Specifications

Currency	Contract Size
	CME
Price Quoted in U.S. Dollars	
Australian dollar	AUD100,000
Brazilian real	BRL100,000
British pound	GBP62,500
Canadian dollar	CAD100,000
Chinese renminbi	CNY1,000,000
Czech koruna	CZK4,000,000
Euro FX	EUR125,000
Hungarian forint	HUF30,000,000
Israeli shekel	ILS1,000,000
Japanese yen	JPY12,500,000
Korean won	KRW125,000,000
Mexican peso	MXN500,000
New Zealand dollar	NZD100,00
Norwegian krone	NOK2,000,000
Polish zloty	PLN500,000
Russian ruble	RUB2,500,000
South African rand	ZAR500,000
Swedish krona	SEK2,000,000
Swiss franc	CHF125,000
Cross-Rate Futures (Underlying Currency/Price Currency)	
Euro FX/British pound	EUR125,000
Euro FX/Japanese yen	EUR125,000
Euro FX/Swiss franc	EUR125,000

Source: CME Group, www.cmegroup.com, website.

PART THREE

Foreign Exchange Exposure and Management

PART THREE is composed of three chapters covering the topics of transaction, economic, and translation exposure management, respectively.

CHAPTER 8 covers the management of transaction exposure that arises from contractual obligations denominated in a foreign currency. Several methods for hedging this exposure are compared and contrasted. The chapter also includes a discussion of why a MNC should hedge, a debatable subject in the minds of both academics and practitioners.

CHAPTER 9 covers economic exposure, that is, the extent to which the value of the firm will be affected by unexpected changes in exchange rates. The chapter provides a way to measure economic exposure, discusses its determinants, and presents methods for managing and hedging economic exposure.

CHAPTER 10 covers translation exposure or, as it is sometimes called, accounting exposure. Translation exposure refers to the effect that changes in exchange rates will have on the consolidated financial reports of a MNC. The chapter discusses, compares, and contrasts the various methods for translating financial statements denominated in foreign currencies, and includes a discussion of managing translation exposure using funds adjustment and the pros and cons of using balance sheet and derivatives hedges.

Forward Market Hedge

Perhaps the most direct and popular way of hedging transaction exposure is by currency forward contracts. Generally speaking, the firm may sell (buy) its foreign currency receivables (payables) forward to eliminate its exchange risk exposure. In the above example, in order to hedge foreign exchange exposure, Boeing may simply sell forward its pounds receivable, £10 million for delivery in one year, in exchange for a given amount of U.S. dollars. On the maturity date of the contract, Boeing will have to deliver £10 million to the bank, which is the counterparty of the contract, and, in return, take delivery of $14.6 million ($1.46 × 10 million), regardless of the spot exchange rate that may prevail on the maturity date. Boeing will, of course, use the £10 million that it is going to receive from British Airways to fulfill the forward contract. Since Boeing's pound receivable is exactly offset by the pound payable (created by the forward contract), the company's net pound exposure becomes zero.

Since Boeing is assured of receiving a given dollar amount, $14.6 million, from the counter-party of the forward contract, the dollar proceeds from this British sale will not be affected at all by future changes in the exchange rate. This point is illustrated in Exhibit 8.1. Once Boeing enters into the forward contract, exchange rate uncertainty becomes irrelevant for Boeing. Exhibit 8.1 also illustrates how the dollar proceeds from the British sale will be affected by the future spot exchange rate when exchange exposure is not hedged. The exhibit shows that the dollar proceeds under the forward hedge will be higher than those under the unhedged position if the future spot exchange rate turns out to be less than the forward rate, that is, $F = \$1.46/\pounds$, and the opposite will hold if the future spot rate becomes higher than the forward rate. In the latter case, Boeing forgoes an opportunity to benefit from a strong pound.

Suppose that on the maturity date of the forward contract, the spot rate turns out to be $\$1.40/\pounds$, which is less than the forward rate, $\$1.46/\pounds$. In this case, Boeing would have received $14.0 million, rather than $14.6 million, had it not entered into the forward contract. Thus, one can say that Boeing gained $0.6 million from forward hedging. Needless to say, Boeing will not always gain in this manner. If the spot rate is, say, $\$1.50/\pounds$ on the maturity date, then Boeing could have received $15.0 million by remaining unhedged. Thus, one can say *ex post* that forward hedging cost Boeing $0.40 million.

The gains and losses from forward hedging can be illustrated as in Exhibits 8.2 and 8.3. The gain/loss is computed as follows:

$$\text{Gain} = (F - S_T) \times \pounds 10 \text{ million} \tag{8.1}$$

Obviously, the gain will be positive as long as the forward exchange rate (F) is greater than the spot rate on the maturity date (S_T), that is, $F > S_T$, and the gain will be negative (that is, a loss will result) if the opposite holds. As Exhibit 8.3 shows, the firm theoretically can gain as much as $14.6 million when the pound becomes worthless, which, of course, is unlikely, whereas there is no limit to possible losses.

It is important, however, to note that the above analysis is *ex post* in nature, and that no one can know for sure what the future spot rate will be beforehand. The firm must decide whether to hedge or not *ex ante*. To help the firm decide, it is useful to consider the following three alternative scenarios:

1. $\bar{S}_T \approx F$
2. $\bar{S}_T < F$
3. $\bar{S}_T > F$

where $\bar{S}_T$ denotes the firm's expected spot exchange rate for the maturity date.

Under the first scenario, where the firm's expected future spot exchange rate, $\bar{S}_T$, is about the same as the forward rate, F, the "expected" gains or losses are approximately zero.

EXHIBIT 8.1

Dollar Proceeds from the British Sale: Forward Hedge versus Unhedged Position

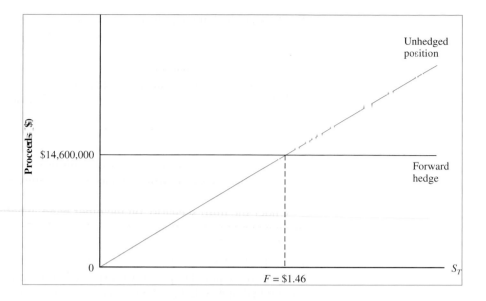

EXHIBIT 8.2

Gains/Losses from Forward Hedge

Receipts from the British Sale

Spot Exchange Rate on the Maturity Date (S_T)	Unhedged Position	Forward Hedge	Gains/Losses from Hedge[b]
$1.30	$13,000,000	$14,600,000	$1,600,000
$1.40	$14,000,000	$14,600,000	$ 600,000
$1.46[a]	$14,600,000	$14,600,000	0
$1.50	$15,000,000	$14,600,000	−$ 400,000
$1.60	$16,000,000	$14,600,000	−$1,400,000

[a]The forward exchange rate (F) is $1.46/£ in this example.

[b]The gains/losses are computed as the proceeds under the forward hedge minus the proceeds from the unhedged position at the various spot exchange rates on the maturity date.

EXHIBIT 8.3

Illustration of Gains and Losses from Forward Hedging

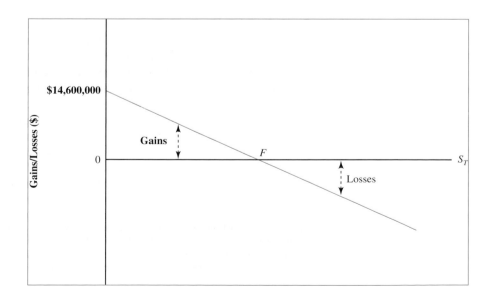

www.sec.gov/info/edgar.shtml
Company files with SEC show
how companies deal with
exchange risk exposure.

exposure management at the corporate level is redundant when stockholders can manage the exposure themselves. Others would argue that what matters in the firm valuation is only systematic risk; corporate risk management may only reduce the total risk. These arguments suggest that corporate exposure management would not necessarily add to the value of the firm.

While the above arguments against corporate risk management may be valid in a "perfect" capital market, one can make a case for it based on various market imperfections:

1. Information asymmetry: Management knows about the firm's exposure position much better than stockholders. Thus, the management of the firm, not its stockholders, should manage exchange exposure.

2. Differential transaction costs: The firm is in a position to acquire low-cost hedges; transaction costs for individual stockholders can be substantial. Also, the firm has hedging tools like the reinvoice center that are not available to stockholders.

3. Default costs: If default costs are significant, corporate hedging would be justifiable because it will reduce the probability of default. Perception of a reduced default risk, in turn, can lead to a better credit rating and lower financing costs.

4. Progressive corporate taxes: Under progressive corporate tax rates, stable before-tax earnings lead to lower corporate taxes than volatile earnings with the same average value. This happens because under progressive tax rates, the firm pays more taxes in high-earning periods than it saves in low-earning periods.

The last point merits elaboration. Suppose the country's corporate income tax system is such that a tax rate of 20 percent applies to the first $10 million of corporate earnings and a 40 percent rate applies to any earnings exceeding $10 million. Firms thus face a simple progressive tax structure. Now consider an exporting firm that expects to earn $15 million if the dollar depreciates, but only $5 million if the dollar appreciates. Let's assume that the dollar may appreciate or depreciate with equal chances. In this case, the firm's expected tax will be $2.5 million:

$$
\begin{aligned}
\text{Expected tax} &= \tfrac{1}{2}\,[(.20)(\$5,000,000)] \\
&\quad + \tfrac{1}{2}\,[(.20)(\$10,000,000) + (.40)(\$5,000,000)] \\
&= \$2,500,000
\end{aligned}
$$

Now consider another firm, B, that is identical to firm A in every respect except that, unlike firm A, firm B aggressively and successfully hedges its risk exposure and, as a result, it can expect to realize certain earnings of $10,000,000, the same as firm A's expected earnings. Firm B, however, expects to pay only $2 million for taxes. Obviously, hedging results in a $500,000 tax saving. Exhibit 8.10 illustrates this situation.

While not every firm is hedging exchange exposure, many firms are engaged in hedging activities, suggesting that corporate risk management is relevant to maximizing the firm's value. To the extent that for various reasons, stockholders themselves cannot properly manage exchange risk, the firm's managers can do it for them, contributing to the firm's value. Some corporate hedging activities, however, might be motivated by managerial objectives; managers may want to stabilize cash flows so that the risk to their human capital can be reduced.

A study by Allayannis and Weston (2001) provides direct evidence on the important issue of whether hedging actually adds to the value of the firm. Specifically, they examine whether firms with currency exposure that use foreign currency derivative contracts, such as currency forward and options, increase their valuation. The authors find that U.S. firms that face currency risk and use currency derivatives for hedging have, on average, about 5 percent higher value than firms that do not use currency

CHAP

CFA
PROBLEMS

CFA
PROBLEMS

5. A Danish company is negoi
delivered to a customer firm l
tion with two payments of I
months. However, the custor
that on the date when the seco
to fulfil its obligation by payi
   Under the modified soluti
a package including the pay
Danish company. Can you ic
interest on the Danish Crown
The current spot exchange ri
deviation of its change is equi
how large a fee should the Dai
acceptance of the new terms c

6. Princess Cruise Company (PC
try for 500 million yen payabl
one-year forward rate is 110/9
8 percent in the United States.
the strike price of $.0081 per y

   a. Compute the future dollar
   market and forward hedges.

   b. Assuming that the forward e
   rate, compute the expected
   the option hedge is used.

   c. At what future spot rate do
   option and forward hedge?

7. Consider a U.S.-based company
pany expects to receive payment
payment will be in Swiss francs,
in the value of the Swiss franc ov
2 percent, and the Swiss risk-fre
expected to remain fixed over the

   a. Indicate whether the U.S. con
   to hedge currency risk.

   b. Calculate the no-arbitrage pri
   forward contract that expires i

   c. It is now 30 days since the U.S
   spot rate is $0.55. Interest rate
   the U.S. company's forward pe

8. Suppose that you are a U.S.-base
You expect the value of the pound
30 days. You will be making paym
and want to hedge your currency
and the U.K. risk-free rate is 4.5
unchanged over the next month. T

   a. Indicate whether you should us
   currency risk.

   b. Calculate the no-arbitrage price
   tract that expires in 30 days.

   c. Move forward 10 days. The sp
   Calculate the value of your forw

   d. Using the text software sprea
   Exhibit 8.8.

EXHIBIT 8.10

Tax Savings from
Hedging Exchange Risk
Exposure

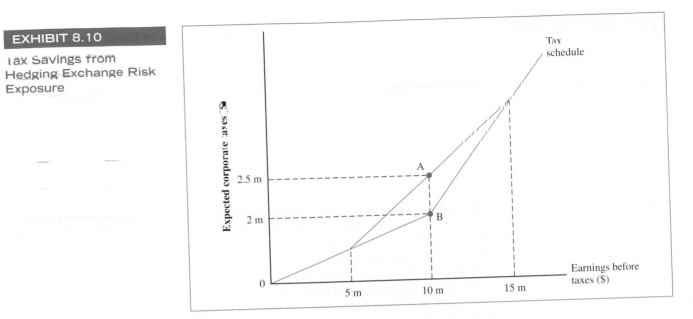

derivatives. For firms that have no direct foreign involvement but may be exposed to
exchange rate movements via export/import competition, they find a small hedging
valuation premium. In addition, they find that firms that stop hedging experience a
decrease in firm valuation compared with those firms that continue to hedge. Their
study thus clearly suggests that corporate hedging contributes to firm value.

What Risk Management Products Do Firms Use?

In an extensive survey, Jesswein, Kwok, and Folks (1995) documented the extent of
knowledge and use of foreign exchange risk management products by U.S. corporations. On the basis of a survey of *Fortune* 500 firms, they found that the traditional
forward contract is the most popular product. As Exhibit 8.11 shows, about 93 percent
of respondents of the survey used forward contracts. This old, traditional instrument

EXHIBIT 8.11

A Survey of Knowledge
and Use of Foreign
Exchange Risk
Management Products
by U.S. Firms[a]

Type of Product	Heard of (Awareness)	Used (Adoption)
Forward contracts	100.0%	93.1%
Foreign currency swaps	98.8	52.6
Foreign currency futures	98.8	20.1
Exchange-traded currency options	96.4	17.3
Exchange-traded futures options	95.8	8.9
Over-the-counter currency options	93.5	48.8
Cylinder options	91.2	28.7
Synthetic forwards	88.0	22.0
Synthetic options	88.0	18.6
Participating forwards, etc.	83.6	15.8
Forward exchange agreements, etc.	81.7	14.8
Foreign currency warrants	77.7	4.2
Break forwards, etc.	65.3	4.9
Compound options	55.8	3.8
Lookback options, etc.	52.1	5.1
Average across products	84.4%	23.9%

[a]The products are ranked by the percentages of respondents who have heard of products. There are 173
respondents in total.

Source: Kurt Jesswein, Chuck Kwok, and William Folks, Jr., "Corporate Use of Innovative Foreign Exchange Risk
Management Products," *Columbia Journal of World Business* (Fall 1995).

PROBLEMS

The spreadsheet TRNSEXP.xls may b...

1. Cray Research sold a supercomp...
   credit and invoiced €10 million...
   forward exchange rate is $1.10...
   Research predicts that the spot ra...

   a. What is the expected gain/loss...

   b. If you were the financial man...
   hedging this euro receivable? V...

   c. Suppose the foreign exchange...
   the same as the forward excha...
   hedging in this case? Why or w...

   d. Suppose now that the future spo...
   you recommend hedging? Why...

2. IBM purchased computer chips fr...
   was billed ¥250 million payable i...
   rate is ¥105/$ and the three-month f...
   market interest rate is 8 percent per...
   annum in Japan. The management...
   to deal with this yen account payab...

   a. Explain the process of a money...
   meeting the yen obligation.

   b. Conduct a cash flow analysis of...

3. You plan to visit Geneva, Switzerla...
   business conference. You expect to...
   meals, and transportation during yo...
   is $0.60/SF and the three-month for...
   month call option on SF with an ex...
   $0.05 per SF. Assume that your exp...
   as the forward rate. The three-mont...
   United States and 4 percent per annu...

   a. Calculate your expected dollar co...
   by a call option on SF.

   b. Calculate the future dollar cost of...
   hedge using a forward contract.

   c. At what future spot exchange rate...
   and option market hedges?

   d. Illustrate the future dollar cost of...
   spot exchange rate under both the c...

4. A financial intermediaty is a party to th...
   maturity in four months from today:

   1. A contract under which the intermed...
   for Singapore dollars.

   2. A contract under which the intermedi...
   for Chinese renminbis.

   The forwards exchange rates on the g...
   CNY4.829/SGD1. The spot exchange ra...
   free interest rates on the Australian Dolla...
   equal to 2.5% and to 6%.

   The intermediaty can enter new forwar...
   exchange rates implied by IRP. How coul...
   contract to realize a cash-flow at maturit...
   very small sums in the other two currencie...

REFERENCE
& SUGGESTE
READINGS

EXHIBIT 10.1A — Comparison of Effects of Translation Methods on Financial Statement Preparation after Appreciation from SF 3.00 to SF 2.00 = $1.00 (in 000 Currency Units)

	Local Currency	Current/ Noncurrent	Monetary/ Nonmonetary	Temporal	Current Rate
Balance Sheet					
Cash	SF 2,100	$1,050	$1,050	$1,050	$1,050
Inventory					
(Current value = SF 1,800)	1,500	750	500	900	750
Net fixed assets	3,000	1,000	1,000	1,000	1,500
Total assets	SF 6,600	$2,800	$2,550	$2,950	$3,300
Current liabilities	SF 1,200	$ 600	$ 600	$ 600	$ 600
Long-term debt	1,800	600	900	900	900
Common stock	2,700	900	900	900	900
Retained earnings	900	700	150	550	360
CTA	—	—	—	—	540
Total liabilities and equity	SF 6,600	$2,800	$2,550	$2,950	$3,300
Income Statement					
Sales revenue	SF10,000	$4,000	$4,000	$4,000	$4,000
COGS	7,500	3,000	2,500	3,000	3,000
Depreciation	1,000	333	333	333	400
Net operating income	1,500	667	1,167	667	600
Income tax (40%)	600	267	467	267	240
Profit after tax	900	400	700	400	360
Foreign exchange gain (loss)	—	300	(550)	150	—
Net income	900	700	150	550	360
Dividends	0	0	0	0	0
Addition to retained earnings	SF 900	$ 700	$ 150	$ 550	$ 360

EXHIBIT 10.1B — Comparison of Effects of Translation Methods on Financial Statement Preparation after Depreciation from SF 3.00 to SF 4.00 = $1.00 (in 000 Currency Units)

	Local Currency	Current/ Noncurrent	Monetary/ Nonmonetary	Temporal	Current Rate
Balance Sheet					
Cash	SF 2,100	$ 525	$ 525	$ 525	$ 525
Inventory					
(Current value = SF1,800)	1,500	375	500	450	375
Net fixed assets	3,000	1,000	1,000	1,000	750
Total assets	SF 6,600	$1,900	$2,025	$1,975	$1,650
Current liabilities	SF 1,200	$ 300	$ 300	$ 300	$ 300
Long-term debt	1,800	600	450	450	450
Common stock	2,700	900	900	900	900
Retained earnings	900	100	375	325	257
CTA	—	—	—	—	(257)
Total liabilities and equity	SF 6,600	$1,900	$2,025	$1,975	$1,650
Income Statement					
Sales revenue	SF10,000	$2,857	$2,857	$2,857	$2,857
COGS	7,500	2,143	2,500	2,143	2,143
Depreciation	1,000	333	333	333	286
Net operating income	1,500	381	24	381	428
Income tax (40%)	600	152	14	152	171
Profit after tax	900	229	14	229	257
Foreign exchange gain (loss)	—	(129)	361	96	—
Net income	900	100	375	325	257
Dividends	0	0	0	0	0
Addition to retained earnings	SF 900	$ 100	$ 375	$ 325	$ 257

Accounting Standards Committee (now the International Accounting Standards Board), and the accounting standards bodies from Canada and the United Kingdom. After many meetings and hearings, FASB 52 was issued in December 1981, and all U.S. MNCs were required to adopt the statement for fiscal years beginning on or after December 15, 1982.

The stated objectives of FASB 52 are to:

a. Provide information that is generally compatible with the expected economic effects of a rate change on an enterprise's cash flows and equity; and
b. Reflect in consolidated statements the financial results and relationships of the individual consolidated entities as measured in their functional currencies in conformity with U.S. generally accepted accounting principles.[1]

Many discussions of FASB 52 claim that it is a current rate method of translation. This, however, is a misnomer, as FASB 52 requires the current rate method of translation in some circumstances and the temporal method in others. Which method of translation is prescribed by FASB 52 depends upon the functional currency used by the foreign subsidiary whose statements are to be translated. The **functional currency** is defined in FASB 52 as "the currency of the primary economic environment in which the entity operates."[2] Normally, that is the local currency of the country in which the entity conducts most of its business. However, under certain circumstances, the functional currency may be the parent firm's home country currency or some third-country currency. Exhibit 10.2 summarizes the method for determining the functional currency.

EXHIBIT 10.2	
Salient Economic Factors for Determining the Functional Currency	**Cash Flow Indicators** Foreign Currency: Foreign entity's cash flows are primarily in foreign currency and they do not directly affect the parent firm's cash flows. Parent's Currency: Foreign entity's cash flows directly affect the parent's cash flows and are readily available for remittance to the parent firm. **Sales Price Indicators** Foreign Currency: Sales prices for the foreign entity's products are generally not responsive on a short-term basis to exchange rate changes, but are determined more by local competition and government regulation. Parent's Currency: Sales prices for the foreign entity's products are responsive on a short-term basis to exchange rate changes, where sales prices are determined through worldwide competition. **Sales Market Indicators** Foreign Currency: There is an active local sales market for the foreign entity's products. Parent's Currency: The sales market is primarily located in the parent's country or sales contracts are denominated in the parent's currency. **Expense Indicators** Foreign Currency: Factor of production costs of the foreign entity are primarily local costs. Parent's Currency: Factor of production costs of the foreign entity are primarily, and on a continuing basis, costs for components obtained from the parent's country. **Financing Indicators** Foreign Currency: Financing of the foreign entity is primarily denominated in the foreign currency and the debt service obligations are normally handled by the foreign entity. Parent's Currency: Financing of the foreign entity is primarily from the parent, with debt service obligations met by the parent, or the debt service obligations incurred by the foreign entity are primarily made by the parent. *(continued)*

[1]See FASB 52, paragraph 4.
[2]See FASB 52, paragraph 5.

EXHIBIT 10.8

Transaction Exposure
Report for Centralia
Corporation and
Its Mexican and
Spanish Affiliates,
December 31, 2013

Affiliate	Amount	Account	Translation Exposure
Parent	CD200,000	Cash	Yes
Parent	Ps3,000,000	Accounts receivable	No
Spanish	SF375,000	Notes payable	Yes

The Ps3,000,000 accounts receivable the parent holds on the Mexican affiliate is also a transaction exposure, but it is not a translation exposure because of the netting of intracompany payables and receivables. The SF375,000 notes payable the Spanish affiliate owes the Swiss bank is both a transaction and a translation exposure.

It is, generally, not possible to eliminate both translation and transaction exposure. In some cases, the elimination of one exposure will also eliminate the other. But in other cases, the elimination of one exposure actually creates the other. Since transaction exposure involves real cash flows, we believe it should be considered the more important of the two. That is, the financial manager would not want to legitimately create transaction exposure at the expense of minimizing or eliminating translation exposure. As previously noted, the translation process has no direct effect on reporting currency cash flows, and will only have a realizable effect on net investment upon the sale or liquidation of the assets. Actual practitioners appear to concur. In a recent survey of exchange risk management practices of U.K., U.S., and Asia Pacific multinational firms, Marshall (2000) found that 83 percent placed a "significant" or the "most" amount of emphasis on managing transaction exposure, whereas only 37 percent placed that much emphasis on managing translation exposure.

Centralia Corporation and its affiliates can take certain measures to reduce its transaction exposure and to simultaneously reduce its translation exposure. One step the parent firm can take is to convert its Canadian dollar cash deposits into U.S. dollar deposits. Secondly, the parent firm can request payment of the Ps3,000,000 owed to it by the Mexican affiliate. Third, the Spanish affiliate has enough cash to pay off the SF375,000 loan to the Swiss bank. If these three steps are taken, all transaction exposure for the MNC will be eliminated. Moreover, translation exposure will be reduced. This can be seen from Exhibit 10.9, which presents a revision of Exhibit 10.6, the translation exposure report for Centralia Corporation and its affiliates. Exhibit 10.9 shows that there is no longer any translation exposure associated with the Canadian dollar or the Swiss franc. Additionally, the exhibit shows that the net exposure has been reduced from Ps25,000,000 to Ps22,000,000 for the peso and from €2,101,000 to €1,826,000 for the euro.

Hedging Translation Exposure

Exhibit 10.9 indicates that there is still considerable translation exposure with respect to changes in the exchange rate of the Mexican peso and the euro against the U.S. dollar. There are two methods for dealing with this remaining exposure, if one desires to attempt to control accounting changes in the historical value of net investment. These methods are a balance sheet hedge or a derivatives hedge.

Balance Sheet Hedge

Note that translation exposure is not entity specific; rather, it is currency specific. Its source is a mismatch of net assets and net liabilities denominated in the same currency. A **balance sheet hedge** eliminates the mismatch. Using the euro as an example, Exhibit 10.9 shows that there are €1,826,000 more exposed assets than liabilities. If the Spanish affiliate, or more practicably the parent firm or the Mexican affiliate, had €1,826,000 more liabilities, or less assets, denominated in euros, there would not be any translation exposure with respect to the euro. A perfect balance sheet hedge would have been created. A change in the €/$ exchange rate would no longer have any effect on the consolidated balance sheet since the change in value of the assets denominated in euros would completely offset the change in value of the liabilities denominated in euros. Nevertheless, if the parent firm or the Mexican affiliate increased its liabilities through, say, euro-denominated borrowings to affect the balance sheet hedge, it would simultaneously be creating transaction exposure in the euro, if the new liability could not be covered from euro cash flows generated by the Spanish affiliate.

Revised Translation Exposure Report for Centralia Corporation and Its Mexican and Spanish Affiliates, December 31, 2013
(in 000 Currency Units)

	Canadian Dollar	Mexican Peso	Euro	Swiss Franc
Assets				
Cash	CD0	Ps 3,000	€ 550	SF0
Accounts receivable	0	9,000	1,045	0
Inventory	0	15,000	1,650	0
Net fixed assets	0	46,000	4,400	0
Exposed assets	CD0	Ps 73,000	€7,645	SF0
Liabilities				
Accounts payable	CD0	Ps 7,000	€1,364	SF0
Notes payable	0	17,000	935	0
Long-term debt	0	27,000	3,520	0
Exposed liabilities	CD0	Ps 51,000	€5,819	SF0
Net exposure	CD0	Ps 22,000	€1,826	SF0

Derivatives Hedge

According to Exhibit 10.6, we determined that when the net exposure for the euro was €2,101,000, a depreciation from €1.1000/$1.00 to €1.1786/$1.00 would create a paper loss of stockholders' equity equal to $127,377. According to the revised translation exposure report shown as Exhibit 10.9, the same depreciation in the euro will result in an equity loss of $110,704, still a sizable amount. (The calculation of this amount is left as an exercise for the reader.) If one desires, a derivative product, such as a forward contract, can be used to attempt to hedge this potential loss. We use the word "attempt" because as the following example demonstrates, using a **derivatives hedge** to control translation exposure really involves speculation about foreign exchange rate changes.

EXAMPLE|10.2: Hedging Translation Exposure with a Forward Contract

To see how a forward contract can be used to hedge the $110,704 potential translation loss in equity, assume that the forward rate coinciding with the date of the consolidation is €1.1393/$1.00. If the expected spot rate on the consolidation date is forecast to be €1.1786/$1.00, a forward sale of €3,782,468 will "hedge" the risk:

$$\frac{\text{Potential translation loss}}{F(\text{reporting/functional}) - \text{Expected}[S(\text{reporting/functional})]}$$

= forward contract position in functional currency,

$$\frac{\$110,704}{1/(€\,1.1393/\$1.00) - 1/(€\,1.1786/\$1.00)} = €3,782,468$$

The purchase of €3,782,468 at the expected spot price will cost $3,209,289. The delivery of €3,782,468 under the forward contract will yield $3,319,993, for a profit of $110,704. If everything goes as expected, the $110,704 profit from the forward hedge will offset the equity loss from the translation adjustment. Note, however, that the hedge will not provide a certain outcome because the size of the forward position is based on the expected future spot rate. Consequently, the forward position taken in euros is actually a speculative position. If the realized spot rate turns out to be less than €1.1393/$1.00, a loss from the forward position will result. Moreover, the hedging procedure violates the hypothesis of the forward rate being the market's unbiased predictor of the future spot rate.

In 1998, FASB 133 was issued. This statement establishes accounting and reporting standards for derivative instruments and hedging activities. To qualify for hedge accounting under FASB 133, a company must identify a clear link between an exposure and a derivative instrument. FASB 133 clarifies which transactions qualify as an acceptable hedge and how to treat an unexpected gain or loss if the hedge is not effective. Under FASB 133, the firm must document the effectiveness of its hedge transactions. Large gains or losses resulting from ineffective hedging are recorded in current income, whereas small gains or losses due to a lack of perfect (but nevertheless effective) hedging are posted to other comprehensive income (OCI), which is an equity account on the balance sheet. Under FASB 52, and prior to FASB 133, a company with an imprecise hedge might be allowed to post all gains or losses from an ineffective translation exposure hedge to the CTA account. However, under FASB 133 this process is modified: Effective hedge results are consolidated along with the CTA in OCI, but differences between total hedge results and the translation exposure being hedged (ineffective hedge results) flow first through current earnings on the income statement. Consequently, as in Example 10.2, if everything goes as expected (i.e., the "hedge" produces effective results), the gain from the derivatives hedge will fully offset the translation loss, resulting in a cumulative translation adjustment of zero.

Translation Exposure versus Operating Exposure

As noted, an unhedged depreciation in the euro will result in an equity loss. Such a loss, however, would only be a paper loss. It would not have any direct effect on reporting currency cash flows. Moreover, it would only have a realizable effect on net investment in the MNC if the affiliate's assets were sold or liquidated. However, as was discussed in Chapter 9, the depreciation of the local currency may, under certain circumstances, have a favorable operating effect. A currency depreciation may, for example, allow the affiliate to raise its sales price because the prices of imported competitive goods are now relatively higher. If costs do not rise proportionately and unit demand remains the same, the affiliate would realize an operating profit as a result of the currency depreciation. It is substantive issues such as these, which result in realizable changes in operating profit, that management should concern itself with.

Empirical Analysis of the Change from FASB 8 to FASB 52

Garlicki, Fabozzi, and Fonfeder (1987) empirically tested a sample of MNCs to determine if there was a change in value when the firms were required to switch from FASB 8 to FASB 52. FASB 8 calls for recognizing translation gains or losses immediately in net income. FASB 52 calls for recognizing translation gains or losses in the cumulative translation adjustment account on the balance sheet. Consequently, the change in the translation process had an effect on reported earnings. "Despite the impact of the change . . . on reported earnings, the actual cash flow of multinationals would not be affected *if managers were not making suboptimal decisions based on accounting rather than economic considerations under Statement 8.* In such circumstances, the mandated switch . . . should not change the value of the firm."[7]

The researchers tested their hypothesis concerning a change in value on the initial exposure draft date and on the date FASB 52 was adopted. They found that there was no significant positive reaction to the change or perceived change in the foreign currency translation process. The results suggest that market agents do not react to cosmetic earnings changes that do not affect value. Other researchers have found similar results when investigating other accounting changes that had only a cosmetic effect on earnings. The results of Garlicki, Fabozzi, and Fonfeder also underline the futility of attempting to manage translation gains and losses.

SUMMARY

In this chapter, we have discussed the nature and management of translation exposure. Translation exposure relates to the effect that an unanticipated change in exchange rates will have on the consolidated financial reports of a MNC.

1. The four recognized methods for consolidating the financial reports of a MNC include the current/noncurrent method, the monetary/nonmonetary method, the temporal method, and the current rate method.

2. An example comparing and contrasting the four translation methods was presented under the assumptions that the foreign currency had appreciated and depreciated. It was

---

[7]Garlicki, Fabozzi, and Fonfeder (1987).

noted that under the current rate method the gain or loss due to translation adjustment does not affect reported cash flows, as it does with the other three translation methods.

3. The old translation method prescribed by the Financial Accounting Standards Board, FASB 8, was discussed and compared with the present prescribed process, FASB 52.

4. In implementing FASB 52, the functional currency of the foreign entity must be translated into the reporting currency in which the consolidated statements are reported. The local currency of a foreign entity may not always be its functional currency. If it is not, the temporal method of translation is used to remeasure the foreign entity's books into the functional currency. The current rate method is used to translate from the functional currency to the reporting currency. In some cases, a foreign entity's functional currency may be the same as the reporting currency, in which case translation is not necessary.

5. It was noted that the European Union follows IAS 21, a monetary/nonmonetary translation method promulgated by the International Accounting Standards Board.

6. A case application illustrating the translation process of the balance sheet of a parent firm with two foreign wholly owned affiliates according to FASB 52 was presented. This was done assuming the foreign exchange rates had not changed since the inception of the businesses, and again after an assumed change, to more thoroughly show the effects of balance sheet consolidation under FASB 52. When a net translation exposure exists, a cumulative translation adjustment account is necessary to bring balance to the consolidated balance sheet after an exchange rate change.

7. Two ways to control translation risk were presented: a balance sheet hedge and a derivatives "hedge." Since translation exposure does not have an immediate direct effect on operating cash flows, its control is relatively unimportant in comparison to transaction exposure, which involves potential real cash flow losses. Since it is, generally, not possible to eliminate both translation and transaction exposure, it is more logical to effectively manage transaction exposure, even at the expense of translation exposure.

KEY WORDS

balance sheet hedge, *256*	current rate method, *246*	reporting currency, *250*
cumulative translation adjustment (CTA), *246*	derivatives hedge, *257*	temporal method, *246*
current/noncurrent method, *245*	functional currency, *249*	translation exposure, *245*
	monetary/nonmonetary method, *246*	translation exposure report, *253*

QUESTIONS

1. Explain the difference in the translation process between the monetary/nonmonetary method and the temporal method.

2. How are translation gains and losses handled differently according to the current rate method in comparison to the other three methods, that is, the current/noncurrent method, the monetary/nonmonetary method, and the temporal method?

3. Identify some instances under FASB 52 when a foreign entity's functional currency would be the same as the parent firm's currency.

4. Describe the remeasurement and translation process under FASB 52 of a wholly owned affiliate that keeps its books in the local currency of the country in which it operates, which is different than its functional currency.

5. It is, generally, not possible to completely eliminate both translation exposure and transaction exposure. In some cases, the elimination of one exposure will also eliminate the other. But in other cases, the elimination of one exposure actually creates the other. Discuss which exposure might be viewed as the most important to effectively manage, if a conflict between controlling both arises. Also, discuss and critique the common methods for controlling translation exposure.

PROBLEMS

1. Assume that FASB 8 is still in effect instead of FASB 52. Construct a translation exposure report for Centralia Corporation and its affiliates that is the counterpart to Exhibit 10.6 in the text. Centralia and its affiliates carry inventory and fixed assets on the books at historical values.

www.mcgraw-hill.co.uk/textbooks/eun

2. Assume that FASB 8 is still in effect instead of FASB 52. Construct a consolidated balance sheet for Centralia Corporation and its affiliates after a depreciation of the euro from €1.1000/$1.00 to €1.1786/$1.00 that is the counterpart to Exhibit 10.7 in the text. Centralia and its affiliates carry inventory and fixed assets on the books at historical values.

3. In Example 10.2, a forward contract was used to establish a derivatives "hedge" to protect Centralia from a translation loss if the euro depreciated from €1.1000/ $1.00 to €1.1786/$1.00. Assume that an over-the-counter put option on the euro with a strike price of €1.1393/$1.00 (or $0.8777/€1.00) can be purchased for $0.0088 per euro. Show how the potential translation loss can be "hedged" with an option contract.

INTERNET EXERCISES

Ford Motor Company manufactures and sells motor vehicles worldwide. Through their worldwide operations they are exposed to all types of foreign currency risk. Their website is www.ford.com. Go to this website and access their 2011 annual report. Scroll through the report until you find the section "Quantitative and Qualitative Disclosures about Market Risk" on page 79. In the subsections titled "Automotive Market and Counterparty Risk" and "Foreign Currency Risk" is a discussion of how Ford hedges economic and transaction exposure, but no mention is made about translation exposure. This is consistent with the discussion in the chapter mentioning that the translation process does not have a direct effect on reporting currency cash flows, and will only have a realizable effect on net investment upon the sale or liquidation of exposed assets.

MINI CASE

Techno Delta NV

Techno Delta NV is a software and computing services company based in Leuven, Belgium, with wholly owned affiliates located in Hong Kong and Turkey. The Hong Kong affiliate serves East Asia; the Turkish affiliate, located in Istanbul, serves Turkey, Central Asia and the Middle East. Each affiliate keeps its books in its local currency, which is also the main currency used in the operations. The relevant spot current exchange rates are:

$$€1.00 = CHF1.22 = HKD10.58 = KZT211.20 = SGD1.73 = TRY3.03.$$

You expect these rates to change to the following during the coming year:

$$€1.00 = CHF1.19 = HKD10.63 = KZT225.00 = SGD1.71 = TRY3.25$$

The nonconsolidated balance sheets for Techno Delta and its two affiliates are reported in the table below.

The corporate treasurer of Techno Delta has asked you to prepare a report analyzing all aspects of the translation exposure faced by Techno Delta as a MNC. In the analysis, you are expected to address the relationship between the firm's translation exposure and its transaction exposure. Given your forecast of the spot rates of exchange, you decide that you must do the following before any sensible report can be written.

1. Using the current exchange rates and the nonconsolidated balance sheets for Techno Delta and its affiliates, prepare a consolidated balance sheet for the MNC according to IAS 21.

2. (a) Prepare a translation exposure report for Techno Delta NV and its two affiliates.

   (b) Using the translation exposure report you have prepared, determine if any reporting currency imbalance will result from a change in exchange rates to which the firm has currency exposure.

3. Prepare a second consolidated balance sheet for the MNC using the new exchange rates that you expect. Determine how any reporting currency imbalance will affect the new consolidated balance sheet for Techno Delta.

4. (a) Prepare a transaction exposure report for Techno Delta and its affiliates. Determine if any transaction exposures are also translation exposures.

   (b) Investigate what Techno Delta and its affiliates can do to control its transaction and translation exposures. Determine if any of the translation exposure should be hedged.

Nonconsolidated Balance Sheet for Techno Delta NV and Its Hong Kong and Turkish Affiliates, December 31, 2013 (in 000 currency units).

	Techno Delta NV (parent)	Hong Kong Affiliate	Turkish Affiliate
Assets			
Cash	€ 31,560	HKD 110,000	TRY 85,000
Accounts receivable	35,400[a]	147,500[b]	43,750[c]
Inventory	620	12,500	6,250
Investment in Hong Kong affiliate	27,552[d]	—	—
Investment in Turkish affiliate	48,102[e]	—	—
Net fixed assets	109,620	105,000	52,500
Total assets	€252,854	HKD 375,000	TRY 187,500
Liabilities and Net Worth			
Accounts payable	€ 18,080	HKD 26,000[a]	TRY 13,000
Notes payable	22,100[f]	27,500	13,750
Long-term debt	31,070	30,000	15,000
Common stock	84,344	200,000[c]	100,000[d]
Retained earnings	97,240	91,500[c]	45,750[d]
Total liabilities and net worth	€252,854	HKD 375,000	TRY 187,500

Unless otherwise claimed in the footnotes, the figures for each company are referred to items denominated in the company's local currency. All translations are made at the current exchange rate (with rounding-ups).

[a]The parent firm is owed HKD250,000 by the Hong Kong affiliate. This sum is included in the parent's accounts receivable as €23,629.

[b]The Hong Kong affiliate has sold on account SGD7,500 of services to a Singapore bank. This sum is carried on the Hong Kong affiliate's books as HKD45,867.

[c]The Turkish affiliate has sold on account KZT1,200,000 of services to an energy company based in Kazakhstan. This sum is carried on the Turkish affiliate's books as TRY17,216.

[d]The Hong Kong affiliate is wholly owned by the parent firm. It is carried on the parent firm's books at €27,552,000. This represents the sum of the common stock (HKD200,000,000) and the retained earnings (HKD91,500,000) on the Hong Kong affiliate's books.

[e]The Turkish affiliate is wholly owned by the parent firm. It is carried on the parent firm's books at €48,102,000. This represents the sum of the common stock (TRY100,000,000) and the retained earnings (TRY45,750,000) on the Turkish affiliate's books.

[f]The parent firm has outstanding notes payable of CHF8,000,000 due to a Swiss bank. This sum is carried on the parent firm's books as €6,557,000.

REFERENCES & SUGGESTED READINGS

Arpan, J. S., and L. H. Radenbaugh. *International Accounting and Multinational Enterprises*, 2nd ed. New York: Wiley, 1985.

Financial Accounting Standards Board. *Accounting for the Translation of Foreign Currency Transactions and Foreign Currency Financial Statements, Statement of Financial Accounting Standards No. 8.* Stamford, CT: Financial Accounting Standards Board, October 1975.

Financial Accounting Standards Board. *Foreign Currency Translation, Statement of Financial Accounting Standards No. 52.* Stamford, Conn.: Financial Accounting Standards Board, December 1981.

Financial Accounting Standards Board. "Summary of Statement No. 133." www.fasb.org.

Garlicki, T. Dessa, Frank J. Fabozzi, and Robert Fonfeder. "The Impact of Earnings under FASB 52 on Equity Returns." *Financial Management* 16 (1987), pp. 36–44.

Haried, Andrew A., Leroy F. Imdieke, and Ralph E. Smith. *Advanced Accounting,* 6th ed. New York: Wiley, 1994.

Kawaller, Ira G. "What Analysts Need to Know about Accounting for Derivatives." *Financial Analysts Journal* 60 (2004), pp. 24–30.

Marshall, Andrew P. "Foreign Exchange Risk Management in UK, USA, and Asia Pacific Multinational Companies." *Journal of Multinational Financial Management* 10 (2000), pp. 185–211.

PART FOUR

World Financial Markets and Institutions

PART FOUR provides a thorough discussion of international financial institutions, assets, and marketplaces, and develops the tools necessary to manage exchange rate uncertainty.

CHAPTER 11 differentiates between international bank and domestic bank operations and examines the institutional differences of various types of international banking offices. International banks and their clients constitute the Eurocurrency market and form the core of the international money market.

CHAPTER 12 distinguishes between foreign bonds and Eurobonds, which together make up the international bond market. The advantages of sourcing funds from the international bond market as opposed to raising funds domestically are discussed. A discussion of the major types of international bonds is included in the chapter.

CHAPTER 13 covers international equity markets. The chapter begins with a statistical documentation of the size of equity markets in both developed and developing countries. Various methods of trading equity shares in the secondary markets are discussed. Additionally, the chapter provides a discussion of the advantages to the firm of cross-listing equity shares in more than one country.

CHAPTER 14 covers interest rate and currency swaps, useful tools for hedging long-term interest rate and currency risk.

CHAPTER 15 covers international portfolio investment. It documents that the potential benefits from international diversification are available to all national investors.

11 International Banking and Money Market

WE BEGIN OUR discussion of world financial markets and institutions in this chapter, which takes up four major topics: international banking; international money market operations, in which banks are dominant players; the international debt crisis; and the global financial crisis. The chapter starts with a discussion of the services international banks provide to their clients. This is appropriate since international banks and domestic banks are characterized by different service mixes. Statistics that show the size and financial strength of the world's largest international banks are presented next. The first part of the chapter concludes with a discussion of the different types of bank operations that encompass international banking. The second part begins with an analysis of the Eurocurrency market, the creation of Eurocurrency deposits by international banks, and the Eurocredit loans they make. These form the foundation of the international money market. Euronotes, Eurocommercial paper, and forward rate agreements are other important money market instruments that are discussed. The third part of the chapter offers a history of the severe international debt crisis of only a few years ago and the dangers of private bank lending to sovereign governments. The chapter concludes with a lengthy discussion of the ongoing global financial crisis.

International Banking Services

International banks can be characterized by the types of services they provide that distinguish them from domestic banks. Foremost, international banks facilitate the imports and exports of their clients by arranging trade financing. Additionally, they serve their clients by arranging for foreign exchange necessary to conduct cross-border transactions and make foreign investments. In conducting foreign exchange transactions, banks often assist their clients in hedging exchange rate risk in foreign currency receivables and payables through forward and options contracts. Since international banks have the facilities to trade foreign exchange, they generally also trade foreign exchange products for their own account.

The major features that distinguish international banks from domestic banks are the types of deposits they accept and the loans and investments they make. Large international banks both borrow and lend in the Eurocurrency market. Additionally, they are frequently members of international loan syndicates, participating with other international banks to lend large sums to MNCs needing project financing and sovereign governments needing funds for economic development. Moreover, depending on the regulations of the country in which it operates and its organizational type, an international bank may participate in the underwriting of Eurobonds and foreign bonds. Today banks are frequently structured as bank holding companies so that they can perform both traditional commercial banking functions, the subject of this chapter, and also engage in investment banking activities.

International banks frequently provide consulting services and advice to their clients. Areas in which international banks typically have expertise are foreign exchange hedging strategies, interest rate and currency swap financing, and international cash management services. All of these international banking services and operations are covered in depth in this and other chapters of the text. Not all international banks provide all services, however. Banks that do provide a majority of these services are commonly known as **universal banks** or **full service banks**.

The World's Largest Banks

Exhibit 11.1 lists the world's 30 largest banks ranked by total assets. The exhibit shows total assets, net income, and market value in billions of U.S. dollars. The exhibit indicates that 5 of the world's 30 largest banks are from the U.S.; 4 are from Australia; 3 each are from Canada, China, Japan, and the U.K.; 2 each are from Brazil, France, Italy, and Spain; and 1 is from Germany.

From Exhibit 11.1, one might correctly surmise that the world's major international finance centers are New York, London, Tokyo, Paris, and increasingly Sydney, Beijing,

| EXHIBIT 11.1 | The World's 30 Largest Banks (in Billions of U.S. Dollars, as of April 2012) | | | | |

Rank	Bank	Country	Total Assets	Net Income	Market Value
1	Deutsch Bank	Germany	2,809.4	5.4	47.3
2	HSBC Holding	United Kingdom	2,550.0	16.2	164.3
3	BNP Paribas	France	2,539.1	7.9	61.5
4	Mitsubishi UFJ Financial	Japan	2,478.8	7.0	74.5
5	Barclays	United Kingdom	2,425.2	4.7	49.1
6	JPMorgan Chase	USA	2,265.8	19.0	170.1
7	Bank of America	USA	2,129.0	1.4	105.2
8	ICBC	China	2,039.1	25.1	237.4
9	Mizuho Financial	Japan	1,934.4	5.0	40.6
10	Citigroup	USA	1,837.9	11.1	107.5
11	Sumitomo Mitsui Financial	Japan	1,654.9	5.7	47.8
12	Banco Santander	Spain	1,624.7	6.9	75.6
13	Bank of China	China	1,583.7	15.8	129.1
14	Société Générale	France	1,531.1	3.3	25.8
15	Wells Fargo	USA	1,313.9	15.9	178.7
16	UniCredit Group	Italy	1,231.8	1.6	31.8
17	Intesa Sanpaolo	Italy	875.7	3.6	33.9
18	Royal Bank of Canada	Canada	812.7	4.7	84.4
19	TD Bank	Canada	771.5	5.8	76.1
20	BBVA-Banco Bilbao Vizcaya	Spain	767.7	3.9	43.1
21	National Australia Bank	Australia	730.4	5.0	56.3
22	Commonwealth Bank	Australia	713.7	6.9	81.6
23	Wesplace Banking Group	Australia	651.7	7.2	67.5
24	Bank of Nova Scotia	Canada	635.2	5.3	62.2
25	Standard Chartered	United Kingdom	598.7	4.7	62.5
26	Bank of Communications	China	598.5	5.9	48.8
27	ANZ	Australia	577.2	5.2	62.6
28	Bando do Brasil	Brazil	516.3	6.5	45.9
29	Itaú Unibanco Holding	Brazil	426.4	7.4	91.2
30	US Bancorp	USA	340.1	4.9	60.5

Source: Compiled from *The Global 2000*, www.forbes.com.

and Shanghai. London, New York, and Tokyo, however, are by far the most important international finance centers because of the relatively liberal banking regulations of their respective countries, the size of their economies, and the importance of their currencies in international transactions. These three financial centers are frequently referred to as *full service centers* because the major banks that operate in them usually provide a full range of services.

Reasons for International Banking

The opening discussion on the services international banks provide implied some of the reasons why a bank may establish multinational operations. Rugman and Kamath (1987) provide a more formal list:

1. *Low marginal costs*—Managerial and marketing knowledge developed at home can be used abroad with low marginal costs.

2. *Knowledge advantage*—The foreign bank subsidiary can draw on the parent bank's knowledge of personal contacts and credit investigations for use in that foreign market.

3. *Home country information services*—Local firms may be able to obtain from a foreign subsidiary bank operating in their country more complete trade and financial market information about the subsidiary's home country than they can obtain from their own domestic banks.

4. *Prestige*—Very large multinational banks have high perceived prestige, liquidity, and deposit safety that can be used to attract clients abroad.

5. *Regulation advantage*—Multinational banks are often not subject to the same regulations as domestic banks. There may be reduced need to publish adequate financial information, lack of required deposit insurance and reserve requirements on foreign currency deposits, and the absence of territorial restrictions.

6. *Wholesale defensive strategy*—Banks follow their multinational customers abroad to prevent the erosion of their clientele to foreign banks seeking to service the multinational's foreign subsidiaries.

7. *Retail defensive strategy*—Multinational banking operations help a bank prevent the erosion of its traveler's check, tourist, and foreign business markets from foreign bank competition.

8. *Transaction costs*—By maintaining foreign branches and foreign currency balances, banks may reduce transaction costs and foreign exchange risk on currency conversion if government controls can be circumvented.

9. *Growth*—Growth prospects in a home nation may be limited by a market largely saturated with the services offered by domestic banks.

10. *Risk reduction*—Greater stability of earnings is possible with international diversification. Offsetting business and monetary policy cycles across nations reduces the country-specific risk a bank faces if it operates in a single nation.

Types of International Banking Offices

The services and operations of international banks are a function of the regulatory environment in which the bank operates and the type of banking facility established. Following is a discussion of the major types of international banking offices, detailing the purpose of each and the regulatory rationale for its existence. The discussion moves from correspondent bank relationships, through which minimal service can be provided to a bank's customers, to a description of offices providing a fuller array of services, to those that have been established by regulatory change for the purpose of leveling the worldwide competitive playing field.[1]

Correspondent Bank

The large banks in the world will generally have a correspondent relationship with other banks in all the major financial centers in which they do not have their own banking operation. A **correspondent bank relationship** is established when two banks maintain a correspondent bank account with one another. For example, a large New York bank will have a correspondent bank account in a London bank, and the London bank will maintain one with the New York bank.

The correspondent banking system enables a bank's MNC client to conduct business worldwide through his local bank or its contacts. Correspondent banking services center around foreign exchange conversions that arise through the international transactions the MNC makes. However, correspondent bank services also include assistance with trade financing, such as honoring letters of credit and accepting drafts drawn on the correspondent bank. Additionally, a MNC needing foreign local financing for one of its subsidiaries may rely on its local bank to provide it with a letter of introduction to the correspondent bank in the foreign country.

The correspondent bank relationship is beneficial because a bank can service its MNC clients at a very low cost and without the need of having bank personnel physically located in many countries. A disadvantage is that the bank's clients may not receive the level of service through the correspondent bank that they would if the bank had its own foreign facilities to service its clients.

Representative Offices

A **representative office** is a small service facility staffed by parent bank personnel that is designed to assist MNC clients of the parent bank in dealings with the bank's correspondents. It is a way for the parent bank to provide its MNC clients with a level of service greater than that provided through merely a correspondent relationship. The parent bank may open a representative office in a country in which it has many MNC clients or at least an important client. Representative offices also assist MNC clients with information about local business practices, economic information, and credit evaluation of the MNC's foreign customers.

Foreign Branches

A **foreign branch bank** operates like a local bank, but legally it is a part of the parent bank. As such, a branch bank is subject to both the banking regulations of its home country and the country in which it operates. U.S. branch banks in foreign countries are regulated from the United States by the Federal Reserve Act and Federal Reserve Regulation K: International Banking Operations, which covers most of the regulations relating to U.S. banks operating in foreign countries and foreign banks operating within the United States.

There are several reasons why a parent bank might establish a branch bank. The primary one is that the bank organization can provide a much fuller range of services for its MNC customers through a branch office than it can through a representative office. For example, branch bank loan limits are based on the capital of the parent bank, not the branch bank. Consequently, a branch bank will likely be able to extend a larger loan to a customer than a locally chartered subsidiary bank of the parent. Additionally, the books of a foreign branch are part of the parent bank's books. Thus, a branch bank system allows customers much faster check clearing than does a correspondent bank network because the debit and credit procedure is handled internally within one organization.

---

[1]Much of the discussion in this section follows Hultman (1990).

Another reason a U.S. parent bank may establish a foreign branch bank is to compete on a local level with the banks of the host country. Branches of U.S. banks are not subject to U.S. reserve requirements on deposits and are not required to have Federal Deposit Insurance Corporation (FDIC) insurance on deposits. Consequently, branch banks are on the same competitive level as local banks in terms of their cost structure in making loans.

Branch banking is the most popular way for U.S. banks to expand operations overseas. Most branch banks are located in Europe, in particular the United Kingdom. Many branch banks are operated as "shell" branches in offshore banking centers, a topic covered later in this section.

The most important piece of legislation affecting the operation of foreign banks in the United States is the International Banking Act of 1978 (IBA). In general, the act specifies that foreign branch banks operating in the United States must comply with U.S. banking regulations just like U.S. banks. In particular, the IBA specifies that foreign branch banks must meet the Fed reserve requirements on deposits and make FDIC insurance available for customer deposits.

Subsidiary and Affiliate Banks

A **subsidiary bank** is a locally incorporated bank that is either wholly owned or owned in major part by a foreign parent. An **affiliate bank** is one that is only partially owned but not controlled by its foreign parent. Both subsidiary and affiliate banks operate under the banking laws of the country in which they are incorporated. U.S. parent banks find subsidiary and affiliate banking structures desirable because they are allowed to underwrite securities.

Foreign-owned subsidiary banks in the United States tend to locate in the states that are major centers of financial activity, as do U.S. branches of foreign parent banks. In the United States, foreign bank offices tend to locate in the highly populous states of New York, California, Illinois, Florida, Georgia, and Texas.[2]

Edge Act Banks

Edge Act banks are federally chartered subsidiaries of U.S. banks that are physically located in the United States and are allowed to engage in a full range of international banking activities. Senator Walter E. Edge of New Jersey sponsored the 1919 amendment to Section 25 of the Federal Reserve Act to allow U.S. banks to be competitive with the services foreign banks could supply their customers. Federal Reserve Regulation K allows Edge Act banks to accept foreign deposits, extend trade credit, finance foreign projects abroad, trade foreign currencies, and engage in investment banking activities with U.S. citizens involving foreign securities. As such, Edge Act banks do not compete directly with the services provided by U.S. commercial banks.

An Edge Act bank is typically located in a state different from that of its parent in order to get around the prohibition on interstate branch banking. However, since 1979, the Federal Reserve has permitted interstate banking by Edge Act banks. Moreover, the IBA permits foreign banks operating in the United States to establish Edge Act banks. Thus, both U.S. and foreign Edge Act banks operate on an equally competitive basis.

Edge Act banks are not prohibited from owning equity in business corporations, unlike domestic commercial banks. Thus, it is *through* the Edge Act that U.S. parent banks own foreign banking subsidiaries and have ownership positions in foreign banking affiliates.

Offshore Banking Centers

A significant portion of the external banking activity takes place through offshore banking centers. An **offshore banking center** is a country whose banking system is organized to permit external accounts beyond the normal economic activity of the country. The International Monetary Fund recognizes the Bahamas, Bahrain, the Cayman Islands, Hong Kong, Sint Maarten, Panama, and Singapore as major offshore banking centers.

---

[2] See Goldberg and Grosse (1994).

Offshore banks operate as branches or subsidiaries of the parent bank. The principal features that make a country attractive for establishing an offshore banking operation are virtually total freedom from host-country governmental banking regulations—for example, low reserve requirements and no deposit insurance, low taxes, a favorable time zone that facilitates international banking transactions, and, to a minor extent, strict banking secrecy laws. It should not be inferred that offshore host governments tolerate or encourage poor banking practices, as entry is usually confined to the largest and most reputable international banks.

The primary activities of offshore banks are to seek deposits and grant loans in currencies other than the currency of the host government. Offshore banking was spawned in the late 1960s when the Federal Reserve authorized U.S. banks to establish "shell" branches, which needs to be nothing more than a post office box in the host country. The actual banking transactions were conducted by the parent bank. The purpose was to allow smaller U.S. banks the opportunity to participate in the growing Eurodollar market without having to bear the expense of setting up operations in a major European money center. Today there are hundreds of offshore bank branches and subsidiaries, about one-third operated by U.S. parent banks.[3] Most offshore banking centers continue to serve as locations for shell branches, but Hong Kong and Singapore have developed into full service banking centers that now rival London, New York, and Tokyo.

International Banking Facilities

In 1981, the Federal Reserve authorized the establishment of **International Banking Facilities (IBF)**. An IBF is a separate set of asset and liability accounts that are segregated on the parent bank's books; it is not a unique physical or legal entity. Any U.S.-chartered depository institution, a U.S. branch or subsidiary of a foreign bank, or a U.S. office of an Edge Act bank may operate an IBF. IBFs operate as foreign banks in the United States. They are not subject to domestic reserve requirements on deposits, nor is FDIC insurance required on deposits. IBFs seek deposits from non-U.S. citizens and can make loans only to foreigners. All nonbank deposits must be nonnegotiable time deposits with a maturity of at least two business days and be of a size of at least $100,000.

IBFs were established largely as a result of the success of offshore banking. The Federal Reserve desired to return a large share of the deposit and loan business of U.S. branches and subsidiaries to the United States. IBFs have been successful in capturing a large portion of the Eurodollar business that was previously handled offshore. However, offshore banking will never be completely eliminated because IBFs are restricted from lending to U.S. citizens, while offshore banks are not.

Exhibit 11.2 summarizes the organizational structure and characteristics of international banking offices from the perspective of the United States.

Capital Adequacy Standards

A concern of bank regulators worldwide and of bank depositors is the safety of bank deposits. **Bank capital adequacy** refers to the amount of equity capital and other securities a bank holds as reserves against risky assets to reduce the probability of a bank failure. In a 1988 agreement known as the **Basel Accord**, after the Swiss city in which it is headquartered, the Bank for International Settlements (BIS) established a framework for measuring bank capital adequacy for banks in the Group of Ten (G-10) countries and Luxembourg. The BIS is the central bank for clearing international transactions between national central banks, and also serves as a facilitator in reaching international banking agreements among its members.

---

[3] See Chapter 10 of Hultman (1990) for an excellent discussion of the development of offshore banking and international banking facilities.

EXHIBIT 11.2 Organizational Structure of International Banking Offices from the U.S. Perspective

Type of Bank	Physical Location	Accept Foreign Deposits	Make Loans to Foreigners	Subject to Fed Reserve Requirements	FDIC Insured Deposits	Separate Legal Equity from Parent
Domestic bank	U.S.	No	No	Yes	Yes	No
Correspondent bank	Foreign	N/A	N/A	No	No	N/A
Representative office	Foreign	No	No	Yes	Yes	No
Foreign branch	Foreign	Yes	Yes	No	No	No
Subsidiary bank	Foreign	Yes	Yes	No	No	Yes
Affiliate bank	Foreign	Yes	Yes	No	No	Yes
Edge Act bank	U.S.	Yes	Yes	No	No	Yes
Offshore banking center	Technically Foreign	Yes	Yes	No	No	No
International banking facility	U.S.	Yes	Yes	No	No	No

www.bis.org

This is the official website of the Bank for International Settlements. It is quite extensive. One can download many papers on international bank policies and reports containing statistics on international banks, capital markets, and derivative securities markets. There is also a link to the websites of most central banks in the world.

The Basel Accord called for a minimum bank capital adequacy ratio of 8 percent of risk-weighted assets for internationally active banks. The accord divides bank capital into two categories: Tier I Core capital, which consists of shareholder equity and retained earnings, and Tier II Supplemental capital, which consists of internationally recognized nonequity items such as preferred stock and subordinated bonds. Supplemental capital could count for no more than 50 percent of total bank capital, or no more than 4 percent of risk-weighted assets. In determining risk-weighted assets, four categories of risky assets are each weighted differently. More risky assets receive a higher weight. Government obligations are weighted at zero percent, short-term interbank assets are weighted at 20 percent, residential mortgages at 50 percent, and other assets at 100 percent. Thus, a bank with $100 million in each of the four asset categories would have the equivalent of $170 million in risk-weighted assets. It would need to maintain $13.6 million in capital against these investments, of which no more than one-half, or $6.8 million, could be Tier II capital.

The 1988 Basel Capital Accord primarily addressed banking in the context of deposit gathering and lending. Thus, its focus was on *credit* risk. The accord was widely adopted throughout the world by national bank regulators. Nevertheless, it had its problems and its critics. One major criticism concerned the arbitrary nature in which the accord was implemented. The 8 percent minimum capital requirement assigned to risk-weighted assets was unchanging regardless of whether the degree of credit risk fluctuated throughout the business cycle, regardless of whether the bank was located in a developed or a developing country, and regardless of the types of risks in which banks were engaged. Bank trading in equity, interest rate, and exchange rate derivative products escalated throughout the 1990s. Many of these products were not even in existence when the Basel Accord was drafted. Consequently, even if the accord was satisfactory in safeguarding bank depositors from traditional credit risks, the capital adequacy requirements were not sufficient to safeguard against the *market* risk from derivatives trading. For example, Barings Bank, which collapsed in 1995 due in part to the activities of a rogue derivatives trader, was considered to be a safe bank by the Basel capital adequacy standards.

Given the shortcomings of the 1988 accord, the Basel Committee concluded in the early 1990s that an updated capital accord was needed. A 1996 amendment, which went into effect in 1998, required commercial banks engaging in significant trading activity to set aside additional capital under the 8 percent rule to cover the market risks inherent in their trading accounts. A new Tier III capital composed of short-term subordinated debt could be used to satisfy the capital requirement on market risk. By this time additional shortcomings of the original accord were becoming evident.

Operational risk, which includes such matters as computer failure, poor documentation, and fraud, was becoming evident as a significant risk. This expanded view of risk reflects the type of business in which banks now engage and the business environment in which banks operate. In 1999, the Basel Committee proposed a new capital accord. In June 2004, after an extensive consultative process, the new capital adequacy framework commonly referred to as Basel II was endorsed by central bank governors and bank supervisors in the G-10 countries. The committee issued an updated version in November 2005, which is currently available for implementation.

Basel II is based on three mutually reinforcing pillars: minimum capital requirements, a supervisory review process, and the effective use of market discipline. The new framework sets out the details for adopting more risk sensitive minimum capital requirements that are extended up to the holding company level of diversified bank groups. With respect to the first pillar, bank capital is defined as per the 1988 accord, but the minimum 8 percent capital ratio is calculated on the sum of the bank's credit, market, and operational risks. In determining adequate capital, the new framework provides a range of options open to banks for valuing credit risk and operational risk. Banks are encouraged to move along the spectrum of approaches as they develop more sophisticated risk measurement systems. Market risk is determined by marking-to-market the value of the bank's trading account, or if that is not possible, marking to a model determined value.

The second pillar is designed to ensure that each bank has a sound internal process in place to properly assess the adequacy of its capital based on a thorough evaluation of its risks. For example, banks are required to conduct meaningful stress tests designed to estimate the extent to which capital requirements could increase in an adverse economic scenario. Banks and supervisors are to use the results of these tests to ensure that banks hold sufficient capital. The third pillar is designed to complement the other two. It is believed that public disclosure of key information will bring greater market discipline to bear on banks and supervisors to better manage risk and improve bank stability.[4]

Throughout the global financial crisis that began in mid-2007, many banks struggled to maintain adequate liquidity.[5] The crisis illustrated how quickly and severely liquidity can crystallize and certain sources of funding can evaporate, compounding concern related to the valuation of assets and capital adequacy. Prior to the onset of the financial crisis, banks built up significant exposures to off-balance-sheet market risks that were not adequately reflected in the capital requirements of Basel II. A number of banking organizations have experienced large losses, most of which were sustained in the banks' trading accounts. These losses have not arisen from actual defaults, but rather from credit agency downgrades, widening credit spreads, and the loss of liquidity.

In July 2009, the Basel Committee on Banking Supervision finalized a package of proposed enhancements to Basel II to strengthen the regulation and supervision of internationally active banks. This package of enhancements is referred to as Basel 2.5. The proposed enhancement to Pillar 1 calls for increasing the minimum capital requirement to cover illiquid credit products in the trading account; complex securitizations, such as asset-backed securities and collateralized debt obligations; and exposures to off-balance-sheet vehicles.[6] Pillar 2 proposals call for more rigorous supervision and risk management; more specifically, the proposals call for clear expectations for the board of directors and senior management to understand firm-wide risk exposure. Pillar 3 proposals call for enhanced disclosure requirements for securitizations and off-balance-sheet vehicles to allow market participants to better assess the firm's risk exposure. Basel 2.5 was due to be implemented by year-end 2011 and at this time has been adopted by most G20 countries.

---

[4]The information in this section is from *International Convergence of Capital Measurement and Capital Standards: A Revised Framework*, Bank for International Settlements, June 2004.

[5]See the section titled "Global Financial Crisis" for an in-depth discussion of the crisis.

[6]See Appendix 11B for an explanation of asset-backed securities and collateralized debt obligations.

Building on Basel 2.5, the Basel Committee on September 12, 2010 announced a third accord, Basel III, which is designed to substantially strengthen the regulatory capital framework and increase the quality of bank capital. Under the committee's reforms, Tier I capital is redefined to include only common equity and retained earnings (i.e., eliminating non-redeemable, non-cumulative preferred stock). Further, Tier I capital is to be increased from 4 to 6 percent. Additionally, the committee introduced a 2.5 percent capital buffer that can be drawn down in periods of financial stress. The 2.5 percent buffer brings Tier I capital to 8.5 percent and total capital to 10.5. These reforms are to be fully in place by January 1, 2019. Implementation is in the early stages among the G20 countries. In the United States, Basel 2.5 and Basel II rulemakings must be coordinated with applicable work on Dodd-Frank regulatory reform legislation. In the European Union, the European Parliament is currently in discussions to agree on the final text of a compromise proposal.

International Money Market

Eurocurrency Market

The core of the international money market is the Eurocurrency market. A **Eurocurrency** is a *time* deposit of money in an international bank located in a country different from the country that issued the currency. For example, Eurodollars are deposits of U.S. dollars in banks located outside of the United States, Eurosterling are deposits of British pound sterling in banks outside of the United Kingdom, and Euroyen are deposits of Japanese yen in banks outside of Japan. The prefix *Euro* is somewhat of a misnomer, since the bank in which the deposit is made does not have to be located in Europe. The depository bank could be located in Europe, the Caribbean, or Asia. Indeed, as we saw in the previous section, Eurodollar deposits can be made in offshore shell branches or IBFs, where the physical dollar deposits are actually with the U.S. parent bank. An "Asian dollar" market exists, with headquarters in Singapore, but it can be viewed as a major division of the Eurocurrency market.

The origin of the Eurocurrency market can be traced back to the 1950s and early 1960s, when the former Soviet Union and Soviet-bloc countries sold gold and commodities to raise hard currency. Because of anti-Soviet sentiment, these Communist countries were afraid of depositing their U.S. dollars in U.S. banks for fear that the deposits could be frozen or taken. Instead they deposited their dollars in a French bank whose telex address was EURO-BANK. Since that time, dollar deposits outside the United States have been called Eurodollars and banks accepting Eurocurrency deposits have been called **Eurobanks**.[7]

The Eurocurrency market is an *external* banking system that runs parallel to the *domestic* banking system of the country that issued the currency. Both banking systems seek deposits and make loans to customers from the deposited funds. In the United States, banks are subject to the Federal Reserve Regulation D, specifying reserve requirements on bank time deposits. Additionally, U.S. banks must pay FDIC insurance premiums on deposited funds. Eurodollar deposits, on the other hand, are not subject to these arbitrary reserve requirements or deposit insurance; hence the cost of operations is less. Because of the reduced cost structure, the Eurocurrency market, and in particular the Eurodollar market, has grown spectacularly since its inception.

The Eurocurrency market operates at the *interbank* and/or *wholesale* level. The majority of Eurocurrency transactions are interbank transactions, representing sums of $1,000,000 or more. Eurobanks with surplus funds and no retail customers to lend to will lend to Eurobanks that have borrowers but need loanable funds. The rate charged by banks with excess funds is referred to as the *interbank offered rate*; they will accept interbank deposits at the *interbank bid rate*. The spread is generally 10–12 basis points for most major Eurocurrencies; however, it has been somewhat higher during the ongoing global economic crisis. Rates on Eurocurrency deposits are quoted for maturities

---

[7]See Rivera-Batiz and Rivera-Batiz (1994) for an account of the historical origin of the Eurocurrency market.

EXHIBIT 11.3	Eurocurrency Interest Rate Quotations: June 5, 2013					
	Short Term	7 Days' Notice	One Month	Three Months	Six Months	One Year
Euro	0.17 to 0.07	0.20 to 0.15	0.11 to 0.01	0.25 to 0.05	0.32 to 0.17	0.55 to 0.35
Danish Krone	0.02 to −0.18	−0.14 to −0.18	1.02 to −0.18	−0.11 to −0.12	0.01 to −0.04	0.19 to 0.14
Sterling	0.51 to 0.41	0.52 to 0.42	0.53 to 0.43	0.64 to 0.54	0.73 to 0.53	0.92 to 0.82
Swiss Franc	0.05 to −0.15	0.05 to −0.15	0.05 to −0.15	0.07 to −0.13	0.16 to −0.04	0.29 to 0.09
Canadian Dollar	0.98 to 0.94	1.12 to 0.97	1.16 to 1.01	1.29 to 1.14	1.41 to 1.26	1.63 to 1.48
US Dollar	0.14 to 0.07	0.31 to 0.26	0.29 to 0.19	0.41 to 0.24	0.53 to 0.43	0.71 to 0.52
Japanese Yen	0.32 to 0.07	0.32 to 0.07	0.18 to 0.03	0.35 to 0.10	0.35 to 0.15	0.29 to 0.17
Singapore $	0.17 to 0.02	0.20 to 0.05	0.32 to 0.22	0.36 to 0.26	0.44 to 0.19	0.56 to 0.31

Note. Short-term rates are call for the U.S. dollar and yen, others, two days' notice.
Source: *Financial Times*, June 6, 2013, p. 19.

ranging from one day to one year; however, more standard maturities are for 1, 2, 3, 6, 9, and 12 months. Exhibit 11.3 shows sample Eurocurrency interest rates. Appendix 11A illustrates the creation of the Eurocurrency.

London has historically been, and remains, the major Eurocurrency financial center. These days, most people have heard of the **London Interbank Offered Rate (LIBOR)**, the reference rate in London for Eurocurrency deposits. To be clear, there is a LIBOR for Eurodollars, Euro–Canadian dollars, Euroyen, and even euros. In other financial centers, other reference rates are used. For example, *SIBOR* is the Singapore Interbank Offered Rate, and *TIBOR* is the Tokyo Interbank Offered Rate. Obviously, competition forces the various interbank rates for a particular Eurocurrency to be close to one another.

The advent of the common euro currency on January 1, 1999, among the 11 countries of the European Union making up the Economic and Monetary Union created a need for a new interbank offered rate designation. It also creates some confusion as to whether one is referring to the common euro currency or another Eurocurrency, such as Eurodollars. Because of this, it is starting to become common practice to refer to *international* currencies instead of Eurocurrencies and *prime* banks instead of Eurobanks. **Euro Interbank Offered Rate (EURIBOR)** is the rate at which interbank deposits of the euro are offered by one prime bank to another in the euro zone.

In the wholesale money market, Eurobanks accept Eurocurrency fixed time deposits and issue **negotiable certificates of deposit (NCDs)**. In fact, these are the preferable ways for Eurobanks to raise loanable funds, as the deposits tend to be for a lengthier period and the acquiring rate is often slightly less than the interbank rate. Denominations are at least $500,000, but sizes of $1,000,000 or larger are more typical.

Exhibit 11.4 shows the year-end values of international bank external liabilities (Eurodeposits and other Euro liabilities) in billions of U.S. dollars for the years 2008–2012. The 2012 column shows that total external liabilities were $24,945.8 billion and that interbank liabilities accounted for $17,233.8 billion of this amount, whereas nonbank deposits were $7,712.0 billion. The major currencies denominating these were the euro, the U.S. dollar, and the British pound sterling.

Approximately 90 percent of wholesale Eurobank external liabilities come from fixed time deposits, the remainder from NCDs. There is an interest penalty for the

www.euribor.org

This website provides a discussion of EURIBOR and related rates.

EXHIBIT 11.4		2008	2009	2010	2011	2012
International Bank External Liabilities (at Year-End in Billions of U.S. Dollars)	*Type Liability*					
	To banks	21,431.2	20,765.1	18,474.6	18,720.1	17,233.8
	To nonbanks	7,636.2	7,309.8	7,163.5	7,182.8	7,712.0
	Total	29,067.4	28,074.8	25,638.0	25,902.9	24,945.8

Source: *International Banking and Financial Market Developments*, Bank for International Settlements, Table 1, p. A7, June 2010 and 2013.

early withdrawal of funds from a fixed time deposit. NCDs, on the other hand, being negotiable, can be sold in the secondary market if the depositor suddenly needs his funds prior to scheduled maturity. The NCD market began in 1967 in London for Eurodollars. NCDs for currencies other than the U.S. dollar are offered by banks in London and in other financial centers, but the secondary market for nondollar NCDs is not very liquid.

BBA LIBOR

www.bba.org.uk

This is the website of the British Bankers Association. Time series of historic LIBOR rates can be obtained from this site.

At 11:00 A.M. every trading day in London, the British Bankers Association (BBA), a private trade association, *fixes* the London Interbank Offered Rate (LIBOR) for ten Eurocurrencies for 15 different maturities. BBA LIBOR serves as the primary daily benchmark used by banks, securities houses, and investors to set payments on at least $350 trillion in the international money, derivatives, and capital markets around the world.[8] The BBA fixes LIBOR for each Eurocurrency it tracks by averaging the middle two quartiles of rates at which a panel of Eurobanks active in the London Eurocurrency market believes they can borrow money from other London prime banks. Hence, the panel banks are estimating their LIBID (London Interbank Bid Rate), or the lending banks' LIBOR. A small variation of the daily fixing represents a substantial amount of money. For example, one basis point of the $350 trillion-worth of financial instruments fixed by BBA LIBOR represents $35 billion on an annual basis. Consequently, a small manipulation of BBA LIBOR has serious consequences and implications.

The International Finance in Practice box "The Rotten Heart of Finance" discusses two LIBOR scandals that have come to light in recent years. One has to do with BBA LIBOR panel banks understating the rates at which they could borrow during the depths of Global Financial Crisis (see the section later in this chapter) so as not to signal to the market any financial weakness implied by the true rate at which they would have to pay to borrow Eurocurrency. During this time Eurobanks did not trust the financial strength of one another and were afraid of what unknown toxic assets may be on a counterparty's balance sheet. As a result, little trading actually took place in the Eurocurrency market. The second scandal has to do with the recently discovered massive collusion among panel banks to manipulate the daily rate fixing in their favor in order to earn excess profit from their financial positions indexed to BBA LIBOR. Barclays was the first international bank to admit wrongdoing and to be penalized in this still-developing scandal. In June 2012, it paid a fine of £250 ($450) million and in July its chairman and CEO was dismissed by the board. And, in December 2012, British, Swiss, and U.S. authorities imposed penalties of CHF1.4 ($1.5) billion on UBS, who admitted "widespread and routine" attempts to manipulate the LIBOR fixing. Several other international banks also stand to be penalized.

Whether banks will be susceptible to civil lawsuits by parties who believe they have been harmed by the rate manipulation is not clear. With respect to the United States, a recent opinion released by a New York federal judge indicates that they will not be. The reason is that LIBOR is not a bid and nothing was bought in a competitive market, thus the laws of competition do not apply. The daily LIBOR fixing is an important and necessary function. Its administration will be transferred from the BBA to a subsidiary of NYSE Euronext in early 2014. The process of "fixing" LIBOR will likely change so that the fix is based on documented transactions rather than mere guesses. Other changes will likely include offering fewer than the current 15 maturities, as most interest is with the one-, three-, and six-month maturities.

Eurocredits

Eurocredits are short- to medium-term loans of Eurocurrency extended by Eurobanks to corporations, sovereign governments, nonprime banks, or international organizations. The loans are denominated in currencies other than the home currency of the

---

[8]Similarly, the Japanese Bankers Association fixes the JBA TIBOR, the Association of Banks in Singapore fixes ABS SIBOR for Eurodollars, and the European Banking Federation fixes EBF EURIBOR.

Eurobank. Because these loans are frequently too large for a single bank to handle, Eurobanks will band together to form a bank lending **syndicate** to share the risk.

The credit risk on these loans is greater than on loans to other banks in the interbank market. Thus, the interest rate on Eurocredits must compensate the bank, or banking syndicate, for the added credit risk. On Eurocredits originating in London the base lending rate is LIBOR. The lending rate on these credits is stated as LIBOR $+X$ percent, where X is the lending margin charged depending upon the creditworthiness of the borrower. Additionally, rollover pricing was created on Eurocredits so that Eurobanks do not end up paying more on Eurocurrency time deposits than they earn from the loans. Thus, a Eurocredit may be viewed as a series of shorter term loans, where at the end of each time period (generally three or six months), the loan is rolled over and the base lending rate is repriced to current LIBOR over the next time interval of the loan.

Exhibit 11.5 shows the relationship among the various interest rates we have discussed in this section. The numbers come from Exhibit 11.3 and the *Market Rates* section of the *Financial Times* (see inside back cover). On June 5, 2013, U.S. domestic banks were paying 0.28 percent for six-month NCDs and the prime lending rate, the base rate charged the bank's most creditworthy corporate clients, was 3.25 percent. This appears to represent a spread of 2.97 percent for the bank to cover operating costs and earn a profit. By comparison, Eurobanks will accept six-month Eurodollar time deposits, say, Eurodollar NCDs, at a LIBID rate of 0.43 percent. The rate charged for Eurodollar credits is LIBOR $+ X$ percent, where any lending margin less than 2.72 percent appears to make the Eurodollar loan more attractive than the prime rate loan. Since lending margins typically fall in the range of ¼ percent to 3 percent, with the median rate being ½ percent to 1½ percent, the exhibit shows the narrow borrowing-lending spreads of Eurobankers in the Eurodollar credit market. This analysis seems to suggest that borrowers can obtain funds somewhat more cheaply in the Eurodollar market. However, international competition in recent years has forced U.S. commercial banks to lend domestically at rates below prime.

EXAMPLE | 11.1: Rollover Pricing of a Eurocredit

Teltrex International can borrow $3,000,000 at LIBOR plus a lending margin of .75 percent per annum on a three-month rollover basis from Barclays in London. Suppose that three-month LIBOR is currently $5\frac{17}{32}$ percent. Further suppose that over the second three-month interval LIBOR falls to $5\frac{1}{8}$ percent. How much will Teltrex pay in interest to Barclays over the six-month period for the Eurodollar loan?

Solution: $3,000,000 × (.0553125 + .0075)/4 + $3,000,000 ×
(.05125 + .0075)/4 = $47,109.38 + $44,062.50
= $91,171.88

EXHIBIT 11.5

Comparison of U.S. Lending and Borrowing Rates with Eurodollar Rates on June 5, 2013

Rate of Interest	
3.25%	U.S. Prime Rate
	LIBOR + X%
0.53%	LIBOR (6-month)
0.43%	LIBID (6-month)
0.28%	U.S. Negotiable CD Rate (6-month)
0.00%	

EXHIBIT 11.7

Size of the Euronote
Market at Year-End
(in Billions of U.S. Dollars)

Instrument	2008	2009	2010	2011	2012
Euronotes	423.2	333.3	403.8	317.2	338.1
Eurocommercial Paper	708.5	598.9	512.0	578.4	502.4
Total	1,131.7	932.2	915.8	895.7	840.5

Source: *International Banking and Financial Market Developments,* Bank for International Settlements, Table 13A, p. A90, June 2009, p. A108, June 2010, p. A118, June 2012, p. A123, June 2013. The compilation methodology changed in December 2012, making the statistics for 2012 not directly comparable to the earlier years.

www.sgx.com

This is the website of the
Singapore Exchange. It
provides detailed information
about the securities and
derivatives traded on it.

The CME Eurodollar futures contract is written on a hypothetical $1,000,000 90-day deposit of Eurodollars. The contract trades in the March, June, September, and December cycle and the four nearest noncycle months. The hypothetical delivery date is the third Wednesday of the delivery month. The last day of trading is two business days prior to the delivery date. The contract is a cash settlement contract. That is, the delivery of a $1,000,000 Eurodollar deposit is not actually made or received. Instead, final settlement is made through realizing profits or losses in the performance bond account on the delivery date based on the final settlement price on the last day of trading. Exhibit 11.8 presents an example of CME Eurodollar futures quotations. Contracts trade out 10 years into the future.

EXHIBIT 11.8

CME Group Eurodollar
Futures Contract
Quotations

	Settle	Change	Open Interest	Volume
Eurodollar (CME)-$1,000,000; pts of 100%				
Jun 13	99.723	−.002	740,914	94,981
Sep	99.685	−.010	746,771	110,598
Dec	99.645	−.005	882,929	128,297
Mar 14	99.600	+.005	762,196	123,005
Jun	99.535	+.005	691,729	150,300
Sep	99.465	+.010	615,745	147,305
Dec	99.385	+.020	726,535	134,870
Mar 15	99.280	+.020	589,494	139,172
Jun	99.155	+.025	717,431	166,453
Sep	99.015	+.035	498,805	152,689
Dec	98.850	+.035	620,247	151,049
Mar 16	98.675	+.040	421,281	114,583
Jun	98.490	+.045	327,040	120,994
Sep	98.295	+.045	245,754	90,801
Dec	98.100	+.050	159,198	63,942
Mar 17	97.920	+.055	145,162	42,151
Jun	97.740	+.055	150,815	34,324
Sep	97.575	+.055	101,973	22,095
Dec	97.405	+.055	134,279	18,873
Mar 18	97.265	+.060	55,866	14,313
Jun	97.125	+.060	32,078	2,171
Sep	96.990	+.060	11,911	1,296
Dec	96.860	+.065	10,519	1,169
Mar 19	96.760	+.065	7,865	1,179
Jun	96.650	+.060	5,126	111
Sep	96.560	+.065	4,556	92

Source: Closing Values on Wednesday, June 5, 2013, from Bloomberg.

EXAMPLE | 11.3: Reading Eurodollar Futures Quotations

Eurodollar futures prices are stated as an index number of three-month LIBOR, calculated as: $F = 100 - \text{LIBOR}$. For example, from Exhibit 11.8 we see that the December 2013 contract (with hypothetical delivery on December 18, 2013) had a settlement price of 99.645 on Wednesday, June 5, 2013. The implied three-month LIBOR yield is thus 0.355 percent. The minimum price change is one-half basis point (bp). On $1,000,000 of face value, a one-basis-point change represents $100 on an annual basis. Since the contract is for a 90-day deposit, one-half basis point corresponds to a $12.50 price change.

EXAMPLE | 11.4: Eurodollar Futures Hedge

As an example of how this contract can be used to hedge interest rate risk, consider the treasurer of a MNC, who on Wednesday, June 5, 2013 learns that his firm expects to receive $20,000,000 in cash from a large sale of merchandise on December 18, 2013. The money will not be needed for a period of 90 days. Thus, the treasurer should invest the excess funds for this period in a money market instrument such as a Eurodollar deposit.

The treasurer notes that three-month LIBOR is currently 0.27445 percent. (See *Money Rates* in the inside back cover.) The implied three-month LIBOR rate in the December 2013 contract is higher at 0.355 percent. Additionally, the treasurer notes that the pattern of future expected three-month LIBOR rates implied by the pattern of Eurodollar futures prices suggests that three-month LIBOR is expected to increase through September 2019. The treasurer believes that a 90-day rate of return of 0.355 percent is a decent rate to "lock in," so he decides to hedge against lower three-month LIBOR in December 2013. By hedging, the treasurer is locking in a certain return of $17,750 (=$20,000,000 × .00355 × 90/360) for the 90-day period the MNC has $20,000,000 in excess funds.

To construct the hedge, the treasurer will need to buy, or take a long position, in Eurodollar futures contracts. At first it may seem counterintuitive that a long position is needed, but remember, a decrease in the implied three-month LIBOR yield causes the Eurodollar futures price to increase. To hedge the interest rate risk in a $20,000,000 deposit, the treasurer will need to buy 20 December 2013 contracts.

Assume that on the last day of trading in the December 2013 contract three-month LIBOR is 0.20 percent. The treasurer is indeed fortunate that he chose to hedge. At 0.20 percent, a 90-day Eurodollar deposit of $20,000,000 will generate only $10,000 of interest income, or $7,750 less than at a rate of 0.355 percent. In fact, the treasurer will have to deposit the excess funds at a rate of 0.20 percent. But the shortfall will be made up by profits from the long futures position. At a rate of 0.20 percent, the final settlement price on the December 2013 contract is 99.80 (=100 − 0.20). The profit earned on the futures position is calculated as: [99.80 − 99.645] × 100 bp × 2 × $12.50 × 20 contracts = $7,750. This is precisely the amount of the shortfall.

International Debt Crisis

Certain principles define sound banking behavior. "At least five of these principles—namely, avoid an undue concentration of loans to single activities, individuals, or groups; expand cautiously into unfamiliar activities; know your counterparty; control mismatches between assets and liabilities; and beware that your collateral is not vulnerable to the same shocks that weaken the borrower—remain as relevant today as in earlier times."[11] Nevertheless, violation of the first two of these principles by some of the largest international banks in the world was responsible for the **international debt**

amount of equity raised. Since yield curves are typically upward sloping, the SIV might normally earn 25 basis points by doing this. Obviously, SIVs are subject to the interest rate risk of the yield curve inverting, that is, short-term rates rising above long-term rates, thus necessitating the SIV to refinance the MBS investment at short-term rates in excess of the rate being earned on the MBS. Default risk is another risk with which SIVs must contend. If the underlying mortgage borrowers default on their home loans, the SIV will lose investment value. Nevertheless, SIVs predominantly invest only in high-grade Aaa/AAA MBS. By investing in a variety of MBS, an SIV further diversifies the credit risk of MBS investment. The SIV's value obviously derives from the value of the portfolio of MBS it represents.

Collateralized Debt Obligations

Collateralized debt obligations (CDOs) have been other big investors in MBS. A CDO is a corporate entity constructed to hold a portfolio of fixed-income assets as collateral. The portfolio of fixed-income assets is divided into different tranches, each representing a different risk class: AAA, AA-BB, or unrated. CDOs serve as an important funding source for fixed-income securities. An investor in a CDO is taking a position in the cash flows of a particular tranche, not in the fixed-income securities directly. The investment is dependent on the metrics used to define the risk and reward of the tranche. Investors include insurance companies, mutual funds, hedge funds, other CDOs, and even SIVs. MBS and other asset-backed securities have served as collateral for many CDOs.

Credit Defaults Swaps

A **credit default swap (CDS)** is the most popular credit derivative. It is a contract that provides insurance against the risk of default of a particular company or sovereignty, known as the *reference entity*. Default is referred to as a *credit event*. For an annual payment, known as the *spread*, the insurance buyer has the right under the terms of the CDS contract to sell bonds issued by the reference entity for full face value to the insurance seller if a credit event occurs. The total face value of bonds that can be sold is the CDS's *notional value*. Consider a 5-year CDS on a notional value of $100 million with a spread of 80 basis points. The buyer pays the seller $800,000 [= .008 × $100 million] per year each and every year if a credit event does not occur. If one does occur, the buyer provides physical delivery of the bonds to the insurance seller in return for $100 million and does not make any further annual payments. Some CDSs require cash settlement, in which case the seller pays the buyer the difference between the face value and the market value in the event of a default.

CDSs allow the buyer of a risky bond the ability to convert it into a risk free bond. Ignoring a difference in liquidity, a long position in a 5-year risky bond plus a long position in a 5-year CDS on the same bond should equal a position in a 5-year risk-free bond. Consequently, it is clear the CDS spread should equal the difference in the yield spread between the 5-year risky bond and a corresponding 5-year risk-free bond. Various financial institutions make a market in CDS in the over-the-counter market, taking either side of the contract. As this example illustrates, a CDS has the characteristics of a put option. However, CDSs were not regulated by the CFTC because they trade in the OTC market. Moreover, since they are classified as a swap instead of an insurance contract, they were not regulated by state insurance commissions either even though insurance companies are frequently market makers. In essence, the CDS market, which grew from virtually nothing into a $58 trillion market in just a few years, was an unregulated market. CDS can be used by bond investors to hedge the credit default risk in their portfolios. Alternatively, speculators without an underlying position in the bond can use CDSs for speculating on the default of a particular reference entity. Prudent risk management suggests that derivative dealers would hold a risk neutral position, but that has not been the case for CDS market makers. As providers of "insurance," they typically carry a large net short position.

From Credit Crunch to Financial Crisis   As the credit crunch escalated, many CDOs found themselves stuck with various tranches of MBS debt, especially the highest risk tranches, which they had not yet placed or were unable to place as subprime foreclosure rates around the country escalated. Commercial and investment banks were forced to write down billions of subprime debt. As the U.S. economy slipped into recession, banks also started to set aside billions for credit-card debt and other consumer loans they feared would go bad. The credit rating firms—Moody's, S&P, and Fitch—lowered their ratings on many CDOs after recognizing that the models they had used to evaluate the risk of the various tranches were mis-specified. Additionally, the credit rating firms downgraded many MBS, especially those containing subprime mortgages, as foreclosures around the country increased. An unsustainable problem arose for bond insurers who sold credit default swap (CDS) contracts and the banks that purchased this credit insurance. As the bond insurers got hit with claims from bank-sponsored SIVs as the MBS debt in their portfolios defaulted, downgrades of the bond insurers by the credit rating agencies required the insurers to put up more collateral with the counterparties who had purchased the CDSs, which put stress on their capital base and prompted additional credit-rating downgrades, which in turn triggered more margin calls. If big bond insurers, such as American International Group (AIG) failed, the banks that relied on the insurance protection would be forced to write down even more mortgage-backed debt which would further erode their Tier I Core capital bases. By September 2008, a worldwide flight to quality investments—primarily short term U.S. Treasury Securities—ensued. On October 10, 2008, the spread between the three-month Eurodollar rate and the three-month U.S. Treasury bill (the TED spread), frequently used as measure of credit risk, reached a record level of 543 basis points. Exhibit 11.11 graphs the TED spread from January 2007 through mid-December 2008. The demand for safety was so great, at one point in November 2008, the one-month U.S. Treasury bill was yielding only one basis point. Investors were essentially willing to accept zero return for a safe place to put their funds! They were not willing to invest in money market funds that invested in commercial paper that banks and industrial corporations needed for survival. The modern day equivalent of a "bank run" was operating in full force and many financial institutions could not survive.

Impact of the Financial Crisis

The financial crisis has had a pronounced effect on the world economy. As a result, dramatic changes have taken place in the financial services industry, the auto industry, and in financial markets worldwide. Some of the most significant changes are detailed here.

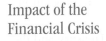

EXHIBIT 11.11

TED Spread (%)

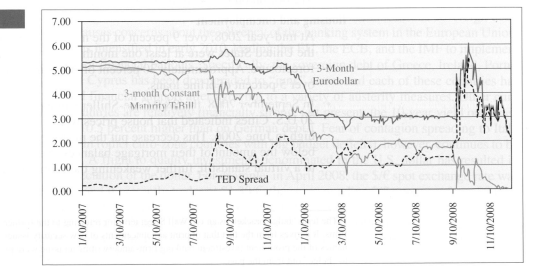

Economic Stimulus

Perhaps the credit crunch could not have been precisely predicted, but at some level the factors that contributed to it did not make sense. Even when the Fed was lowering the Fed Funds rate, Fed Chairman Alan Greenspan said, "I don't know what it is, but we're doing some damage because this is not the way credit markets should operate."[14] Lowering interest rates to such a low level and keeping them there for such a long period of time was a mistake. In retrospect, the global savings glut likely would have supplied a good deal of the liquidity needed by the U.S. and world economies after the dot-com bubble burst. It is difficult to understand how the Fed did not recognize this given the economic data available to it for analysis. Lowering the fed funds rate only added additional liquidity to the U.S. economy and exacerbated Americans' unsustainable buying binge. When the Fed started increasing interest rates, the party came to an end. In testimony before Congress on October 13, 2008, former Fed Chairman Greenspan admitted that he made a mistake with the hands-off regulatory environment he helped foster and further acknowledged that he made a critical forecasting error in his assumption about the resilience of home prices and never anticipated that they could fall so much.

Many new initiatives were made in 2008 to spur U.S. and world economic activity:

- Under the guidance of current Federal Reserve Chairman Ben Bernanke, the Fed began reducing the fed funds rate from the recent high of 5 ¼ percent at its meeting on September 18, 2007 to 0–25 basis points on December 16, 2008, where it remains. Obviously, the Fed had run out of ammo in this pouch as a means of increasing the money supply and stimulating the economy through normal open market operations. As a consequence, the Fed began a massive program of *quantitative easing*, that is, buying long-term Treasuries and mortgage-backed-securities, that at the time of this writing buys $85 billion of securities a month.

- Similarly, central banks around the world have reduced their short-term rates. A coordinated effort of rate cuts involving the Fed, European Central Bank, Bank of England, and the People's Bank of China took place on October 8, 2008. And, on December 17, 2008, central banks in Norway, the Czech Republic, Hong Kong, Saudi Arabia, Oman, and Kuwait cut interest rates. Quantitative easing programs have also been implemented in the U.K., the euro zone, and in Japan.

- As a result of frozen credit markets, corporations encountered problems obtaining working capital. In an effort to provide credit, the Fed established the Commercial Paper Facility to buy $1.3 trillion in commercial paper directly from U.S. companies.

- The Fed established the $540 billion Money Market Investor Funding Facility to buy commercial paper and certificates of deposit from money market funds to restore the public's confidence in these funds.

- Congress authorized the Federal Deposit Insurance Corporation (FDIC) to increase the level of bank deposit insurance from $100,000 to $250,000, which will likely be made permanent.

- The $700 billion Troubled Assets Relief Program (TARP), spearheaded by former U.S. Treasury Secretary Henry (Hank) Paulson to purchase poor performing mortgages and MBS from financial institutions, was signed into law in October 3, 2008. The idea behind the bailout plan was to get poor performing assets off of banks' books to alleviate the fears of depositors. In a startling change in tactics, Secretary Paulson announced on November 12 that

---

[14] Greg Ip and Jon E. Hilsenrath, "How Credit Got So Easy and Why It's Tightening." *The Wall Street Journal*, August 7, 2007, pp. A1 and A7.

the government would no longer use TARP funds to buy distressed mortgage-related assets from banks, but instead it would concentrate on direct capital injections into banks. In total, $418.80 billion of the TARP funds have been disbursed. At present, repayments and income earned on investment positions total $411.51 billion. Hence, the program has been largely self-supporting.

The Aftermath

The global economic crisis is ongoing. At this stage, virtually every economic entity has experienced a downturn. Many lessons should be learned from these experiences. One lesson is that bankers seem not to scrutinize credit risk as closely when they serve only as mortgage originators and then pass it on to MBS investors rather than hold the paper themselves. As things have turned out, when the subprime mortgage crisis hit, commercial and investment banks found themselves exposed, in one fashion or another, to more mortgage debt than they realized they held. This outcome is partially a result of the repeal of the Glass-Steagall Act, which allowed commercial banks to engage in investment banking functions. As we have seen, the market has spoken with respect to investment banking as a viable business model—the bulge bracket Wall Street firms no longer exist. It remains doubtful, however, if the subprime credit crunch has taught commercial bankers a lasting lesson. As during the international debt crisis in the 1980s or the Asian crisis in the 1990s, for some reason, bankers always seem willing to lend huge amounts to borrowers with a limited potential to repay. There is no excuse for bankers not properly evaluating the potential risks of an investment or loan. In lending to a sovereign government or making loans to private parties in distant parts of the world, the risks are unique and proper analysis is warranted.

The decision to allow the CDS market to operate without supervision of the CFTC or some other regulatory agency was a serious error in judgment. CDSs are a potentially useful vehicle for offsetting credit risk, but the market is in need of more transparency with respect to OTC derivatives, and market makers need to fully understand the extent of the risk of their positions. Another lesson is that credit rating agencies need to refine their models for evaluating esoteric credit risk in securities such as MBS and CDOs and borrowers must be more wary of putting complete faith in credit ratings.

As anyone would expect, more political and regulatory scrutiny of banking operations and the functioning of financial markets was a virtual certainty in the aftermath of the crisis. In this regard, as previously mentioned, a package of enhancements known as Basel 2.5 proposed by the Basel Committee on Banking Supervision to strengthen the regulation and supervision of internationally active banks has been largely adopted. Additionally, a new accord, named Basel III, aims to strengthen the regulatory capital framework of international banks. At the country level, in the U.K., the Financial Services Act of 2012 created two new financial regulatory bodies that began operation on April 1, 2013. The Financial Policy Committee is charged with a primary objective of identifying, monitoring and taking action to remove or reduce systemic risks and the Prudential Regulation Authority is responsible for the supervision of banks, depository financial institutions, insurers, and major investment firms. In the European Union, existing supervisory architecture was replaced with a system of three European Supervisory Authorities that have been mandated to implement a single rulebook. These three authorities are the European Banking Authority, the European Securities and Markets Authority, and the European Insurance and Occupational Authority. They will operate in conjunction with the European Systemic Risk Board to regulate all financial markets, products, and institutions.

In the United States, on July 21, 2010, President Barack Obama signed into law the Dodd-Frank Wall Street Reform and Consumer Protection Act. This legislation institutes new broad financial regulations that rewrite the rules covering all aspects of finance and expands the power of the government over banking and financial markets. Such sweeping new regulation has not been seen since the Great Depression.

8. The global financial crisis began in the United States in the summer of 2007 as a credit crunch, or the inability of borrowers to easily obtain credit. The origin of the credit crunch can be traced back to three key contributing factors: liberalization of banking and securities regulation, a global savings glut, and the low interest rate environment created by the Federal Reserve in the earlier part of the decade. Low interest rates created the means for first-time homeowners to afford mortgage financing and for existing homeowners to trade up to more expensive homes. During this time, many banks and mortgage financers lowered their credit standards to attract new home buyers who could afford to make mortgage payments at current low interest rates. These so-called subprime mortgages were typically not held by the originating bank making the loan, but instead were resold for packaging into mortgage-backed securities (MBSs) to be sold to investors. As the economy cooled, many subprime borrowers found it difficult, if not impossible, to make mortgage payments, especially when their adjustable-rate mortgages were reset at higher rates. As matters unfolded, it was discovered that the amount of subprime debt held in exotic investment vehicles, and who exactly held it, was essentially unknown. When subprime debtors began defaulting on their mortgages, liquidity worldwide essentially dried up. Commercial and investment banks suffered huge losses, and many were forced into mergers with stronger banks or had to receive government bailout funds to stay in business. A deep, worldwide recession resulted. At this stage, virtually every economic entity has experienced a downtown. Many lessons should be learned from these experiences. One lesson is that bankers seem not to scrutinize credit risk as closely when they serve only as mortgage originators and then pass it on to MBS investors rather than hold the paper themselves. New banking regulations and financial regulations are currently being implemented to try and prevent or mitigate future financial crises.

KEY WORDS

affiliate bank, 268	Eurocurrency, 272	mortgage-backed
bank capital	Euronote, 279	securities (MBSs), 287
adequacy, 269	Euro Interbank Offered	negotiable certificate of
Basel Accord, 269	Rate (EURIBOR), 273	deposit (NCD), 273
Brady bonds, 284	foreign branch bank, 267	offshore banking
collateraliged debt	forward rate agreement	center, 268
obligations (CDOs), 287	(FRA), 276	representative office, 267
correspondent bank	full service bank, 265	shadow banking
relationship, 267	International Banking	system, 286
credit default swap	Facility (IBF), 269	sovereign debt crisis, 291
(CDS), 288	international debt	structured investment
debt-for-equity swap, 283	crisis, 281	vechicles (SIVs), 287
Edge Act bank, 268	less-developed countries	subsidiary bank, 268
Eurobank, 272	(LDCs), 282	syndicate, 275
Eurocommercial paper, 279	London Interbank Offered	universal bank, 265
Eurocredit, 274	Rate (LIBOR), 273	

QUESTIONS

1. Briefly discuss some of the services that international banks provide their customers and the marketplace.

2. Briefly discuss the various types of international banking offices.

3. How does the deposit-loan rate spread in the Eurodollar market compare with the deposit-loan rate spread in the domestic U.S. banking system? Why?

4. What is the difference between the Euronote market and the Eurocommercial paper market?

5. Briefly discuss the cause and the solution(s) to the international bank crisis involving less-developed countries.

6. What were the weaknesses of Basel II that became apparent during the global financial crisis that began in mid-2007?

7. Discuss the regulatory and macroeconomic factors that contributed to the credit crunch of 2007–2008.

8. How did the credit crunch become a global financial crisis?

9. What is a structured investment vehicle and what effect did they have on the credit crunch?

10. What is a collateralized debt obligation and what effect did they have on the credit crunch?

11. What is a credit default swap and what effect did they have on the credit crunch?

PROBLEMS

1. Grecian Tile Manufacturing of Athens, Georgia, borrows $1,500,000 at LIBOR plus a lending margin of 1.25 percent per annum on a six-month rollover basis from a London bank. If six-month LIBOR is 4½ percent over the first six-month interval and 5⅜ percent over the second six-month interval, how much will Grecian Tile pay in interest over the first year of its Eurodollar loan?

2. A bank sells a "three against six" $3,000,000 FRA for a three-month period beginning three months from today and ending six months from today. The purpose of the FRA is to cover the interest rate risk caused by the maturity mismatch from having made a three-month Eurodollar loan and having accepted a six-month Eurodollar deposit. The agreement rate with the buyer is 5.5 percent. There are actually 92 days in the three-month FRA period. Assume that three months from today the settlement rate is 4⅞ percent. Determine how much the FRA is worth and who pays who—the buyer pays the seller or the seller pays the buyer.

3. Assume the settlement rate in problem 2 is 6⅛ percent. What is the solution now?

4. A "three against nine" FRA has an agreement rate of 4.75 percent. You believe six-month LIBOR in three months will be 5.125 percent. You decide to take a speculative position in a FRA with a $1,000,000 notional value. There are 183 days in the FRA period. Determine whether you should buy or sell the FRA and what your expected profit will be if your forecast is correct about the six-month LIBOR rate.

5. Recall the FRA problem presented as Example 11.2. Show how the bank can alternatively use a position in Eurodollar futures contracts to hedge the interest rate risk created by the maturity mismatch it has with the $3,000,000 six-month Eurodollar deposit and rollover Eurocredit position indexed to three-month LIBOR. Assume that the bank can take a position in Eurodollar futures contracts that mature in three months and have a futures price of 94.00.

6. The Fisher effect (Chapter 6) suggests that nominal interest rates differ between countries because of differences in the respective rates of inflation. According to the Fisher effect and your examination of the one-year Eurocurrency interest rates presented in Exhibit 11.3, order the currencies from the eight countries from highest to lowest in terms of the size of the inflation premium embedded in the nominal ask interest rates for June 5, 2013.

CFA® PROBLEMS

7. George Johnson is considering a possible six-month $100 million LIBOR-based, floating-rate bank loan to fund a project at terms shown in the table below. Johnson fears a possible rise in the LIBOR rate by December and wants to use the December Eurodollar futures contract to hedge this risk. The contract expires December 20, 2009, has a US$1 million contract size, and a discount yield of 7.3 percent. Johnson will ignore the cash flow implications of marking-to-market,

3. *Tier 2 Capital*, which includes cumulative preferred shares and subordinated debt with original maturity of at least five years and loan loss provisions against presently unidentified losses.

The sum of deferred tax-assets and other specified assets can only account for a limited percentage of the total Tier 1 capital. Adequacy is evaluated against the *risk-weighted exposures*. Bank Eins' on balance sheet exposures are calculated by using the weights reported in the table below, the off balance sheet (weighted) exposures have already been estimated in CHF 184,990.

The risk-weights of assets belonging to different categories:

Cash and secure/liquid credit instruments with maturity below 1 year	0%
Debt issued by sovereigns and other qualified institutions	5%
Corporate bonds or covered bonds rated AA− or higher	20%
Highly liquid equity securities and corporate bonds rated between A− and A+	50%
Residential mortgages of any maturity	65%
Loans to retail and small business customers with maturity below 1 year	85%
Other assets	100%

Unless otherwise specified, the instruments have maturities above 1 year.

The lowest acceptable values of the capital adequacy ratios faced by Bank Eins are as follows:

$$\frac{\text{Common Equity Tier 1 Capital}}{\text{Risk-weighted exposures}} = 4.5\%,$$

$$\frac{\text{Total Tier 1 Capital}}{\text{Risk-weighted exposures}} = 6\%,$$

$$\frac{\text{Tier 1 Capital + Tier 2 Capital}}{\text{Risk-weighted exposures}} = 8\%.$$

Does Bank Eins meet the capital adequacy requirements?

REFERENCES & SUGGESTED READINGS

Acharya, Viral V., Thomas F. Cooley, Matthew P. Richardson, and Ingo Walter. *Regulating Wall Street: The Dodd-Frank Act and the New Architecture of Global Finance.* Hoboken, N.J.: John Wiley & Sons, 2011.

Bank for International Settlements. "Supervisory Lessons to Be Drawn from the Asian Crisis." Basel: Bank for International Settlements, June 1999.

Bank for International Settlements. *International Convergence of Capital Measurement and Capital Standards: A Revised Framework.* Basel: Bank for International Settlements, July 2004.

Bodie, Zvi, Alex Kane, and Alan J. Marcus. *Investments*, 9th ed. New York: McGraw-Hill/Irwin, 2011.

Dufey, Gunter, and Ian Giddy. *The International Money Market*, 2nd ed. Upper Saddle River, N.J.: Prentice Hall, 1994.

Goldberg, Lawrence G., and Robert Grosse. "Location Choice of Foreign Banks in the United States." *Journal of Economics and Business* 46 (1994), pp. 367–79.

Hultman, Charles W. *The Environment of International Banking.* Englewood Cliffs, N.J.: Prentice Hall, 1990.

International Monetary Fund. *International Capital Markets: Part II. Systemic Issues in International Finance.* Washington, D.C.: International Monetary Fund, August 1993.

International Monetary Fund. *International Capital Markets: Developments, Prospects, and Key Policy Issues.* Washington, D.C.: International Monetary Fund, September 1998.

Ip, Greg, and Jan E. Hilsenrath, "How Credit Got So Easy and Why It's Tightening," *The Wall Street Journal*, August 7, 2007, pp. A1 and A7.

Resnick, Bruce G., and Gary L. Shoesmith. "Information Transmission in the World Money Markets." *European Financial Management* 17 (2011), pp. 183–200.

Rivera-Batiz, Francisco L., and Luis Rivera-Batiz. *International Finance and Open Economy Macroeconomics*, 2nd ed. Upper Saddle River, N.J.: Prentice Hall, 1994.

Rugman, Alan M., and Shyan J. Kamath. "International Diversification and Multinational Banking." In Sarkis J. Khoury and Alo Ghosh, eds., *Recent Developments in International Banking and Finance.* Lexington, Mass.: Lexington Books, 1987.

11A Eurocurrency Creation

As an illustration, consider the following simplified example of the creation of Euro-dollars. Assume a U.S. Importer purchases $100 of merchandise from a German Exporter and pays for the purchase by drawing a $100 check on his U.S. checking account (demand deposit). Further assume the German Exporter deposits the $100 check received as payment in a demand deposit in the U.S. bank (which in actuality represents the entire U.S. commercial banking system). This transaction can be represented by T accounts, where changes in assets are on the left and changes in liabilities are on the right side of the T, as follows:

U.S. Commercial Bank		
	Demand Deposits	
	U.S. Importer	−$100
	German Exporter	+$100

At this point, all that has changed in the U.S. banking system is that ownership of $100 of demand deposits has been transferred from domestic to foreign control.

The German Exporter is not likely to leave his deposit in the form of a demand deposit for long, as no interest is being earned on this type of account. If the funds are not needed for the operation of the business, the German Exporter can deposit the $100 in a time deposit in a bank outside the United States and receive a greater rate of interest than if the funds were put in a U.S. time deposit. Assume the German Exporter closes out his demand deposit in the U.S. Bank and redeposits the funds in a London Eurobank. The London Eurobank credits the German Exporter with a $100 time deposit and deposits the $100 into its correspondent bank account (demand deposit) with the U.S. Bank (banking system). These transactions are represented as follows by T accounts:

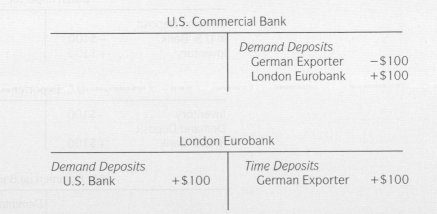

U.S. Commercial Bank		
	Demand Deposits	
	German Exporter	−$100
	London Eurobank	+$100

London Eurobank				
Demand Deposits			*Time Deposits*	
U.S. Bank	+$100		German Exporter	+$100

Two points are noteworthy from these transactions. First, ownership of $100 of demand deposits has again been transferred (from the German Exporter to the London

12 International Bond Market

THIS CHAPTER CONTINUES the discussion of international capital markets and institutions, focusing on the international bond market. The chapter is designed to be useful for the financial officer of a MNC interested in sourcing new debt capital in the international bond market, as well as for the international investor interested in international fixed-income securities.

The chapter opens with a brief statistical presentation showing the size of the world's bond markets and the major currencies in which bonds are denominated. The next section presents some useful definitions that describe exactly what is meant by the international bond market. The accompanying discussion elaborates on the features that distinguish these market segments and the various types of bond instruments traded in them. Included in the discussion is a decomposition of the international bond market by currency denomination, nationality of issuer, and the type of borrower. Trading practices in the Eurobond market are discussed next. The chapter concludes with a discussion of international bond credit ratings and bond market indexes that are useful for performance analysis.

The World's Bond Markets: A Statistical Perspective

Exhibit 12.1 presents an overview of the world's bond markets. It shows the amounts of domestic and international bonds outstanding denominated in the major currencies. The exhibit shows that at year-end 2011 the face value of bonds outstanding in the world was approximately $97,492.4 billion. Domestic bonds account for the largest share of outstanding bonds, equaling $69,912.7 billion, or 71.7 percent, of the total. The remaining $27,579.7 billion, 28.3 percent, are international bonds.

Exhibit 12.1 shows that the U.S. dollar, the euro, the pound sterling, and the yen are the four currencies in which the majority of domestic and international bonds are denominated. Proportionately more domestic bonds than international bonds are denominated in the yen (21.4 percent versus 2.7 percent) while more international bonds than domestic bonds are denominated in the dollar (41.0 percent versus 37.7 percent), the euro (42.5 percent versus 18.8 percent), and the pound sterling (7.5 percent versus 2.5 percent).

Foreign Bonds and Eurobonds

The international bond market encompasses two basic market segments: foreign bonds and Eurobonds. A **foreign bond** issue is one offered by a foreign borrower to the investors in a national capital market and denominated in that nation's currency.

EXHIBIT 12.1	Amounts of Domestic and International Bonds Outstanding (As of Year-End 2011 in Billions of U.S. Dollars)					
Currency	Domestic	Percent	International	Percent	Total	Percent
U.S. dollar	26,333.1	37.7	11,313.0	41.0	57,646.1	58.6
Euro	13,122.4	18.8	11,723.2	42.5	24,845.6	25.5
Pound sterling	1,743.8	2.5	2,061.6	7.5	3,805.4	3.9
Yen	14,952.5	21.4	758.1	2.7	15,710.6	16.1
Other	13,760.9	19.7	1,723.8	6.3	15,484.7	15.9
Total	69,912.7	100.0	27,579.7	100.0	97,492.4	100.0

Source: Derived from data in Tables 13B and 16A, pp. A119 and A124, respectively, in *International Banking and Financial Market Developments*, Bank for International Settlements, June 2012.

An example is a German MNC issuing dollar-denominated bonds to U.S. investors. A **Eurobond** issue is one denominated in a particular currency but sold to investors in national capital markets other than the country that issued the denominating currency. An example is a Dutch borrower issuing dollar-denominated bonds to investors in the U.K., Switzerland, and the Netherlands. The markets for foreign bonds and Eurobonds operate in parallel with the domestic national bond markets, and all three market groups compete with one another.[1] A "Dragon bond" market exists where non-Japanese Asian issuers sell bonds typically denominated in the U.S. dollar through Asian syndication. This market can be viewed as a segment of the Eurobond market.

Exhibit 12.2 presents the year end amounts of international bonds outstanding for 2008 through 2012. The exhibit classifies the amounts by type of issue. As the exhibit shows, the amounts of international bonds have increased steadily each year. At year-end 2008, $22,717.1 billion in bonds were outstanding; at year-end 2011 the amount was $27,579.7 billion, a 21 percent increase. A change in the compilation method by the Bank for International Settlements makes comparisons of 2012 with the earlier years difficult.

In any given year, roughly 80 percent of new international bonds are likely to be Eurobonds rather than foreign bonds. Eurobonds are known by the currency in which they are denominated, for example, U.S. dollar Eurobonds, yen Eurobonds, and Swiss franc Eurobonds, or, correspondingly, Eurodollar bonds, Euroyen bonds, and EuroSF bonds. Foreign bonds, on the other hand, frequently have colorful names that designate the country in which they are issued. For example, *Yankee* bonds are dollar–denominated foreign bonds originally sold to U.S. investors, *Samurai* bonds are yen-denominated foreign bonds sold in Japan, and *Bulldogs* are pound sterling–denominated foreign bonds sold in the U.K.

Bearer Bonds and Registered Bonds

Eurobonds are usually bearer bonds. With a **bearer bond**, possession is evidence of ownership. The issuer does not keep any records indicating who is the current owner of a bond. With **registered bonds**, the owner's name is on the bond and it is also recorded by the issuer, or else the owner's name is assigned to a bond serial number recorded by the issuer. When a registered bond is sold, a new bond certificate is issued with the new owner's name, or the new owner's name is assigned to the bond serial number.

U.S. security regulations require Yankee bonds and U.S. corporate bonds sold to U.S. citizens to be registered. Bearer bonds are very attractive to investors desiring privacy and anonymity. One reason for this is that they enable tax evasion. Consequently, investors will generally accept a lower yield on bearer bonds than on registered bonds of comparable terms, making them a less costly source of funds for the issuer to service.

---

[1]In this chapter the terms *market segment, market group,* and *market* are used interchangeably when referring to the foreign bond and Eurobond divisions of the international bond market.

EXHIBIT 12.2	**2008**	**2009**	**2010**	**2011**	**2012**
International Bond Amounts Outstanding Classified by Major Instruments (At Year-End in Billions of U.S. Dollars)	*Instrument*				
	Straight fixed-rate				
	14,428.4	17,274.2	18,406.3	19,404.5	14,770.0
	Floating-rate notes 7,892.0	8,357.2	7,892.6	7,687.9	5,990.7
	Convertible issues 391.5	442.9	481.8	485.2	319.6
	With equity warrants 5.2	4.2	4.2	2.2	0.9
	Total 22,717.1	26,078.5	26,783.9	27,579.7	21,081.2

Source: Derived from *International Banking and Financial Market Developments,* Bank for International Settlements, Table 13B, p. A109, June 2010, p. A113, June 2012, and p. A151, June 2013. The compilation methodology changed in December 2012, making the statistics for 2012 not directly comparable to the earlier years.

National Security Regulations

Foreign bonds must meet the security regulations of the country in which they are issued. This means that publicly traded Yankee bonds must meet the same regulations as U.S. domestic bonds. The U.S. Securities Act of 1933 requires full disclosure of relevant information relating to a security issue. The U.S. Securities Exchange Act of 1934 established the Securities and Exchange Commission (SEC) to administer the 1933 Act. According to the 1933 Act, securities sold in the United States to public investors must be registered with the SEC, and a prospectus disclosing detailed financial information about the issuer must be provided and made available to prospective investors. The expense of the registration process, the time delay it creates in bringing a new issue to market (four additional weeks), and the disclosure of information that many foreign borrowers consider private have historically made it more desirable for foreign borrowers to raise U.S. dollars in the Eurobond market, which, in general, is not subject to registration under the 1933 Act. The shorter length of time in bringing a Eurodollar bond issue to market, coupled with the lower rate of interest that borrowers pay for Eurodollar bond financing in comparison to Yankee bond financing, are two major reasons why the Eurobond segment of the international bond market is roughly four times the size of the foreign bond segment. Because Eurobonds do not have to meet national security regulations, name recognition of the issuer is an extremely important factor in being able to source funds in the international capital market.

Transactional restrictions prohibit offers and sales of Eurobonds in the United States or to U.S. investors during a 40-day restriction period that allows for the security to become seasoned in the secondary market. The purpose of the restriction period is to protect U.S. investors from investing in unregistered bonds where little investment information is known until "the market" has had the opportunity to evaluate them rather than to prevent U.S. investors from investing in bearer bonds which may facilitate tax avoidance or evasion through the bearer feature.

Withholding Taxes

Prior to 1984, the United States required a 30 percent withholding tax on interest paid to nonresidents who held U.S. government or corporate bonds. Moreover, U.S. firms issuing Eurodollar bonds from the United States were required to withhold the tax on interest paid to foreigners. In 1984, the withholding tax law was repealed. Additionally, U.S. corporations were allowed to issue domestic bearer bonds to nonresidents, but Congress would not grant this privilege to the Treasury.

The repeal of the withholding tax law caused a substantial shift in the relative yields on U.S. government and Eurodollar bonds. Prior to 1984, top-quality Eurodollar bonds sold overseas traded at lower yields than U.S. Treasury bonds of similar maturities that were subject to the withholding tax. Afterward the situation was reversed; foreign investors found the safety of registered U.S. Treasury bonds without the withholding tax more attractive than higher yields on corporate Eurodollar bond issues.

Security Regulations that Ease Bond Issuance

Two other U.S. security regulations have had an effect on the international bond market. One is *Rule 415,* which the SEC instituted in 1982 to allow shelf registration. **Shelf registration** allows an issuer to preregister a securities issue, and then shelve the securities for later sale when financing is actually needed. Shelf registration has thus eliminated the time delay in bringing a foreign bond issue to market in the United States, but it has not eliminated the information disclosure that many foreign borrowers find too expensive and/or objectionable. In 1990, the SEC instituted *Rule 144A*, which allows *qualified institutional buyers (QIBs)* in the United States to trade in private placement issues that do not have to meet the strict information disclosure requirements of publicly traded issues. Rule 144A was designed to make the U.S. capital markets more competitive with the Eurobond market. Rule 144A issues are non-registered and may only trade among QIBs. A large portion of the 144A market is composed of Yankee bonds. The International Finance in Practice box, "SOX and Bonds," discusses how international companies are starting to prefer issuing Yankee bonds in the private placement market in the United States to avoid costly information disclosure required of registered bonds by the Sarbanes-Oxley Act.

Global Bonds

Global bond issues were first offered in 1989. A **global bond** issue is a very large bond issue that would be difficult to sell in any one country or region of the world. Consequently, it is simultaneously sold and subsequently traded in major markets worldwide. Global bonds are fully fungible because the identical instrument trades in all markets without restriction. The average size of global bond issues has been about one billion dollars. Most have been denominated in the U.S. dollar. The portion of a U.S. dollar global bond sold by a U.S. (foreign) borrower in the United States is classified as a domestic (Yankee) bond and the portion sold elsewhere is a Eurodollar bond. If the larger issue size and the worldwide marketability of a global bond issue enhances its liquidity, investors might, ceteris paribus, be willing to accept a lower yield than they would require from smaller issues of domestic, foreign or Eurobonds. This does not appear to be the case, however. In a recent study, Resnick (2012) shows that, ceteris paribus, investors demand an equivalent yield from dollar denominated domestic, Yankee, Eurodollar, and global bonds. Hence, global bond investors demand a competitive yield with other bond market segments. On the other hand, Resnick does find that the gross underwriting spread, a common measure of the costs of bond issuance paid to underwriters, is, ceteris paribus, lower for a global issue in comparison to smaller domestic, Yankee, or Eurodollar bond issues. These cost savings are attributed entirely to economies of scale that result from the large size of the global issue. Miller and Puthenpurackal (2005) also document a cost savings from issuing global bonds. The largest corporate global bond issue to date is the $14.6 billion Deutsche Telekom multicurrency offering. The issue includes three U.S. dollar tranches with 5-, 10-, and 30-year maturities totaling $9.5 billion, two euro tranches with 5- and 10-year maturities totaling €3 billion, two British pound sterling tranches with 5- and 30-year maturities totaling £950 million, and one 5-year Japanese yen tranche of ¥90 billion. Another large global bond issue is the AT&T package of $2 billion of 5.625 percent notes due 2004, $3 billion of 6.000 percent notes due 2009, and $3 billion of 6.500 percent notes due 2029 issued in March 1999. The Republic of Italy issued one of the largest sovereign global bond issues in September 1993, a package of $2 billion of 6.000 percent notes due 2003 and $3.5 billion of 6.875 percent debentures due 2023. One of the largest emerging markets global bond issues to date is the Republic of Korea package issued April 1998 of $1 billion of 8.750 percent notes due 2003 and $3 billion of 8.875 percent bonds due 2008. SEC Rule 415 and Rule 144A have likely facilitated global bond offerings, and more offerings in the future can be expected.

Types of Instruments

The international bond market has been much more innovative than the domestic bond market in the types of instruments offered to investors. In this section, we examine the major types of international bonds. We begin with a discussion of the more standard types of instruments and conclude with the more exotic innovations that have appeared in recent years.

SOX and Bonds

The Sarbanes-Oxley Act (SOX) of 2002 is the U.S. law designed to eliminate corporate fraud. SOX was named for Michael Oxley, the former House Financial Services Committee Chairman, and former Maryland Democratic Senator Paul Sarbanes of Maryland. It was passed after the collapse of Enron and WorldCom.

A recent article by Bloomberg News* reports that its existence is prompting more companies to issue unregistered bonds. "At least 100 . . . companies are selling bonds that aren't registered with the Securities and Exchange Commission instead of debt that requires more disclosure." The sale of unregistered bonds " . . . increased 50 percent in the past two years, five times faster than the rest of the U.S. market."

According to Bloomberg News, private bond placements are surging because companies face little penalty for keeping their finances away from the public. Investors demand only 11 basis points more in yield to buy unregistered securities, whereas it costs millions of dollars to comply with the Sarbanes-Oxley.

SOX compliance costs can easily erase any yield savings from issuing public debt. SOX requires companies to hire external auditors to evaluate their financial reports. The law also applies to foreign borrowers desiring to sell so-called Yankee bonds to the American public. According to Bloomberg News, "international companies that used to sell public debt in the U.S. are staying away to avoid Sarbanes-Oxley."

SOX is consistent with attempts to make the bond market more transparent. Unregistered bonds can only trade between institutions. These trades are not reported on the NASD's Trade Reporting and Compliance Engine.

However, according to Bloomberg News, investors are willing to trade more yield for additional documentation or registration requirements. The market value of unregistered bonds has risen 28 percent a year since 2004, compared with only a 5 percent increase for all corporate debt.

Sellers of unregistered bonds need only to disclose information to owners of their securities. According to Bloomberg News, companies selling unregistered bonds include closely held issuers that have traditionally used private placements to borrow.

For example, "Cargill Inc., the largest U.S. agricultural company, has at least $8.3 billion in unregistered securities. The closely held company only sells debt in private placements or through an SEC exemption known as Rule 144a." A Cargill spokesperson notes "'we have access to a limited pool of investors because we're not selling registered debt. We pay a slightly higher interest rate, and our disclosure goes only to those *qualified institutional buyers* that purchase the debt.'"

*Mark Pittman, "Sarbanes-Oxley Backfires in Unregistered Bond Sales," Bloomberg News, February 14, 2007.

Straight Fixed-Rate Issues

Straight fixed-rate bond issues have a designated maturity date at which the principal of the bond issue is promised to be repaid. During the life of the bond, fixed coupon payments, which are a percentage of the face value, are paid as interest to the bondholders. In contrast to many domestic bonds, which make semiannual coupon payments, coupon interest on Eurobonds is typically paid annually. The reason is that the Eurobonds are usually bearer bonds, and annual coupon redemption is more convenient for the bondholders and less costly for the bond issuer because the bondholders are scattered geographically. Exhibit 12.2 shows that the vast majority of new international bond offerings in any year are straight fixed-rate issues. The euro, U.S. dollar, British pound sterling, and Japanese yen have been the most common currencies denominating straight fixed-rate bonds in recent years.

Euro-Medium-Term Notes

Euro-Medium-Term Notes (Euro-MTNs) are (typically) fixed-rate notes issued by a corporation with maturities ranging from less than a year to about 10 years. Like fixed-rate bonds, Euro-MTNs have a fixed maturity and pay coupon interest on periodic dates. Unlike a bond issue, in which the entire issue is brought to market at once, a Euro-MTN issue is partially sold on a continuous basis through an issuance facility that allows the borrower to obtain funds only as needed on a flexible basis. This feature is very attractive to issuers. Euro-MTNs have become a very popular means of raising medium-term funds since they were first introduced in 1986. All the statistical exhibits in this chapter include the amounts outstanding of MTNs.

An example of straight fixed-rate Euro-MTNs is the $600,000,000 of 5.15 percent notes due January 2013, issued in December 2007 by BT Group Plc of the United Kingdom.

and Polfliet (2002) report that approxi
AAA and 30 percent are AA. One exp
ratings invoke their publication rights
nation. Kim and Stulz (1988) sugges
likely. That is, the Eurobond market is
ratings and name recognition to begin
is beneficial to know about the ratings
bond issues.

Gande and Parsley (2005) study cro
ining changes in foreign U.S. dollar
(i.e., sovereign yield above comparal
ings events abroad. They find an asyn
ratings events in one country have no
tries; however, negative ratings events
spreads. On average, a one-notch dow
a 12 basis point increase in spreads
attribute the spillover among countrie
trade flows.

Exhibit 12.6 presents a guide to
sovereigns, municipalities, corporatio
Exhibit 12.5, sovereigns issue a sizable
sovereign government, S&P's analysis
profiled in Exhibit 12.7. The rating ass
because it frequently represents the ceili
of an entity domiciled within that count

Eurobond Market Structure and Practices

Given that in any year the Eurobond seg
for approximately 80 percent of new
about the Eurobond market structure and

Primary Market

A borrower desiring to raise funds by i
contact an investment banker and ask it
ing syndicate that will bring the bonds
group of investment banks, merchant b
mercial banks that specialize in some p
will sometimes invite comanagers to for
with the borrower, ascertain market conc
provides the 2011 and 2012 rankings f
bonds and other debt products. Ranking
(based on service to clients) and by curr

The managing group, along with o
the issue, that is, they will commit th
borrower at a discount from the issue pr
is typically in the 2 to 2.5 percent range
1 percent for domestic issues. Most of th
be part of a **selling group** that sells the
members of the underwriting syndicate
on the number and type of functions the
receive the full spread, but a bank serv
will receive a smaller portion. The tota
borrower to issue Eurobonds until the
typically five to six weeks. Exhibit 12.

Floating-Rate Notes

The first floating-rate notes were introduced in 1970. **Floating-rate notes (FRNs)** are typically medium-term bonds with coupon payments indexed to some reference rate. Common reference rates are either three-month or six-month U.S. dollar LIBOR. Coupon payments on FRNs are usually quarterly or semiannual and in accord with the reference rate. For example, consider a five-year FRN with coupons referenced to six-month dollar LIBOR paying coupon interest semiannually. At the beginning of every six-month period, the next semiannual coupon payment is *reset* to be $.5 \times (\text{LIBOR} + X \text{ percent})$ of face value, where X represents the default risk premium above LIBOR the issuer must pay based on its creditworthiness. The premium is typically no larger than 1/8 percent for top-quality issuers. As an example, if X equals 1/8 percent and the current six-month LIBOR is 6.6 percent, the next period's coupon rate on a $1,000 face value FRN will be $.5 \times (.066 + .00125) \times \$1,000 = \$33.625$. If on the next reset date six-month LIBOR is 5.7 percent, the following semiannual coupon will be set at $29.125.

Obviously, FRNs behave differently in response to interest rate risk than straight fixed-rate bonds. All bonds experience an inverse price change when the market rate of interest changes. Accordingly, the price of straight fixed-rate bonds may vary significantly if interest rates are extremely volatile. FRNs, on the other hand, experience only mild price changes between reset dates, over which time the next period's coupon payment is fixed (assuming, of course, that the reference rate corresponds to the market rate applicable to the issuer). On the reset date, the market price will gravitate back close to par value when the next period's coupon payment is reset to the new market value of the reference rate, and subsequent coupon payments are repriced to market expectations of future values of the reference rate. (The actual FRN market price may deviate somewhat from exact par value because the default risk premium portion of the coupon payment is fixed at inception, whereas the credit quality of the borrower may change through time.) FRNs make attractive investments for investors with a strong need to preserve the principal value of the investment should they need to liquidate the investment prior to the maturity of the bonds. Exhibit 12.2 shows that FRNs are the second most common type of international bond issue. The euro and the U.S. dollar are the two currencies denominating most outstanding FRNs.

As an example of fixed/FRNs, in May 2006 General Electric Capital Corporation issued $500,000 of four-year notes with interest paid at the fixed rate of 5.464 percent the first year and indexed to three-month LIBOR plus 6 basis points the last three years.

Equity-Related Bonds

There are two types of **equity-related bonds**: convertible bonds and bonds with equity warrants. A **convertible bond** issue allows the investor to exchange the bond for a predetermined number of equity shares of the issuer. The *floor-value* of a convertible bond is its straight fixed-rate bond value. Convertibles usually sell at a premium above the larger of their straight debt value and their conversion value. Additionally, investors are usually willing to accept a lower coupon rate of interest than the comparable straight fixed coupon bond rate because they find the conversion feature attractive. **Bonds with equity warrants** can be viewed as straight fixed-rate bonds with the addition of a call option (or warrant) feature. The warrant entitles the bondholder to purchase a certain number of equity shares in the issuer at a prestated price over a predetermined period of time.

Dual-Currency Bonds

Dual-currency bonds became popular in the mid-1980s. A **dual-currency bond** is a straight fixed-rate bond issued in one currency, say, Swiss francs, that pays coupon interest in that same currency. At maturity, the principal is repaid in another currency, say, U.S. dollars. Coupon interest is frequently at a higher rate than comparable straight fixed-rate bonds. The amount of the dollar principal repayment at maturity is set at inception; frequently, the amount allows for some appreciation in the exchange rate of the stronger currency. From the investor's perspective, a dual-currency bond

INTERNATIONAL FINAN[...]

Heineken Refreshes Euromarket with Spectacular Unrated Bonds

Heineken launched the euro market's largest unrated bond this week with a spectacular two tranche Eu1.1bn debut transaction. The deal, in 6- and 10-year tranches, was more than four times oversubscribed and priced well inside price guidance. Heineken's success demonstrates the depth of demand for unrated credits in the Eurobond market, despite the growing prevalence of ratings and well publicized investor calls for borrowers to have at least two ratings. The major factor in Heineken's favour was the global reach of its brand—the brewer has operations in over 170 countries.

The 10-year bond—the first from an unrated corporate—was five times oversubscribed, enabling bookrunners Barclays Capital, Citigroup, Credit Suisse First Boston and JP Morgan to increase it from Eu500m to Eu600m. "There was no clear guidance in the market about what we could achieve for Heineken or where they could be positioned as a credit—we had to convince people," said Chris Tuffey, head of corporate syndicate at CSFB in London. "Unrated issues are typically tough to sell investors on, but the Heineken transaction was exactly the opposite—both tranches were heavily oversubscribed." Although the lead managers looked at brand names such as Louis Vuitton Moet Hennessy, McDonald's and Carlsberg in pricing the transaction, the price was decided by investors' perception of the credit. Heineken was priced as a single-A credit, although it paid a small premium for the absence of a rating.

Rene Hooft Graafland, a member of Heineken's executive board, said the Heineken family retains a controlling interest in the company and maintains a very conservative approach in running it. He said the diversity of the company's cashflows and profit sources made Heineken an attractive credit. Explaining why Heineken is not rated, Hooft Graafland said the bond was a one-off issue to partially finance the Eu1.9bn acquisition of Brau-Beteiligung AG, Austria's largest brewer, which was completed on October 15. Heineken does not intend

to become a [...]
obtain a rating [...]
indications tha[...]
the Heineken [...]
Graafland. "Th[...]
straightforwar[...]
way the compa[...]

The acquisi[...]
regional player[...]
share of 27%. [...]
concerned by [...]
the possibility t[...]
to the compar[...]
tackled by ma[...]
successfully so,[...]

The reason [...]
concentrated i[...]
the holding co[...]
effective under[...]
last month. "H[...]
level is modes[...]
three big oper[...]
"In addition t[...]
bond has a cov[...]
indebtedness a[...]
assets." The m[...]
Switzerland tak[...]
and the Benelu[...]
bid for the sh[...]
agers and insu[...]
respectively. Uk[...]
in the 2013s, [...]
accounts with [...]
took 10%. Fund[...]
of the book, th[...]
ance companie[...]

Source: Excerpted [...]

Standard & Poor's rates bond issues (and [...] ers, the categories are AAA, AA, A, BBB, [...] Categories AAA to BBB are investment gr[...] regulatory supervision owing to its financial [...] failed to pay one or more of its financial obli[...] AA to CCC may be modified with a plus (+) [...] ing of an issue to others in the category. Fi[...] similar to S&P's.

It has been noted that a disproportionate [...] ings in comparison to domestic and foreign [...]

EXHIBIT 12.8

Ranking of Top International Bond and Debt Product Underwriters

Overall		
2012	2011	Bank
1	5	Barclays
2	4	Deutsche Bank
3	1	HSBC
4	7	Société Générale
5	2	JPMorgan
6	6	RBS
7	5	BNP Paribas
8	9	Citi
9	8	Bank of America Merrill Lynch
10	10	Credit Agricole CIB
11	13	Morgan Stanley
12	11	Credit Suisse
13	16	UBS
14	12	Goldman Sachs
15	15	Commerzbank

Best by Currency ($ Issues)		
2012	2011	Bank
1	1	JPMorgan
2	2	Citi
3	3	Bank of America Merrill Lynch
4	4	HSBC
5	9	Barclays

Best by Currency (Sterling Issues)		
2012	2011	Bank
1	1	RBS
2	2	Barclays
3	3	HSBC
4	6	Deutsche Bank
5	13	JPMorgan

Best by Currency (Euro Issues)		
2012	2011	Bank
1	1	Deutsche Bank
2	3	Société Générale
3	2	BNP Paribas
4	7	Barclays
5	4	HSBC

Best by Currency (Yen Issues)		
2012	2011	Bank
1	1	Nomura
2	2	Mitsubishi UFJ
3	3	Mizuho
4	4	Daiwa Securities
5	7	HSBC

continued

EXHIBIT 12.8

Ranking of Top
International Bond
and Debt Product
Underwriters (continued)

Best by Currency (Noncore Currencies)		
2012	2011	Bank
1	1	HSBC
2	3	Citi
3	7	Deutsche Bank
4	4	JPMorgan
5	14	Barclays

Source. *Euromoney*, June 2012.

EXHIBIT 12.9

Eurobond Tombstone

This announcement appears as a matter of record only

Hamburgische Landesbank

Hamburgische Landesbank – Girozentrale –
(incorporated as a credit institution under public law in the Federal Republic of Germany)

Hamburgische Landesbank London Branch
Hamburgische LB Finance (Guernsey) Limited
(incorporated in Guernsey)

U.S.$2,000,000,000

Euro Medium Term Note Programme

Guaranteed in respect of Notes issued by
Hamburgische LB Finance (Guernsey) Limited by
Hamburgische Landesbank – Girozentrale –

The Programme is rated Aa1 by Moody's and AAA by Fitch IBCA

NOW RATED Aa1 BY MOODY'S

Arrangers

Merrill Lynch International

Merrill Lynch Capital Markets Bank Limited,
Frankfurt/Main Branch

Merrill Lynch Finance SA

Dealers

Credit Suisse First Boston
Hamburgische Landesbank – Girozentrale –
Merrill Lynch International
Morgan Stanley Dean Witter
Salomon Smith Barney

Deutsche Morgan Grenfell
Merrill Lynch Finance SA
J.P. Morgan Securities Ltd.
Nomura International
Warburg Dillon Read

Source: *Euromoney*, January 1999, p. 11.

International Government Bond Market Data Provided Daily in the Financial Times

| EXHIBIT 12.11 | |

BENCHMARK GOVERNMENT BONDS

Jun 5	Redemption Date	Coupon	Bid Price	Bid Yield	Day Chg Yield	Wk Chg Yield	Month Chg Yld	Year Chg Yld
Australia	04/15	6.25	106.70	2.51	−0.07	−0.08	−0.08	0.37
	04/23	5.50	117.76	3.37	−0.05	−0.03	0.23	0.54
Austria	07/15	3.50	106.85	0.22	0.01	0.05	0.13	−0.20
	10/23	1.75	98.58	1.90	−0.02	0.04	0.25	−0.13
Belgium	03/15	3.50	105.77	0.28	0.02	0.10	0.17	0.53
	06/23	2.25	100.08	2.24	−0.01	0.08	0.29	−0.72
Canada	05/15	1.00	99.89	1.06	−0.02	−0.01	0.09	0.10
	06/23	1.50	94.01	2.07	0.01	0.01	0.50	0.58
Denmark	11/16	2.50	107.62	0.27	0.01	0.06	0.16	0.41
	11/23	1.50	98.90	1.62	−0.04	0.06	0.26	0.60
Finland	07/15	4.25	108.36	0.19	−0.01	0.06	0.12	−0.01
	04/23	1.50	97.67	1.76	0.00	0.05	0.27	0.28
France	04/15	3.50	106.12	0.22	0.01	0.06	0.13	−0.11
	05/18	1.00	100.38	0.92	−0.01	0.09	0.22	−0.27
	05/23	1.75	97.23	2.06	−0.03	0.05	0.35	−0.22
	04/41	4.50	126.13	3.09	−0.02	0.05	0.26	0.07
Germany	06/15		99.78	0.11	0.01	0.05	0.11	0.10
	04/18	0.25	98.62	0.54	0.01	0.04	0.21	0.18
	05/23	1.50	99.81	1.52	0.00	0.02	0.28	0.31
	07/44	2.50	102.56	2.38	−0.01	0.00	0.22	0.68
Greece	02/23	2.00	60.98	9.25	−0.14	0.58	−0.95	−20.75
	02/33	2.00	50.43	8.78	−0.22	0.09	−0.70	−16.66
Ireland	10/17	5.50	112.33	2.48	0.04	0.32	0.23	−4.84
	03/23	3.90	100.44	3.84	−0.04	0.36	0.39	−3.59
Italy	06/15	3.00	102.73	1.62	−0.07	0.03	0.35	−2.72
	06/18	3.50	102.38	3.00	−0.05	0.09	0.26	−2.20
	05/23	4.50	103.47	4.11	−0.05	0.09	0.30	−1.56
	09/40	5.00	102.91	4.86	−0.01	0.08	0.24	−1.21
Japan	06/15	0.20	100.15	0.13	−0.01	−0.01	0.01	0.02
	03/18	0.40	100.50	0.30	−0.01	−0.11	0.08	0.09
	06/23	0.80	99.42	0.86	0.05	−0.05	0.29	0.04
	03/33	1.60	98.69	1.69	0.09	−0.01	0.22	0.04
Netherlands	01/15	2.75	104.14	0.16	0.01	0.05	0.10	0.00
	07/23	1.75	98.98	1.86	0.01	0.05	0.27	0.29
New Zealand	04/15	6.00	106.00	2.65	0.05	0.07	0.18	0.50
	04/23	5.50	115.18	3.65	0.05	0.13	0.47	0.33
Norway	05/17	4.25	110.05	1.60	0.06	0.23	0.34	0.23
	05/23	2.00	97.52	2.28	0.00	0.12	0.26	0.39
Portugal	10/14	3.60	100.92	2.88	−0.05	0.29	0.29	−8.09
	10/23	4.95	93.48	5.80	−0.02	0.39	0.30	−6.17
Spain	03/15	2.75	101.45	1.92	−0.05	0.09	0.39	−2.99
	01/23	5.40	107.53	4.42	−0.06	0.12	0.39	−1.98
Sweden	08/15	4.50	107.65	0.92	−0.04	0.09	0.11	0.21
	11/23	1.50	95.75	1.95	0.00	0.09	0.28	0.81
Switzerland	06/15	3.75	107.45	0.02	0.02	0.09	0.09	0.25
	02/23	4.00	129.48	0.82	0.07	0.14	0.25	0.28
UK	03/14	2.25	101.40	0.38	0.00	0.02	0.10	0.05
	07/18	1.25	100.85	1.08	0.01	0.20	0.36	0.45
	09/22	1.75	97.76	2.02	0.00	0.07	0.27	0.48
	01/44	3.25	97.53	3.38	0.01	0.15	0.35	0.52
US	05/15	0.25	99.91	0.29	0.00	0.01	0.07	0.04
	05/18	1.00	99.88	1.02	0.00	0.03	0.30	0.35
	05/23	1.75	96.78	2.11	−0.02	−0.03	0.37	0.59
	05/43	2.88	92.31	3.28	0.01	−0.01	0.32	0.71

London close.

Yields: Local market standard Annualised yield basis. Yields shown for Italy exclude withholding tax at 12.5 percent payable by nonresidents.

Source: *Financial Times*, June 6, 2013, p. 19.

CHAPTER 1

MINI CASE

REFERENCES & SUGGESTED READINGS

SUMMARY

This chapter introduces and discusses the international bond market. The chapter presents a statistical perspective of the market, noting its size, an analysis of the market segments, the types of instruments issued, the major currencies used to denominate international bonds, and the major borrowers by nationality and type. Trading practices of the Eurobond market are examined, as are credit ratings for international bonds and international bond market indexes.

1. At year-end 2011, there were $69.9 trillion in domestic bonds outstanding and $27.6 trillion in international bonds. The four major currencies that are used to denominate bonds are the euro, U.S. dollar, British pound sterling, and Japanese yen.

2. A foreign bond issue is one offered by a foreign borrower to investors in a national capital market and denominated in that nation's currency. A Eurobond issue is one denominated in a particular currency but sold to investors in national capital markets other than the country that issues the denominating currency.

3. The Eurobond segment of the international bond market is roughly four times the size of the foreign bond segment. The two major reasons for this stem from the fact that the U.S. dollar is the currency most frequently sought in international bond financing. First, Eurodollar bonds can be brought to market more quickly than Yankee bonds because they are not offered to U.S. investors and thus do not have to meet the strict SEC registration requirements. Second, Eurobonds are typically bearer bonds that provide anonymity to the owner and thus allow a means for avoiding taxes on the interest received. Because of this feature, investors are generally willing to accept a lower yield on Eurodollar bonds in comparison to registered Yankee bonds of comparable terms, where ownership is recorded. For borrowers, the lower yield means a lower cost of debt service.

4. Straight fixed-rate bonds are the most frequent type of international bond issue, and floating-rate notes are the second. Other types of issues found in the international bond market are convertible bonds, bonds with equity warrants, and dual-currency bonds.

5. Fitch Ratings, Moody's Investors Service, and Standard & Poor's provide credit ratings on most international bond issues. It has been noted that a disproportionate share of Eurobonds have high credit ratings. The evidence suggests that a logical reason for this is that the Eurobond market is accessible only to firms that have good credit ratings to begin with. An entity's credit rating is usually never higher than the rating assigned to the sovereign government of the country in which it resides. S&P's analysis of a sovereign includes an examination of political risk and economic risk.

6. New Eurobond issues are offered in the primary market through an underwriting syndicate hired by the borrower to bring the bonds to market. The secondary market for Eurobonds is an over-the-counter arrangement with principal trading done in London.

7. The investment banking firm of J.P. Morgan and Company provides some of the best international bond market indexes that are frequently used for performance evaluations. J.P. Morgan publishes Developed Markets Indexes, Emerging Markets Indexes, and a Global Aggregate Bond Index.

KEY WORDS

CHAPTER
13 International Equity Markets

THIS CHAPTER FOCUSES on equity markets, or how ownership in publicly owned corporations is traded throughout the world. It discusses both the *primary* sale of new common stock by corporations to initial investors and how previously issued common stock is traded between investors in the *secondary* markets. This chapter is useful for understanding how companies source new equity capital and provides useful institutional information for investors interested in diversifying their portfolio internationally.

The chapter begins with an overview of the world's equity markets. Statistics are provided that show the comparative sizes and trading opportunities in various secondary equity marketplaces in both developed and developing countries. Differences in market structures are also explored, and comparative transaction costs of equity trading are presented. Following this, the discussion moves to the benefits of multiple listing of a corporation's stock on more than one national stock exchange. The related issue of sourcing new equity capital from primary investors in more than the home national market is also examined. The chapter concludes with a discussion of the factors that affect equity valuation. An examination of the historical market performances and the risks of investing in foreign national equity markets is not presented here, but rather in Chapter 15, where a strong case is made for international diversification of investment funds.

A Statistical Perspective

Before we can intelligently discuss international equity markets, it is helpful to understand where the major national equity markets are located, some information about their relative sizes, and the opportunities for trading and ownership. This section provides these background data, along with a statistical summary of emerging equity markets in Eastern Europe, the Middle East, Africa, Latin America, and Asia.

Market Capitalization of Developed Countries

At year-end 2012, total market capitalization of the world's equity markets stood at $53,164 billion. Of this amount, 75 percent is accounted for by the market capitalization of the major equity markets from 31 developed countries. Exhibit 13.1 shows the market capitalizations for these 31 developed countries for 2008 through 2012. As the exhibit indicates, their total market capitalization increased nearly 51 percent over the five-year period, from $26,534 billion to $40,016 billion. This increase is a result of countries recovering from the global financial crisis.

The change in market capitalization was somewhat unevenly spread among the developed countries. For example, the United States registered an increase of 59 percent over the five-year period, whereas the increase in European markets was only 38 percent. The Far East registered a 43 percent increase.

QUESTIONS

PROBLEMS

INTERNET EXERCISES

EXHIBIT 13.1

Market Capitalization of Equity Markets in Developed Countries (in Billions of U.S. Dollars)

Region or Country	2008	2009	2010	2011	2012
Europe	8,362	10,842	11,879	10,391	11,580
Austria	72	54	68	82	106
Belgium	167	261	269	230	300
Cyprus	8	5	7	3	2
Denmark	132	187	232	180	225
Finland	154	91	118	143	159
France	1,492	1,972	1,926	1,569	1,823
Germany	1,108	1,298	1,430	1,184	1,486
Greece	90	55	73	34	45
Iceland	6	1	2	2	3
Ireland	49	30	34	108	109
Israel	–	–	218	145	148
Italy	521	317	318	431	480
Luxembourg	66	106	101	68	70
Netherlands	388	543	661	595	651
Norway	126	227	251	219	253
Portugal	69	99	82	62	66
Spain	946	1,297	1,172	1,031	995
Sweden	253	432	581	470	561
Switzerland	863	1,071	1,229	932	1,079
United Kingdom	1,852	2,796	3,107	2,903	3,019
Far East	5,429	7,306	8,130	7,003	7,749
Australia	676	1,258	1,455	1,198	1,286
Hong Kong	1,329	2,292	1,080	890	1,108
Japan	3,220	3,378	4,100	3,541	3,681
Korea	–	–	1,089	994	1,180
New Zealand	24	67	36	72	80
Singapore	180	311	370	308	414
Atlantic	3	2	2	2	1
Bermuda	2	1	2	1	1
Cayman Islands	< 1	< 1	–	–	–
St. Kitts and Nevis	< 1	< 1	< 1	< 1	–
North America	12,740	16,758	19,299	17,548	20,684
Canada	1,002	1,681	2,160	1,907	2,016
United States	11,738	15,077	17,139	15,641	18,668
Total Developed Markets[a]	26,534	34,907	39,310	34,943	40,016

[a]Column total may not sum due to rounding error.

Source: Various issues of *Global Stock Markets Factbook,* Standard & Poor's, Israel and Korea became classified as developed markets in 2012.

Market Capitalization of Developing Countries

Exhibit 13.2 presents the market capitalization of 37 emerging secondary equity markets from developing countries for 2008 through 2012. In general, Standard & Poor's Emerging Markets Data Base classifies a stock market as "emerging" if it meets at least one of two general criteria: (i) it is located in a low- or middle-income economy as defined by the World Bank, and/or (ii) its investable market capitalization is low relative to its most recent GNI figures.

Exhibit 13.2 indicates that the majority of emerging markets have grown significantly over the five-year period. The 2012 market capitalizations indicate that presently there are several tiny national equity markets in Latin America, Europe, the Middle East, and Africa. However, many of the national equity markets in Latin America (principally Brazil and Mexico) and in Asia (China, India, and Taiwan) have market capitalizations far in excess of the size of some of the smaller equity markets in the developed countries presented in Exhibit 13.1. This is indicative of investment opportunities in these emerging national markets.

EXHIBIT 13.2

Market Capitalization of Equity Markets in Selected Developing Countries (in Billions of U.S. Dollars)

Region or Country	2008	2009	2010	2011	2012
Latin America					
Argentina	52	49	64	44	34
Brazil	589	1,167	1,546	1,229	1,230
Chile	132	209	342	270	313
Colombia	87	133	209	201	262
Mexico	233	341	454	409	525
Peru	56	70	100	79	97
Asia					
China	2,794	5,008	4,763	3,389	3,697
India	645	1,179	1,616	1,015	4,263
Indonesia	99	178	360	390	397
Korea	495	836	–	–	–
Malaysia	187	256	441	395	476
Pakistan	23	33	38	33	44
Philippines	52	80	157	165	264
Sri Lanka	4	8	20	19	17
Taiwan	381	696	804	623	712
Thailand	103	138	278	268	383
Europe					
Croatia	27	26	25	22	22
Czech Republic	49	53	43	38	37
Hungary	19	28	28	19	21
Poland	90	135	190	138	178
Russia	397	861	1,005	796	875
Slovak Republic	5	5	4	5	5
Turkey	118	226	307	202	309
Ukraine	24	17	39	26	21
Mideast/Africa					
Bahrain	21	17	20	17	16
Egypt	86	90	82	49	58
Iran	49	63	87	107	141
Israel	134	182	–	–	–
Jordan	36	32	31	27	27
Kuwait	107	96	120	101	97
Morocco	66	63	69	60	53
Nigeria	50	33	51	39	56
Oman	15	17	20	20	20
Qatar	76	88	124	125	126
Saudi Arabia	246	319	353	339	373
South Africa	491	705	1,013	523	612
UAE	98	110	105	71	68

Source: Various issues of *Global Stock Markets Factbook*, Standard & Poor's. Israel and Korea became classified as developed markets in 2010.

Investment in foreign equity markets became common practice in the 1980s as investors became aware of the benefits of international portfolio diversification (our topic in Chapter 15). However, during the 1980s, cross-border equity investment was largely confined to the equity markets of developed countries. Only in the 1990s did world investors start to invest sizable amounts in the emerging equity markets, as the economic growth and prospects of the developing countries improved.

Measure of Liquidity

A liquid stock market is one in which investors can buy and sell stocks quickly at close to the current quoted prices. A measure of **liquidity** for a stock market is the turnover ratio; that is, the ratio of stock market transactions over a period of time divided by the

EXHIBIT 13.3

Turnover Ratio of Equity Markets in Developed Countries (Transactions in U.S. $/Year End Market Capitalization in U.S. $)

Region or Country	2008	2009	2010	2011	2012
Europe					
Austria	69	41	79	52	50
Belgium	76	60	42	43	39
Cyprus	NA	15	11	10	12
Denmark	105	97	69	73	52
Finland	155	74	97	134	84
France	152	79	43	84	66
Germany	192	107	103	135	92
Greece	59	71	68	47	38
Iceland	67	12	10	28	28
Ireland	85	47	53	45	11
Israel	–	–	67	65	46
Italy	284	110	170	237	167
Luxembourg	3	< 1	–	–	–
Netherlands	169	130	98	88	71
Norway	152	140	91	89	56
Portugal	82	55	35	50	42
Spain	178	143	76	129	106
Sweden	157	114	87	96	73
Switzerland	146	82	76	86	64
United Kingdom	227	146	102	138	84
Far East					
Australia	103	79	90	94	85
Hong Kong	82	82	64	158	123
Japan	153	129	115	109	100
Korea	–	–	169	195	139
New Zealand	46	82	21	40	33
Singapore	101	103	83	75	43
Atlantic					
Bermuda	NA	3	7	2	2
North America					
Canada	123	92	71	75	62
United States	232	349	189	188	125

Source: Various issues of *Global Stock Markets Factbook*, Standard & Poor's. Israel and Korea became classified as developed markets in 2010.

size, or market capitalization, of the stock market. Generally, the higher the turnover ratio, the more liquid the secondary stock market, indicating ease in trading.

Exhibit 13.3 presents turnover ratio percentages for 29 equity markets of developed countries for the five years beginning with 2008. The table indicates that the turnover ratio varies considerably over time for most national equity markets. The table also indicates that most national equity markets had very high turnover ratios, with the great majority in excess of 50 percent turnover per year.

Exhibit 13.4 presents the turnover ratio percentages for 35 emerging stock markets for the five years from 2008 through 2012. The exhibit indicates a considerable difference in turnover ratios among the developing countries. Many of the small equity markets in each region (e.g., Argentina, Peru, Sri Lanka, Slovak Republic, Croatia, and Bahrain) have relatively low turnover ratios, indicating poor liquidity at present. Nevertheless, the larger emerging equity markets (China, India, and Taiwan) demonstrate fairly strong liquidity. For the majority of countries, the turnover ratio was less in 2012 than it was in 2008, indicating poor liquidity in most emerging equity markets.

in the market when the order is received, that is, the *market price*. A **limit order** is an order *away from the market* price that is held in a **limit order book** until it can be executed at the desired price.

There are many different designs for secondary markets that allow for efficient trading of shares between buyers and sellers. Generally, however, a secondary market is structured as a dealer or agency market. In a **dealer market**, the broker takes the trade through the dealer, who participates in trades as a principal by buying and selling the security for his own account. Public traders do not trade directly with one another in a dealer market. In an **agency market**, the broker takes the client's order through the agent, who matches it with another public order. The agent can be viewed as a *broker's broker*. Other names for the agent are *official broker* and *central broker*.

Both dealer and agency structures exist in the United States. The **over-the-counter (OTC)** market is a dealer market. Almost all OTC stocks trade on the National Association of Security Dealers Automated Quotation System (NASDAQ), which is a computer-linked system that shows the **bid** (buy) and **ask** (sell) **prices** of all dealers in a security. As many as 20 dealers may make a market in the most actively traded issues.

In the United States, firms must meet certain listing requirements in order to have their stock traded on one of several organized stock exchanges. The two largest of these exchanges, the New York Stock Exchange (NYSE) and the American Stock Exchange (AMEX), are both national exchanges on which the stocks of the largest companies of most interest to investors are traded. Shares of firms of regional interest are traded on several regional exchanges.

The exchange markets in the United States are agency/auction markets. Each stock traded on the exchange is represented by a **specialist**, who makes a market by holding an inventory of the security. Each specialist has a designated station (desk) on the exchange trading floor where trades in his stock are conducted. Floor brokers bring the flow of public market orders for a security to the specialist's desk for execution. Serving as a dealer, the specialist is obligated to post bid and ask prices for the stock he represents and to stand willing to buy or sell for his own account at these prices. Through an auction process, the "crowd" of floor brokers may arrive at a more favorable market price for their clients between the specialist's bid and ask prices and thus transact among themselves. The specialist also holds the limit order book. In executing these orders, the specialist serves as an agent. Limit order prices receive preference in establishing the posted bid and ask prices if they are more favorable than the specialist's, and he must fill a limit order, if possible, from the flow of public orders before trading for his own account. Both the OTC and the exchange markets in the United States are **continuous markets** where market and limit orders can be executed at any time during business hours.

In recent years, most national stock markets have become automated for at least some of the issues traded on them. The first was the Toronto Stock Exchange (TMX), which in 1977 instituted the Computer Assisted Trading System (CATS). An automated trading system electronically stores and displays public orders on a continuous basis, and allows public traders to cross orders with one another to execute a trade without the assistance of exchange personnel. Automated systems are successful largely because orders can be filled faster and fewer exchange personnel are needed. Indeed, automated trading that bypasses the specialist system now accounts for more than half of all NYSE transactions. In some countries the exchange trading floor has been completely eliminated.

Not all stock market systems provide continuous trading. For example, the Paris Bourse was traditionally a call market. In a **call market**, an agent of the exchange accumulates, over a period of time, a batch of orders that are periodically executed by written or verbal auction throughout the trading day. Both market and limit orders are handled in this way. The major disadvantage of a call market is that traders are not certain about the price at which their orders will transact because bid and ask quotations

---

www.nasdaq.com

This is the official website of the NASDAQ stock exchange. It provides information about the exchange, stock screening software, and price quotations.

www.nyse.com

This is the website of the New York Stock Exchange. Information about the NYSE, its operation, membership, and listed companies is provided here. U.S. stock price quotations are available at this site.

www.tmx.com

This is the website of TMX Group, which operates the Toronto Stock Exchange. Information about the exchange, its operation, membership, and listed companies is provided here. Canadian stock and mutual fund prices are available at this site.

EXHIBIT 13.6

Characteristics of Major
Equity Trading Systems

Equity Trading System	Market Characteristics		
	Public Orders	**Order Flow**	**Example**
Dealer	Trade with dealer	Continuous	NASDAQ OTC
Agency	Agent assists with matching of public orders	Continuous or periodic	NYSE specialist system[a] (continuous) Old Paris Bourse (noncontinuous)
Fully automated	Electronic matching of public orders	Continuous	Toronto Stock Exchange

[a]As noted in the text, a specialist may at times also serve as a dealer.

are not available prior to the call. On September 22, 2000, the Paris Bourse merged with the Brussels and Amsterdam exchanges to form Euronext, discussed in a later section in this chapter.

A second type of noncontinuous exchange trading system is **crowd trading**. Typically, crowd trading is organized as follows: In a trading ring, an agent of the exchange periodically calls out the name of the issue. At this point, traders announce their bid and ask prices for the issue, and seek counterparts to a trade. Between counterparts a deal may be struck and a trade executed. Unlike a call market in which there is a common price for all trades, several bilateral trades may take place at different prices. Crowd trading was once the system of trading on the Zurich Stock Exchange, but the Swiss exchange moved to an automated system in August 1996. At present, crowd trading is practiced at the Madrid Stock Exchange for a small percentage of trading.

Continuous trading systems are desirable for actively traded issues, whereas call markets and crowd trading offer advantages for thinly traded issues because they mitigate the possibility of sparse order flow over short time periods. Exhibit 13.6 provides a summary of the major equity trading systems found worldwide.

Market Consolidations and Mergers

www.nyx.com

This is the official website of NYSE Euronext.

There are approximately 80 major national stock markets. Western and Eastern Europe once had more than 20 national stock exchanges where at least 15 different languages were spoken. Today, stock markets around the world are under pressure from clients to combine or buy stakes in one another to trade shares of companies anywhere, at a faster pace. To satisfy investors' needs, several combinations and trading arrangements have been formed. One of the most promising arrangements is Euronext. Euronext was formed on September 22, 2000, as a result of a merger of the Amsterdam Exchanges, Brussels Exchanges, and the Paris Bourse. Euronext creates a single trading platform serving all members at each of the three subsidiary exchanges. Access to all shares and products is provided. Additionally, a single order book exists for each stock, allowing for transparency and liquidity. A single clearinghouse and payment and delivery system facilitates trading. In June 2001, the Lisbon stock exchange merged with Euronext. Possibly, over time a European stock exchange will develop. However, a lack of common securities regulations, even among the countries of the European Union, hinders this development. Nevertheless, the April 4, 2007, merger of Euronext with the New York Stock Exchange, to form NYSE Euronext, creates the potential for internationalizing trading arrangements in the future. Additionally, on October 1, 2008, NYSE Euronext acquired the American Stock Exchange to form NYSE AMEX. On November 13, 2013, Intercontinental Exchange (ICE), the 12-year-old energy and commodities futures exchange, acquired NYSE Euronext for $11 billion.

Another noteworthy European trading arrangement is Norex. Norex is an alliance among the Nordic and Baltic exchanges in Denmark, Estonia, Finland, Latvia, Lithuania, Sweden (all owned and operated by OMX, the largest integrated securities

www.nasdaqomx.com

This is the official website of NASDAQ OMX.

market in Northern Europe), Iceland, and Norway. Trading on Norex exchanges is carried out through the Stockholm Automated Exchange (SAXESS), a state-of-the-art computerized and electronic trading system capable of handling 2,000 orders per second. On May 25, 2007, NASDAQ acquired OMX to form NASDAQ OMX, and on July 24, 2008, NASDAQ OMX acquired the Philadelphia Stock Exchange.

Trading in International Equities

During the 1980s world capital markets began a trend toward greater global integration. Several factors account for this movement. First, investors began to realize the benefits of international portfolio diversification. Second, major capital markets became more liberalized through the elimination of fixed trading commissions, the reduction in governmental regulation, and measures taken by the European Union to integrate their capital markets. Third, new computer and communications technology facilitated efficient and fair securities trading through order routing and execution, information dissemination, and clearance and settlement. Fourth, MNCs realized the benefits of sourcing new capital internationally. In this section, we explore some of the major effects that greater global integration has had on the world's equity markets. We begin by examining the cross-listing of shares.

Cross-Listing of Shares

Cross-listing refers to a firm having its equity shares listed on one or more foreign exchanges, in addition to the home country stock exchange. Cross-listing is not a new concept; however, with the increased globalization of world equity markets, the amount of cross-listing has exploded in recent years. In particular, MNCs often cross-list their shares, but non-MNCs also cross-list.

Exhibit 13.7 presents the total number of companies listed on various national stock exchanges in the world and the breakdown of the listings between domestic and foreign for 2011.[2] The exhibit also shows the number of new listings and the domestic-foreign split for 2011. The exhibit shows that there are some foreign companies listed on virtually all national stock exchanges from developed countries. Several exchanges have a large proportion of foreign listings. In fact, the Luxembourg Stock Exchange has more foreign than domestic listings, while on the Singapore Stock Exchange foreign listings represent more than 40 percent of the total.

A firm may decide to cross-list its shares for many reasons:

1. Cross-listing provides a means for expanding the investor base for a firm's stock, thus potentially increasing its demand. Increased demand for a company's stock may increase the market price. Additionally, greater market demand and a broader investor base improve the price liquidity of the security.

2. Cross-listing establishes name recognition of the company in a new capital market, thus paving the way for the firm to source new equity or debt capital from local investors as demands dictate. This is an especially important reason for firms from emerging market countries with limited capital markets to cross-list their shares on exchanges in developed countries with enhanced capital market access.

3. Cross-listing brings the firm's name before more investor and consumer groups. Local consumers (investors) may more likely become investors in (consumers of) the company's stock (products) if the company's stock is (products are) locally available. International portfolio diversification is facilitated for investors if they can trade the security on their own stock exchange.

---

[2]For the purpose of this discussion, NASDAQ OMX OTC stocks will be referred to as listed shares.

EXHIBIT 13.7

Total, Domestic, and Foreign Company Listings on Major National Stock Exchanges for 2011

Exchange	Total Listings 2011			New Listings 2011		
	Total	Domestic	Foreign	Total	Domestic	Foreign
Americas						
Bermuda SE	40	13	27	2	0	2
BM&FBOVESPA	373	366	7	15	15	0
Buenos Aires SE	105	99	6	1	1	0
Colombia SE	83	79	4	4	1	3
Lima SE	254	202	52	11	6	5
Mexican Exchange	476	128	348	63	3	60
NASDAQ OMX	2,680	2,383	297	151	124	27
NYSE Euronext (US)	2,308	1,788	520	144	109	35
Santiago SE	267	229	38	49	9	40
TMX Group	3,945	3,845	100	369	350	19
Total Region	10,531	9,132	1,399	809	618	191
Asia, Pacific						
Australian Securities Exchange	2,079	1,983	96	121	108	13
Bombay SE	5,112	5,112	0	39	39	0
Bursa Malaysia	940	932	8	28	28	0
Colombo SE	272	272	0	31	31	0
GreTai Securities Market	608	607	1	52	51	1
Hong Kong Exchanges	1,496	1,472	24	101	93	8
Indonesia SE	440	440	0	25	25	0
Korea Exchange	1,816	1,799	17	72	70	2
National Stock Exchange of India	1,640	1,639	1	107	107	0
Osaka Securities Exchange	1,229	1,228	1	16	16	0
Philippine SE	253	251	2	6	6	0
Shanghai SE	931	931	0	39	39	0
Shenzhen SE	1,411	1,411	0	243	243	0
Singapore Exchange	773	462	311	24	10	14
Taiwan SE Corp.	824	772	52	48	27	21
Thailand SE	545	545	0	12	12	0
Tokyo SE Group	2,291	2,280	11	50	50	0
Total Region	22,660	22,136	524	1,014	955	59
Europe - Africa - Middle East						
Amman SE	247	247	0	2	2	0
Athens Exchange	272	269	3	0	0	0
BME Spanish Exchanges	3,276	3,241	35	88	87	1
Budapest SE	54	52	2	6	6	0
Casablanca SE	76	75	1	3	3	0
Cyprus SE	106	106	0	0	0	0
Deutsche Börse	746	670	76	216	29	187
Egyptian Exchange	233	232	1	9	9	0
Irish SE	55	48	7	2	1	1
IMKB	264	263	1	25	25	0
Johannesburg SE	395	347	48	16	12	4
Ljubljana SE	66	66	0	1	1	0
London SE Group	2,886	2,288	598	163	120	43
Luxembourg SE	298	27	271	21	2	19
Malta SE	21	21	0	0	0	0
Mauritius SE	64	63	1	1	1	0
MICEX	284	283	1	96	96	0
NASDAQ OMX Nordic Exchange	773	743	30	26	22	4
NYSE Euronext (Europe)	1,112	969	143	45	40	5
Oslo Børs	238	194	44	13	8	5
RTS Stock Exchange	252	251	1	8	8	0
Saudi Stock Market-Tadawul	150	150	0	4	4	0
SIX Swiss Exchange	280	246	34	0	0	0
Tel-Aviv SE	593	576	17	11	10	1
Warsaw SE	777	757	20	204	198	6
Wiener Börse	105	88	17	4	3	1
Total Region	13,623	12,272	1,351	964	687	277
WFE Total	46,814	43,540	3,274	2,787	2,260	527

Source: Table 1.3, p. 94 and Table 1.4., p. 95 from *Annual Report and Statistics* 2011. World Federation of Exchanges.

4. Cross-listing into developed capital markets with strict securities regulations and information disclosure requirements may be seen as a signal to investors that improved corporate governance is forthcoming.

5. Cross-listing may mitigate the possibility of a hostile takeover of the firm through the broader investor base created for the firm's shares.

Cross-listing of a firm's stock obligates the firm to adhere to the securities regulations of its home country as well as the regulations of the countries in which it is cross-listed. Cross-listing in the United States means the firm must meet the reporting and disclosure requirements of the U.S. Securities and Exchange Commission. According to the **bonding theory**, a U.S. cross-listing both restricts the ability of corporate insiders of the cross-listed firm from consuming private benefits and also publicly benefits the firm by allowing it to finance new growth opportunities at more advantageous terms. Reconciliation of a company's financial statements to U.S. standards can be a laborious process, and some foreign firms are reluctant to disclose hidden reserves. For foreign firms desiring to have their shares traded only among large institutional investors rather than listed on an exchange, less rigorous accounting and disclosure requirements apply under SEC Rule 144A. Rule 144A share sales are often acceptable to family-owned companies, which for privacy or tax reasons operate their businesses with more lax accounting standards.

Yankee Stock Offerings

The introduction to this section indicated that in recent years U.S. investors have bought and sold a large amount of foreign stock. Since the beginning of the 1990s, many foreign companies, Latin American in particular, have listed their stocks on U.S. exchanges to prime the U.S. equity market for future **Yankee stock** offerings, that is, the direct sale of new equity capital to U.S. public investors. This was a break from the past for the Latin American companies, which typically sold restricted 144A shares to large investors. Three factors appear to be fueling the sale of Yankee stocks. One is the push for privatization by many Latin American and Eastern European government-owned companies. A second factor is the rapid growth in the economies of the developing countries. The third reason is the large demand for new capital by Mexican companies following approval of the North American Free Trade Agreement.

American Depository Receipts

Foreign stocks can be traded directly on a national stock market, but frequently they are traded in the form of a *depository receipt*. For example, Yankee stock issues often trade on the U.S. exchanges as **American Depository Receipts (ADRs)**. An ADR is a receipt representing a number of foreign shares that remain on deposit with the U.S. depository's custodian in the issuer's home market. The bank serves as the transfer agent for the ADRs, which are traded on the listed exchanges in the United States or in the OTC market. The first ADRs began trading in 1927 as a means of eliminating some of the risks, delays, inconveniences, and expenses of trading the actual shares. At year-end 2012, 396 ADRs traded on U.S. listed exchanges. Several hundred more ADRs trade on the U.S. OTC market. Similarly, *Singapore Depository Receipts* trade on the Singapore Stock Exchange. *Global Depository Receipts (GDRs)* allow a foreign firm to simultaneously cross-list on several national exchanges. Many GDRs are traded on the London and Luxembourg stock exchanges. The DR market has grown significantly over the years; at year-end 2012, there were 3,678 DR programs, representing issuers from 82 countries, trading on the world's exchanges. Exhibit 13.8 shows a tombstone for a Global Depository Receipt.

ADRs offer the U.S. investor many advantages over trading directly in the underlying stock on the foreign exchange. Non-U.S. investors can also invest in ADRs, and

EXHIBIT 13.8

Global Depository
Receipt Tombstone

CIB

COMMERCIAL INTERNATIONAL BANK
(EGYPT) S.A.E.

International Offering of
9,999,000 Global Depository Receipts

corresponding to
999,900 Shares (nominal Value of E£100 per Share)

at an
Offer price of US$11.875 per Global Depository Receipt

Seller
National Bank of Egypt

Global Co-ordinator
Co Lead Managers
Robert Fleming & Co. Limited Salomon Brothers International Limited
UBS Limited

Domestic Advisor
Commercial International Investment Company S.A.E.

ING 🦁 BARINGS

July 1996

Source: *Euromoney,* October 1998, p. 127.

frequently do so rather than invest in the underlying stock because of the investment advantages. These advantages include:

1. ADRs are denominated in dollars, trade on a U.S. stock exchange, and can be purchased through the investor's regular broker. By contrast, trading in the underlying shares would likely require the investor to: set up an account with a broker from the country where the company issuing the stock is located; make a currency exchange; and arrange for the shipment of the stock certificates or the establishment of a custodial account.

2. Dividends received on the underlying shares are collected and converted to dollars by the custodian and paid to the ADR investor, whereas investment in the underlying shares requires the investor to collect the foreign dividends and make a currency conversion. Moreover, tax treaties between the United States and some countries lower the dividend tax rate paid by nonresident investors. Consequently, U.S. investors in the underlying shares need to file a form to get a refund on the tax difference withheld. ADR investors, however, receive the full dollar equivalent dividend, less only the applicable taxes.

3. ADR trades clear in three business days as do U.S. equities, whereas settlement practices for the underlying stock vary in foreign countries.

4. ADR price quotes are in U.S. dollars.

5. ADRs (except Rule 144A issues) are registered securities that provide for the protection of ownership rights, whereas most underlying stocks are bearer securities. Exhibit 13.9 describes the various types of ADR programs.

6. An ADR investment can be sold by trading the depository receipt to another investor in the U.S. stock market, or the underlying shares can be sold in the local stock market. In this case the ADR is delivered for cancellation

EXHIBIT 13.9

Types of ADRs

	Level I	Level II	Level III	Rule 144A
Description	Unlisted program in the U.S.	Listed on a U.S. exchange	Shares offered and listed on a U.S. exchange	Private placement to Qualified Institutional Buyers
Trading	OTC	NASDAQ, AMEX, NYSE	NASDAQ, AMEX, NYSE	U.S. private placement
SEC Registration	Form F-6	Form F-6	Forms F-1 and F-6	None
U.S. Reporting Requirements	Exempt under Rule 12g3-2(b)	Form 20-F*	Form 20-F*	Exempt under Rule 12g3-2(b)

*Financial statements must be partially reconciled to U.S. GAAP.
Level I: The most basic type of ADR program.
The issuer is not seeking to raise new equity capital in the U.S. and/or cannot list on NASDAQ.
Level II: The issuer is not seeking to raise new equity capital in the U.S. and ADRs can be listed on NASDAQ, AMEX, or NYSE.
Level III: The issuer floats a public offering of new equity in the U.S. and lists the ADRs on NASDAQ, AMEX, or NYSE.
Rule 144A: This type of ADR program is a private placement of equity to Qualified Institutional Buyers (QIBs). It can only be traded among QIBs.

Source: Excerpted from www.adr.com.

to the bank depository, which delivers the underlying shares to the buyer. Exhibit 13.10 charts the mechanics of issuance and cancellation of ADRs.

7. ADRs frequently represent a multiple of the underlying shares, rather than a one-for-one correspondence, to allow the ADR to trade in a price range customary for U.S. investors. A single ADR may represent more or less than one underlying share, depending upon the underlying share value.

8. ADR holders give instructions to the depository bank as to how to vote the rights associated with the underlying shares. Voting rights are not exercised by the depository bank in the absence of specific instructions from the ADR holders.

There are two types of ADRs: sponsored and unsponsored. *Sponsored* ADRs are created by a bank at the request of the foreign company that issued the underlying security. The sponsoring bank often offers ADR holders an assortment of services, including investment information and portions of the annual report translated into English. Sponsored ADRs are the only ones that can be listed on the U.S. stock markets. All new ADR programs must be sponsored. *Unsponsored* ADRs—some dating back prior to 1980 still exist—were usually created at the request of a U.S. investment banking firm without direct involvement by the foreign issuing firm. Consequently, the foreign company may not provide investment information or financial reports to the depository on a regular basis or in a timely manner. The depository fees of sponsored ADRs are paid by the foreign company. ADR investors pay the depository fees on unsponsored ADRs. Unsponsored ADRs may have several issuing banks, with the terms of the offering varying from bank to bank. In general, only sponsored ADRs trade on NASDAQ or the major stock exchanges.

The 396 sponsored ADRs that traded on U.S. listed exchanges at year-end 2012 represent a decline from 403 a year earlier. Many of the issuers that have delisted in recent years have continued to offer their depository receipts to investors by converting them to a Level I OTC-traded ADR program. After delisting, the cross-listed firm can apply for deregistration of its securities with the U.S. SEC and the termination of all the reporting requirements under the Securities Exchange Act of 1934. Delisting was facilitated by the March 21, 2007, adoption by the SEC of the Exchange Act Rule 12h-6, which makes it much easier for foreign firms to deregister. It has been widely debated whether the recent surge in delisting indicates that foreign listed firms no

EXHIBIT 13.10   Mechanics of Issuance and Cancellation of ADRs

A broker-dealer can purchase existing ADRs in the United States or purchase underlying shares in an issuer's home market and have new ADRs created, or issued, by the depository bank. While the pool of available ADRs is constantly changing, the broker-dealer decides whether to purchase existing ADRs or have new ones issued, depending on such factors as availability, pricing, and market conditions in the United States and the issuer's home market.

To create new ADRs, underlying shares are deposited with a custodian bank in the issuer's home market. The depository then issues ADRs representing those shares. The process for canceling ADRs is similar to the issuance process, but the steps are reversed. The following chart and description provide a more detailed explanation, including the parties and steps involved.

The ADR purchase and issuance process: two scenarios

EXISTING ADRs

A1 Investor places order with broker in the United States.

A2 Broker in the United States purchases ADRs in the applicable market.

A3 Settlement and delivery of the ADRs (in book-entry or certificate form).

NEW ADRs

B1 Investor places order with broker in the United States.

B2 Broker in the United States places order with local broker (outside U.S.) for equivalent shares.

B3 Local broker purchases shares in local market.

B4 Local shares are deposited with the depository's custodian.

B5 Depository receives confirmation of share deposit.

B6 Depository issues new ADRs and delivers them to broker in the U.S.

B7 Settlement and delivery of the ADRs (in book-entry or certificate form).

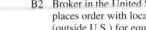
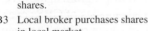

longer see benefits from cross-listing in the United States or that U.S. markets have lost their competitiveness because of new regulation such as the Sarbanes-Oxley Act of 2002 (SOX), which instituted a broad set of new reforms regarding corporate governance of publicly held corporations.

There has been much anecdotal evidence that compliance with SOX has been particularly onerous and expensive. Additionally, a particular concern for the United States is the fact that new initial public offerings (IPOs) by Chinese firms, the major source of new IPOs, have been cross-listed in Hong Kong rather than in the United States. For example, in 2005 nine of the ten largest Chinese IPOs were cross-listed in Hong Kong, and in 2006 the $9.7 billion Bank of China IPO was cross-listed there. Again, the anecdotal evidence is that company executives find the burden of compliance with U.S. regulation to be responsible. Alternatively, the reason may simply be that the Chinese government prefers to promote its own stock exchanges. Cross-listed firms that trade in the United States as Level I ADRs are exempt from the reporting requirements of the Securities Exchange Act of 1934 and from the accountability requirements under SOX. Thus, the fact that in recent years the majority of cross-listed firms that delisted from U.S. exchanges continue to trade on the U.S. OTC market suggests that these firms do find the burden of complying with U.S. regulation onerous and expensive, but nevertheless value U.S. markets as a venue for cross-listing.

Global Registered Shares

The merger of Daimler Benz AG and Chrysler Corporation in November 1998 created DaimlerChrysler AG, a German firm. The merger was hailed as a landmark event for global equity markets because it simultaneously created a new type of equity share called Global Registered Shares (GRSs). GRSs are shares that are traded globally, unlike ADRs, which are receipts for bank deposits of home-market shares and traded on foreign markets. The primary exchanges for DaimlerChrysler GRSs were the Frankfurt Stock Exchange and the NYSE; however, they were traded on a total of 20 exchanges worldwide. GRSs are fully fungible—a GRS purchased on one exchange can be sold on another. DaimlerChrysler GRSs traded in both euros and U.S. dollars. A global share registrar that linked the German and U.S. transfer agents and registrars facilitated clearing. In October 2007, the company was renamed Daimler AG, when it spun off Chrysler. Daimler AG continued to trade as a GRS. In May 2010, Daimler decided to delist from the NYSE and submitted a request to that effect with the U.S. SEC. The delisting became effective on June 7, 2010, and Daimler GRSs began trading on the OTC market. As a result, Daimler is no longer subject to the reporting requirements under the U.S. Securities Exchange Act of 1934 or the accountability requirements of the Sarbanes-Oxley Act of 2002, thus saving it millions of euros per year. Daimler reasoned that in today's global marketplace, with high-volume trading platforms, it no longer made sense to be listed on a large number of stock exchanges. On September 23, 2010, Daimler established a Level I ADR program in the OTC market in the U.S., with one ADR equaling one GRS. The main advantages of GRSs over ADRs appear to be that all shareholders have equal status and direct voting rights. The main disadvantage of GRSs appears to be the greater expense in establishing the global registrar and clearing facility. GRSs have met with limited success; many companies that considered them opted for ADRs.[3] Deutsche Bank and UBS also trade as GRSs.

EXAMPLE | 13.1: Daimler AG

Stock in Daimler AG, the famous German automobile manufacturer, trades on both the Frankfurt Stock Exchange in Germany and as a Level I ADR on the OTC market in the United States. On the Frankfurt bourse, Daimler closed at a price of EUR41.26 on Thursday, April 11, 2013. On the same day, Daimler closed in the United States at $54.13 per share. To prevent arbitrage trading between the two markets, the shares have to trade at the same price when adjusted for the exchange rate. We see that this is true. The $/EUR exchange rate on April 11 was $1.3104/EUR1.00. Thus, EUR41.26 $\times$ $1.3104 = $54.07, an amount very close to the closing price in the United States of $54.13. The difference is easily explainable by the fact that the U.S. OTC market closes several hours after the Frankfurt exchange, and thus market prices had changed slightly.

Empirical Findings on Cross-Listing and ADRs

Several empirical studies document important findings on cross-listing in general and on ADRs in particular.

Park (1990) found that a substantial portion of the variability in (i.e., change in) ADR returns is accounted for by variation in the share price of the underlying security in the home market. However, information observed in the U.S. market is also an important factor in the ADR return generating process.

---

[3]Much of the information in this section is from the 2003 clinical study by G. Andrew Karolyi.

Kao, Wenchi, Wei, and Vu (1991) examined ADRs as vehicles for constructing diversified equity portfolios. They used 10 years of monthly return data covering the period 1979 through 1989 for ADRs with underlying shares in the U.K., Australia, Japan, the Netherlands, and Sweden. They found that an internationally diversified portfolio of ADRs outperforms both a U.S. stock market and a world stock market benchmark on a risk-adjusted basis.

Jayaraman, Shastri, and Tandon (1993) examined the effect of the listing of ADRs on the risk and return of the underlying stock. They found positive abnormal performance (i.e., return in excess of the expected equilibrium return) of the underlying security on the initial listing date. They interpreted this as evidence that an ADR listing provides the issuing firm with another market from which to source new equity capital. Additionally, they found an increase in the volatility of (i.e., change in) returns of the underlying stock. They interpreted this as consistent with the theory that traders with proprietary information will attempt to profit from their knowledge by taking advantage of price discrepancies caused by information differentials between the ADR and underlying security markets.

Gagnon and Karolyi (2004) compared synchronous intraday prices of ADRs and other types of cross-listed shares in U.S. markets relative to home-market prices after currency adjustment for 581 companies from 39 countries. They discovered that for most stocks, prices of cross-listed shares are within 20 to 85 basis points of the home-market shares, thus limiting arbitrage opportunities after transaction costs. However, when institutional barriers that limit arbitrage exist, prices can deviate by as much as a 66 percent premium and an 87 percent discount. Large deviations seldom exist for more than a day. They also discovered that cross-listed shares trading in the United States are relatively more (less) correlated with the U.S. market index than with the home market when there is proportionately more (less) trading in the U.S. market.

Berkman and Nguyen (2010) studied the impact of cross-listing in the United States on domestic liquidity for a sample of 277 firms from 30 countries over the period 1996 through 2005. Their results indicate that cross-listed firms from countries with poor corporate governance and/or weak accounting standards gain from improvements in domestic liquidity in the first two years after cross-listing but tend to diminish later on. In general, they found little evidence that cross-listing results in significant improvements in domestic liquidity. Their results are seemingly inconsistent with the bonding theory, which predicts that firms from countries with weak investor protection should experience permanent improvements in domestic liquidity.

Abdallah and Ioannidis (2010) reexamined prior work. They found that firms cross-list in a period of good performance in their local market to take advantage of an overvaluation of share prices to raise new capital in the cross-listed country. Additionally, they found that abnormal return exhibits a significant decline after cross-listing, which is more pronounced the higher the level of the pre-cross-listing abnormal return. Their results support earlier findings that local market beta (risk) declines after cross-listing, but that the decrease diminishes over time. These findings are consistent for firms that cross-list on either regulated U.S. exchanges or on the OTC market and for firms from both civil and common law countries. Overall, their results do not support the bonding theory's prediction that cross-listing signals the firm's commitment to protect minority shareholders' interests and thus increase the value of the firm by reducing the required rate of return.

Doidge, Karolyi, and Stulz (2010) studied why foreign cross-listed firms choose to delist from a U.S. exchange. The Exchange Act Rule 12h-6 adopted by the SEC on March 21, 2007, facilitates foreign firms delisting from U.S. exchanges. Two theories present predictions why a firm might choose to delist. The bonding theory predicts that firms with poor growth opportunities, who have little need for new external capital, and those which perform poorly might be likely candidates for delisting. The loss of competitiveness theory predicts that the compliance costs of SOX and possibly other regulatory developments so reduced the net benefits of a U.S. listing that for some firms the value of the cross-listing became negative. The strongest evidence they found concluded that firms that delist and leave U.S. markets (i.e., are not subsequently traded on the U.S. OTC market) do so because they do not foresee the need to raise new external funds. They did not find that SOX is a major determinant in decisions to leave U.S. markets.

International Equity Market Benchmarks

As a benchmark of activity or performance of a given national equity market, an index of the stocks traded on the secondary exchange (or exchanges) of a country is used. Several national equity indexes are available for use by investors.

To this point, the exhibits of this chapter have presented data from stock market indexes prepared by Standard & Poor's. Each year S&P publishes its *Global Stock Markets Factbook*, which provides a variety of statistical data on both emerging and developed country stock markets. The *Factbook* is an excellent source that is carried by many university libraries and provides annual comparative statistics in an easy-to-read format.

www.msci.com

This website provides detailed information about the construction of MSCI international stock market indexes.

The indexes constructed and published by MSCI are an excellent source of national stock market performance. MSCI presents return and price level data for 24 national stock market indexes from developed countries, 21 emerging market countries, and 31 frontier markets that cover investment opportunities beyond traditional developed and emerging markets. In constructing each of these indexes, an attempt is made to include equity issues representing at least 85 percent of the free-float market capitalization of each industry within the country. The stocks in each country index are market-value weighted, that is, the proportion of the index a stock represents is determined by its proportion of the total market capitalization of all stocks in the index. Additionally, MSCI publishes a market-value-weighted World Index comprising 24 of its country indexes. The World Index includes approximately 2,600 stock issues of major corporations in the world. MSCI also publishes several regional indexes: the European, Australasia, Far East (EAFE) Index comprising approximately 1,000 stocks from 22 countries; the North American Index composed of the United States and Canada; the Far East Index (three countries); several Europe Indexes (depending upon whether individual constituent countries are included); the Nordic Countries Index (four countries); the Pacific Index (five countries); and the Emerging Markets Index (21 countries). The EAFE Index is widely followed, and it is representative of World Index excluding North American stock market performance. MSCI also publishes dozens of industry indexes, each of which includes equity issues from the respective industry from the countries it follows. Most recently, MSCI introduced two new indexes: the All Country World Investable Market Index (ACW) and the All Country World ex U.S.A. Investable Market Index (ACW ex US) provide a better representation of the stock market. The ACW Index includes more than 9,000 stock issues represented by the 45 MSCI developed and emerging market country indexes and the ACW ex US includes more that 6,000 issues, which covers 98 percent of the world's non-U.S. markets.

The *Financial Times* reports values in local currency of the major stock market indexes of the national exchanges or markets from various countries in the world. Many of these indexes are prepared by the stock markets themselves or well-known investment advisory firms. Exhibit 13.11 presents a list of the indexes that appear daily in the *Financial Times*.

Standard & Poor's publishes the S&P ADR Index, an investable index designed to allow investors to benchmark international stock performance traded on U.S. stock exchanges. The S&P ADR index includes foreign firms that are members of the S&P Global 1200 Index that trade as Level II or Level III ADRs, global shares, or ordinary shares, in the case of Canadian equities. The index is market-value weighted and includes about 260 securities from 29 countries.

EXHIBIT 13.11   Major National Stock Market Indexes

Country	Index	Country	Index	Country	Index
Argentina	Merval	Israel	Tel Aviv 100	Thailand	Bangkok SET
Australia	All Ordinaries	Italy	FTSE MIB	Turkey	ISE 100
	S&P/ASX 200 Res		FTSE Italia Mid Cap	UK	FTSE 100
	NIKKEI 200		FTSE Italia All-Sh		FT 30
Austria	AIX	Japan	Nikkei 225		FTSE All Share
Belgium	BEL 20		Topix		FTSE techMARK 100
	BEL Mid		S&P Topix 150		FTSE4Good UK
Brazil	Bovespa		2nd Section	USA	S&P 500
Canada	S&P/TSX Met & Min	Jordan	Amman SE		FTSE NASDAQ 500
	S&P/TSX 60	Kenya	NSE 20		NASDAQ Cmp
	S&P/TSX Comp	Latvia	OMX Riga		NASDAQ 100
Chile	IGPA Gen	Lithuania	OMX Vilnius		Russell 2000
China	Shanghai A	Luxembourg	Luxembourg General		NYSE Comp.
	Shanghai B	Malaysia	FTSE Bursa KLCI		Wilshire 5000
	Shanghai Comp	Mexico	IPC		DJ Industrial
	Shenzhen A	Morocco	MASI		DJ Composite
	Shenzhen B	Netherlands	AEX		DJ Transport
	FTSE A200		AEX All Share		DJ Utilities
	FTSE B35	New Zealand	NZX 50	Venezuela	IBC
Colombia	CSE Index	Nigeria	SE All Share	Vietnam	VNI
Creatia	CROBEX	Norway	Oslo All Share	CROSS-	Stoxx 50 €
Cyprus	CSE M&P Gen	Pakistan	KSE 100	BORDER	Euro Stoxx 50 €
Czech Republic	PX	Philippines	Manila Comp		DJ Global Titans $
Denmark	OMX Copenhagen				Euronext 100 ID
	20	Poland	Wig		FTSE Multinatts $
Egypt	EGX 30	Portugal	PSI General		FTSE Global 100 $
Estonia	OMX Tallinn		PSI 20		FTSE 4Good Glob $
Finland	OMX Helsinki	Romania	BET Index		FTSE E300
	General	Russia	RTS		FTSEurofirst 80 €
France	CAC 40		MICEX Comp.		FTSEurofirst 100 €
	SBF 120	Singapore	FTSE Straits Times		FTSE Lattbex Top €
Germany	M-DAX	Slovakia	SAX		FTSE Eurotop 100
	XETRA Dax	Slovenia	SBI TOP		FTSE Gold Min $
	TecDAX	South Africa	FTSE/JSE All Share		FTSE All World
Greece	Athens Gen		FTSE/JSE Top 40		FTSE World $
	FTSE/ASE 20		FTSE/JSE Res 20		MSCI All World $
Hong Kong	Hang Seng	South Korea	Kospi		MSCI ACWI Fr $
	HS China		Kospi 200		MSCI Europe €
	Enterprise	Spain	Madrid SE		MSCI Pacific $
	HSCC Red Chip		IBEX 35		SAP Global 1200 $
Hungary	Bux	Sri Lanka	CSE All Share		SAP Europe 350 €
India	BSE Sens	Sweden	OMX Stockholm 30		SAP Euro €
	S&P CNX 500		OMX Stockholm AS		
Indonesia	Jakarta Comp	Switzerland	SMI Index		
Ireland	ISEQ Overall	Taiwan	Weighted Pr		

Source: *Financial Times* April 18, 2013, p. 21.

iShares MSCI

BlackRock, Inc., an international investment management firm, operates iShares MSCI as vehicles to facilitate investment in country, regional, and world funds. iShares MSCI are baskets of stocks designed to replicate various MSCI stock indexes. Currently there are 63 iShares MSCI, of which 31 are country-specific funds and the remaining 32 replicate other MSCI indexes, such as the World, EAFE, and Emerging Markets Index. iShares are exchange-traded funds; most trade on NYSE AMEX.

industries, there is little difference in cross-country covariances between firms in the same industry and those in different industries.

Phylaktis and Xia (2006) examined the roles of country and industry effects on international equity returns using a database covering 50 industry groups from 34 countries over the period 1992 to 2001. Their study focuses on the evolving process of those effects over time and on geographical differences. Their main results are that country effects dominate industry effects over the full study period, but since 1999 there has been a shift toward industry effects. The degree of the shift varies across regions and is more pronounced in Europe and North America, whereas country effects dominate in Asia Pacific and Latin America.

SUMMARY

This chapter provides an overview of international equity markets. The material is designed to provide an understanding of how MNCs source new equity capital outside of their own domestic primary market and to provide useful institutional information to investors interested in diversifying their portfolios internationally.

1. The chapter began with a statistical perspective of the major equity markets in developed countries and of emerging equity markets in developing countries. Market capitalization and turnover figures were provided for each marketplace. Examination of Exhibit 13.1 reveals that the market capitalization of a most national equity markets in developed countries increased from 2008 to 2012 as a result of countries recovering from the global financial crisis. Similarly, Exhibit 13.2 reveals that the market capitalization of a majority of developing countries increased in value over the same time period. Additionally, turnover ratios in many emerging markets remained low and market concentration ratios remained high, indicating that investment opportunities in these markets have not been improving.

2. A considerable amount of discussion was devoted to differences in secondary equity market structures. Secondary markets have historically been structured as dealer or agency markets. Both of these types of market structure can provide for continuous market trading, but noncontinuous markets tend to be agency markets. Over-the-counter trading, specialist markets, and automated markets allow for continuous market trading. Call markets and crowd trading are each types of noncontinuous trading market systems. It was noted that most national stock markets are now automated for at least some of the issues traded on them.

3. Cross-listing of a company's shares on foreign exchanges was extensively discussed. A firm may cross-list its shares to: establish a broader investor base for its stock; establish name recognition in foreign capital markets; and pave the way for sourcing new equity and debt capital from investors in these markets. Yankee stock offerings, or sale of foreign stock to U.S. investors, was also discussed. Yankee shares trade on U.S. markets as American depository receipts (ADRs), which are bank receipts representing a multiple of foreign shares deposited in a foreign bank. ADRs eliminate some of the risks, delays, inconveniences, and expenses of trading actual shares.

4. A variety of international equity benchmarks was also presented. Knowledge of where to find comparative equity market performance data is useful. Specifically, Standard & Poor's and MSCI indexes were discussed. Also, a list of the major national stock market indexes prepared by the national exchanges or major investment advisory services was presented.

5. Several empirical studies that tested for factors that might influence equity returns indicate that domestic factors, such as the level of domestic interest rates and

expected changes in domestic inflation, as opposed to international monetary variables, had the greatest effect on national equity returns. Industrial structure did not appear to be of primary importance. Equity returns were also found to be sensitive to own-currency exchange rate changes.

KEY WORDS

agency market, 330	call market, 330	liquidity, 326
American Depository Receipts (ADRs), 334	continuous markets, 330	market order, 330
	cross listing, 332	over-the-counter (OTC), 330
ask price, 330	crowd trading, 331	primary market, 329
bid price, 330	dealer market, 330	secondary market, 329
bonding theory, 334	limit order, 330	specialist, 330
broker, 329	limit order book, 330	Yankee stock, 334

QUESTIONS

1. Exhibit 13.11 presents a listing of major national stock market indexes as displayed daily in the print edition of the *Financial Times*. At www.ft.com, you can find an online tracking of these national stock market indexes that shows performance over the past day, month, and year. Go to this website and compare the performance for several stock market indexes from various regions of the world. How does the performance compare? What do you think accounts for differences?

2. As an investor, what factors would you consider before investing in the emerging stock market of a developing country?

3. Compare and contrast the various types of secondary market trading structures.

4. Discuss any benefits you can think of for a company to (a) cross-list its equity shares on more than one national exchange, and (b) to source new equity capital from foreign investors as well as domestic investors.

5. Why might it be easier for an investor desiring to diversify his portfolio internationally to buy depository receipts rather than the actual shares of the company?

6. Why do you think the empirical studies about factors affecting equity returns basically showed that domestic factors were more important than international factors, and, secondly, that industrial membership of a firm was of little importance in forecasting the international correlation structure of a set of international stocks?

PROBLEMS

1. On the Tokyo Stock Exchange, Honda Motor Company stock closed at ¥3,945 per share on Thursday, April 11, 2013. Honda trades as an ADR on the NYSE. One underlying Honda share equals one ADR. On April 11, 2013, the ¥/$ exchange rate was ¥99.8270/$1.00.

   a. At this exchange rate, what is the no-arbitrage U.S. dollar price of one ADR?

   b. By comparison, Honda ADRs traded at $39.97. Do you think an arbitrage opportunity exists?

2. If Honda ADRs were trading at $44 when the underlying shares were trading in Tokyo at ¥3,945, what could you do to earn a trading profit? Use the information in problem 1 to help you, and assume that transaction costs are negligible.

INTERNET EXERCISES

1. Bloomberg provides current values of many of the international stock indexes presented in Exhibit 13.11 at the website www.bloomberg.com. Go to this website and determine what country's stock markets are trading higher and lower today. Is there any current news event that might influence the way different national markets are trading today?

2. The J.P. Morgan website www.adr.com provides online data on trading in ADRs. From this website, what are the top 10 individual ADRs by ownership value?

By ownership increases? Does there seem to be a similarity in industry (such as telecom) represented by the top ADRs, or are they from a variety of different industries? Recall from the chapter that the effect of industrial structure on international stock returns is an unresolved issue.

MINI CASE

San Pico's New Stock Exchange

San Pico is a rapidly growing Latin American developing country. The country is blessed with miles of scenic beaches that have attracted tourists by the thousands in recent years to new resort hotels financed by joint ventures of San Pico businessmen and moneymen from the Middle East, Japan, and the United States. Additionally, San Pico has good natural harbors that are conducive to receiving imported merchandise from abroad and exporting merchandise produced in San Pico and other surrounding countries that lack access to the sea. Because of these advantages, many new businesses are being started in San Pico.

Presently, stock is traded in a cramped building in La Cobijio, the nation's capital. Admittedly, the San Pico Stock Exchange system is rather archaic. Twice a day an official of the exchange will call out the name of each of the 43 companies whose stock trades on the exchange. Brokers wanting to buy or sell shares for their clients then attempt to make a trade with one another. This crowd trading system has worked well for over one hundred years, but the government desires to replace it with a new modern system that will allow greater and more frequent opportunities for trading in each company, and will allow for trading the shares of the many new start-up companies that are expected to trade in the secondary market. Additionally, the government administration is rapidly privatizing many state-owned businesses in an attempt to foster their efficiency, obtain foreign exchange from the sale, and convert the country to a more capitalist economy. The government believes that it could conduct this privatization faster and perhaps at more attractive prices if it had a modern stock exchange facility where the shares of the newly privatized companies will eventually trade.

You are an expert in the operation of secondary stock markets and have been retained as a consultant to the San Pico Stock Exchange to offer your expertise in modernizing the stock market. What would you advise?

REFERENCES & SUGGESTED READINGS

Abdallah, Abed Al-Nasser, and Christos Ioannidis. "Why Do Firms Cross-List? Evidence from the U.S. Market." *Quarterly Review of Economics and Finance* 50 (2010), pp. 202–13.

Adler, Michael, and David Simon. "Exchange Rate Surprises in International Portfolios." *The Journal of Portfolio Management* 12 (1986), pp. 44–53.

Asprem, Mads. "Stock Prices, Assets Portfolios and Macroeconomic Variables in Ten European Countries." *Journal of Banking and Finance* 13 (1989), pp. 589–612.

Beckers, Stan. "Investment Implications of a Single European Capital Market." *Journal of Portfolio Management*, Spring (1999), pp. 9–17.

Berkman, Henk, and Nhut H. Nguyen. "Domestic Liquidity and Cross-Listing in the United States." *Journal of Banking and Finance* 34 (2010), pp. 1139–51.

Doidge, Craig, G. Andrew Karolyi, and Rene M. Stulz. "Why Do Foreign Firms Leave U.S. Equity Markets?" *Journal of Finance* 65 (2010), pp. 1507–53.

Eun, Cheol S., and Bruce G. Resnick. "Estimating the Correlation Structure of International Share Prices." *Journal of Finance* 39 (1984), pp. 1311–24.

Eun, Cheol S., and Bruce G. Resnick. "Exchange Rate Uncertainty, Forward Contracts, and International Portfolio Selection." *Journal of Finance* 43 (1988), pp. 197–215.

Gagnon, Louis, and G. Andrew Karolyi. "Multi-Market Trading and Arbitrage." Ohio State University working paper (July 2004).

Griffin, John M., and G. Andrew Karolyi. "Another Look at the Role of the Industrial Structure of Markets for International Diversification Strategies." *Journal of Financial Economics* 50 (1998), pp. 351–73.

Gupta, Manoj, and Joseph E. Finnerty. "The Currency Risk Factor in International Equity Pricing." *Review of Quantitative Finance and Account* 2 (1992), pp. 245–57.

Heston, Steven L., and K. Geert Rouwenhorst. "Does Industrial Structure Explain the Benefits of International Diversification?" *Journal of Financial Economics* 36 (1994), pp. 3–27.

Jayaraman, Narayanan, Kuldeep Shastri, and Kishore Tandon. "The Impact of International Cross-Listings on Risk and Return: The Evidence from American Depository Receipts." *Journal of Banking and Finance* 17 (1993), pp. 91–103.

Kao, G., K. C. Wenchi, John Wei, and Joseph Vu. "Risk-Return Characteristics of the American Depository Receipts," unpublished working paper, 1991.

Karolyi, G. Andrew. "DaimlerChrysler AG, The First Truly Global Share." *Journal of Corporate Finance* 9 (2003), pp. 409–30.

Miller, Darius P. "The Market Reaction to International Cross-Listings: Evidence from Depository Receipts." *Journal of Financial Economics* 51 (1999), pp. 103–23.

Park, Jinwoo. *The Impact of Information on ADR Returns and Variances: Some Implications,* unpublished Ph.D. dissertation from The University of Iowa, 1990.

Phylaktis, Kate, and Lichuan Xia. "The Changing Roles of Industry and Country Effects in the Global Equity Markets." *European Journal of Finance* 12 (2006), pp. 627–48.

Roll, Richard. "Industrial Structure and the Comparative Behavior of International Stock Market Indexes." *Journal of Finance* 47 (1992), pp. 3–42.

Rouwenhorst, K. Geert. "European Equity Markets and the EMU." *Financial Analysts Journal*, May/June (1999), pp. 57–64.

Schwartz, Robert A. *Equity Markets.* New York: Harper and Row, 1988.

Solnik, Bruno. "Capital Markets and International Monetary Variables." *Financial Analysts Journal* 40 (1984), pp. 69–73.

14 Interest Rate and Currency Swaps

CHAPTER 5 INTRODUCED forward contracts as a vehicle for hedging exchange rate risk; Chapter 7 introduced futures and options contracts on foreign exchange as alternative tools to hedge foreign exchange exposure. These types of instruments seldom have terms longer than a few years, however. Chapter 7 also discussed Eurodollar futures contracts for hedging short-term U.S.-dollar-denominated interest rate risk. In this chapter, we examine interest rate swaps, both single-currency and cross-currency, which are techniques for hedging long-term interest rate risk and foreign exchange risk.

The chapter begins with some useful definitions that define and distinguish between interest rate and currency swaps. Data on the size of the interest rate and currency swap markets are presented. The next section illustrates the usefulness of interest rate swaps. The following section illustrates the construction of currency swaps. The chapter also details the risks confronting a swap dealer in maintaining a portfolio of interest rate and currency swaps and shows how swaps are priced.

Types of Swaps

In interest rate swap financing, two parties, called **counterparties**, make a contractual agreement to exchange cash flows at periodic intervals. There are two types of interest rate swaps. One is a **single-currency interest rate swap**. The name of this type is typically shortened to *interest rate swap*. The other type can be called a **cross-currency interest rate swap**. This type is usually just called a *currency swap*.

In the basic ("plain vanilla") *fixed-for-floating rate* interest rate swap, one counterparty exchanges the interest payments of a floating-rate debt obligation for the fixed-rate interest payments of the other counterparty. Both debt obligations are denominated in the same currency. Some reasons for using an interest rate swap are to better match cash inflows and outflows and/or to obtain a cost savings. There are many variants of the basic interest rate swap, some of which are discussed below.

In a **currency swap**, one counterparty exchanges the debt service obligations of a bond denominated in one currency for the debt service obligations of the other counterparty denominated in another currency. The basic currency swap involves the exchange of *fixed-for-fixed rate* debt service. Some reasons for using currency swaps are to obtain debt financing in the swapped denomination at a cost savings and/or to hedge long-term foreign exchange rate risk. The International Finance in Practice box "The World Bank's First Currency Swap" discusses the first currency swap.

The World Bank's First Currency Swap

The World Bank frequently borrows in the national capital markets around the world and in the Eurobond market. It prefers to borrow currencies with low nominal interest rates, such as the (former) deutsche mark and the Swiss franc. In 1981, the World Bank was near the official borrowing limits in these currencies but desired to borrow more. By coincidence, IBM had a large amount of deutsche mark and Swiss franc debt that it had incurred a few years earlier. The proceeds of these borrowings had been converted to dollars for corporate use. Salomon Brothers convinced the World Bank to issue Eurodollar debt with maturities matching the IBM debt in order to enter into a currency swap with IBM. IBM agreed to pay the debt service (interest and principal) on the World Bank's Eurodollar bonds, and in turn the World Bank agreed to pay the debt service on IBM's deutsche mark and Swiss franc debt. While the details of the swap were not made public, both counterparties benefited through a lower all-in cost (interest expense, transaction costs, and service charges) than they otherwise would have had. Additionally, the World Bank benefited by developing an indirect way to obtain desired currencies without going directly to the German and Swiss capital markets.

Size of the Swap Market

As the International Finance in Practice box suggests, the market for currency swaps developed first. Today, however, the interest rate swap market is larger. Exhibit 14.1 provides some statistics on the size and growth in the interest rate and currency swap markets. Size is measured by **notional principal**, a reference amount of principal for determining interest payments. The exhibit indicates that both markets have grown significantly since 2003. The total amount of interest rate swaps outstanding increased from $111.2 trillion at year-end 2003 to $370.0 trillion by year-end 2012, an increase of 233 percent. Total outstanding currency swaps increased 299 percent, from $6,371 billion at year-end 2003 to over $25.4 trillion by year-end 2012.

While not shown in Exhibit 14.1, the four most common currencies used to denominate interest rate and currency swaps were the euro, U.S. dollar, Japanese yen, and the British pound sterling, with the fifth most common currency being the Swedish krona for interest rate swaps and the Swiss franc for currency swaps.

EXHIBIT 14.1		
Size of Interest Rate and Currency Swap Markets: Total Notional Principal Outstanding Amounts in Billions of U.S. Dollars*		

Year	Interest Rate Swaps	Currency Swaps
2003	111,209	6,371
2004	150,631	8,223
2005	169,106	8,504
2006	229,780	10,772
2007	309,588	14,347
2008	309,760	13,322
2009	349,236	16,509
2010	364,377	19,271
2011	402,611	22,791
2012	369,999	25,420

*Notional principal is used only as a reference measure to which interest rates are applied for determining interest payments. In an interest rate swap, principal does not actually change hands. At the inception date of a swap, the market value of both sides of the swap are of equivalent value. As interest rates change, the value of the cash flows will change, and both sides may no longer be equal. This is interest rate risk. The deviation can amount to 2 to 4 percent of notional principal. Only this small fraction is subject to credit (or default) risk.

Sources: *International Banking and Financial Market Developments,* Bank for International Settlements, Table 19, p. A103, June 2007, p. A121, June 2010, and p. A141, June 2013.

The Swap Bank

A **swap bank** is a generic term to describe a financial institution that facilitates swaps between counterparties. A swap bank can be an international commercial bank, an investment bank, a merchant bank, or an independent operator. The swap bank serves as either a **swap broker** or **swap dealer**. As a broker, the swap bank matches counterparties but does not assume any risk of the swap. The swap broker receives a commission for this service. Today, most swap banks serve as dealers or market makers. As a market maker, the swap bank stands willing to accept either side of a currency swap, and then later lay it off, or match it with a counterparty. In this capacity, the swap bank assumes a position in the swap and therefore assumes certain risks. The dealer capacity is obviously more risky, and the swap bank would receive a portion of the cash flows passed through it to compensate it for bearing this risk.

The market for interest rate and currency swaps are subject to the regulation of over-the-counter swaps as defined under the Commodities Exchange Act, as amended by the Dodd-Frank Act. The Dodd-Frank Act covers several key aspects of the functionality of swaps markets, including clearing, transparency, reporting requirements, bankruptcy-related issues, trading and risk mitigation, and coordination of international enforcement. At the time of this writing, most of this regulation has yet to be implemented.

Swap Market Quotations

www.bis.org

This is the website of the Bank for International Settlements. This site describes the activities and purpose of the BIS. Many online publications about foreign exchange and OTC derivatives are available at this site.

Swap banks will tailor the terms of interest rate and currency swaps to customers' needs. They also make a market in generic "plain vanilla" swaps and provide current market quotations applicable to counterparties with Aa or Aaa credit ratings. Consider a basic U.S. dollar fixed-for-floating interest rate swap indexed to dollar LIBOR. A swap bank will typically quote a fixed-rate bid-ask spread (either semiannual or annual) versus three-month or six-month dollar LIBOR flat, that is, no credit premium. Suppose the quote for a five-year swap with semiannual payments is 8.50–8.60 percent against six-month LIBOR flat. This means the swap bank will pay semiannual fixed-rate dollar payments of 8.50 percent against receiving six-month dollar LIBOR, or it will receive semiannual fixed-rate dollar payments at 8.60 percent against paying six-month dollar LIBOR.

It is convention for swap banks to quote interest rate swap rates for a currency against a local standard reference in the same currency and currency swap rates against dollar LIBOR. For example, for a five-year swap with semiannual payments in Swiss francs, suppose the bid-ask swap quotation is 6.60–6.70 percent against six-month LIBOR flat. This means the swap bank will pay semiannual fixed-rate SF payments at 6.60 percent against receiving six-month SF (dollar) LIBOR in an interest rate (a currency) swap, or it will receive semiannual fixed-rate SF payments at 6.70 percent against paying six-month SF (dollar) LIBOR in an interest rate (a currency) swap.

It follows that if the swap bank is quoting 8.50–8.60 percent in dollars and 6.60–6.70 percent in SF against six-month dollar LIBOR, it will enter into a currency swap in which it would pay semiannual fixed-rate dollar payments of 8.50 percent in return for receiving semiannual fixed-rate SF payments at 6.70 percent, or it will receive semiannual fixed-rate dollar payments at 8.60 percent against paying semiannual fixed-rate SF payments at 6.60 percent.

Exhibit 14.2 provides an illustration of interest rate swap quotations. Swap banks typically build swap yield curves such as this from the 90-day LIBOR rates implied in the Eurodollar interest rate futures contracts we discussed in Chapter 7.

Interest Rate Swaps

Basic Interest Rate Swap

As an example of a basic, often called "plain vanilla," interest rate swap, consider the following example of a fixed-for-floating rate swap. Bank A is a AAA-rated international bank located in the United Kingdom. The bank needs $10,000,000 to finance

EXHIBIT 14.2		Interest Rate Swap Quotations							
	Euro-€		£ Stlg.		SwFr		US $		Yen	
Jun 5	Bid	Ask	Bid	Ask	Bid	Ask	Bid	Ask	Bid	Ask
1 year	0.32	0.36	0.51	0.54	0.06	0.12	0.32	0.35	0.22	0.28
2 year	0.44	0.48	0.68	0.72	0.11	0.19	0.43	0.46	0.24	0.30
3 year	0.59	0.63	0.81	0.85	0.20	0.28	0.03	0.66	0.29	0.35
4 year	0.77	0.81	0.97	1.02	0.34	0.42	0.89	0.92	0.36	0.42
5 year	0.95	0.99	1.13	1.20	0.49	0.57	1.17	1.20	0.45	0.51
6 year	1.14	1.18	1.35	1.40	0.66	0.74	1.45	1.10	0.58	0.62
7 year	1.30	1.34	1.55	1.60	0.83	0.91	1.64	1.72	0.68	0.74
8 year	1.46	1.50	1.74	1.79	0.98	1.06	1.91	1.94	0.79	0.85
9 year	1.60	1.64	1.93	1.97	1.11	1.19	2.09	2.12	0.89	0.95
10 year	1.74	1.78	2.08	2.13	1.21	1.29	2.25	2.28	0.99	1.05
12 year	1.95	1.99	2.35	2.40	1.38	1.48	2.52	2.55	1.16	1.24
15 year	2.18	2.22	2.59	2.68	1.55	1.65	2.78	2.81	1.41	1.49
20 year	2.33	2.37	2.84	2.97	1.67	1.77	3.00	3.03	1.70	1.78
25 year	2.38	2.42	2.98	3.11	1.71	1.81	3.11	3.14	1.84	1.92
30 year	2.39	2.43	3.05	3.18	1.73	1.83	3.17	3.20	1.90	1.98

Bid and Ask rates as of close of London business. £ and Yen quoted on a semi-annual actual/365 basis against 6 month Libor with the exception of the 1 Year GBP rate which is quoted annual actual against 3M Libor. Euro/Swiss Franc quoted on an annual bond 30/360 basis against 6 month Euribor/Libor.

Source: *Financial Times*, June 6, 2013, p. 19.

floating-rate Eurodollar term loans to its clients. It is considering issuing five-year floating-rate notes indexed to LIBOR. Alternatively, the bank could issue five-year fixed-rate Eurodollar bonds at 10 percent. The FRNs make the most sense for Bank A, since it would be using a floating-rate liability to finance a floating-rate asset. In this manner, the bank avoids the interest rate risk associated with a fixed-rate issue. Without this hedge, Bank A could end up paying a higher rate than it is receiving on its loans should LIBOR fall substantially.

Company B is a BBB-rated U.S. company. It needs $10,000,000 to finance a capital expenditure with a five-year economic life. It can issue five-year fixed-rate bonds at a rate of 11.25 percent in the U.S. bond market. Alternatively, it can issue five-year FRNs at LIBOR plus .50 percent. The fixed-rate debt makes the most sense for Company B because it locks in a financing cost. The FRN alternative could prove very unwise should LIBOR increase substantially over the life of the note, and could possibly result in the project being unprofitable.

A swap bank familiar with the financing needs of Bank A and Company B has the opportunity to set up a fixed-for-floating interest rate swap that will benefit each counterparty and the swap bank. Assume that the swap bank is quoting five-year U.S. dollar interest rate swaps at 10.375–10.50 percent against LIBOR flat. The key, or necessary condition, giving rise to the swap is that a **quality spread differential (QSD)** exists. A QSD is the difference between the default-risk premium differential on the fixed-rate debt and the default-risk premium differential on the floating-rate debt. In general, the former is greater than the latter. The reason for this is that the yield curve for lower-quality debt tends to be steeper than the yield curve for higher-rated debt. Financial theorists have offered a variety of explanations for this phenomenon, none of which is completely satisfactory. Exhibit 14.3 shows the calculation of the QSD.

Given that a QSD exists, it is possible for each counterparty to issue the debt alternative that is least advantageous for it (given its financing needs), then swap interest payments, such that each counterparty ends up with the type of interest payment desired, but at a lower all-in cost than it could arrange on its own. Exhibit 14.4 diagrams a possible scenario the swap bank could arrange for the two counterparties. The interest rates used in Exhibit 14.4 refer to the percentage rate paid per annum on the notional principal of $10,000,000.

	Company B	Bank A	Differential
Fixed-rate	11.25%	10.00%	1.25%
Floating-rate	LIBOR + .50%	LIBOR	.50%
			QSD = .75%

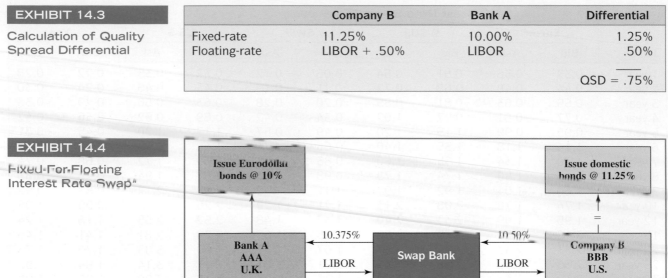

Net Cash Outflows

	Bank A	Swap Bank	Company B
Pays	LIBOR	10.375%	10.50%
	10%	LIBOR	LIBOR + .50%
Receives	−10.375%	−10.50%	−LIBOR
		−LIBOR	
Net	LIBOR − .375%	−.125%	11%

*Debt service expressed as a percentage of $10,000,000 notional value.

From Exhibit 14.4, we see that the swap bank has instructed Company B to issue FRNs at LIBOR plus .50 percent rather than the more suitable fixed-rate debt at 11.25 percent. Company B passes through to the swap bank 10.50 percent (on the notional principal of $10,000,000) and receives LIBOR in return. In total, Company B pays 10.50 percent (to the swap bank) plus LIBOR + .50 percent (to the floating-rate bondholders) and receives LIBOR percent (from the swap bank) for an **all-in cost** (interest expense, transaction costs, and service charges) of 11 percent. Thus, through the swap, Company B has converted floating-rate debt into fixed-rate debt at an all-in cost .25 percent lower than the 11.25 percent fixed rate it could arrange on its own.

Similarly, Bank A was instructed to issue fixed-rate debt at 10 percent rather than the more suitable FRNs. Bank A passes through to the swap bank LIBOR percent and receives 10.375 percent in return. In total, Bank A pays 10 percent (to the fixed-rate Eurodollar bondholders) plus LIBOR percent (to the swap bank) and receives 10.375 percent (from the swap bank) for an all-in cost of LIBOR −.375 percent. Through the swap, Bank A has converted fixed-rate debt into floating-rate debt at an all-in cost .375 percent lower than the floating rate of LIBOR it could arrange on its own.

The swap bank also benefits because it pays out less than it receives from each counterparty to the other counterparty. Note from Exhibit 14.4 that it receives 10.50 percent (from Company B) plus LIBOR percent (from Bank A) and pays 10.375 percent (to Bank A) and LIBOR percent (to Company B). The net inflow to the swap bank is .125 percent per annum on the notional principal of $10,000,000. In sum, Bank A has saved .375 percent, Company B has saved .25 percent, and the swap bank has earned .125 percent. This totals .75 percent, which equals the QSD. Thus, if a QSD exists, it can be split in some fashion among the swap parties resulting in lower all-in costs for the counterparties.

In an interest rate swap, the principal sums the two counterparties raise are not exchanged, since both counterparties have borrowed in the same currency. The amount of interest payments that are exchanged are based on a notional sum, which may not equal the exact amount actually borrowed by each counterparty. Moreover, while Exhibit 14.4 portrays a gross exchange of interest payments based on the notional principal, in practice only the net difference is actually exchanged. For example, Company B would pay to the swap bank the net difference between 10.50 percent and LIBOR percent on the notional value of $10,000,000.

In More Depth

Pricing the Basic Interest Rate Swap

After the inception of an interest rate swap, it may become desirable for one and/or the other counterparty to unwind or reverse the swap. The value of an interest rate swap to a counterparty should be the difference in the present values of the payment streams the counterparty will receive and pay on the notional principal. As an example, consider Company B from our previous example. Company B pays 10.50 percent to the swap bank and receives LIBOR percent from the swap bank on a notional value of $10,000,000. It has an all-in cost of 11 percent because it has issued FRNs at LIBOR + .50 percent.

Assume that one year later, the swap bank is quoting four-year dollar swaps at 9.00–9.125 percent versus LIBOR flat. This will also be a reset date for the FRNs. On any reset date, the present value of the future floating-rate payments paid or received at LIBOR on the notional value will always be $10,000,000. The present value of a hypothetical bond issue of $10,000,000 with four remaining 10.50 percent coupon payments at the new swap bid rate of 9 percent is $10,485,958 = $1,050,000 × $PVIFA_{9\%,4}$ + $10,000,000 × $PVIF_{9\%,4}$. The value of the swap is $10,000,000 − $10,485,958 = −$485,958. Thus, Company B should be willing to pay $485,958 to the swap bank to unwind or reverse the original swap. In essence, the market value of the swap is the present value of the difference between paying 10.50 percent and receiving 9 percent on the $10,000,000 notional value discounted at the new swap bid rate of 9 percent. That is: −$150,000 × $PVIFA_{9\%,4}$ = −$485,958.

Currency Swaps

Basic Currency Swap

As an example of a basic currency swap, consider the following example. A U.S. MNC desires to finance a capital expenditure of its German subsidiary. The project has an economic life of five years. The cost of the project is €40,000,000. At the current exchange rate of $1.30/€1.00, the parent firm could raise $52,000,000 in the U.S. capital market by issuing five-year bonds at 8 percent. The parent would then convert the dollars to euros to pay the project cost. The German subsidiary would be expected to earn enough on the project to meet the annual dollar debt service and to repay the principal in five years. The only problem with this situation is that a long-term transaction

EXHIBIT 14.8

Cross-Currency Swap
Analyzer, CURSWAP.xls
Output

	A	B	C	D	E	F	G
1							
2							
3			FC Bond	FC	$	Actual	
4			Cash Flow	Received	Paid	$ Cash Flow	
5							
6		0	40,000,000	−40,000,000	30,769,231	30,769,231	
7		1	−2,400,000	2,400,000	−2,507,692	−2,507,692	
8		2	−2,400,000	2,400,000	−2,507,692	−2,507,692	
9		3	−2,400,000	2,400,000	−2,507,692	−2,507,692	
10		4	−2,400,000	2,400,000	−2,507,692	−2,507,692	
11		5	−42,400,000	42,400,000	−33,276,923	−33,276,923	
12							
13		AIC	6.00%	6.00%	8.15%	8.15%	
14							
15		Face value:	40,000,000				
16						Bid	Ask
17		Coupon rate:	6.000%		Spot FX rate:	1.30000	1.30000
18							
19		OP as % of par:	100.000%		FC swap rate:	6.00%	6.10%
20							
21		Underwriting fee:	0.000%		$ swap rate:	8.00%	8.15%

Variations of Basic Interest Rate and Currency Swaps

There are several variants of the basic interest rate and currency swaps we have discussed. For example, a fixed-for-floating interest rate swap does not require a fixed-rate coupon bond. A variant is a *zero-coupon-for-floating* rate swap where the floating-rate payer makes the standard periodic floating-rate payments over the life of the swap, but the fixed-rate payer makes a single payment at the end of the swap. Another variation is the *floating-for-floating* interest rate swap. In this swap, each side is tied to a different floating rate index (e.g., LIBOR and Treasury bills) or a different frequency of the same index (such as three-month and six-month LIBOR). For a swap to be possible, a QSD must still exist. Additionally, interest rate swaps can be established on an amortizing basis, where the debt service exchanges decrease periodically through time as the hypothetical notional principal is amortized. Currency swaps need not involve the swap of fixed-rate debt. *Fixed-for-floating* and *floating-for-floating* currency rate swaps are also frequently arranged. Additionally, *amortizing* currency swaps incorporate an amortization feature in which periodically the amortized portions of the notional principals are reexchanged. The International Finance in Practice box "Fallout from Greece's Swap" describes how Greece used a currency swap in an unethical manner to hide the amount of its sovereign debt. While interesting from a current events perspective, we do not advocate this use of currency swaps.

Risks of Interest Rate and Currency Swaps

Some of the major risks that a swap dealer confronts are discussed here.

Interest-rate risk refers to the risk of interest rates changing unfavorably before the swap bank can lay off on an opposing counterparty the other side of an interest rate swap entered into with a counterparty. As an illustration, reconsider the interest rate swap example outlined in Exhibit 14.4. To recap, in that example, the swap bank earns a spread of .125 percent. Company B passes through to the swap bank 10.50 percent per annum (on the notional principal of $10,000,000) and receives LIBOR percent in return.

Fallout from Greece's Swap

Greek debt is a hot topic, and Goldman has suffered attacks on, among other things, its role in subprime credit derivatives and the bailout of U.S. insurance giant American International Group. But what gets lost amid the furor is the real context— a decade long tango between financial innovators at investment banks and institutional clients, including governments, which were anxious to skirt various restrictions. The most significant restraints are accounting rules.

Since their invention in the 1980s, over-the-counter derivatives such as swaps have had legitimate uses. Take the cross currency swap, the tool that Goldman adapted for Greece. Borrowing in a foreign currency can seem attractive when interest rates are comparatively low abroad, as they are in Japan. The catch is that if your home currency weakens, the size of your debt can balloon. A swap removes this risk by converting all the future foreign currency payments of interest and principal into an obligation denominated in your home currency. The borrower has bought an instrument that turns foreign debt into domestic debt.

In the corporate world, accountants allow firms to treat liabilities that have been fully hedged from foreign to domestic currency as if they had been issued in their home currency. When the euro zone was conceived, its member states were already big borrowers in foreign currencies. It would have seemed odd for Eurostat, the European Union's statistics agency and watchdog, not to allow the corporate accounting rules to apply. But, as so often happens, the gatekeeper got captured.

Suppose you had borrowed US$10 billion at a time when the U.S. dollar and euro were at parity. Now imagine a swap that did not use the prevailing market exchange rate, but instead assumed your home currency was stronger than it really was—say two dollars to one euro. That would shrink your US$10 billion debt to US$5 billion. In essence, that was how Goldman's customized swap deal for Greece worked. The derivative, hatched in 2001, reduced Greece's public debt by almost $3 billion. The balancing of this paper gain would come later, in a further series of swap payments to Goldman. The economic reality of the transaction was that Goldman was lending to the Greek government and getting paid back over 20 years.

Eurostat's bean counters understood the implications of allowing Greece, and other EU states, to legitimately hide debt in this way from the wider world. Debt managers, presumably from the most indebted countries,

successfully lobbied Eurostat to amend its rulebook to make the disappearing trick possible. The willingness of Eurostat to sanction off-balance-sheet transactions and pressure from the EU's weakest members exposes it as an irresponsible steward of accounting integrity.

It is unclear precisely how widely the transaction was known, or its implications understood. If the credit rating agencies were aware of it, as has been suggested, they certainly did not reflect Greece's true off-balance-sheet debt position in their ratings.

Having made what economically amounted to a loan for Greece—although it was off the Greek balance sheet—what did Goldman do with it? Displaying its characteristic aversion to risk, the bank promptly bought credit protection from Depfa, now part of Germany's Hypo Real Estate.

In total, Greece paid an eye-watering $500 million for the instrument. The cost of the off-balance-sheet loan was widely criticized in Greece after the Risk article. Shortly before the change of Greek government in 2005, Goldman restructured the deal, unwinding the Depfa credit protection and transferring the swap to the National Bank of Greece. In 2008, a securitization transaction, called Titlos, reduced the cost of the original deal for Greece.

Clearly, investment banks are in the often lucrative business of advising clients how to use rules to their advantage. And with EU governance permitting Greece and other states to hobble Eurostat in the way they did, it was hard for Goldman's publicity-shy derivatives innovators to resist applying their skills. Better oversight of derivatives dealers is long overdue. But it makes even more sense to focus on client governance. In the 1990s, weak accounting rules contributed to a wave of derivatives scandals across corporate America. When these rules were tightened up—to exclude customized derivatives from hedge accounting and to enforce disclosure—the problem went away.

The same thing happened to European companies after the introduction of IFRS hedge accounting. Greece and Goldman simply took advantage of the then-generous rules in the 2001 transaction. They would have to break the rules to do the same today.

The currency outcry over Greece makes reform of EU governance mechanisms inevitable.

Source: Excerpted from Nicholas Dunbar, Thomson Reuters, February 19, 2010. Reprinted with permission of LexisNexis.

Bank A passes through to the swap bank LIBOR percent and receives 10.375 percent in return. Suppose the swap bank entered into the position with Company B first. If fixed rates increase substantially, say, by .50 percent, Bank A will not be willing to enter into the opposite side of the swap unless it receives, say, 10.875 percent. This would make the swap unprofitable for the swap bank.

Basis risk refers to a situation in which the floating rates of the two counterparties are not pegged to the same index. Any difference in the indexes is known as the basis. For example, one counterparty could have its FRNs pegged to LIBOR, while the other counterparty has its FRNs pegged to the U.S. Treasury bill rate. In this event, the indexes are not perfectly positively correlated and the swap may periodically be unprofitable for the swap bank. In our example, this would occur if the Treasury bill rate was substantially larger than LIBOR and the swap bank receives LIBOR from one counterparty and pays the Treasury bill rate to the other.

Exchange-rate risk refers to the risk the swap bank faces from fluctuating exchange rates during the time it takes for the bank to lay off a swap it undertakes with one counterparty with an opposing counterparty.

Credit risk is the major risk faced by a swap dealer. It refers to the probability that a counterparty will default. The swap bank that stands between the two counterparties is not obligated to the defaulting counterparty, only to the nondefaulting counterparty. There is a separate agreement between the swap bank and each counterparty.

Mismatch risk refers to the difficulty of finding an exact opposite match for a swap the bank has agreed to take. The mismatch may be with respect to the size of the principal sums the counterparties need, the maturity dates of the individual debt issues, or the debt service dates. Textbook illustrations typically ignore these real-life problems.

Sovereign risk refers to the probability that a country will impose exchange restrictions on a currency involved in a swap. This may make it very costly, or perhaps impossible, for a counterparty to fulfill its obligation to the dealer. In this event, provisions exist for terminating the swap, which results in a loss of revenue for the swap bank.

To facilitate the operation of the swap market, the International Swaps and Derivatives Association (ISDA) has standardized two swap agreements. One is the "Interest Rate and Currency Swap Agreement" that covers currency swaps, and the other is the "Interest Rate Swap Agreement" that lays out standard terms for U.S.-dollar- denominated interest rate swaps. The standardized agreements have reduced the time necessary to establish swaps and also provided terms under which swaps can be terminated early by a counterparty.

Is the Swap Market Efficient?

The two primary reasons for a counterparty to use a currency swap are to obtain debt financing in the swapped currency at an interest cost reduction brought about through comparative advantages each counterparty has in its national capital market, and/or the benefit of hedging long-run exchange rate exposure. These reasons seem straightforward and difficult to argue with, especially to the extent that name recognition is truly important in raising funds in the international bond market.

The two primary reasons for swapping interest rates are to better match maturities of assets and liabilities and/or to obtain a cost savings via the quality spread differential. In an efficient market without barriers to capital flows, the cost-savings argument through a QSD is difficult to accept. It implies that an arbitrage opportunity exists because of some mispricing of the default risk premiums on different types of debt instruments. If the QSD is one of the primary reasons for the existence of interest rate swaps, one would expect arbitrage to eliminate it over time and that the growth of the swap market would decrease. Quite the contrary has happened as Exhibit 14.1 shows; growth in interest rate swaps has been extremely large in recent years. Thus, the arbitrage argument does not seem to have much merit. Consequently, one must rely on an argument of **market completeness** for the existence and growth of interest rate swaps. That is, all types of debt instruments are not regularly available for all borrowers. Thus, the interest rate swap market assists in tailoring financing to the type desired by a particular borrower. Both counterparties can benefit (as well as the swap dealer) through financing that is more suitable for their asset maturity structures.

SUMMARY

This chapter provides a presentation of currency and interest rate swaps. The discussion details how swaps might be used and the risks associated with each.

1. The chapter opened with definitions of an interest rate swap and a currency swap. The basic interest rate swap is a fixed-for-floating rate swap in which one counterparty exchanges the interest payments of a fixed-rate debt obligation for the floating-interest payments of the other counterparty. Both debt obligations are denominated in the same currency. In a currency swap, one counterparty exchanges the debt service obligations of a bond denominated in one currency for the debt service obligations of the other counterparty, which are denominated in another currency.

2. The function of a swap bank was discussed. A swap bank is a generic term to describe a financial institution that facilitates the swap between counterparties. The swap bank serves as either a broker or a dealer. When serving as a broker, the swap bank matches counterparties, but does not assume any risk of the swap. When serving as a dealer, the swap bank stands willing to accept either side of a currency swap.

3. An example of a basic interest rate swap was presented. It was noted that a necessary condition for a swap to be feasible was the existence of a quality spread differential between the default-risk premiums on the fixed-rate and floating-rate interest rates of the two counterparties. Additionally, it was noted that there was not an exchange of principal sums between the counterparties to an interest rate swap because both debt issues were denominated in the same currency. Interest rate exchanges were based on a notional principal.

4. Pricing an interest rate swap after inception was illustrated. It was shown that after inception, the value of an interest rate swap to a counterparty should be the difference in the present values of the payment streams the counterparty will receive and pay on the notional principal.

5. A detailed example of a basic currency swap was presented. It was shown that the debt service obligations of the counterparties in a currency swap are effectively equivalent to one another in cost. Nominal differences can be explained by the set of international parity relationships.

6. Pricing a currency swap after inception was illustrated. It was shown that after inception, the value of a currency swap to a counterparty should be the difference in the present values of the payment stream the counterparty will receive in one currency and pay in the other currency, converted to one or the other currency denomination.

7. In addition to the basic fixed-for-floating interest rate swap and fixed-for-fixed currency swap, many other variants exist. One variant is the amortizing swap, which incorporates an amortization of the notional principles. Another variant is a zero-coupon-for-floating rate swap in which the floating-rate payer makes the standard periodic floating-rate payments over the life of the swap, but the fixed-rate payer makes a single payment at the end of the swap. Another is the floating-for-floating rate swap. In this type of swap, each side is tied to a different floating-rate index or a different frequency of the same index.

8. Reasons for the development and growth of the swap market were critically examined. It was argued that one must rely on an argument of market completeness for the existence and growth of interest rate swaps. That is, the interest rate swap market assists in tailoring financing to the type desired by a particular borrower when all types of debt instruments are not regularly available to all borrowers.

www.mcgraw-hill.co.uk/textbooks/eun

Two years ago, Rone issued a $25 million (U.S.$), five-year floating-rate note (FRN). The FRN pays an annual coupon equal to one-year LIBOR plus 75 basis points. The FRN is noncallable and will be repaid at par at maturity.

Scott expects interest rates to increase, and she recognizes that Rone could protect itself against the increase by using a pay-fixed swap. However, Rone's board of directors prohibits both short sales of securities and swap transactions. Scott decides to replicate a pay-fixed swap using a combination of capital market instruments.

a. Identify the instruments needed by Scott to replicate a pay-fixed swap and describe the required transactions.

b. Explain how the transactions in part a are equivalent to using a pay-fixed swap.

CFA® PROBLEMS

8. A company based in the United Kingdom has an Italian subsidiary. The subsidiary generates €25,000,000 a year, received in equivalent semiannual installments of €12,500,000. The British company wishes to convert the euro cash flows to pounds twice a year. It plans to engage in a currency swap in order to lock in the exchange rate at which it can convert the euros to pounds. The current exchange rate is €1.5/£. The fixed rate on a plain vanilla currency swap in pounds is 7.5 percent per year, and the fixed rate on a plain vanilla currency swap in euros is 6.5 percent per year.

a. Determine the notional principals in euros and pounds for a swap with semiannual payments that will help achieve the objective.

b. Determine the semiannual cash flows from this swap.

CFA® PROBLEMS

9. Ashton Bishop is the debt manager for World Telephone, which needs €3.33 billion Euro financing for its operations. Bishop is considering the choice between issuance of debt denominated in:

- Euros (€), or

- U.S. dollars, accompanied by a combined interest rate and currency swap.

a. Explain *one* risk World would assume by entering into the combined interest rate and currency swap.

Bishop believes that issuing the U.S.-dollar debt and entering into the swap can lower World's cost of debt by 45 basis points. Immediately after selling the debt issue, World would swap the U.S. dollar payments for Euro payments throughout the maturity of the debt. She assumes a constant currency exchange rate throughout the tenor of the swap.

Exhibit 1 gives details for the two alternative debt issues. Exhibit 2 provides current information about spot currency exchange rates and the 3-year tenor Euro/U.S. Dollar currency and interest rate swap.

EXHIBIT 1	Characteristic	Euro Currency Debt	U.S. Dollar Currency Debt
World Telephone Debt Details	Par value	€3.33 billion	$3 billion
	Term to maturity	3 years	3 years
	Fixed interest rate	6.25%	7.75%
	Interest payment	Annual	Annual

EXHIBIT 2		
Currency Exchange Rate and Swap Information	Spot currency exchange rate	$0.90 per Euro ($0.90/€1.00)
	3-year tenor Euro/U.S. Dollar fixed interest rates	5.80% Euro/7.30% U.S. Dollar

b. Show the notional principal and interest payment cash flows of the combined interest rate and currency swap.

Note: Your response should show both the correct currency ($ or €) and amount for *each* cash flow.

Answer problem b in the template provided.

Template for problem b

Cash Flows of the Swap				
World pays				
Notional principal				
Interest payment				
World receives				
Notional principal				
Interest payment				

c. State whether or not World would reduce its borrowing cost by issuing the debt denominated in U.S. dollars, accompanied by the combined interest rate and currency swap. Justify your response with *one* reason.

INTERNET EXERCISES

The website www.finpipe.com/intrateswaps.htm provides a brief description of interest rate swaps. Links at the bottom of the screen lead to other descriptions of derivative products, including currency swaps and other types of swaps that you will find interesting. It is a good idea to bookmark this site for future reference. Use it now to see how well you understand interest rate and currency swaps. If you cannot follow the discussions, go back and reread Chapter 14.

MINI CASE

Groene Stad Ltd.'s Currency Swap

Groene Stad Ltd., a South African company specialized in environment-friendly infrastructure engineering, has decided to participate in a development project in Brisbane, Australia. Groene Stad is expected to raise a sum of AUD 8,000,000 in the credit market to finance the project. The principal amount of the loan should be repaid in four years, with yearly interest payments. The company has hitherto been mostly active on a national scale, and faces more favorable credit terms in the South African market than in the Australian market, for loans in the respective currencies. The lowest rates for loans denominated in AUD and in ZAR are respectively 6.5% and 6%.

Study Questions

1. An Australian MNC must borrow 80,000,000 Rands to finance the capital expenditures of its South African subsidiaries over a four-year time-period. The lowest rates faced by this MNC for loans denominated in AUD and in ZAR are respectively 5% and 7%, and the spot exchange rate is AUD 1.00/Rand 1.00. Construct a currency swap that would benefit both the Australian MNC and Groene Stad, and indicate the currency in which each company should borrow.

2. Two years after the start of the project, Groene Stad has negotiated its participation in two new projects. The company has been offered a loan in AUD on very favorable terms from a major Australian bank. It is thus planning to refinance the loan initially taken out to finance the first project, taking advantage of a specific clause included in the contract. Upon extinguishing the loan, Groene Stad would also unwind the currency swap, which would otherwise drive imbalances between the cash in- and out-flows denominated in Rands and in AUD. The AUD and the Rand fixed rates quoted on the date when the decision is made are respectively 3.5% and 5%, and the spot exchange rate is AUD 1.06/Rand 1.00. Which payment should Groene Stad expect to make or to receive? Indicate the value of the payment both in AUD and in Rands.

EXHIBIT 15.5   Selection of the Optimal International Portfolio

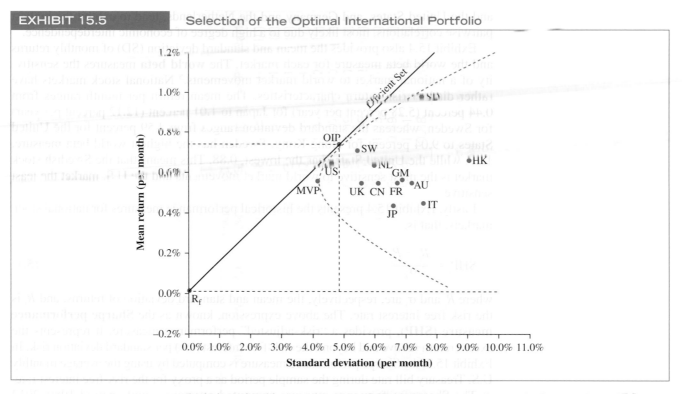

In their optimal international portfolio, U.S. investors allocate the largest share, 47.72 percent, of funds to the U.S. home market, followed by the Swedish (24.31 percent) and Swiss (27.97 percent) markets. Other markets are not included in U.S. investors' OIP[7]. Apart from OIP, Exhibit 15.5 also shows the minimum variance portfolio (MVP), which is the portfolio with the lowest possible risk among all risky portfolios.[8]

Similarly, we can solve for the composition of the optimal international portfolio from the perspective of each of the national investors. Since the risk-return characteristics of international stock markets vary depending on the numeraire currency used to measure returns, the composition of the optimal international portfolio will also vary across national investors using different numeraire currencies. Exhibit 15.6 presents the composition of the optimal international portfolio from the currency perspective of each national investor. In Exhibit 15.6, we use the stock market parameters computed over the period 1980–2012 and the risk-free rate faced by investors in December 2012.

For instance, the U.K. (or British pound–based) investors' optimal international portfolio comprises Sweden (30.73%), Switzerland (45.41%), the U.K. (7.70%), and the United States (16.16%). It is clear from the table that the two of the best-performing markets, Switzerland and Sweden, are most heavily represented in the optimal international portfolios. In fact, the Swiss and Swedish markets are included in every national investor's optimal international portfolio and receive large weights. It is noted that the U.S. market is also included in most national investor's optimal portfolio, with

---

[7]It is noted that in Exhibit 15.6, short sales are not allowed in any market and that optimal international portfolios are solved based on the historical (ex post) parameter values. We conduct our portfolio analysis here in order to estimate the "potential gains" from international portfolio diversification. It is noted that when we want to construct an "ex ante" optimal international portfolio to hold for a future period, we need to use estimated (predicted) parameter values.

[8] During the period 1980–2012, U.S. investors' MVP consists of Japan (19.20%), Switzerland (15.96%), and the United States (64.84%). By comparison, Australian MVP consists of Australia (28.23%), Italy (1.68%), Japan (15.29%), Switzerland (15.92%), the U.K. (2.02%), and the United States (36.87%). Compared to OIPs, MVPs tend to be move diversified and assign greater weights to investors' respective home markets. It is noted that Japan tends to receive significant weights in MVPs, most likely due to its relatively low correlations with other markets. Also, the United States tends to receive more weights in MVPs than in OIPs due to its low return volatility.

EXHIBIT 15.6 Composition of the Optimal International Portfolio by Investors' Domicile (Holding Period: 1980–2010)

Stock Market	From the Perspective of Investors Domiciled in												
	AU	CN	FR	GM	HK	IT	JP	NL	SD	SW	UK	US	LC[a]
Australia (AU)	0.0650												0.0099
Canada (CN)													
France (FR)													
Germany (GM)													
Hong Kong (HK)		0.0020	0.0043		0.0307								0.0171
Italy (IT)													
Japan (JP)		0.0015			0.0054	0.0104			0.0053				
Netherlands (NL)													
Sweden (SD)	0.4372	0.2962	0.2596	0.3210	0.1950	0.2558	0.6409	0.3121	0.3220	0.3319	0.1773	0.2431	0.5378
Switzerland (SW)	0.2688	0.2365	0.6338	0.6233	0.3239	0.5654	0.3591	0.6245	0.5322	0.6681	0.4341	0.2797	
United Kingdom (UK)											0.0770		0.0748
United States (US)	0.2290	0.4638	0.1022	0.0558	0.4450	0.1684		0.0635	0.1404		0.3116	0.4772	0.3604
Total	1.0000	1.0000	1.0000	1.0000	1.0000	1.0000	1.0000	1.0000	1.0000	1.0000	1.0000	1.0000	1.0000
Risk-free rate (%)[b]	0.1958	0.0817	0.0050	0.0050	0.0192	0.0053	0.0075	0.0050	0.0032	−0.0129	0.0032	0.0179	0.0179

[a]LC column provides the composition of the optimal international portfolio without considering exchange rate changes.

[b]The risk-free rate denotes the risk-free interest rate faced by investors domiciled in the corresponding country in December 2012. It is proxied by the one-month Treasury bill rate or eurocurrency interest rate.

data presented in Exhibit 15.7 suggest that, regardless of domicile and numeraire currency, investors can potentially benefit from IPD to a varying degree.[9]

Effects of Changes in the Exchange Rate

The realized dollar returns for a U.S. resident investing in a foreign market will depend not only on the return in the foreign market but also on the change in the exchange rate between the dollar and the local (foreign) currency. Thus, the success of foreign investment rests on the performances of both the foreign security market and the foreign currency.

Formally, the rate of return in dollar terms from investing in the ith foreign market, $R_{i\$}$, is given by

$$R_{i\$} = (1 + R_i)(1 + e_i) - 1$$
$$= R_i + e_i + R_i e_i \qquad (15.4)$$

where R_i is the local currency rate of return from the ith foreign market and e_i is the rate of change in the exchange rate between the local currency and the dollar; e_i will be positive (negative) if the foreign currency appreciates (depreciates) against the dollar. Suppose that a U.S. resident just sold shares of British Petroleum (BP) she had purchased a year ago, and that the share price of BP rose 15 percent in terms of the British pound (i.e., $R = .15$), whereas the British pound depreciated 5 percent against the dollar over the one-year period (i.e., $e = -.05$). Then the rate of return, in dollar terms, from this investment will be calculated as: $R_{i\$} = (1 + .15)(1 - .05) - 1 = .0925$, or 9.25 percent.

The above expression suggests that exchange rate changes affect the risk of foreign investment as follows:

$$\text{Var}(R_{i\$}) = \text{Var}(R_i) + \text{Var}(e_i) + 2\text{Cov}(R_i, e_i) + \Delta\text{Var} \qquad (15.5)$$

where the ΔVar term represents the contribution of the cross-product term, $R_i e_i$, to the risk of foreign investment. Should the exchange rate be certain, only one term, $\text{Var}(R_i)$, would remain in the right-hand side of the equation. Equation 15.5 demonstrates that exchange rate fluctuations contribute to the risk of foreign investment through three possible channels:

1. Its own volatility, $\text{Var}(e_i)$.
2. Its covariance with the local market returns, $\text{Cov}(R_i, e_i)$.
3. The contribution of the cross-product term, ΔVar.

Exhibit 15.8 provides the breakdown of the variance of dollar returns into different components for both the bond and stock markets of six major foreign countries during the period 1990–2012: Australia, Canada, Germany, Japan, Switzerland, and the United Kingdom. Let us first examine the case of bond markets. The exhibit clearly indicates that a large portion of the risk associated with investing in foreign bonds arises from the exchange rate uncertainty. Consider investing in a German bond. As can be seen from the exhibit, the variance of German bond returns is only 2.91 percent squared in terms of the local currency, but jumps to 11.58 percent squared when measured

---

[9]In analyzing the gains from international investments, it was implicitly assumed that investors fully bear exchange risk. As will be discussed later, investors can hedge exchange risk using, say, forward contracts, therefore enhancing the gains. It is also pointed out that the preceding analyses are strictly "ex-post" in the sense that the risk-return characteristics of securities are assumed to be known to investors. In reality, of course, investors will have to estimate these characteristics, and estimation errors may lead to an inefficient allocation of funds.

| EXHIBIT 15.8 | Decomposition of the Variance of International Security Returns in U.S. Dollar (Monthly Data: 1990.1–2012.12) |

		Components of Var(R_{is})[b]			
	VAR(R_{is})	VAR(R_i)	VAR(e_i)	2Cov(R_i, e_i)	ΔVar
Bonds					
Australia	14.18	4.70 (33.82%)	11.59 (81.73%)	−2.28 (−16.00%)	0.08 (0.54%)
Canada	7.96	3.51 (44.16%)	4.85 (60.90%)	0.40 (5.00%)	0.00 (−0.06%)
Germany	11.50	2.91 (25.12%)	9.57 (82.65%)	−0.91 (−7.86%)	0.01 (0.08%)
Japan	13.15	2.16 (16.42%)	10.33 (78.55%)	0.53 (4.03%)	0.13 (1.00%)
Switzerland	13.02	2.18 (16.75%)	11.44 (87.89%)	−0.78 (−6.00%)	0.18 (1.36%)
U.K.	10.45	4.25 (40.70%)	7.94 (75.99%)	−1.87 (−17.86%)	0.12 (1.17%)
U.S.	4.72	4.72 (100.00%)	0.00 (n.a.)	0.00 (n.a.)	0.00 (n.a.)
Stocks					
Australia	40.05	17.41 (43.48%)	11.59 (28.94%)	10.60 (26.47%)	0.45 (1.11%)
Canada	36.05	22.04 (61.13%)	4.85 (13.44%)	9.60 (26.62%)	−0.43 (−1.19%)
Germany	46.38	38.53 (83.07%)	9.57 (20.63%)	−1.82 (−3.92%)	0.10 (0.22%)
Japan	42.57	35.21 (82.72%)	10.33 (24.26%)	−3.57 (−8.39%)	0.60 (1.41%)
Switzerland	27.79	24.15 (86.90%)	11.44 (41.16%)	−8.02 (−28.85%)	0.22 (0.80%)
U.K.	26.74	19.88 (74.36%)	7.94 (29.70%)	−1.27 (−4.76%)	0.19 (0.70%)
U.S.	20.67	20.67 (100.00%)	0.00 (n.a.)	0.00 (n.a.)	0.00 (n.a.)

[a]The portfolio variances are computed using the monthly percentage returns.
[b]The relative contributions of individual components to the total risk appear in parentheses.

Source: Monthly stock and bond returns data are obtained from the *Datastream* database. Specifically, Morgan Stanley Capital International (MSCI) stock market indexes and *Datastream* benchmark 10-year government bond indexes are used.

in dollar terms. This change in volatility is due to the volatility of the exchange rate, Var(e_i) = 9.57, as well as its covariance with the local bond market returns, that is 2Cov(R_i, e_i) = −0.91. As can be expected, the cross-product term contributes relatively little. In the case of investing in the Swiss bond, the local bond market returns account for only 16.75 percent of the volatility of returns in dollar terms. This means that investing in Swiss bonds largely amounts to investing in the Swiss currency.

Without exception, exchange rate volatility is much greater than bond market volatility. And exchange rate changes may covary positively or negatively with local bond market returns. Empirical evidence regarding bond markets suggests that it is essential to control exchange risk to enhance the efficiency of international bond portfolios.

Compared with bond markets, the risk of investing in foreign stock markets is, to a lesser degree, attributable to exchange rate uncertainty. Again, consider investing in the German market. The variance of the German stock market is 38.53 percent squared in terms of the local currency, but it increases to 46.38 percent squared when measured in terms of the U.S. dollar. The local market return volatility accounts for 83.07 percent of the volatility of German stock market returns in dollar terms. In comparison, exchange rate volatility accounts for 20.63 percent of the dollar return variance, still a significant portion. Interestingly, the exchange rate covaries negatively with local stock market returns, partially offsetting the effect of exchange rate volatility. In the case of investing in the Swiss stock market, the local market variance, 24.15, is only modestly less than the dollar return variance, 27.79. In other words, U.S. and Swiss investors face similar risk when they invest in the Swiss stock market. This result is due to the fact that the exchange rate volatility is largely offset by a significantly negative comovement between the local market return and exchange rate change. In the case of Australian stocks, the exchange rate contributes to the dollar return variance through its strongly positive co-movement with the local stock market return, as well as through its own volatility. The same largely holds for Canadian stocks.

International Bond Investment

Although the world bond market is comparable in terms of capitalization value to the world stock market, so far it has not received as much attention in international investment literature. This may reflect, at least in part, the perception that exchange risk makes it difficult to realize significant gains from international bond diversification. It is worthwhile to explore this issue and determine if this perception has merit.

Exhibit 15.9 provides summary statistics of monthly returns, in U.S. dollar terms, on long-term government bond indexes from seven major countries: Australia, Canada, Germany, Japan, Switzerland, the United Kingdom, and the United States. It also presents the composition of the optimal international portfolio for U.S. (dollar-based) investors. Note that European bond markets have relatively high correlations. For instance, the correlation of the German bond market is 0.82 with the Swiss bond market and 0.71 with the U.K. bond market. These high correlations reflect the fact that as a group these European currencies tend to float against the U.S. dollar. Similarly, two "commodity currency" bonds, i.e., the Australian bond and the Canadian bond, exhibit a relatively high correlation, 0.68. In contrast, the Japanese bond tends to have relatively low correlations with other bonds. For example, its correlation is 0.27 with the Australian bond, 0.19 with the Canadian bond, and 0.36 with the U.S. bond. Exhibit 15.9 further shows that the U.S. bond market has the lowest mean return and also the lowest risk among the seven markets during the study period 1990–2012. Japan has the highest Sharpe ratio, 0.119, followed by Switzerland (0.117), Australia (0.101), and Canada (0.100).

In the optimal international portfolio, the Swiss, Canadian, and Japanese bonds receive the most weights, followed by the Australian, U.S., and U.K. bonds. The German bond receives a negative weight, implying that U.S. investors should have borrowed in the German currency (i.e., German mark till the end of 1998 and the euro thereafter). The optimal portfolio has a monthly mean return of 0.46 percent and a standard deviation of 2.64 percent, resulting in a Sharpe performance measure of 0.167. Considering that the U.S. bond has a mean return of 0.16 percent, a standard deviation of 2.17 percent, and a Sharpe measure of 0.065, U.S. investors could have benefited very substantially from holding the optimal international bond portfolio.

The preponderance of exchange risk in foreign bond investment suggests that investors may be able to increase their gains from international bond diversification if they can properly control the exchange risk. Existing studies indeed show that when

Summary Statistics of the Monthly Returns to Bonds and the Composition of the Optimal International Bond Portfolio

| EXHIBIT 15.9 | | | | | | | (in U.S. dollars 1990.1–2012.12) | | | |

Bond Market	Correlation Coefficient						Mean (%)	SD (%)	SHP	Optimal International Portfolio[a] (Weights)
	AU	CN	GM	JP	SW	UK				
Australia (AU)							0.40	3.77	0.101	0.1439
Canada (CN)	0.68						0.30	2.82	0.100	0.3629
Germany (GM)	0.50	0.42					0.27	3.40	0.074	−0.6597
Japan (JP)	0.27	0.19	0.45				0.45	3.63	0.119	0.3456
Switzerland (SW)	0.42	0.32	0.82	0.50			0.44	3.61	0.117	0.6329
United Kingdom (UK)	0.46	0.48	0.71	0.33	0.60		0.27	3.23	0.078	0.0731
United States (US)	0.35	0.36	0.49	0.36	0.36	0.41	0.16	2.17	0.065	0.1014
Optimal International Portfolio :							0.46	2.64	0.167	

[a]The optimal international bond portfolio is solved allowing for short sales and using one-month U.S. Treasury-bill rate as the monthly risk-free interest rate. The risk-free interest rate is 0.018% for December 2012. Benchmark 10-year *Datastream* government bond indexes are used.

Source: Bond returns data are obtained from *Datastream*.

investors control exchange risk by using currency forward contracts, they can substantially enhance the efficiency of international bond portfolios. Eun and Resnick (1994), for instance, show that when exchange risk is hedged, international bond portfolios tend to dominate international stock portfolios in terms of risk-return efficiency.[10]

The advent of the *euro,* the common European currency, altered the risk-return characteristics of the euro zone markets. Before the euro was introduced, for instance, the Italian and German bonds had quite different characteristics; the former was generally viewed as a high-risk and high-return investment, whereas the latter a low-risk and low-return investment, largely because the German mark was a hard currency while the Italian lira was a weak one. In the post-euro period, however, both German and Italian bonds (and all the other euro zone bonds) became denominated and transacted in the common currency, rendering nationality of bonds a somewhat less significant factor. Although euro zone bonds differ in terms of credit risk, their risk-return characteristics converged to a certain extent. This implies that non-euro currency bonds like British bonds would play an enhanced role in international diversification strategies as they would retain their unique risk-return characteristics.

International Mutual Funds: A Performance Evaluation

Currently, U.S. investors can achieve international diversification at home simply by investing in U.S.-based international mutual funds, which have proliferated in recent years. By investing in international mutual funds, investors can (i) save any extra transaction and/or information costs they may have to incur when they attempt to invest directly in foreign markets, (ii) circumvent many legal and institutional barriers to direct portfolio investments in foreign markets, and (iii) potentially benefit from the expertise of professional fund managers.

These advantages of international mutual funds should be particularly appealing to small individual investors who would like to diversify internationally but have neither the necessary expertise nor the direct access to foreign markets. It is thus relevant to ask the following question: Can investors benefit from international diversification by investing in existing U.S.-based international mutual funds? To provide an answer to the above question, we are going to examine the historical performance of international mutual funds that invest a substantial portion of their assets in foreign markets.

Exhibit 15.10 provides the risk-return profiles of a sample of U.S.-based international mutual funds that have sufficient track records. Three funds—the ASA (which invests in South African gold-mining stocks), the Canadian Fund, and the Japan Fund—are single-country funds. Other funds invest more broadly. The table shows that all but one fund have a higher mean return than the U.S. stock market index, proxied by the Standard & Poor 500 Index, during the period of 1977.1–1986.12. The average mean return of the international mutual funds is 1.58 percent per month (18.96 percent per year). In comparison, the mean return on the S&P 500 is 1.17 percent per month (14.04 percent per year). The standard deviation of the international mutual funds ranges from 3.36 percent to 11.88 percent, with an average of 5.78 percent. In comparison, the S&P has a standard deviation of 4.25 percent.[11]

Exhibit 15.10 also provides the U.S. beta measures of the international funds and the associated coefficient of determination (R^2) values.[12] Note that most funds have a U.S. beta value that is much less than unity. On average, U.S. stock market movements

---

[10]For further discussion of exchange risk hedging, readers are referred to Appendix 15A.

[11]It is noted that no existing studies provide current, comprehensive evaluation of international mutual fund performances.

[12]The U.S. beta measures the sensitivity of the fund returns to the U.S. stock market returns. The coefficient of determination (R^2) measures the fraction of the variance of fund returns that can be explained by the U.S. market returns.

International
Mutual Funds: A
Performance Evaluation
(Monthly Returns:
1977.1–1986.12)

Fund	Mean (%)	SD (%)	β_{US}	R^2	SHP[a]
ASA	1.75	11.88	0.80	0.08	0.084
Canadian Fund	0.91	4.64	0.75	0.47	0.035
International Investors	2.34	10.09	0.72	0.09	0.157
Japan Fund	1.72	7.02	0.59	0.13	0.138
Keystone International	1.14	4.29	0.69	0.47	0.091
Merrill Lynch Pacific	1.82	5.45	0.32	0.06	0.100
New Perspective	1.47	3.99	0.80	0.73	0.179
Oppenheimer Global	1.94	6.35	1.02	0.47	0.186
Putnam International	1.64	5.91	0.62	0.20	0.150
Scudder International	1.46	4.23	0.50	0.26	0.168
Sogen International	1.48	3.36	0.70	0.78	0.217
Templeton Growth	1.48	4.13	0.84	0.74	0.176
United International Growth	1.41	3.86	0.71	0.61	0.172
Average	1.58	5.78	0.69	0.39	0.150
U.S. MNC Index	1.34	4.38	0.98	0.90	0.135
S&P 500	1.17	4.25	1.00	1.00	0.099
MSCI World Index	1.46	3.80	0.70	0.61	0.186

[a]The Sharpe measure is computed using the risk-free rate of 0.752%, which is the average monthly Treasury bill rate during the sample period.

Source: C. Eun, R. Kolodny, and B. Resnick, "U.S.-Based International Mutual Funds: A Performance Evaluation." This copyrighted material is reprinted with permission from the *Journal of Portfolio Management*, 488 Madison Avenue, New York, NY 10022.

account for less than 40 percent of the fluctuations in the international fund returns. In contrast, U.S. stock market movements are known to account for about 90 percent of the fluctuations in U.S. domestic stock fund returns.[13] These results show that the sample funds provided U.S. investors with a valuable opportunity to diversify internationally. In contrast, the U.S. MNC Index, which comprises 60 U.S. multinational corporations with the highest proportions of international revenue, has a U.S. beta value of 0.98 and an R^2 value of 90 percent. This means that the share prices of MNCs behave much like those of domestic firms, without providing effective international diversification.[14]

Lastly, Exhibit 15.10 provides the Sharpe performance measures of international mutual funds. As the table shows, 10 out of 13 international funds outperformed the U.S. stock market index based on the Sharpe measure. The same point is illustrated in Exhibit 15.11, showing that only three international funds lie below the U.S. capital market line (CML).[15] This is in sharp contrast to the findings of previous studies showing that the majority of U.S. domestic mutual funds lie below the U.S. capital market line. Against the alternative benchmark of the World Index, however, the sample funds performed rather poorly. The average SHP value for the international funds, 0.15, is substantially less than the value for the World Index, 0.186. This seems to suggest that it is desirable to invest in a world index fund if available.[16]

---

[13]See, for example, Sharpe (1966), pp. 127–28.

[14]This result is consistent with Jacquillat and Solnik's study (1978), showing that multinational corporations of various countries have very low exposure (beta) to foreign stock market indexes.

[15]The capital market line (CML) is the straight line obtained by connecting the risk-free interest rate and the market portfolio.

[16]The capital asset pricing model (CAPM) suggests that if the world market portfolio is indeed mean-variance efficient, then the expected return on a portfolio will be determined by its world beta. This, in turn, implies that if investors hold parochial portfolios that are less than fully diversified globally, they are bearing some diversifiable risk for which there will be no compensation in terms of extra returns. Under this situation it would be optimal for investors to hold the world market portfolio, proxied by a world index fund, together with the risk-free asset, to achieve the desired combination of risk and return.

EXHIBIT 15.11

Performance of
International Mutual
Funds: 1977.1–1986.12

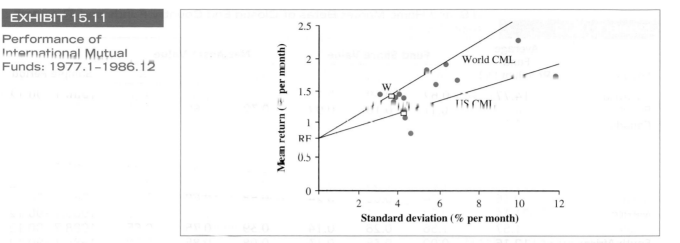

Note: Each international fund is denoted by a round dot (•). The risk-free rate (RF) is 7.52%, which is the average T-bill rate during the sample period. W and US, respectively, denote the MSCI World Index and the S&P 500.

In More Depth

In addition to international mutual funds, investors may achieve international portfolio diversification "at home" by investing in (i) country funds, (ii) American depository receipts (ADRs), (iii) exchange-traded funds (ETFs), or (iv) hedge funds without having to invest directly in foreign stock markets. In the next section, we discuss each of these instruments.

International Diversification through Country Funds

Recently, country funds have emerged as one of the most popular means of international investment in the United States as well as in other developed countries. As the name suggests, a country fund invests exclusively in stocks of a single country. Using country funds, investors can

1. Speculate in a single foreign market with minimum costs.
2. Construct their own *personal* international portfolios using country funds as building blocks.
3. Diversify into *emerging markets* that are otherwise practically inaccessible.

Many emerging markets, such as India, China, and Russia, still remain substantially segmented. As a result, country funds often provide international investors with the most practical, if not the only, way of diversifying into these foreign markets.

The majority of country funds available, however, have a *closed-end* status. Like other closed-end funds, a **closed-end country fund (CECF)** issues a given number of shares that trade on the stock exchange of the host country as if the fund were an individual stock by itself. Unlike shares of open-end mutual funds, shares of a closed-end country fund cannot be redeemed at the underlying net asset value set at the home market of the fund. Currently, about 30 countries offer CECFs, a partial list of which is provided in Exhibit 15.12. In the United States, the majority of CECFs are listed on the New York Stock Exchange, with a few listed on the American Stock Exchange.

Since the share value of a fund is set on a U.S. stock exchange, it may very well diverge from the underlying net asset value (NAV) set in the fund's home market. The difference is known as a *premium* if the fund share value exceeds the NAV, or a *discount* in the opposite case. Exhibit 15.12 provides the magnitude of premiums/discounts

EXHIBIT 15.13	Summary Statistics of the Weekly Returns for Closed-End Country Funds and Their Net Asset Values and the Compositions of Optimal Portfolios (in U.S. Dollar Terms: 1989.1–1990.12)							
	Country Fund Share			**Net Asset Value**			**Optimal Portfolio**	
Country	Mean (%)	SD (%)	Correlation with U.S.	Mean (%)	SD (%)	Correlation with U.S	CECF (Weight)	NAV (Weight)
Australia	0.46	5.64	0.12	0.01	1.78	0.25	0.0033	0.0000
Brazil	0.73	6.31	−0.01	0.29	7.55	−0.02	0.1271	0.0023
Canada	0.14	4.91	−0.31	−0.19	1.98	−0.19	0.0660	0.0000
Germany	0.78	9.70	0.22	0.30	4.67	−0.11	0.0253	0.0000
India	0.36	5.93	0.18	0.15	3.92	−0.21	0.0750	0.0882
Italy	0.44	7.00	0.22	0.39	2.20	0.25	0.0000	0.1044
Korea	−0.37	6.79	0.25	0.00	2.91	0.08	0.0000	0.0000
Malaysia	0.72	7.89	0.35	0.37	3.21	0.29	0.0000	0.0000
Mexico	1.11	6.07	0.50	0.77	2.63	0.24	0.2427	0.6026
Spain	0.39	8.76	0.40	0.03	3.08	0.29	0.0000	0.0000
South Africa	0.43	4.00	−0.13	0.36	5.06	−0.03	0.2993	0.0954
Switzerland	0.27	4.50	0.46	0.20	2.48	0.36	0.0000	0.0000
Taiwan	0.57	7.42	0.31	−0.06	7.95	0.05	0.0000	0.0000
Thailand	0.71	8.42	0.29	0.50	5.14	0.23	0.0000	0.0000
U.K.	0.35	4.01	0.44	0.27	4.08	0.23	0.0424	0.0616
U.S. Index	0.18	2.06	1.00	0.18	2.06	1.00	0.1189	0.0454
						Total =	1.0000	1.0000
						Mean =	0.58%	0.58%
						SD =	2.49%	1.81%
						SHP =	0.233	0.320

Source: E. Chang, C. Eun, and R. Kolodny, "International Diversification through Closed-End Country Funds," *Journal of Banking and Finance* (October 1995). Reprinted with permission of Elsevier Science.

EXHIBIT 15.14

Efficient Sets: Country Funds versus Net Assets: 1989.1–1990.12

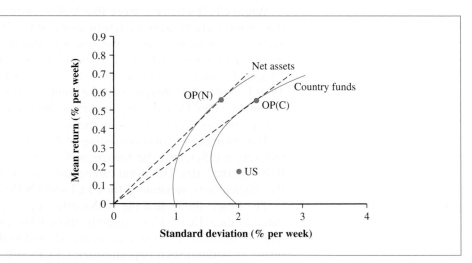

Note: OP(N) and OP(C) denote, respectively, the optimal portfolios comprising net assets and country funds. The efficient sets are illustrated by the dotted lines.

International Diversification with ADRs

U.S. investors can achieve international diversification at home using American depository receipts (ADRs), as well as country funds. As explained in Chapter 13, ADRs represent receipts for foreign shares held in the U.S. (depository) banks' foreign branches or custodians. Like closed-end country funds, ADRs are traded on U.S. exchanges like domestic American securities. Consequently, U.S. investors can save transaction costs and also benefit from speedy and dependable disclosures, settlements, and custody

www.adr.com

This website, managed by J.P. Morgan & Co., is a comprehensive source of information on American depository receipts.

services. It is noted that like American investors, British and European investors may achieve international diversification at home using global depository receipts (GDRs), which represent ownership claims on those foreign shares that are listed on the London Stock Exchange.

A few studies examined the potential benefits of international diversification with ADRs. Officer and Hoffmeister (1987) found that adding ADRs to a domestic portfolio had substantial risk reduction benefits. Including as few as four ADRs in a representative U.S. stock portfolio reduced risk, measured by the standard deviation of returns, by as much as 25 percent without reducing the expected return. They also found that ADRs tend to have very low beta exposure to the U.S. stock market. During the sample period 1973–1983, ADRs were found to have an average U.S. beta of only 0.264.

Wahab and Khandwala (1993) found similar results. They reported that when investors hold an equally weighted portfolio of seven ADRs and the S&P 500, the annualized standard deviation of daily returns drops from 30.2 percent (for a purely domestic port-folio) to 17.5 percent. They also reported that most of the nonsystematic risk of the port-folio is eliminated by adding only seven ADRs to the S&P 500. Adding ADRs beyond seven did not reduce the portfolio risk materially, regardless of portfolio weights.

Considering that the majority of ADRs are from such developed countries as Australia, Japan, and the United Kingdom, U.S. investors have a limited opportunity to diversify into emerging markets using ADRs. However, in a few emerging markets like Mexico, investors can choose from several ADRs. In this situation, investors should consider the relative advantages and disadvantages of ADRs and CECFs as a means of international diversification. Compared with ADRs, CECFs are likely to provide more complete diversification. As shown previously, however, the potential gains from investing in them tend to be reduced by premiums/discounts.

International Diversification with Exchange-Traded Funds (ETFs)

www.ishares.com

Provides extensive coverage of exchange-traded funds, including WEBS.

In April 1996, the American Stock Exchange (AMEX) introduced a class of securities called **World Equity Benchmark Shares (WEBS)**, originally designed and managed by Barclays Global Investors. In essence, WEBS are exchange-traded funds (ETFs) that are designed to closely track foreign stock market indexes. Currently, there are WEBS track-ing the Morgan Stanley Capital International (MSCI) indexes for the following individual countries: Australia, Austria, Belgium, Brazil, Canada, Chile, China, France, Germany, Hong Kong, Indonesia, Ireland, Israel, Italy, Japan, Korea, Malaysia, Mexico, the Netherlands, Peru, Poland, Singapore, South Africa, Spain, Sweden, Switzerland, Taiwan, Thailand, Turkey, and the United Kingdom. The AMEX had previously introduced a similar security for the U.S. market, Standard & Poor's Depository Receipts (SPDRs), known as "spiders," that is designed to track the S&P 500 Index. Using **exchange-traded funds (ETFs)** like WEBS and spiders, investors can trade a whole stock market index as if it were a single stock. Being open-end funds, WEBS trade at prices that are very close to their net asset values. In addition to single-country index funds, investors can achieve global diversification instantaneously just by holding shares of the S&P Global 100 Index Fund that is also trading on the AMEX with other WEBS. WEBS were later re-named as iShares, which are listed on multiple exchanges, including the New York Stock Exchange, London Stock Exchange, and Hong Kong Stock Exchange.

A study by Khorana, Nelling, and Trester (1998) found that WEBS indeed track the underlying MSCI country indexes very closely. For example, the average correlation of daily returns between WEBS and the underlying country indexes is 0.97. They also found that the average correlation of WEBS with the S&P 500 Index is quite low, 0.22, which makes WEBS an excellent tool for international risk diversification. For those investors who desire international equity exposure, WEBS may well serve as a major alternative to such traditional tools as international mutual funds, ADRs, and closed-end country funds.

International Diversification with Hedge Funds

Hedge funds that represent privately pooled investment funds have experienced a phenomenal growth in recent years. This growth of hedge funds has been mainly driven by the desire of institutional investors, such as pension plans, endowments, and private foundations, to achieve positive or absolute returns, regardless of whether markets are rising or falling. Unlike traditional mutual funds that generally depend on "buy and hold" investment strategies, hedge funds may adopt flexible, dynamic trading strategies, often aggressively using leverages, short positions, and derivative contracts, in order to achieve their investment objectives. These funds may invest in a wide spectrum of securities, such as currencies, domestic and foreign bonds and stocks, commodities, real estate, and so forth. Many hedge funds aim to realize positive returns, regardless of market conditions.

Legally, hedge funds are private investment partnerships. As such, these funds generally do not register as investment companies under the Investment Company Act and are not subject to any reporting or disclosure requirements. As a result, many hedge funds operate in rather opaque environments. Hedge fund advisors typically receive a management fee, often 1–2 percent of the fund asset value as compensation, plus performance fee that can be 20–25 percent of capital appreciation. Investors may not be allowed to liquidate their investments during a certain lock-up period. In the United States, only institutional investors and wealthy individuals are allowed to invest in hedge funds. In many European countries, however, retail investors are also allowed to invest in these funds.

Hedge funds tend to have relatively low correlations with various stock market benchmarks and thus allow investors to diversify their portfolio risk. In addition, hedge funds allow investors to access foreign markets that are not easily accessible. For example, J.P. Morgan provides access to the Jayhawk China Fund, a hedge fund investing in Chinese stocks not readily available in U.S. markets. Also, hedge funds may allow investors to benefit from certain global macroeconomic events. In fact, many hedge funds are classified as "global/macro" funds. Examples of global/macro funds include such well-known names as George Soros' Quantum Fund, Julian Robertson's Jaguar Fund, and Louis Bacon's Moore Global Fund. Some hedge funds were active during the British pound crisis of 1992 and Asian financial crisis of 1997. As is well known, George Soros correctly anticipated the withdrawal of the British pound from the European Monetary System (EMS) and bet on the pound depreciation upon the withdrawal. His funds reportedly took a $10 billion short position on the British pound and made about $1 billion profit during September 1992. Soros funds also had short positions in the Thai baht and Malaysian ringgit during the Asian currency crisis of 1997. This touched off a series of acrimonious exchanges between the Malaysian Prime Minister Mahatir Mohamad and George Soros on whether hedge funds were responsible for the currency crisis.

While investors may benefit from hedge funds, they need to be aware of the associated risk as well. Hedge funds may make wrong bets based on the incorrect prediction of future events and wrong models. The failure of Long Term Capital Management (LTCM) provides an example of the risk associated with hedge fund investing. John Meriwether, a former fixed income trader at Salomon Brothers, founded LTCM in 1993. Teamed up with a group of veteran Wall Street traders and two Nobel laureates, Myron Scholes and Robert Merton, LTCM enjoyed a solid credibility and respectability among the investment community. Using its good name, LTCM pursued highly leveraged fixed income arbitrage strategies. Among other things, LTCM borrowed heavily and bet on international interest convergence between high- and low-quality debts. For example, LTCM bought Italian government bonds and sold German Bund futures. Initially, LTCM did well, realizing about 40 percent annual returns on equity in the first few years. But following the Asian and Russian currency crises, gradual convergence turned into a dramatic divergence. As a result, LTCM's debts increased and its capital base depleted, eventually leading to its downfall. Investors lost large sums of money.

Why Home Bias in Portfolio Holdings?

As previously documented, investors can potentially benefit a great deal from international diversification. The actual portfolios that investors hold, however, are quite different from those predicted by the theory of international portfolio investment. Recently, various researchers, such as French and Poterba (1991), Cooper and Kaplanis (1994), Tesar and Werner (1993), Glassman and Riddick (1993), and Chan, Covrig, and Ng (2005), documented the extent to which portfolio investments are concentrated in domestic equities.

Exhibit 15.15, which is adopted from Lau, Ng, and Zhang (2010), shows the extent of **home bias in portfolio holdings**. U.S. mutual funds, for instance, invested about 87 percent of their funds in domestic equities on average during 1998–2007, when the U.S. stock market accounted for about 45 percent of the world market capitalization value during the period. Relatively speaking, German mutual funds seem to invest more internationally—they put 71 percent of their funds in foreign equities and 29 percent in domestic equities. Considering, however, that the German share in the world market value is only 3.2 percent, German funds also display a striking degree of home bias in their portfolio holdings. It is noted that Brazilian mutual funds invested exclusively in domestic equities, probably due to regulatory restrictions. In recent years, investors have begun to invest in foreign securities in earnest. But, most investors still exhibit a strong home bias in portfolio holdings.

This home bias in actual portfolio holdings obviously runs counter to the strand of literature, including Grubel (1968), Levy and Sarnat (1970), Solnik (1974), Lessard (1976), and Eun and Resnick (1988), that collectively established a strong case for international diversification. This points to the following possibilities. First, domestic securities may provide investors with certain extra services, such as hedging against domestic inflation, that foreign securities do not. Second, there may be barriers, formal or informal, to investing in foreign securities that keep investors from realizing gains from international diversification. In what follows, we are going to examine possible reasons for the home bias in portfolio holdings.[20]

EXHIBIT 15.15

The Home Bias in Equity Portfolios: Selected Countries, 1998–2007

Country	Share in the World Market Value (%)	Proportion of Local Equities in Domestic Mutual Funds (%)
Australia	1.70	78.91
Brazil	0.71	100.00
Canada	2.67	28.67
France	4.13	55.48
Germany	3.21	29.35
Japan	9.29	98.50
Sweden	1.00	48.56
United Kingdom	7.64	42.95
United States	44.86	86.88

Source: Adopted from S.T. Lau et al., "The World Price of Home Bias," *Journal of Financial Economics* 97 (2010), pp. 191–217.

---

[20]For a survey of this issue, readers are referred to Uppal (1992).

First, consider the possibility that investors face country-specific inflation risk due to the violations of purchasing power parity and that domestic equities may provide a hedging service against domestic inflation risk. In this case, investors who would like to hedge domestic inflation risk may allocate a disproportionate share of their investment funds to domestic equities, resulting in home bias. This, however, is not a likely scenario. Those investors who are averse to inflation risk are likely to invest in domestic risk-free bonds rather than domestic equities, as the latter tends to be a poor hedge against inflation.[21] In addition, a study by Cooper and Kaplanis (1994) rules out inflation hedging as a primary cause for home bias.

Second, the observed home bias may reflect institutional and legal restrictions on foreign investments. For example, many countries used to restrict foreigners' ownership share of domestic firms. In Finland, foreigners could own at most 30 percent of the shares outstanding of any Finnish firm. In Korea, foreigners' ownership proportion was restricted to 20 percent of any Korean firm. As a result, foreigners had to pay premiums for local shares, which may reduce the gains from investing in those restricted markets. At the same time, some institutional investors may not invest more than a certain fraction of their funds overseas under the so-called *prudent man rule*. For example, Japanese insurance companies and Spanish pension funds may invest at most 30 percent of their funds in foreign securities. These inflow and outflow restrictions may contribute to the home bias in actual portfolio holdings.

Third, extra taxes and transaction/information costs for foreign securities can inhibit cross-border investments, giving rise to home bias. Investors often have to pay withholding taxes on dividends from foreign securities for which they may or may not receive tax credits in their home country. Transaction costs can be higher for foreign securities partly because many foreign markets are relatively thin and illiquid and partly because investment in foreign securities often involves transactions in foreign exchange markets. What's more, as argued by Merton (1987), investors tend not to hold securities with which they do not feel familiar. To the extent that investors feel familiar with domestic securities, but not with foreign securities, they are going to allocate funds to domestic, but not to foreign, securities. Consistent with the familiarity bias, Chan, Covrig, and Ng (2005) found that when a country is more remote from the rest of the world and has an uncommon language, domestic (foreign) investors tend to invest more (less) in the country's market. It is even possible that some investors may not be fully aware of the potential gains from international investments. Bailey, Kumar, and Ng (2004) found that the degree of home bias varies across investors. Using brokerage records of tens of thousands of U.S. individual investors, they examined ownership and trading of U.S.-listed foreign stocks and closed-end country funds. They found that wealthier, more experienced, and sophisticated investors are more likely to invest in foreign securities.

The observed home bias in asset holdings is likely to reflect a combination of some of the factors mentioned above. Considering the ongoing integration of international financial markets, coupled with the active financial innovations introducing new financial products such as country funds and international mutual funds, home bias may be substantially mitigated in the near future.

International Diversification with Small-Cap Stocks

To the extent that investors diversify internationally, well-known, large-cap stocks receive the dominant share of fund allocation. There is no doubt "large-cap bias" as well as home bias in international investment. These biases are broadly consistent with

---

[21]Fama and Schwert (1975) showed that common stocks are a perverse hedge against domestic inflation in that returns to common stocks are significantly negatively correlated with the inflation rate. In comparison, bond returns are positively correlated with the inflation rate.

The Average Return Correlation among 10 Major International Stock Markets Over Time, 1981–2012[a]

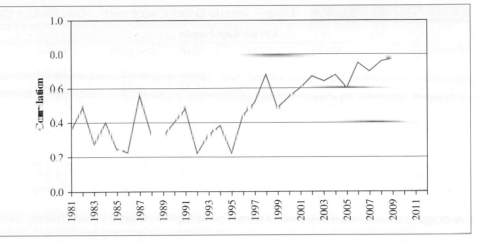

[a]The 10 markets are Australia, Canada, France, Germany, Hong Kong, Italy, Japan, the Netherlands, the United Kingdom, and the United States. Weekly stock market index returns, in U.S. dollars, are used to compute the correlations for each year of the study period.

Source: *Datastream.*

the proposition that "familiarity breeds investment."[22] Increasingly, however, returns to large-cap stocks or stock market indexes that are dominated by large-cap stocks tend to co-move, mitigating the benefit from international diversification. This point is illustrated in Exhibit 15.16, which plots the average return correlation among 10 major international stock markets over time. As can be seen in the exhibit, the average correlation among international stock market returns was fluctuating around 0.37 until the mid-1990s, but it has been generally increasing since then. It is noted that the average correlation reached nearly 0.80 in 2009, when the global financial crisis was at its height. The rising tendency of international correlations in recent years led many investors to become doubtful about the benefit and wisdom of international diversification.

Many well-known large-cap stocks that are popular among international investors are likely to be those of multinational firms with a substantial foreign customer and investor base. In contrast, small-cap firms are likely to be locally oriented with a limited international exposure. As a result, returns on large-cap stocks would be substantially driven by common "global factors," whereas returns on small-cap stocks are likely to be primarily driven by "local factors." This implies that locally oriented, small-cap stocks may be an effective vehicle for international diversification. In a recent study, Eun, Huang, and Lai (2008) confirmed that this is indeed the case.

Exhibit 15.17, which is based on the aforementioned study, provides a summary of the risk-return characteristics of large-cap versus small-cap funds of 10 major markets during the study period 1980–1999. For each fund, the exhibit provides the annualized mean return (Mean), standard deviation of return (SD), the Sharpe performance measure (SHP), and the correlation with the U.S. stock market index [Cor(US)]. As can be seen from the last row of the exhibit, small-cap funds, on average, have a much higher mean return (21.1%) than large-cap funds (16.6%). This confirms the existence of the so-called "small-cap premium" in most countries, with the exception of two countries: the Netherlands and the United States. As expected, the standard deviation of returns is, on average, higher for small-cap funds (25.3%) than for large-cap funds (22.3%). The Sharpe performance measure indicates that the small-cap fund outperformed the large-cap counterpart in each country, except for the same two countries: the Netherlands and the United States.

---

[22]This proposition is due to Huberman (2001). In a similar vein, Leuz, Lins, and Warnock (2009) show that foreigners tend to invest less in firms with poor disclosure (less reliable information) and governance standards.

EXHIBIT 15.17				Large- versus Small-Cap Funds: Risk-Return Characteristics			
	Large-Cap Funds				**Small-Cap Funds**		
Countries	Mean	SD	SHP	Cor (US)	Mean	SD	SHP	Cor (US)
Australia	14.9%	25.7%	0.32	0.45	24.9%	33.1%	0.55	0.22
Canada	10.9%	17.9%	0.24	0.71	24.6%	22.5%	0.80	0.45
France	15.3%	21.9%	0.40	0.46	17.2%	21.9%	0.48	0.27
Germany	14.4%	20.1%	0.39	0.41	14.6%	16.5%	0.48	0.19
Hong Kong	22.1%	34.3%	0.45	0.38	27.6%	39.7%	0.53	0.26
Italy	20.0%	27.7%	0.48	0.46	18.2%	27.2%	0.61	0.21
Japan	15.6%	24.2%	0.37	0.22	23.1%	27.8%	0.59	0.13
Netherlands	18.4%	16.2%	0.73	0.61	16.3%	18.4%	0.52	0.20
U.K.	17.3%	19.1%	0.56	0.54	24.0%	23.7%	0.73	0.31
U.S.	17.4%	15.1%	0.71	0.99	15.9%	21.7%	0.43	0.55
Average	16.6%	22.2%	0.46	0.50	21.1%	25.3%	0.57	0.28

Source: Cheol Eun, Victor Huang, and Sandy Lai, "International Diversification with Large- and Small-Cap Stocks," *Journal of Financial and Quantitative Analysis* 43 (2008), pp. 489–524.

Importantly, the small-cap fund is much less correlated with the U.S. stock market index than its large-cap counterpart in each of the 10 countries examined, without exception. For instance, the correlation of the Netherlands small-cap (large-cap) fund with the U.S. market index is 0.20 (0.61). Although not shown in the exhibit, small-cap funds have low correlations not only with large-cap funds but also with each other. For instance, the correlation of the Netherlands small-cap fund with the U.S. small-cap fund is only 0.17. In contrast, large-cap funds tend to have relatively high correlations with each other, reflecting their common exposure to global factors. Thus, small-cap stocks can potentially be a very effective vehicle for international diversification.

Against this backdrop, investment companies recently have introduced many small-cap-oriented international mutual funds, allowing investors to diversify into foreign small-cap stocks without incurring excessive transaction costs. Investment companies, including Fidelity, ING, Lazard, Merrill Lynch, Morgan Stanley, Oppenheimer, and Templeton, currently offer a variety of small-cap-focused international funds. In terms of geographical coverage, some funds are global and international, such as Templeton Global Smaller Companies Fund and Fidelity International Small Cap Fund, while others are regional and national, such as AIM Europe Small Company Fund and DFA Japanese Small Company Fund. To conclude, investors can clearly enhance the gains from international investment by augmenting their portfolios with foreign small-cap stocks.

SUMMARY

This chapter discusses the gains from international portfolio diversification, which emerged as a major form of cross-border investment in the 1980s, rivaling foreign direct investment by firms.

1. International portfolio investment (IPI) has been growing rapidly in recent years due to (a) the deregulation of financial markets, and (b) the introduction of such investment vehicles as international mutual funds, country funds, and internationally cross-listed stocks, which allow investors to achieve international diversification without incurring excessive costs.

2. Investors diversify to reduce risk; the extent to which the risk is reduced by diversification depends on the covariances among individual securities making up the portfolio. Since security returns tend to covary much less across countries than

within a country, investors can reduce portfolio risk more by diversifying internationally than purely domestically.

3. In a full-fledged risk-return analysis, investors can gain from international diversification in terms of "extra" returns at the "domestic-equivalent" risk level. Empirical evidence indicates that regardless of domicile and the numeraire currency used to measure returns, investors can capture extra returns when they hold their optimal international portfolios.

4. Foreign exchange rate uncertainty contributes to the risk of foreign investment through its own volatility as well as through its covariance with local market returns. Generally speaking, exchange rates are substantially more volatile than bond market returns but less so than stock market returns. This suggests that investors can enhance their gains from international diversification, especially in the case of bond investment, when they hedge exchange risk using, say, forward contracts.

5. U.S.-based international mutual funds that investors actually held did provide investors with an effective global risk diversification. In addition, the majority of them outperformed the U.S. stock market index in terms of the Sharpe performance measure. Closed-end country funds (CECFs) also provided U.S. investors with an opportunity to achieve international diversification at home. CECFs, however, were found to behave more like U.S. securities in comparison with their underlying net asset values (NAVs).

6. Despite sizable potential gains from international diversification, investors allocate a disproportionate share of their funds to domestic securities, displaying so-called home bias. Home bias is likely to reflect imperfections in the international financial markets such as excessive transaction/information costs, discriminatory taxes for foreigners, and legal/institutional barriers to international investments.

KEY WORDS

closed-end country fund (CECF), *381*
exchange-traded funds (ETFs), *385*
gains from international diversification, *367*
home bias in portfolio holdings, *387*

international correlation structure, *367*
optimal international portfolios, *369*
portfolio risk diversification, *367*
Sharpe performance measure (SHP), *371*

systematic risk, *368*
world beta, *371*
World Equity Benchmark Shares (WEBS), *385*

QUESTIONS

1. What factors are responsible for the recent surge in international portfolio investment?

2. Security returns are found to be less correlated across countries than within a country. Why can this be?

3. Explain the concept of the world beta of a security.

4. Explain the concept of the Sharpe performance measure.

5. Explain how exchange rate fluctuations affect the return from a foreign market, measured in dollar terms. Discuss the empirical evidence for the effect of exchange rate uncertainty on the risk of foreign investment.

6. Would exchange rate changes always increase the risk of foreign investment? Discuss the condition under which exchange rate changes may actually reduce the risk of foreign investment.

7. Evaluate a home country's multinational corporations as a tool for international diversification.

8. Discuss the advantages and disadvantages of closed-end country funds (CECFs) relative to American depository receipts (ADRs) as a means of international diversification.

9. Why do you think closed-end country funds often trade at a premium or discount?

10. Why do investors invest the lion's share of their funds in domestic securities?

11. What are the advantages of investing via international mutual funds?

12. Discuss how the advent of the euro would affect international diversification strategies.

PROBLEMS

1. Suppose you are a euro-based investor who just sold Microsoft shares that you had bought six months ago. You had invested 10,000 euros to buy Microsoft shares for $120 per share; the exchange rate was $1.15 per euro. You sold the stock for $135 per share and converted the dollar proceeds into euro at the exchange rate of $1.06 per euro. First, determine the profit from this investment in euro terms. Second, compute the rate of return on your investment in euro terms. How much of the return is due to the exchange rate movement?

2. Mr. James K. Silber, an avid international investor, just sold a share of Nestlé, a Swiss firm, for SF5,080. The share was bought for SF4,600 a year ago. The exchange rate is SF1.60 per U.S. dollar now and was SF1.78 per dollar a year ago. Mr. Silber received SF120 as a cash dividend immediately before the share was sold. Compute the rate of return on this investment in terms of U.S. dollars.

3. In problem 2, suppose that Mr. Silber sold SF4,600, his principal investment amount, forward at the forward exchange rate of SF1.62 per dollar. How would this affect the dollar rate of return on this Swiss stock investment? In hindsight, should Mr. Silber have sold the Swiss franc amount forward or not? Why or why not?

4. Japan Life Insurance Company invested $10,000,000 in pure-discount U.S. bonds in May 1995 when the exchange rate was 80 yen per dollar. The company liquidated the investment one year later for $10,650,000. The exchange rate turned out to be 110 yen per dollar at the time of liquidation. What rate of return did Japan Life realize on this investment in yen terms?

5. At the start of 1996, the annual interest rate was 6 percent in the United States and 2.8 percent in Japan. The exchange rate was 95 yen per dollar at the time. Mr. Jorus, who is the manager of a Bermuda-based hedge fund, thought that the substantial interest advantage associated with investing in the United States relative to investing in Japan was not likely to be offset by the decline of the dollar against the yen. He thus concluded that it might be a good idea to borrow in Japan and invest in the United States. At the start of 1996, in fact, he borrowed ¥1,000 million for one year and invested in the United States. At the end of 1996, the exchange rate became 105 yen per dollar. How much profit did Mr. Jorus make in dollar terms?

6. Suppose we obtain the following data in dollar terms:

Stock Market	Return (Mean)	Risk (SD)
United States	1.26% per month	4.43%
United Kingdom	1.23% per month	5.55%

The correlation coefficient between the two markets is 0.58. Suppose that you invest equally, that is, 50 percent in each of the two markets. Determine the expected return and standard deviation risk of the resulting international portfolio.[23] This problem can be solved using the spreadsheet MPTSolver.xls.

7. Suppose you are interested in investing in the stock markets of seven countries—i.e., Australia, Canada, Germany, Japan, Switzerland, the United Kingdom, and the United States—the same seven countries that appear in Exhibit 15.9. Specifically, you would like to solve for the optimal (tangency) portfolio comprising the above seven stock markets. In solving the optimal portfolio, use the input data (i.e., correlation coefficients, means, and standard deviations) provided in Exhibit 15.4. The risk-free interest rate is assumed to be 0.2 percent per month and you can take a short position in any stock market. What are the optimal weights for each of the seven stock markets? What are the risk and return of the optimal portfolio? This problem can be solved using the MPT-Solver.xls spreadsheet.

CFA®
PROBLEMS

8. The HFS Trustees have solicited input from three consultants concerning the risks and rewards of an allocation to international equities. Two of them strongly favor such action, while the third consultant commented as follows:

"The risk reduction benefits of international investing have been significantly overstated. Recent studies relating to the cross-country correlation structure of equity returns during different market phases cast serious doubt on the ability of international investing to reduce risk, especially in situations when risk reduction is needed the most."

a. Describe the behavior of cross-country equity return correlations to which the consultant is referring. Explain how that behavior may diminish the ability of international investing to reduce risk in the short run.

Assume the consultant's assertion is correct.

b. Explain why it might still be more efficient on a risk/reward basis to invest internationally rather than only domestically in the long run.

The HFS Trustees have decided to invest in non-U.S. equity markets and have hired Jacob Hind, a specialist manager, to implement this decision. He has recommended that an unhedged equities position be taken in Japan, providing the following comment and the table data to support his views:

"Appreciation of a foreign currency increases the returns to a U.S. dollar investor. Since appreciation of the Yen from 100¥/$U.S. to 98¥/$U.S. is expected, the Japanese stock position should not be hedged."

---

[23]The mean return on the portfolio is simply the weighted average of the returns on the individual securities that are included in the portfolio. The portfolio variance, on the other hand, can be computed using the following formula:

$$\text{Var}(R_p) = \Sigma_i \Sigma_j x_i x_j \sigma_{ij}$$

where x_i represents an investment weight for the ith security, and σ_{ij} denotes the variances and covariances among individual securities. In the case where the portfolio is composed of two securities, its variance is computed as follows:

$$\text{Var}(R_p) = x_1^2 \sigma_1^2 + x_2^2 \sigma_2^2 + 2x_1 x_2 \sigma_{12}$$

The standard deviation, of course, is the square root of the variance. It is also noted that the covariance σ_{ij} is related to the correlation coefficient ρ_{ij} via $\sigma_{ij} = \rho_{ij} \sigma_i \sigma_j$, where σ_i is the standard deviation of returns on the ith security.

Market Rates and Hind's Expectations

	U.S.	Japan
Spot rate (yen per $U.S.)	n/a	100
Hind's 12-month currency forecast (yen per $U.S.)	n/a	98
1-year Eurocurrency rate (% per annum)	6.00	0.80
Hind's 1-year inflation forecast (% per annum)	3.00	0.50

Assume that the investment horizon is one year and that there are no costs associated with currency hedging.

c. State and justify whether Hind's recommendation (not to hedge) should be followed. Show any calculations.

9. Rebecca Taylor, an international equity portfolio manager, recognizes that an optimal country allocation strategy combined with an optimal currency strategy should produce optimal portfolio performance. To develop her strategies, Taylor produced the following table, which provides expected return data for the three countries and three currencies in which she may invest. The table contains the information she needs to make market strategy (country allocation) decisions and currency strategy (currency allocation) decisions.

Expected Returns for a U.S.-Based Investor

Country	Local Currency Equity Returns	Exchange Rate Returns	Local Currency Eurodeposit Returns
Japan	7.0%	1.0%	5.0%
United Kingdom	10.5	−3.0	11.0
United States	8.4	0.0	7.5

a. Prepare a ranking of the three countries in terms of expected equity-market return premiums. Show your calculations.

b. Prepare a ranking of the three countries in terms of expected currency return premiums from the perspective of a U.S. investor. Show your calculations.

c. Explain *one* advantage a portfolio manager obtains, in formulating a global investment strategy, by calculating both expected market premiums and expected currency premiums.

10. The Glover Scholastic Aid Foundation has received a €20 million global government bond portfolio from a Greek donor. This bond portfolio will be held in euros and managed separately from Glover's existing U.S. dollar-denominated assets. Although the bond portfolio is currently unhedged, the portfolio manager, Raine Sofia, is investigating various alternatives to hedge the currency risk of the portfolio. The bond portfolio's current allocation and the relevant country performance data are given in Exhibits 1 and 2. Historical correlations for the currencies being considered by Sofia are given in Exhibit 3. Sofia expects that future returns and correlations will be approximately equal to those given in Exhibits 2 and 3.

Exhibit 1. Glover Scholastic Aid Foundation Current Allocation Global Government Bond Portfolio

Country	Allocation (%)	Maturity (years)
Greece	25	5
A	40	5
B	10	10
C	10	5
D	15	10

Exhibit 2. Country Performance Data (in local currency)

Country	Cash Return (%)	5-year Excess Bond Return (%)	10-year Excess Bond Return (%)	Unhedged Currency Return (%)	Liquidity of 90-day Currency Forward Contracts
Greece	2.0	1.5	2.0	—	Good
A	1.0	2.0	3.0	−4.0	Good
B	4.0	0.5	1.0	2.0	Fair
C	3.0	1.0	2.0	−2.0	Fair
D	2.6	1.4	2.4	3.0	Good

Exhibit 3. Historical Currency Correlation Table
(1998–2003, weekly observations)

Currency	€ (Greece)	A	B	C	D
€ (Greece)	1.00	−0.77	0.45	−0.57	0.77
A	—	1.00	−0.61	0.56	−0.70
B	—	—	1.00	−0.79	0.88
C	—	—	—	1.00	−0.59
D	—	—	—	—	1.00

a. Calculate the expected total annual return (euro-based) of the current bond portfolio if Sofia decides to leave the currency risk unhedged. Show your calculations.

b. Explain, with respect to currency exposure and forward rates, the circumstance in which Sofia should use a currency forward contact to hedge the current bond portfolio's exposure to a given currency.

c. Determine which *one* of the currencies being considered by Sofia should be the *best* proxy hedge for Country B bonds. Justify your response with *two* reasons.

Sofia has been disappointed with the low returns on the current bond portfolio relative to the benchmark—a diversified global bond index—and is exploring general strategies to generate excess returns on the portfolio. She has already researched two such strategies: duration management and investing in markets outside the benchmark index.

d. Identify *three* general strategies (other than duration management and investing in markets outside the benchmark index) that Sofia could use to generate excess returns on the current bond portfolio. Give, for *each* of the three strategies, a potential benefit specific to the current bond portfolio.

INTERNET EXERCISES

1. You would like to invest in the Mexican stock market and consider two alternative ways of investing in Mexico: (i) the Mexican closed-end country fund trading on the New York Stock Exchange (NYSE) and (ii) the iShares MSCI Mexico ETF trading on the NYSE/Arca. Their websites are:

www.themexicofund.com

http://us.ishares.com/product_info/fund/overview/EWW.htm

Study all the relevant information from the websites and evaluate the relative merits and demerits of the two securities for your Mexican investment. Which one would you prefer?

www.mcgraw-hill.co.uk/textbooks/eun

MINI CASE

Solving for the Optimal International Portfolio

Suppose you are a financial adviser and your client, who is currently investing only in the U.S. stock market, is considering diversifying into the U.K. stock market. At the moment, there are neither particular barriers nor restrictions on investing in the U.K. stock market. Your client would like to know what kinds of benefits can be expected from doing so. Using the data provided in problem 6, solve the following problems:

1. Graphically illustrate various combinations of portfolio risk and return that can be generated by investing in the U.S. and U.K. stock markets with different proportions. Two extreme proportions are (a) investing 100 percent in the United States with no position in the U.K. market, and (b) investing 100 percent in the U.K. market with no position in the U.S. market.

2. Solve for the optimal international portfolio comprising the U.S. and U.K. markets. Assume that the monthly risk-free interest rate is 0.5 percent and that investors can take a short (negative) position in either market. This problem can be solved using the spreadsheet MPTSolver.xls.

3. What is the extra return that U.S. investors can expect to capture at the U.S.-equivalent risk level? Also trace out the efficient set. Appendix 15.B provides an example.

REFERENCES & SUGGESTED READINGS

Adler, Michael, and Bernard Dumas. "International Portfolio Choice and Corporation Finance: A Synthesis." *Journal of Finance* 38 (1983), pp. 925–84.

Bailey, Warren, and J. Lim. "Evaluating the Diversification Benefits of the New Country Funds." *Journal of Portfolio Management* 18 (1992), pp. 74–80.

Bailey, Warren, Alok Kumar, and David Ng. "Venturing Abroad: Foreign Investments of U.S. Individual Investors." Working Paper (2004).

Bonser-Neal, C., G. Brauer, R. Neal, and S. Wheatley. "International Investment Restriction and Closed-End Country Fund Prices." *Journal of Finance* 45 (1990), pp. 523–47.

Chan, Kalok, Vicentiu Covrig, and Lilian Ng. "What Determines the Domestic Bias and Foreign Bias? Evidence from Mutual Fund Equity Allocations Worldwide." *Journal of Finance* 60 (2005), pp. 1495–1534.

Chuppe, T., H. Haworth, and M. Watkins. "Global Finance: Causes, Consequences and Prospects for the Future." *Global Finance Journal* 1 (1989), pp. 1–20.

Cooper, Ian, and Evi Kaplanis. "Home Bias in Equity Portfolios, Inflation Hedging, and International Capital Market Equilibrium." *Review of Financial Studies* 7 (1994), pp. 45–60.

Cumby, R., and J. Glen. "Evaluating the Performance of International Mutual Funds." *Journal of Finance* 45 (1990), pp. 497–521.

Errunza, Vihang, Ked Hogan, and Mao-Wei Hung. "Can the Gains from International Diversification Be Achieved without Trading Abroad?" *Journal of Finance* (1999), 2075–2107.

Eun, Cheol, and Bruce Resnick. "Exchange Rate Uncertainty, Forward Contracts and International Portfolio Selection." *Journal of Finance* 43 (1988), pp. 197–215.

Eun, Cheol, and Bruce Resnick. "International Diversification of Investment Portfolios: U.S. and Japanese Perspectives." *Management Science* 40 (1994), pp. 140–61.

Eun, Cheol, and Bruce Resnick. "International Equity Investments with Selective Hedging Strategies." *Journal of International Financial Markets,* Institutions and Money 7 (1997), pp. 21–42.

Eun, Cheol, Richard Kolodny, and Bruce Resnick. "Performance of U.S.-Based International Mutual Funds." *Journal of Portfolio Management* 17 (1991), pp. 88–94.

Eun, Cheol, Victor Huang, and Sandy Lai. "International Diversification with Large- and Small-Cap Stocks." *Journal of Financial and Quantitative Analysis* 43 (2008), pp. 489–524.

Fama, Eugene, and W. G. Schwert. "Asset Returns and Inflation." *Journal of Financial Economics* 5 (1975), pp. 115–46.

French, K., and J. Poterba. "Investor Diversification and International Equity Markets." *American Economic Review* 81 (1991), pp. 222–26.

Fung, William, and David Hsieh. "A Primer on Hedge Funds." *Journal of Empirical Finance* 6 (1999), pp. 309–31.

Glassman, Debra, and Leigh Riddick. "Why Empirical Portfolio Models Fail: Evidence That Model Misspecification Creates Home Asset Bias." Unpublished manuscript, 1993.

Grubel, H. G. "Internationally Diversified Portfolios." *American Economic Review* 58 (1968), pp. 1299–1314.

Huberman, G. "Familiarity Breeds Investment." *Review of Financial Studies* 14 (2001), pp. 659–80.

Jacquillat, B., and B. Solnik. "Multinationals Are Poor Tools for Diversification." *Journal of Portfolio Management* 4 (1978), pp. 8–12.

Jorion, Philippe. "Asset Allocation with Hedged and Unhedged Foreign Stocks and Bonds." *Journal of Portfolio Management* 15 (Summer 1989), pp. 49–54.

Khorana, A., E. Nelling, and J. Trester. "The Emergence of Country Index Funds." *Journal of Portfolio Management* (Summer 1998), pp. 78–84.

Larsen, Glen, Jr., and Bruce Resnick. "Universal Currency Hedging for International Equity Portfolios under Parameter Uncertainty." *International Journal of Business* 4 (1999), pp. 1–17.

Larsen, Glen, Jr., and Bruce Resnick. "The Optimal Construction of Internationally Diversified Equity Portfolios Hedged against Exchange Rate Uncertainty." *European Financial Management* 6 (2000), pp. 479–514.

Lessard, D. "World, Country and Industry Relationship in Equity Returns: Implications for Risk Reduction through International Diversification." *Financial Analyst Journal* 32 (1976), pp. 22–28.

Leuz, C., Karl Lins, and Francis Warnock. "Do Foreigners Invest Less in Poorly Governed Firms?" *Reivew of Financial Studies* 22 (2009), pp. 3245–85.

Levy, H., and L. Sarnat. "International Diversification of Investment Portfolios." *American Economic Review* 60 (1970), pp. 668–75.

Longin, Francois, and Bruneo Solnik. "Is the Correlation in International Equity Returns Constant?: 1960–1990." *Journal of International Money and Finance* 14 (1995), pp. 3–26.

Merton, R. "A Simple Model of Capital Market Equilibrium with Incomplete Information." *Journal of Finance* 42 (1987), pp. 483–510.

Officer, Dennis, and Ronald Hoffmeister. "ADRs: A Substitute for the Real Thing?" *Journal of Portfolio Management* (Winter 1987), pp. 61–65.

Roll, Richard. "The International Crash of 1987." *Financial Analyst Journal* 44 (1988), pp. 19–35.

Sener, T. "Objectives of Hedging and Optimal Hedge Ratios: U.S. vs. Japanese Investors." *Journal of Multinational Financial Management* 8 (1998), pp. 137–53.

Sharpe, W. "Mutual Fund Performance." *Journal of Business,* A Supplement, No. 1, Part 2 (1966), pp. 119–38.

Solnik, Bruno. "Why Not Diversify Internationally?" *Financial Analyst Journal* 20 (1974), pp. 48–54.

Solnik, Bruno, and J. Roulet. "Dispersion as Cross-sectional, Correlation." *Financial Analyst Journal* 56 (2000), pp. 54–61.

Tesar, L., and I. Werner. "Home Bias and High Turnover." Unpublished manuscript, 1993.

Uppal, Raman. "The Economic Determinants of the Home Country Bias in Investors' Portfolios: A Survey." *Journal of International Financial Management and Accounting* 4 (1992), pp. 171–89.

Wahab, Mahmood, and Amit Khandwala. "Why Not Diversify Internationally with ADRs?" *Journal of Portfolio Management* (Winter 1993), pp. 75–82.

15A International Investment with Exchange Risk Hedging

In this appendix we show how hedging the exchange rate risk in an international portfolio can enhance the risk-return efficiency of an internationally diversified portfolio of financial assets. We begin by restating Equations 15.4 and 15.5 from the text that state the return and variance of return to a U.S. dollar investor from investing in individual foreign security i:

$$R_{i\$} = (1 + R_i)(1 + e_i) - 1 \tag{15A.1a}$$

$$= R_i + e_i + R_i e_i \tag{15A.1b}$$

$$\approx R_i + e_i. \tag{15A.1c}$$

In Equation 15A.1c, we ignore the cross-product term, $R_i e_i$, which is generally small, for discussion purposes. Consequently, the expected return to the U.S. dollar investor from investing in foreign security i can be approximated as:

$$\overline{R}_{i\$} \approx \overline{R}_i + \overline{e}_i \tag{15A.2}$$

Also, we can express the variance of dollar returns from the ith foreign security as follows:

$$\text{Var}(R_{i\$}) = \text{Var}(R_i) + \text{Var}(e_i) + 2\text{Cov}(R_i, e_i) \tag{15A.3}$$

Similarly, we can state the covariance between dollar returns from two different foreign securities as follows:

$$\text{Cov}(R_{i\$}, R_{j\$}) = \text{Cov}(R_i, R_j) + \text{Cov}(e_i, e_j) + \text{Cov}(R_i, e_j) + \text{Cov}(R_j, e_i) \tag{15A.4}$$

Now consider a simple exchange risk hedging strategy in which the U.S. dollar investor sells the expected foreign currency proceeds forward. In dollar terms, it amounts to exchanging the "uncertain" dollar return, $(1 + \overline{R}_i)(1 + e_i) - 1$, for the "certain" dollar return, $(1 + \overline{R}_i)(1 + f_i) - 1$, where $f_i = (F_i - S_i)/S_i$ is the forward exchange premium of the currency denominating security i. Although the expected foreign investment proceeds will be converted into U.S. dollars at the known forward exchange rate under this strategy, the unexpected foreign investment proceeds will have to be converted into U.S. dollars at the uncertain future spot exchange rate. The dollar rate of return under the hedging (H) strategy is thus given by

$$\overline{R}_{i\$H} = [1 + \overline{R}_i](1 + f_i) + [R_i - \overline{R}_i](1 + e_i) - 1 \tag{15A.5a}$$

$$= R_i + f_i + R_i e_i + \overline{R}_i(f_i - e_i) \tag{15A.5b}$$

Since the third and fourth terms of Equation 15A.5b are likely to be small in magnitude, the expected hedged return for the U.S. dollar investor can be approximated as follows:

$$\overline{R}_{i\$H} \approx \overline{R}_i + f_i \tag{15A.6}$$

Recall from the forward expectations parity discussion in Chapter 6 that f_i can be an unbiased estimate of $\overline{e}_i$, i.e., $f_i = \overline{e}_i$. Comparison of Equations 15A.1c and 15A.6 thus indicates that the expected return to the U.S. dollar investor is approximately the same whether the investor hedges the exchange rate risk in the investment, or remains unhedged.

To the extent that the investor establishes an effective hedge to eliminate exchange rate uncertainty, the $\text{Var}(e_i)$ and $\text{Cov}(R_i, e_i)$ terms in Equation 15A.3 will be close to zero. Similarly, the $\text{Cov}(e_i, e_j)$, $\text{Cov}(R_i, e_j)$, and $\text{Cov}(R_j, e_i)$ terms in Equation 15A.4 will be close to zero. Consequently, given that f_i is a constant, it follows that

$$\text{Var}(R_{i\$H}) < \text{Var}(R_{i\$}), \text{ and}$$

$$\text{Cov}(R_{i\$H}, R_{j\$H}) < \text{Cov}(R_{i\$}, R_{j\$}).$$

The empirical results presented in Exhibit 15.8 generally support these relationships. It thus follows that the risk-return efficiency is likely to be superior if the investor hedges the exchange rate risk when investing internationally.

15B Solving for the Optimal Portfolio

Here we explain how to solve for the optimal portfolio of risky securities when there exists a risk-free asset paying a certain risk-free interest rate, R_f. Once we assume that investors prefer more wealth to less and are averse to risk, we can solve for the "optimal" portfolio by maximizing the Sharpe ratio (SHPp) of the excess portfolio return to the standard deviation risk. In other words,

$$\text{Max SHPp} = [\overline{R}_p - R_f]/\sigma_p \tag{15B.1}$$

where $\overline{R}_p$ is the expected rate of return on the portfolio and σ_p is the standard deviation of the portfolio returns.

The expected portfolio return, $\overline{R}_p$, is just the weighted average of the expected returns to individual assets, $\overline{R}_i$, included in the portfolio, that is,

$$\overline{R}_p = \Sigma_i x_i \overline{R}_i \tag{15B.2}$$

where x_i denotes a fraction of wealth invested in the ith individual asset; the sum of fractions should add up to 1, that is, $\Sigma_i x_i = 1$. The portfolio risk, σ_p, on the other hand, is related to the variances and covariances of individual asset returns as follows:

$$\sigma_p = [\Sigma_i \Sigma_j x_i x_j \sigma_{ij}]^{1/2} \tag{15B.3}$$

where σ_{ij} denotes the covariance of returns to the ith and jth assets. What's inside the bracket is the variance of portfolio return.

Now let us consider a simple case where the portfolio includes only two risky assets, A and B. In this case, the risk and return of the portfolio will be determined as follows:

$$\overline{R}_p = x_A \overline{R}_A + x_B \overline{R}_B \tag{15B.4}$$

$$\sigma_p = [x_A^2 \sigma_A^2 + x_B^2 \sigma_B^2 + 2x_A x_B \sigma_{AB}]^{1/2} \tag{15B.5}$$

Suppose we now want to solve for the optimal portfolio using the two assets. We then first substitute Equations 15B.4 and 15B.5 in Equation 15B.1 and maximize SHPp with respect to the portfolio weights x's to obtain the following solution:

$$x_A = \frac{[\overline{R}_A - R_f]\sigma_B^2 - [\overline{R}_B - R_f]\sigma_{AB}}{[\overline{R}_A - R_f]\sigma_B^2 + [\overline{R}_B - R_f]\sigma_A^2 - [\overline{R}_A - R_f + \overline{R}_B - R_f]\sigma_{AB}}$$

$$x_B = 1 - x_A \tag{15B.6}$$

EXAMPLE Suppose we are trying to construct the optimal international portfolio using the U.S. (US) and Netherlands (NL) stock market indexes. From the period 1980.1–2012.12, we obtain the following data (in percentage per month) for the two stock markets:

$$\overline{R}_{US} = 0.647; \qquad \sigma_{US}^2 = 21.07$$

$$\overline{R}_{NL} = 0.635; \qquad \sigma_{NL}^2 = 35.64$$

$$\sigma_{US,NL} = \sigma_{US}\sigma_{NL}\rho_{US,NL} = (4.59)(5.97)(0.73) = 20.00$$

Using the monthly risk-free rate of 0.023 percent, we can substitute the given data into Equation 15B.6 to obtain

$$x_{US} \frac{(0.647 \quad 0.023)(35.64) - (0.635 - 0.023)(20.0)}{(0.647 - 0.023)(35.64) + (0.635 - 0.023)(21.07) - (0.647 - 0.023 + 0.635 - 0.023)(20.0)}$$

$$= 0.9606$$

$$x_{NL} = 1 - x_{US} = 1 - 0.9606 = 0.0394$$

The optimal international portfolio thus comprises 96.06 percent in the U.S. market and 3.96 percent in the Dutch market. The expected return and risk of the optimal portfolio can be computed as follows:

$$\overline{R}_{OP} = (0.9606)(0.647) + (0.0396)(0.635) = 0.647\%$$

$$\sigma_{OP} = [(0.9606)^2 (21.07) + (0.0394)^2 (35.64) + 2(0.9606)(0.0394)(20.0)]^{1/2}$$

$$= 4.58\%$$

16 Foreign Direct Investment and Cross-Border Acquisitions

IN THE EARLY 1980s, Honda, a Japanese automobile company, built an assembly plant in Marysville, Ohio, and began to produce cars for the North American market. These cars were substitutes for imports from Japan. As the production capacity at the Ohio plant expanded, Honda began to export its U.S.-manufactured cars to other markets, including its home market, Japan. A few key factors seem to have motivated Honda to make investments in America. First, Honda wanted to circumvent trade barriers imposed on Japanese automobile manufacturers; under the 1981 *Voluntary Restraint Agreement*, Japanese manufacturers were not allowed to increase their automobile exports to the U.S. market. Second, direct investments in America might have been an integral part of Honda's overall corporate strategy designed to bolster its competitive position vis-à-vis its domestic rivals, such as Toyota and Nissan. Following Honda's lead, Toyota and Nissan themselves subsequently made direct investments in America.

It is noteworthy that the Japanese government had been urging the automobile companies to begin production in the United States. In the early 1980s, Japan exported about two million cars a year to the United States, compared to about 20,000 cars imported from the United States. The Japanese government wished to forestall the kind of protectionist sentiment that led to U.S. import quotas on Japanese-made TVs. When TV import quotas were introduced in 1977, virtually all Japanese TV makers were forced to build plants in the United States.

Honda's decision to build a plant in Ohio was welcomed by the United Auto Workers (UAW), an American labor union, which regarded the plant as a major job opportunity for its members. Honda also received several forms of assistance from the state of Ohio, including improved infrastructure around the plant site, access to the Transportation Research Center operated by Ohio State University, abatement of property taxes, and setting up a special foreign trade zone that allowed Honda to import automobile parts from Japan at a reduced tariff rate.

Firms become *multinational* when they undertake **foreign direct investments (FDI)**. FDI often involves the establishment of new production facilities in foreign countries such as Honda's Ohio plant. FDI may also involve mergers with and acquisitions of existing foreign businesses. An example is provided by Ford, which acquired effective control of Mazda, a Japanese car manufacturer. Whether FDI involves a **greenfield investment** (that is, building brand-new production facilities) or **cross-border mergers and acquisitions**, it affords the multinational corporation (MNC) a measure of *control*. FDI thus represents an internal organizational expansion by MNCs.

According to a recent UN survey, the world FDI stock grew about twice as fast as worldwide exports of goods and services, which themselves grew faster than the

http://unctadstat.unctad.org

Provides FDI data in an interactive format.

world GDP by about 50 percent.[1] Indeed, FDI by MNCs now plays a vital role in linking national economies and defining the nature of the emerging global economy. By undertaking FDI on a global basis, such MNCs as General Electric, Toyota, British Petroleum, IBM, GM, Coca-Cola, McDonald's, Volkswagen, Siemens, and Nestlé have established their presence worldwide and become familiar household names. These MNCs deploy their formidable resources, tangible and intangible, irrespective of national boundaries, to pursue profits and bolster their competitive positions.

In this chapter, we discuss competing theories of FDI for the purpose of understanding the reasons firms undertake it. We also discuss in detail an increasingly popular mode of FDI, namely, cross-border mergers and acquisitions. In addition, we are going to discuss an extra dimension in FDI that would not particularly matter in domestic investments: how to measure and manage political risk associated with FDI. Our analysis of political risk is largely applicable to international portfolio investment as well. Once a MNC acquires a production facility in a foreign country, its operation will be subject to the "rules of the game" set by the host government. Political risk ranges from (unexpected) restrictions on the repatriation of foreign earnings to outright confiscation of foreign-owned assets. Needless to say, it is essential to the welfare of MNCs to effectively manage political risk. Before we discuss these issues, however, let us briefly review the global trends in FDI in recent years.

Global Trends in FDI

The recent trends in **FDI flows** are presented in Exhibit 16.1 and Exhibit 16.2. FDI flows represent new additions to the existing stock of FDI. As the exhibits show, during the five-year period 2007–2011, total annual worldwide FDI outflows amounted to about $1,698 billion on average. As can be expected, several developed countries are the dominant sources of FDI *outflows*. During the five-year period 2007–2011, the United States, on average, invested about $334 billion per year overseas, followed by the U.K., which invested about $125 billion per year. France is the third most important source of FDI outflows, investing about $118 billion per year on average during the five-year period. Germany ($97 billion) and Japan ($89 billion) also invested heavily overseas. After these "big five" come Spain ($60 billion), Canada ($54 billion), China ($53 billion), Italy ($53 billion), and Switzerland ($52 billion). The top 10 countries mentioned above account for about 62 percent of the total worldwide FDI outflows during this five-year period. This implies that MNCs domiciled in these countries should have certain comparative advantages in undertaking overseas investment projects. It is noted that China emerged as one of the top ten source countries for FDI.

Exhibits 16.1 and 16.2 also show FDI *inflows* by country. During the five-year period 2007–2011, the United States received the largest amount of FDI inflows, $218 billion per year on average, among all countries. The next most popular destinations of FDI flows were China ($105 billion), U.K. ($93 billion), Canada ($52 billion), France ($51 billion), Spain ($45 billion), Germany ($40 billion), Australia ($39 billion), the Netherlands ($34 billion), and Mexico ($23 billion). These 10 countries account for about 45 percent of the total worldwide FDI inflows, suggesting these countries must have locational advantages for FDI over other countries. In contrast to its substantial role as an originating country of FDI outflows, Japan plays a relatively minor role as a host of FDI inflows; Japan received only about $11 billion worth of FDI, on average, per year during the period 2007–2011, reflecting a variety of legal, economic, and cultural barriers to foreign investment in Japan.

It is noteworthy that FDI flows into China have dramatically increased in recent years. The amount of inflow increased from $3.5 billion in 1990 to $124 billion in 2011. By 2011, China had emerged as the second most important host country for FDI,

---

[1]Source: *World Investment Report 2004*, UNCTAD, United Nations.

EXHIBIT 16.1		Foreign Direct Investment–Outflows (Inflows) in Billions of Dollars				
Country	2007	2008	2009	2010	2011	Annual Average
Australia	16.9	33.6	16.7	12.8	20.0	20.0
	(45.5)	(47.2)	(26.6)	(35.0)	(41.5)	(39.2)
Canada	57.7	79.8	41.7	38.6	49.6	53.5
	(114.7)	(57.2)	(21.4)	(23.4)	(40.9)	(51.5)
China	22.5	52.2	56.5	68.8	65.1	53.0
	(83.5)	(100.3)	(95.0)	(114.7)	(124.0)	(105.1)
France	164.3	155.0	107.1	76.9	90.1	118.7
	(96.2)	(64.2)	(24.2)	(30.6)	(40.9)	(51.2)
Germany	170.6	72.8	75.4	109.3	54.4	96.5
	(80.2)	(8.1)	(24.2)	(46.9)	(40.4)	(40.0)
Italy	96.2	67.0	21.3	32.7	47.2	52.9
	(43.8)	(−10.8)	(20.1)	(9.2)	(29.1)	(18.3)
Japan	73.5	128.0	74.7	56.3	114.4	89.4
	(22.5)	(24.4)	(11.9)	(−1.3)	(−1.8)	(11.1)
Mexico	8.3	1.2	7.0	13.6	8.9	7.8
	(31.5)	(27.1)	(16.1)	(20.7)	(19.6)	(23.0)
Netherlands	55.6	68.3	28.1	55.2	31.9	47.8
	(119.4)	(4.5)	(36.0)	(−9.0)	(17.1)	(33.6)
Spain	137.1	74.7	13.1	38.3	37.3	60.1
	(64.3)	(80.0)	(10.4)	(40.8)	(29.5)	(45.0)
Sweden	38.8	31.3	25.9	18.0	26.9	28.2
	(27.7)	(37.2)	(10.0)	(−1.3)	(12.1)	(17.1)
Switzerland	51.0	45.3	27.8	64.8	69.6	51.7
	(32.4)	(15.1)	(28.6)	(20.4)	(−0.2)	(19.3)
United Kingdom	272.4	161.1	44.4	39.5	107.1	124.9
	(196.4)	(91.5)	(71.1)	(50.6)	(53.9)	(92.7)
United States	393.5	308.3	267.0	304.4	396.7	334.0
	(216.0)	(306.4)	(143.6)	(197.9)	(226.9)	(218.2)
World	2,198.0	1,969.3	1,175.1	1,451.4	1,694.4	1,697.6
	(1,975.5)	(1,790.7)	(1,197.8)	(1,309.0)	(1,524.4)	(1,559.5)

Note: FDI flows with a negative sign indicate that at least one of the three components of FDI (equity capital, reinvested earnings, or intra-company loans) is negative and is not offset by positive amounts of the other components. There are instances of reverse investment or disinvestment.
Source: Adapted from *World Investment Report 2009, 2012,* UNCTAD.

trailing only the United States. MNCs might have been lured to invest in China not only by lower labor and efficient manufacturing infrastructure but also by the desire to pre-empt the entry of rivals into China's potentially huge market.

Among developing countries, Mexico is another country that experienced substantial FDI inflows, $23 billion on average per year. It is well known that MNCs are invest-ing in Mexico, a low-cost country, to serve the North American as well as Mexican markets. Considering that the wage rate in China has been rising fast in recent years, Mexico and other developing countries like Indonesia and Vietnam may attract more FDI inflows in the future. It is also noteworthy that MNCs invested heavily, $45 billion per year, in Spain, where the costs of production are relatively low compared to other European countries such as France and Germany. Most likely, MNCs invested in Spain to gain a foothold in the huge single market created by the European Union, of which Spain is a member country.

As can be seen in Exhibit 16.1, world-wide FDI, both inflows and outflows, declined significantly in 2008–2009 due to the global recession. However, it began to recover gradually since 2010.

Now, let us turn our attention to **FDI stocks**, which are the accumulation of previous FDI flows. The overall cross-border production activities of MNCs are best captured by FDI stocks. Exhibit 16.3 provides a summary of FDI stocks, both outward and

EXHIBIT 16.2

Average Foreign Direct
Investment per Year
during 2007–2011
($ Billions)

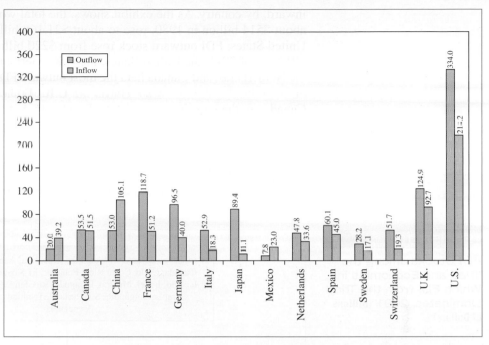

Source: Adapted from *World Investment Report 2009, 2012*, UNCTAD.

EXHIBIT 16.3

Foreign Direct
Investment—Outward
(Inward) Stocks in
Billions of Dollars

Country	1990	1995	2000	2005	2008	2011
Australia	30.1	41.3	85.4	159.2	194.7	385.5
	(75.8)	(104.2)	(111.1)	(210.9)	(272.2)	(499.7)
Canada	78.9	110.4	237.6	399.4	520.4	670.4
	(113.1)	(116.8)	(212.7)	(356.9)	(412.3)	(595.0)
China	2.5	17.3	27.8	46.3	147.9	366.0
	(14.1)	(129.0)	(193.3)	(317.9)	(378.1)	(711.8)
France	110.1	200.9	445.1	853.2	1,397.0	1,372.7
	(86.5)	(162.4)	(259.8)	(600.8)	(991.4)	(963.8)
Germany	151.6	235.0	541.9	967.3	1,450.9	1,441.6
	(111.2)	(134.0)	(271.6)	(502.8)	(700.5)	(713.7)
Italy	56.1	86.7	180.3	293.5	517.1	512.2
	(58.0)	(64.7)	(121.2)	(219.9)	(343.2)	(332.7)
Japan	201.4	305.5	278.4	386.6	680.3	962.8
	(9.9)	(17.8)	(50.3)	(100.9)	(203.4)	(225.8)
Mexico	0.6	2.7	8.3	28.0	45.4	112.1
	(27.9)	(61.3)	(97.2)	(209.6)	(294.7)	(302.3)
Netherlands	109.1	158.6	305.5	641.3	843.7	943.1
	(73.7)	(102.6)	(243.7)	(463.4)	(644.6)	(589.1)
Spain	14.9	34.3	129.2	381.3	601.8	640.3
	(66.3)	(128.9)	(156.3)	(367.7)	(634.8)	(634.5)
Sweden	49.5	61.6	123.3	202.8	319.3	358.9
	(12.5)	(32.8)	(94.0)	(171.5)	(253.5)	(338.5)
Switzerland	65.7	108.3	232.2	394.8	724.7	992.0
	(33.7)	(43.1)	(86.8)	(172.5)	(374.1)	(583.5)
United Kingdom	230.8	319.0	897.8	1,238.0	1,510.6	1,731.1
	(218.0)	(244.1)	(438.6)	(816.7)	(982.9)	(1,198.9)
United States	435.2	705.6	1,316.2	2,051.3	3,162.0	4,500.0
	(394.9)	(564.6)	(1,256.9)	(1,625.7)	(2,278.9)	(3,509.4)
World	1,758.2	2,897.6	6,069.9	10,671.9	16,205.7	21,168.5
	(1,950.3)	(2,992.1)	(5,757.4)	(10,129.7)	(14,909.3)	(20,438.2)

Source: Adapted from *World Investment Report 2009, 2012*, UNCTAD.

inward, by country. As the exhibit shows, the total worldwide FDI stock, which was about $514 billion in 1980, rose to about $21,168 billion in 2011. In the case of the United States, FDI outward stock rose from $220 billion in 1980 to $4,500 billion in 2011. As of 2011, the United States, the U.K., Germany, France, Switzerland, Japan, the Netherlands, and Canada held the most outward FDI stocks. For FDI inward stock, on the other hand, the United States, the U.K., France, Germany, China, Spain and Canada are the most important hosts. Exhibit 16.4 shows the direction of FDI stocks among the three major economic centers, that is, the United States, the European Union, and Japan. Clearly, much of the FDI stocks are concentrated in these three major economic centers.

EXHIBIT 16.4

FDI Stocks among the Triad and Economies in Which FDI from the Triad Dominates, 2001 (Billions of Dollars)

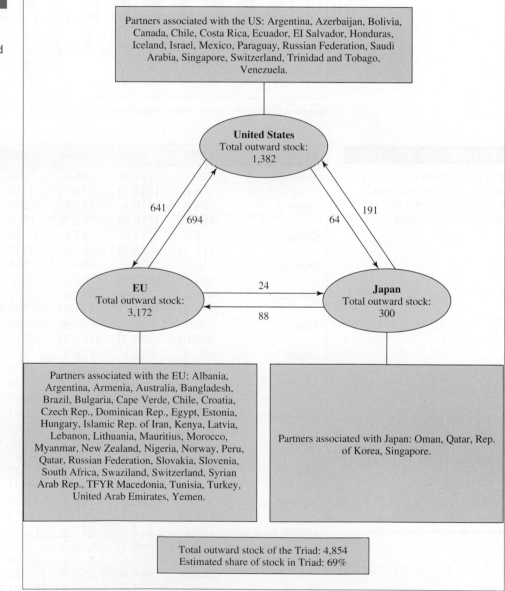

Note: Associate partners are the host economies in which the Triad member accounts for total FDI inward stocks or of total FDI inward flows within a 3-year average.

Source: UNCTAD *World Investment Report 2003:* www.unctad.org/wir.

Why Do Firms Invest Overseas?

Why do firms locate production overseas rather than exporting from the home country or licensing production to a local firm in the host country? In other words, why do firms seek to extend corporate *control* overseas by forming multinational corporations? Unlike the theory of international trade or the theory of international portfolio investment, we do not have a well-developed, comprehensive theory of FDI. But several theories can shed light on certain aspects of the FDI phenomenon. Many of the existing theories, such as Kindleberger (1969) and Hymer (1976), emphasize various *market imperfections*, that is, imperfections in product, factor, and capital markets, as the key motivating forces driving FDI.

In what follows, we are going to discuss some of the key factors that are important in firms' decisions to invest overseas:

- Trade barriers
- Imperfect labor market
- Intangible assets
- Vertical integration
- Product life cycle
- Shareholder diversification services

Trade Barriers

International markets for goods and services are often rendered imperfect by acts of governments. Governments may impose tariffs, quotas, and other restrictions on exports and imports of goods and services, hindering the free flow of these products across national boundaries. Sometimes, governments may even impose complete bans on the international trade of certain products. Governments regulate international trade to raise revenue, protect domestic industries, and pursue other economic policy objectives.

Facing barriers to exporting its products to foreign markets, a firm may decide to move production to foreign countries as a means of circumventing the trade barriers. A classic example for trade barrier–motivated FDI is Honda's investment in Ohio. Since the cars produced in Ohio would not be subject to U.S. tariffs and quotas, Honda could circumvent these barriers by establishing production facilities in the United States. The recent surge in FDI in countries like Mexico and Spain can be explained, at least in part, by the desire of MNCs to circumvent external trade barriers set up by NAFTA and the European Union.

Trade barriers can also arise *naturally* from transportation costs. Such products as mineral ore and cement that are bulky relative to their economic values may not be suitable for exporting because high transportation costs will substantially reduce profit margins. In these cases, FDI can be made in the foreign markets to reduce transportation costs.

Imperfect Labor Market

Suppose Samsung, a Korean conglomerate, would like to build production facilities for its consumer electronics products to serve the North American markets. Samsung could locate its production facilities anywhere in North America if the firm is concerned only with circumventing trade barriers imposed by NAFTA. Samsung initially chose to locate its production facilities in northern Mexico rather than in Canada or the United States, mainly because it wanted to take advantage of the lower costs of labor in Mexico.

Labor services in a country can be severely underpriced relative to their productivity because workers are not allowed to freely move across national boundaries to seek higher wages. Among all factor markets, the labor market is the most imperfect. Severe imperfections in the labor market lead to persistent wage differentials among countries. Exhibit 16.5 provides the hourly labor costs in the manufacturing sector for selected countries in 2011. Compared with Belgium, hourly compensation for factory workers is about $26 less in Spain. The hourly compensation is only $6.48 in Mexico, compared with $35.53 in the United States. The exhibit shows that the average hourly labor cost ranged from $60.40 in Switzerland to $0.37(!) in Bangladesh.

EXHIBIT 16.5

Labor Costs around the Globe (2011)

Country	Average Hourly Cost ($)
Switzerland	60.40
Belgium	54.77
Sweden	49.12
Germany	47.38
Australia	46.29
France	42.12
Canada	36.56
Italy	36.17
Japan	35.71
United States	35.53
United Kingdom	30.77
Spain	28.44
Singapore	22.60
Israel	21.42
Korea	18.91
Brazil	11.65
Taiwan	9.34
Mexico	6.48
Philippines	2.01
China	1.64
India	1.45
Indonesia	1.15
Vietnam	0.73
Bangladesh	0.37

Note: The data for China, India, Indonesia, Vietnam, and Bangladesh are for 2012.
Source: U.S. Department of Labor, Bureau of Labor Statistics and Japan External Trade Organization.

When workers are not mobile because of immigration barriers, firms themselves should move to the workers in order to benefit from the underpriced labor services. This is one of the main reasons MNCs are making FDIs in less-developed countries such as Mexico, China, India, and Southeast Asian countries like Thailand, Malaysia, and Indonesia, where labor services are underpriced relative to their productivity. The recent surge in investment in China by companies from Japan, South Korea, and Taiwan can be attributable, in part, to the highly productive, low-cost workforces in China. However, as labor costs in China began to rise, some of the manufacturing operations there have relocated to other Asian countries, where the wage rates are extremely low, such as Bangladesh, Cambodia, and Vietnam.

Intangible Assets

Coca-Cola has invested in bottling plants all over the world rather than, say, licensing local firms to produce Coke. Coca-Cola chose FDI as a mode of entry into foreign markets for an obvious reason—it wanted to protect the formula for its famed soft drink. If Coca-Cola licenses a local firm to produce Coke, it has no guarantee that the secrets of the formula will be maintained. Once the formula is leaked to other local firms, they may come up with similar products, which will hurt Coca-Cola's sales. This possibility is known as the *boomerang* effect. In the 1960s, Coca-Cola, which had bottling plants in India, faced strong pressure from the Indian government to reveal the Coke formula as a condition for continued operations in India. Instead of revealing the formula, Coca-Cola chose to withdraw from India.[2]

MNCs may undertake overseas investment projects in a foreign country, despite the fact that local firms may enjoy inherent advantages. This implies that MNCs should have significant advantages over local firms. Indeed, MNCs often enjoy comparative

---

[2]Coca-Cola reentered the Indian market as India gradually liberalized its economy, improving the climate for foreign investments.

advantages due to special **intangible assets** they possess. Examples include technological, managerial, and marketing know-how, superior R&D capabilities, and brand power. These intangible assets are often hard to package and sell to foreigners. In addition, the property rights in intangible assets are difficult to establish and protect, especially in foreign countries where legal recourse may not be readily available. As a result, firms may find it more profitable to establish foreign subsidiaries and capture returns directly by internalizing transactions in these assets. The internalization theory can help explain why MNCs, not local firms, undertake investment projects in foreign countries.

A strand of literature, including Caves (1982) and Magee (1977), places special emphasis on the role of market imperfections for intangible assets in motivating firms to undertake FDI. According to the **internalization theory** of FDI, firms that have intangible assets with a *public good* property tend to invest directly in foreign countries in order to use these assets on a larger scale and, at the same time, avoid the misappropriations of intangible assets that may occur while transacting in foreign markets through a market mechanism.[3]

Vertical Integration

Suppose Royal Dutch Shell purchases a significant portion of crude oil for its refinery facilities from a Saudi oil company that owns the oil fields. In this situation, Royal Dutch Shell can experience a number of problems. For example, Royal Dutch Shell, the downstream firm, would like to hold the crude oil price down, whereas the Saudi oil company, an upstream firm, would like to push the price up. If the Saudi company has stronger bargaining power, Royal Dutch Shell may be forced to pay a higher price than it would like to, adversely affecting the firm's profits. In addition, as the world's demand for refined oil fluctuates, one of the two firms may have to bear excessive risk. The conflicts between the upstream and downstream firms can be resolved, however, if the two firms form a vertically integrated firm. Obviously, if Royal Dutch Shell controls the oil fields, the problems will disappear. In recent years, Chinese firms actively pursued vertical integrations through overseas merger and acquisition (M&A) deals, especially in mining and resources sectors. For instance, Shandong Iron & Steel Group invested $1.5 billion to acquire a major stake in African Minerals of Sierra Leone in 2010. Also, Aluminum Corporation of China (Chinalco) recently bought 9 percent of Rio Tinto, a major Australian mining firm, for $14 billion, to ensure a reliable supply of minerals at reasonable prices. China's overseas M&A activities so far are heavily concentrated in resource-rich countries, such as Australia, Brazil, Canada, Mongolia, Sierra Leone, Guinea, and Indonesia.

Generally speaking, MNCs may undertake FDI in countries where inputs are available in order to secure the supply of inputs at a stable price. Furthermore, if MNCs have monopolistic/oligopolistic control over the input market, this can serve as a barrier to entry to the industry. Many MNCs involved in extractive/natural resources industries tend to directly own oil fields, mine deposits, and forests for these reasons. Also, MNCs often find it profitable to locate manufacturing/processing facilities near the natural resources in order to save transportation costs. It would be costly to bring bulky bauxite ore to the home country and then extract the aluminum.

Although the majority of vertical FDIs are *backward* in that FDI involves an industry abroad that produces inputs for MNCs, foreign investments can take the form of *forward* vertical FDI when they involve an industry abroad that sells a MNC's outputs. As is well known, U.S. car makers found it difficult to market their products in Japan. This is partly because most car dealers in Japan have a long and close business relationship with the Japanese car makers and are reluctant to carry foreign imports. To overcome this problem, U.S. car makers began to build their own network of dealerships in Japan to help sell their cars. This is an example of forward vertical FDI.

---

[3]Examples of public goods include public parks, lighthouses, and radio/TV broadcasting services. Once these goods are produced, it is difficult to preclude the public from using them, whether they are paying or not.

Outsourcing: A Passage Out of India

As U.S. corporations try to outsource more-skilled white-collar jobs, they're looking beyond India. Savings can reach 50 percent.

For years there was pretty much one choice for U.S. companies seeking to move jobs offshore: India. Outsourcing grew to a $69 billion business there and transformed backwaters such as Chennai and Hyderabad into teeming cities. That wave has crested. In 2011 companies in Latin America and eastern Europe opened 54 new outsourcing facilities, versus 49 for India, according to industry tracker Everest Group.

The two regions are challenging the subcontinent's dominance in outsourcing as American corporations increasingly ship higher-level jobs offshore. India had substantial advantages in offshoring's first phase: plenty of English speakers to staff call centers and enough technology talent to run remote data-processing and computer support centers—all at about a 60 percent discount to stateside workers. But having wrung substantial costs out of back-office functions, U.S. companies are exporting skilled white-collar jobs in research, accounting, procurement, and financial analysis.

Because these jobs aren't mass-processing functions, India's forte, there are greater opportunities for countries such as Argentina and Poland, which have higher labor costs than India. Using an outsourcing firm to hire an entry-level accountant in Argentina, for example, costs 13 percent less than a similar U.S. worker, while an Indian worker would cost 51 percent less. But many employers moving higher-end jobs offshore care about more than just getting the lowest wage. "The higher-value outsourcing jobs require a greater understanding of business context and a higher amount of interaction with clients," says Phil Fersht, chief executive officer of HfS Research, a Boston outsourcing research firm.

It helps that the region's time zones are more in sync with those of North America. That's why Copal Partners, which since 2002 has built up its investment-research outsourcing business in Gurgaon, India, added an office in Buenos Aires. It's only a two-hour time difference for Copal's clients in New York. "If you're working with a hedge fund manager where you have to interact with him 10 to 15 times a day, having someone in about the same time zone is important," says Rishi Khosla, Copal's CEO.

Product Life Cycle

According to Raymond Vernon (1966), firms undertake FDI at a particular stage in the life cycle of the products that they initially introduced. Vernon observed that throughout the 20th century, the majority of new products, such as computers, televisions, and mass-produced cars, were developed by U.S. firms and first marketed in the United States. According to Vernon's **product life-cycle theory**, when U.S. firms first introduce new products, they choose to keep production facilities at home, close to customers. In the early stage of the product life cycle, the demand for the new product is relatively insensitive to the price and thus the pioneering firm can charge a relatively high price. At the same time, the firm can continuously improve the product based on feedback from its customers at home.

As demand for the new product develops in foreign countries, the pioneering U.S. firm begins to export to those countries. As the foreign demand for the product continues to grow, U.S. firms, as well as foreign firms, may be induced to start production in foreign countries to serve local markets. As the product becomes standardized and mature, it becomes important to cut the cost of production to stay competitive. A foreign producer operating in a low-cost country may start to export the product to the United States. At the same time, cost considerations may induce the U.S. firms to set up production facilities in a low-cost foreign country and export the product back to the United States. In other words, FDI takes place when the product reaches maturity and cost becomes an important consideration. FDI can thus be interpreted as a *defensive* move to maintain the firm's competitive position against its domestic and foreign rivals. The International Finance in Practice box "Outsourcing: A Passage Out of India" provides an interesting example of FDI.

The product life-cycle theory predicts that over time the United States switches from an exporting country of new products to an importing country. The dynamic changes in the international trade pattern are illustrated in Exhibit 16.6. The prediction of the product life-cycle theory is consistent with the pattern of dynamic changes observed for many products. For instance, personal computers (PCs) were first developed by U.S. firms (such as IBM and Apple Computer) and exported to overseas markets. As PCs became a standardized commodity, however, the United States became a net

Even Tata Consultancy Services—India's outsourcing leader, with estimated sales of $9.8 billion in 2011—has 8,500 employees in South America, including Peru and Paraguay. And Genpact (G), the subcontinent's biggest business-process outsourcer, opened a finance and accounting center in São Paulo last year for U.K. drugmaker AstraZeneca.

Such "nearshoring" of jobs is also benefiting eastern Europe. The economy of Wroclaw, Poland's fourth-largest city, revolved around heavy industry during the Communist years. Now it's an outsourcing center, with 30 local colleges providing a skilled labor pool. Local outsourcing jobs doubled from 2008 to 2010, when centers were opened there by IBM, Microsoft, and Ernst & Young. The auditing firm in 2011 added a second center in Wroclaw, where workers provide legal, real estate, and human resources services to European clients. Ernst & Young employs 1,300 people in six Polish centers.

Poland's Gen Y population is highly educated—about 50 percent of its 20- to 24-year-olds are in college, says Hersht, versus 10 percent in India—and prolifically multilingual. The 26 languages spoken at Hewlett-Packard's Wroclaw center make it ideal for serving its European, African, and Middle Eastern operations, says Jacek Levernes, who oversees outsourcing for those regions. The Wroclaw center employs more than twice as many workers as HP expected when it opened in 2005—2,300, versus 1,000—and they perform higher functions. The Polish workers originally provided basic financial and accounting support; now they handle marketing services and supply-chain analysis as well.

France's Capgemini has staked much of its outsourcing future on nearshoring, including financial and accounting centers in Guatemala City and Kraków, Poland. Bottler Coca-Cola Enterprises pulled jobs out of its Tampa, Dallas, and Toronto offices in favor of Capgemini's Guatemala center, for instance, and out of Paris, Brussels, and London in favor of Kraków. HfS's Fersht, who's visited both, says each could pass for a U.S. office, except for the rich stew of languages and the workers' nearly uniform youth. Fersht cites another benefit: Capgemini's clients get the services of Polish and Guatemalan college graduates for the price of U.S. high school graduates.

Source: Adapted from 'Outsourcing: A Passage Out of India' by John Helyar, with Mehul Srivastava, *Bloomberg Businessweek*, March 15, 2012. ©2014 BLOOMBERG L.P. ALL RIGHTS RESERVED.

importer of PCs from foreign producers based in such countries as Japan, Korea, and Taiwan, as well as foreign subsidiaries of U.S. firms.

It should be pointed out that Vernon's theory was developed in the 1960s when the United States was the unquestioned leader in R&D capabilities and product innovations. Increasingly, product innovations are taking place outside the United States as well, and new products are introduced simultaneously in many advanced countries. Production facilities may be located in multiple countries from the inception of a new product. The international system of production is becoming too complicated to be explained by a simple version of the product life-cycle theory.

Shareholder Diversification Services

If investors cannot effectively diversify their portfolio holdings internationally because of barriers to cross-border capital flows, firms may be able to provide their shareholders with indirect diversification services by making direct investments in foreign countries. When a firm holds assets in many countries, the firm's cash flows are internationally diversified. Thus, shareholders of the firm can indirectly benefit from international diversification even if they are not directly holding foreign shares. Capital market imperfections thus may motivate firms to undertake FDI.

Although shareholders of MNCs may indirectly benefit from corporate international diversification, it is not clear that firms are motivated to undertake FDI for the purpose of providing shareholders with diversification services. Considering the fact that many barriers to international portfolio investments have been dismantled in recent years, enabling investors to diversify internationally by themselves, capital market imperfections as a motivating factor for FDI are likely to become less relevant.

Cross-Border Mergers and Acquisitions

As previously mentioned, FDI can take place either through *greenfield investments*, which involve building new production facilities in a foreign country, or through *cross-border mergers and acquisitions*, which involve combining with or buying

EXHIBIT 16.12   Corruption Perceptions Index 2012 - Transparency International

Rank	Country/Territory	Score	Rank	Country/Territory	Score	Rank	Country/Territory	Score
1	Denmark	90	58	Namibia	48	118	Ecuador	32
1	Finland	90	61	Oman	47	118	Egypt	32
1	New Zealand	90	62	Croatia	46	118	Indonesia	32
4	Sweden	88	62	Slovakia	46	118	Madagascar	32
5	Singapore	87	64	Ghana	45	123	Belarus	31
6	Switzerland	86	64	Lesotho	45	123	Mauritania	31
7	Australia	85	66	Kuwait	44	123	Mozambique	31
7	Norway	85	66	Romania	44	123	Sierra Leone	31
9	Canada	84	66	Saudi Arabia	44	123	Vietnam	31
9	Netherlands	84	69	Brazil	43	128	Lebanon	30
11	Iceland	82	69	Macedonia, FYR	43	128	Togo	30
12	Luxembourg	80	69	South Africa	43	130	Côte d'Ivoire	29
13	Germany	79	72	Bosnia and Herzegovina	42	130	Nicaragua	29
14	Hong Kong	77	72	Italy	42	130	Uganda	29
15	Barbados	76	72	Sao Tome and Principe	42	133	Comoros	28
16	Belgium	75	75	Bulgaria	41	133	Guyana	28
17	Japan	74	75	Liberia	41	133	Honduras	28
17	United Kingdom	74	75	Montenegro	41	133	Iran	28
19	United States	73	75	Tunisia	41	133	Kazakhstan	28
20	Chile	72	79	Sri Lanka	40	133	Russia	28
20	Uruguay	72	80	China	39	139	Azerbaijan	27
22	Bahamas	71	80	Serbia	39	139	Kenya	27
22	France	71	80	Trinidad and Tobago	39	139	Nepal	27
22	Saint Lucia	71	83	Burkina Faso	38	139	Nigeria	27
25	Austria	69	83	El Salvador	38	139	Pakistan	27
25	Ireland	69	83	Jamaica	38	144	Bangladesh	26
27	Qatar	68	83	Panama	38	144	Cameroon	26
27	United Arab Emirates	68	83	Peru	38	144	Central African Republic	26
29	Cyprus	66	88	Malawi	37	144	Congo Republic	26
30	Botswana	65	88	Morocco	37	144	Syria	26
30	Spain	65	88	Suriname	37	144	Ukraine	26
32	Estonia	64	88	Swaziland	37	150	Eritrea	25
33	Bhutan	63	88	Thailand	37	150	Guinea-Bissau	25
33	Portugal	63	88	Zambia	37	150	Papua New Guinea	25
33	Puerto Rico	63	94	Benin	36	150	Paraguay	25
36	St. Vincent & Grenadines	62	94	Colombia	36	154	Guinea	24
37	Slovenia	61	94	Djibouti	36	154	Kyrgyzstan	24
37	Taiwan	61	94	Greece	36	156	Yemen	23
39	Cape Verde	60	94	India	36	157	Angola	22
39	Israel	60	94	Moldova	36	157	Cambodia	22
41	Dominica	58	94	Mongolia	36	157	Tajikistan	22
41	Poland	58	94	Senegal	36	160	Congo, D.R.	21
43	Malta	57	102	Argentina	35	160	Laos	21
43	Mauritius	57	102	Gabon	35	160	Libya	21
45	Korea (South)	56	102	Tanzania	35	163	Equatorial Guinea	20
46	Brunei	55	105	Algeria	34	163	Zimbabwe	20
46	Hungary	55	105	Armenia	34	165	Burundi	19
48	Costa Rica	54	105	Bolivia	34	165	Chad	19
48	Lithuania	54	105	Gambia	34	165	Haiti	19
50	Rwanda	53	105	Kosovo	34	165	Venezuela	19
51	Georgia	52	105	Mali	34	169	Iraq	18
51	Seychelles	52	105	Mexico	34	170	Turkmenistan	17
53	Bahrain	51	105	Philippines	34	170	Uzbekistan	17
54	Czech Republic	49	113	Albania	33	172	Myanmar	15
54	Latvia	49	113	Ethiopia	33	173	Sudan	13
54	Malaysia	49	113	Guatemala	33	174	Afghanistan	8
54	Turkey	49	113	Niger	33	174	Korea (North)	8
58	Cuba	48	113	Timor-Leste	33	174	Somalia	8
58	Jordan	48	118	Dominican Republic	32			

foreign countries, and (iv) loss of business income due to political violence. OPIC's primary goal is to encourage U.S. private investments in the economies of developing countries. Alternatively, MNCs may also purchase tailor-made insurance policies from private insurers such as Lloyd's of London.

When the political risk faced by a MNC can be fully covered by an insurance contract, the MNC can subtract the insurance premium from the expected cash flows from the project in computing its NPV. The MNC then can use the usual cost of capital, which would be used to evaluate domestic investment projects, in discounting the expected cash flows from foreign projects. Lastly, it is pointed out that many countries have concluded bilateral or multilateral investment protection agreements, effectively eliminating most political risk. As a result, if a MNC invests in a country that signed the investment protection agreement with the MNC's home country, it need not be overly concerned with political risk.

One particular type of political risk that MNCs and investors may face is corruption associated with the abuse of public offices for private benefits. Investors may often encounter demands for bribes from politicians and government officials for contracts and smooth bureaucratic processes. If companies refuse to make *grease payments*, they may lose business opportunities or face difficult bureaucratic red tape. If companies pay, on the other hand, they may risk violating laws or being embarrassed when the payments are discovered and reported in the media. Corruption can be found anywhere in the world. But it is a much more serious problem in many developing and transition economies where the state sector is large, democratic institutions are weak, and the press is often muzzled. U.S. companies are legally prohibited from bribing foreign officials by the Foreign Corrupt Practices Act (FCPA). In 1997, the OECD also adopted a treaty to criminalize the bribery of foreign officials by companies. Bribery thus is both morally and legally wrong for companies from most developed countries. Another particular risk that companies may face is extortion demands from Mafia-style criminal organizations. For example, the majority of companies in Russia are known to have paid extortion demands. To deal with this kind of situation, it is important for companies to hire people who are familiar with local operating environments, to strengthen local support for the company, and to enhance physical security measures.

SUMMARY

This chapter discusses various issues associated with foreign direct investments (FDI) by MNCs, which play a key role in shaping the nature of the emerging global economy.

1. Firms become *multinational* when they undertake FDI. FDI may involve either the establishment of new production facilities in foreign countries or acquisitions of existing foreign businesses.

2. During the five-year period 2004–2008, total annual worldwide FDI out-flows amounted to about $1,423 billion on average. The United States is the largest recipient, as well as initiator, of FDI. Besides the United States, France, Germany, Spain, and the United Kingdom are the leading sources of FDI outflows, whereas the United States, United Kingdom, France, China, Canada, and Spain are the major destinations for FDI in recent years.

3. Most existing theories of FDI emphasize various market imperfections, that is, imperfections in product, factor, and capital markets, as the key motivating forces driving FDI.

4. The *internalization* theory of FDI holds that firms that have intangible assets with a public good property tend to invest directly in foreign countries in order to use these assets on a larger scale and, at the same time, avoid the misappropriations that may occur while transacting in foreign markets through a market mechanism.

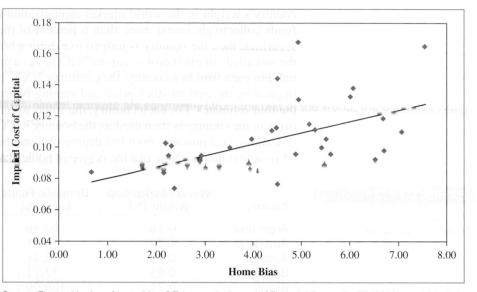

Source: The world price of home bias, S.T. Lau et al., *Journal of Financial Economics* 97 (2010), pp. 191–217.

the percentage of domestic mutual funds' holdings in domestic securities in a country divided by the percentage weight of the country in the world market capitalization and is expressed in natural log. As can be seen from the exhibit, the degree of home bias ranges from 0.70 for the United States to 7.56 for Peru. The United States exhibits the lowest degree of home bias and, at the same time, has the lowest cost of capital (8.5%), whereas Peru exhibits the highest degree of home bias and has the second-highest cost of capital (16.5%), after Brazil (16.8%). Exhibit 17.3 plots the implicit cost of capital and the degree of home bias for different countries, showing that the two variables are positively related to each other. A higher home bias is associated with a higher cost of capital.

When a country exhibits a high degree of home bias, as Peru does, the global risk sharing is hampered, thereby increasing the cost of capital for the country. Based on this finding, Lau et al. suggest that reduced home bias and greater global risk sharing would help reduce the cost of capital. In addition, they report that accounting transparency also helps reduce the cost of capital.

In perfect markets, firms would be indifferent between raising funds abroad or at home. When markets are imperfect, however, international financing can lower the firm's cost of capital. In Chapter 12, for example, we saw that Eurobond financing was typically a less expensive form of debt financing than domestic bond financing. We continue with this line of thinking in this chapter, where we explore ways of lowering the cost of equity capital through internationalizing the firm's ownership structure. Let us first examine the historical experiences of one firm, Novo Industri, that has successfully internationalized its cost of capital by cross-border listings. Our discussion here draws on Stonehill and Dullum (1982).[5]

CASE APPLICATION

Novo Industri

Novo Industri A/S is a Danish multinational corporation that controls about 50 percent of the world industrial enzyme market. The company also produces health care products, including insulin. On July 8, 1981, Novo listed its stock on the New York Stock Exchange, thereby becoming the first Scandinavian company to directly raise equity capital in the United States.

---

[5]Stonehill and Dullum (1982) provide a detailed analysis of the Novo case.

EXHIBIT 17.4

Process of
Internationalizing the
Capital Structure: Novo

1977:	Novo increased the level of its financial and technical disclosure in both Danish and English versions. Grieveson, Grant and Co, a British stock brokerage firm, started to follow Novo's stock and issued the first professional security analyst report in English. Novo's stock price: DKr200–225.
1978:	Novo raised $20 million by offering convertible Eurobond underwritten by Morgan Grenfell. Novo listed on the London Stock Exchange.
1980 April:	Novo organized a marketing seminar in New York City promoting its stock to U.S. investors.
1980 December:	Novo's stock price reached DKr600 level; P/E ratio rose to around 16.
1981 April:	Novo ADRs were listed on NASDAQ (5 ADRs = one share) Morgan Guaranty Trust Co. served as the depository bank.
1981 July:	Novo listed on NYSE. Novo stock price reached DKr1400.Foreign ownership increased to over 50 percent of the shares outstanding. U.S. institutional investors began to hold Novo shares.

Source: Arthur Stonehill and Kare Dullum, *Internationalizing the Cost of Capital* (New York: John Wiley & Sons, 1982).

www.novo.dk

The homepage of Novo provides basic information about the company.

In the late 1970s, Novo management decided that in order to finance the planned future growth of the company, it had to tap into international capital markets. Novo could not expect to raise all the necessary funds exclusively from the Danish stock market, which is relatively small and illiquid. In addition, Novo management felt that the company faced a higher cost of capital than its main competitors, such as Eli Lilly and Miles Lab, because of the segmented nature of the Danish stock market.

Novo thus decided to internationalize its cost of capital in order to gain access to additional sources of capital and, at the same time, lower its cost of capital. Initially, Novo increased the level of financial and technical disclosure, followed by Eurobond issue and the listing of its stock on the London Stock Exchange in 1978. In pursuing its goals further, Novo management decided to sponsor an American depository receipt (ADR) so that U.S. investors could invest in the company's stock using U.S. dollars rather than Danish kroners. Morgan Guarantee issued the ADR shares, which began trading in the over-the-counter (OTC) market in April 1981. On July 8, 1981, Novo sold 1.8 million ADR shares, raising Dkr. 450 million, and, at the same time, listed its ADR shares on the New York Stock Exchange. The chronology of these events is provided in Exhibit 17.4.

As can be seen from Exhibit 17.5, Novo's stock price reacted very positively to the U.S. listing.[6] Other Danish stocks, though, did not experience comparable price increases. The sharp increase in Novo's stock price indicates that the stock became fully priced internationally upon U.S. listing. This, in turn, implies that the Danish stock market was indeed segmented from the rest of the world. From the experiences of Novo, we can derive the following lesson: *Firms operating in a small, segmented domestic capital market can gain access to new capital and lower the cost of capital by listing their stocks on large, liquid capital markets like the New York and London Stock Exchanges.*

---

[6]It is noted that Novo has dual-class shares: A-shares that are held by the Novo Foundation and are nontradable and B-shares that are publicly tradable.

EXHIBIT 17.7

Foreign Firms Listed
on the New York Stock
Exchange (Selected)

Country	Firms
Australia	BHP Billiton, Coles Myer, Telstra, Westpac Banking
Brazil	Banco Itaú, Embraer, Petrobras, Telebras, Unibanco, VALE
Canada	Alcan, Barrick Gold, Canadian Pacific, Domtar, Fairfax Financial, Mitel, Northern Telecom, Toronto Dominion Bank
Chile	Banco de Chile, Macedo, Vina Concha y Toro
China	China Eastern Airlines, China Life Insurance, Huaneng Power, PetroChina, China Mobile
Finland	Nokia Corp., Stora Enso
France	Alstom, Alcatel-Lucent, Technicolor, France Telecom, Sanofi-Aventis, Suez, Total, Vivendi
Germany	Deutsche Bank, Infineon, SAP, Siemens
India	ICICI Bank, Tata Communications, Wipro
Israel	Blue Square, Elscint, Tefron
Italy	ENI, Luxottica, Natuzzi, Telecom Italia
Japan	Canon, Honda Motor, Hitachi, Kubota, Kyocera, NTT Docomo, Sony, Panasonic, Toyota Motor
Korea	Korea Electric Power, Korea Telecom, Pohang Iron & Steel, SK Telecom
Mexico	Cemex, Empresas ICA, Grupo Televisa, Telefonos de Mexico
Netherlands	Aegon, Arcelor Mittal, Reed Elsevier, Unilever, CNH Global, ING, Royal Dutch Petroleum
Norway	Norsk Hydro, Smedvig, Statoil
South Africa	ASA, Anglo Gold Ashanti, Sasol
Spain	Banco Santander, Repsol
Switzerland	ABB, Novartis, UBS
United Kingdom	Barclays, BP, BT Group, Diageo, GlaxoSmithKlein, HSBC, Lloyds, Prudential, Royal Bank of Scotland, Vodafone

Source: Datastream.

EXHIBIT 17.8

Foreign Firms Listed
on the London Stock
Exchange (Selected)

Country	Firms
Australia	Allied Gold, Medusa Mining, Platinum Australia, Range Resources
Canada	Canadian Pacific Railways, Greystar Resources, Ondine Biopharma, Turbo Power Systems, Western Coal
China	Air China, China Petroleum & Chemical, Datang Intl Power Generation, Zhejiang Expressway
Czech Republic	Komercni Banka, Telefonica O2 Czech Republic
Egypt	Commercial Intl Bank, Suez Cement, Telecom Egypt
France	Compagnie de St-Gobain, Groupe Eurotunnel, Total FinaElf
Germany	BASF, Deutsche Bank, Siemens, Volkswagen
India	Lloyd Electric & Engineering, Reliance Infrastructure, State Bank of India, Tata Motors
Ireland	Abbey Plc, Aer Lingus Group Plc, Bank of Ireland, Ryanair Hldgs
Israel	Bank Hapoalim, Dori Media Group, Metal-Tech
Japan	Fujitsu, Nippon Tel & Tel, Sony, Toyota Motor
Korea	Hyundai Motor, LG Electronics, Posco, Samsung Electronics
Netherlands	Aegon, European Assets Trust, New World Resources
Poland	Bank Pekao, Polski Koncern Naftowy Orlen, Telekomunikacja Polska
Russia	Gazprom, Lukoil, Severstal, Rosneft
Taiwan	Acer, Evergreen Marine, Hon Hai Precision Industry
Turkey	Turk Ekonomi Bankasi, Turkiye Petrol Rafinerileri, Uzel Makina Sanayi
United States	Abbott Laboratories, Bank of America, Boeing, Caterpillar, Dow Chemical, General Motors, General Electric, IBM, Pfizer, Verizon Communications

Source: London Stock Exchange.

CHAPTER

18

Generally speaking, a company can benefit from cross-border listings of its shares in the following ways:

1. The company can expand its potential investor base, which will lead to a higher stock price and a lower cost of capital.
2. Cross-listing creates a secondary market for the company's shares, which facilitates raising new capital in foreign markets.[7]
3. Cross-listing can enhance the liquidity of the company's stock.
4. Cross-listing enhances the visibility of the company's name and its products in foreign marketplaces.
5. Cross-listed shares may be used as the "acquisition currency" for taking over foreign companies.
6. Cross-listing may improve the company's corporate governance and transparency.

The last point deserves detailed discussion here. Consider a company domiciled in a country where shareholders' rights are not well protected, and controlling shareholders (e.g., founding families and large shareholders) derive substantial private benefits, such as perks, inflated salaries, bonuses, and even thefts, from controlling the company. Once the company cross-lists its shares on the New York Stock Exchange (NYSE), London Stock Exchange (LSE), or other foreign exchanges that impose stringent disclosure and listing requirements, controlling shareholders may not be able to continue to divert company resources to their private benefit. As argued by Doidge, Karolyi, and Stulz (2001), in spite of the "inconveniences" associated with a greater public scrutiny and enhanced transparency, controlling shareholders may choose to cross-list the company shares overseas, as it can be ultimately in their best interest to bond themselves to "good behavior" and to be able to raise funds to undertake profitable investment projects (thereby increasing share prices). This implies that if a foreign company does not need to raise capital, it may choose not to pursue U.S. listings, so that controlling shareholders can continue to extract private benefits from the company. The aforementioned study shows that other things being equal, those foreign companies that are listed on U.S. exchanges are valued nearly 17 percent higher, on average, than those that are not, reflecting investors' recognition of the enhanced corporate governance associated with U.S. listings. Since the London Stock Exchange also imposes stringent disclosure and listing requirements, foreign firms cross-listed on the exchange may also experience positive revaluation due to the effect of enhanced corporate governance.[8]

A study by Lang, Lins, and Miller (2003) shows that cross-listing can enhance firm value through improving the firm's overall information environments. Specifically, they show that foreign firms that cross-list in U.S. exchanges enjoy greater analyst coverage and increased forecast accuracy for firms' future earnings relative to those firms that are not cross-listed. They further show that firms that have greater analyst coverage and higher forecasting accuracy have a higher valuation, other things equal. These findings are consistent with the findings of other studies that cross-listed firms generally enjoy a lower cost of capital and better corporate governance.

---

[7]Chaplinsky and Ramchand (1995) report that, compared with exclusively domestic offerings, global equity offerings enable firms to raise capital at advantageous terms. In addition, they report that the negative stock price reaction that equity issue often elicits is reduced if firms have a foreign tranche in their offer.

[8]As Dahya, McConnell, and Travlos (2002) point out, the standard of corporate governance has been raised significantly in the United Kingdom since the "Cadbury Committee" issued the *Code of Best Practice* in 1992, recommending that corporate boards include at least three outside directors and that the positions of chairman and CEO be held by different individuals.

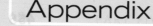

17A

SUMMA

REFERENCES
& SUGGESTED

P.
A
S

KEY WO

EXHIBIT 17A.1

International Capital
Market Equilibria: The
Effect of Cross-Listings

Asset
A. Equ
D1
D2
D3
D4
F1
F2
F3
F4
B. Cos
D1
D2
D3
D4
F1
F2
F3
F4

QUEST

One of the major benefits of the APV framework is the ease with which difficult cash flow terms, such as tax savings or deferrals and the repatriation of restricted funds, can be handled. The analyst can first analyze the capital expenditure as if these terms did not exist. Additional cash flow terms do not need to be explicitly considered unless the APV is negative. If the APV is negative, the analyst can calculate how large the cash flows from other sources need to be to make the APV positive, and then estimate whether these other cash inflows will likely be that large

Estimating the Future Expected Exchange Rate

The financial manager must estimate the future expected exchange rates, $\overline{S}_t$, in order to implement the APV framework. Chapter 6 provided a wide variety of methods for estimating exchange rates. One quick and simple way to do this is to rely on PPP and estimate the future expected spot rate for year t as:

$$\overline{S}_t = S_0 (1 + \overline{\pi}_d)^t/(1 + \overline{\pi}_f)^t \qquad (18.8)$$

where $\overline{\pi}_d$ is the expected long-run annual rate of inflation in the (home) domestic country of the MNC and $\overline{\pi}_f$ is the rate in the foreign land.

As noted in Chapter 6, PPP is not likely to hold precisely in reality. Nevertheless, unless the financial manager suspects that there is some systematic long-run bias in using PPP to estimate $\overline{S}_t$ that would result in a systematic over- or underestimate of the series of expected exchange rates, then PPP should prove to be an acceptable tool. Alternatively, the analyst may choose to use long-dated forward prices to estimate the future expected spot exchange rates, or use an IRP forecast.

CASE APPLICATION

The Centralia Corporation

The Centralia Corporation is a midwestern manufacturer of small kitchen electrical appliances. The market segment it caters to is the midprice range. It specializes in small and medium-size microwave ovens suitable for small homes, apartment dwellers, or office coffee lounges. In recent years it has been exporting microwave ovens to Spain, where they are sold through a sales affiliate in Madrid. Because of different electrical standards in various European countries, the ovens Centralia manufactured for the Spanish market could not be used everywhere in Europe without an electrical converter. Thus, the sales affiliate concentrated its marketing effort just in Spain. Sales are currently 9,600 units a year and have been increasing at a rate of 5 percent.

Centralia's marketing manager has been keeping abreast of integration activities in the European Union. All obstacles to the free movement of goods, services, people, and capital among the member states of the EU have been removed. Additionally, further integration promises a commonality among member states of rail track size, telephone and electrical equipment, and a host of other items. These developments have led the marketing manager to believe that a substantial number of microwave oven units could be sold throughout the EU and that the idea of a manufacturing facility should be explored.

The marketing and production managers have jointly drawn up plans for a wholly owned manufacturing facility in Zaragoza, which is located about 325 kilometers northeast of Madrid. Zaragoza is located just a couple hundred kilometers from the French border, thus facilitating shipment out of Spain into other EU countries. Additionally, Zaragoza is located close enough to the major population centers in Spain so that internal shipments should not pose a problem. A major attraction of locating the manufacturing facility in Zaragoza, however, is that the Spanish government has promised to arrange for a large portion of the construction cost of the production facility to be financed at a very attractive interest rate if the plant is built there. Any type of industry that will improve the employment situation would be a benefit, as the current unemployment rate in Spain exceeds 19 percent. Centralia's executive committee has instructed the financial manager to determine if the plan has financial merit. If the manufacturing facility is built, Centralia will no longer export units for sale in Europe. The necessary information follows.

On its current exports, Centralia receives $180 per unit, of which $35 represents contribution margin. The sales forecast predicts that 25,000 units will be sold within the EU during the first year of operation and that this volume will increase at the rate of 12 percent per year. All sales will be invoiced in euros. When the plant begins operation, units will be priced at €200 each. It is estimated that the current production cost will be €160 per unit. The sales price and production costs are expected to keep pace with inflation, which is forecast to be 2.1 percent per annum for the foreseeable future. By comparison, long-run U.S. inflation is forecast at 3 percent per annum. The current exchange rate is $1.32/€1.00.

The cost of constructing the manufacturing plant is estimated at €5,500,000. The borrowing capacity created by a capital expenditure of this amount is $2,904,000. The Madrid sales affiliate has accumulated a net amount of €750,000 from its operations, which can be used to partially finance the construction cost. The marginal corporate tax rate in Spain and the United States is 35 percent. The accumulated funds were carried under special tax concessions offered during the initial years of the sales operation, and taxed at a marginal rate of 20 percent. If they were repatriated, additional tax at the 35 percent marginal rate would be due, but with a foreign tax credit given for the Spanish taxes already paid.

The Spanish government will allow the plant to be depreciated over an eight-year period. Little, if any, additional investment will be required over that time. At the end of this period, the market value of the facility is difficult to estimate, but Centralia believes that the plant should still be in good condition for its age and that it should therefore have reasonable market value. All after-tax operating cash flows from the new facility will be immediately repatriated to the United States.

One of the most attractive features of the proposal is the special financing the Spanish government is willing to arrange. If the plant is built in Zaragoza, Centralia will be eligible to borrow €4,000,000 at a concessionary loan rate of 5 percent per annum. The normal borrowing rate for Centralia is 8 percent in dollars and 7 percent in euros. The loan schedule calls for the principal to be repaid in eight equal installments. In dollar terms, Centralia uses 12 percent as its **all-equity cost of capital**.

Here is a summary of the key points:

The current exchange rate in American terms is $S_0 = \$1.32/€1.00$.

$\bar{\pi}_f = 2.1\%$.

$\bar{\pi}_d = 3\%$.

The initial cost of the project in U.S. dollars is

$S_0 C_0 = \$1.32 \times €5,500,000 = \$7,260,000$.

For simplicity, we will assume that PPP holds and use it to estimate future expected spot exchange rates in American terms as:

$\bar{S}_t = 1.32(1.03)^t/(1.021)^t$.

The before-tax incremental operating cash flow per unit at $t = 1$ is €200 − 160 = €40. The nominal contribution margin in year t equals €40$(1.021)^{t-1}$.

Incremental lost sales in units for year t equals 9,600$(1.05)^t$.

Contribution margin per unit of lost sales in year t equals $35(1.03)^t$.

The marginal tax rate, τ equals the Spanish (or U.S.) rate of 35 percent.

Terminal value will initially be assumed to equal zero.

Straight-line depreciation is assumed; $D_t = €687,500 = €5,500,000/8$ years.

$K_{ud} = 12\%$.

$i_c = 5\%$.

$i_d = 8\%$.

In Exhibit 18.2 the present value of the expected after-tax operating cash flows from Centralia establishing the manufacturing facility in Spain is calculated. Column (a)

EXHIBIT 18.2   Calculation of the Present Value of the After-Tax Operating Cash Flows

Year (t)	$\bar{S}_t$	Quantity	$\bar{S}_t \times$ Quantity $\times$ €40 $\times (1.021^{t-1})$ (a) $	Quantity Lost Sales	Quantity Lost Sales $\times$ \$35.00 $\times (1.03)^t$ (b) $	$\bar{S}_t OCF_t$ (a + b) $	$\dfrac{\bar{S}_t OCF_t(1-\tau)}{(1+K_{ud})^t}$ $
1	1.3316	25,000	1,331,636	(10,080)	(363,384)	968,252	561,932
2	1.3434	28,000	1,536,175	(10,584)	(393,000)	1,143,175	592,366
3	1.3552	31,360	1,772,131	(11,113)	(425,029)	1,347,102	623,246
4	1.3672	35,123	2,044,331	(11,669)	(459,669)	1,584,662	654,603
5	1.3792	39,338	2,358,340	(12,252)	(497,131)	1,861,208	686,465
6	1.3914	44,059	2,720,581	(12,865)	(537,640)	2,182,952	718,062
7	1.4036	49,346	3,138,462	(13,508)	(581,467)	2,556,995	751,826
8	1.4160	55,267	3,620,530	(14,184)	(628,856)	2,991,674	785,386
							5,374,685

presents the annual revenue in dollars from operating the new manufacturing facility. These are calculated each year by multiplying the expected quantity of microwave ovens to be sold times the year one incremental operating cash flow of €40 per unit. This product is in turn multiplied by the euro zone price inflation factor of 2.1 percent. For example, for year $t = 2$ the factor is $(1.021)^{t-1} = (1.021)$. The euro sales estimates are then converted to dollars at the expected spot exchange rates. Column (b) presents the annual lost sales revenues in dollars that are expected to result if the manufacturing facility is built and the parent firm no longer sells part of its production through the Spanish sales affiliate. These are calculated by multiplying the estimated quantity of lost sales in units by the current contribution margin of \$35 per unit, which is in turn multiplied by a 3 percent U.S. price inflation factor. The incremental dollar operating cash flows are the sum of columns (a) and (b), which are converted to their after-tax value and discounted at K_{ud}. The sum of their present values is \$5,374,685.

The present value of the depreciation tax shields τD_t is calculated in Exhibit 18.3. The tax savings on the annual straight-line depreciation of €687,500 is converted to dollars at the expected future spot exchange rates and discounted to the present at the domestic borrowing rate of 8 percent. The present value of these tax shields is \$1,892,502.

The present value of the benefit of the concessionary loan is calculated in Exhibits 18.4 and 18.5. Exhibit 18.4 finds the present value of the concessionary loan payments in dollars. Since the annual principal payment on the €4,000,000 concessionary loan is the same each year, the interest payments decline as the loan

EXHIBIT 18.3

Calculation of the Present Value of the Depreciation Tax Shields

Year (t)	$\bar{S}_t$	D_t €	$\dfrac{\bar{S}_t \tau D_t}{(1+i_d)^t}$ \$
1	1.3316	687,500	296,690
2	1.3434	687,500	277,134
3	1.3552	687,500	258,868
4	1.3672	687,500	241,805
5	1.3792	687,500	225,867
6	1.3914	687,500	210,980
7	1.4036	687,500	197,074
8	1.4160	687,500	184,084
			1,892,502

EXHIBIT 18.4

Calculation of the
Present Value of the
Concessionary Loan
Payments

Year (t)	$\overline{S}_t$ (a)	Principal Payment (b) €	I_t (c) €	$\overline{S}_t\,LP_t$ (a) × (b + c) $	$\dfrac{\overline{S}_t LP_t}{(1 + i_d)^t}$ $
1	1.3316	500,000	200,000	932,145	863,097
2	1.3434	500,000	175,000	906,777	777,415
3	1.3552	500,000	150,000	880,890	699,279
4	1.3672	500,000	125,000	854,476	628,065
5	1.3792	500,000	100,000	827,528	563,202
6	1.3914	500,000	75,000	800,030	504,160
7	1.4036	500,000	50,000	771,999	450,454
8	1.4160	500,000	25,000	743,404	401,638
		4,000,000			4,887,311

EXHIBIT 18.5

Calculation of the Present Value of the Benefit from the
Concessionary Loan

$$S_0 CL_0 - \sum_{t=1}^{T} \frac{\overline{S}_t LP_t}{(1 + i_d)^t} = \$1.32 \times €4,000,000 - \$4,887,311 = \$392,689$$

balance declines. For example, during the first year, interest of €200,000 (= .05 × €4,000,000) is paid on the full amount borrowed. During the second year interest of €175,000 (= .05 × (€4,000,000 − 500,000)) is paid on the outstanding balance over year two. The annual loan payment equals the sum of the annual principal payment and the annual interest charge. The sum of their present values in dollars, converted at the expected spot exchange rates, discounted at the domestic borrowing rate of 8 percent, is $4,887,311. This sum represents the size of the equivalent loan available (in dollars) from borrowing at the normal borrowing rate with a debt service schedule equivalent to that of the concessionary loan.

Exhibit 18.5 concludes the analysis of the concessionary loan. It shows the difference between the dollar value of the concessionary loan and the equivalent dollar loan value calculated in Exhibit 18.4. The difference of $392,689 represents the present value of the benefit of the below-market-rate financing of the concessionary loan.

The present value of the interest tax shields is calculated in Exhibit 18.6. The interest payments in column (b) of Exhibit 18.6 are drawn from column (c) of Exhibit 18.4. That is, we follow a conservative approach and base the interest tax shields on using the concessionary loan interest rate of 5 percent. The concessionary loan of €4,000,000

EXHIBIT 18.6

Calculation of the
Present Value of the
Interest Tax Shields

Year (t)	$\overline{S}_t$ (a)	I_t (b) €	λ/Project Debt Ratio (c)	$\overline{S}_t \tau(.55)I_t$ (a × b × c × τ) $	$\dfrac{\overline{S}_t \tau(.55)I_t}{(1 + i_d)^t}$ $
1	1.3316	200,000	0.55	51,268	47,470
2	1.3434	175,000	0.55	45,255	38,799
3	1.3552	150,000	0.55	39,132	31,064
4	1.3672	125,000	0.55	32,897	24,181
5	1.3792	100,000	0.55	26,550	18,069
6	1.3914	75,000	0.55	20,088	12,659
7	1.4036	50,000	0.55	13,510	7,883
8	1.4160	25,000	0.55	6,815	3,682
					183,807

represents 72.73 percent of the project cost of €5,500,000. By comparison, the borrowing capacity created by the project is $2,904,000, which implies an optimal debt ratio λ for the parent firm of 40.0 percent = $2,904,000/$7,260,000 of the dollar cost of the project. Thus, only 55.0 percent (= 40.0%/72.73%) of the interest payments on the concessionary loan should be used to calculate the interest tax shields. At the domestic borrowing rate of 8 percent, the present value of the interest tax shields is $183,807.

To calculate the amount of the freed-up restricted remittances it is first necessary to gross up the after-tax value of the net accumulation of €750,000, on which the Madrid sales affiliate has previously paid taxes at the rate of 20 percent. This amount is €937,500 = €750,000/(1 − .20). The dollar value of this sum at the current spot exchange rate S_0 is $1,237,500 = $1.32 (€937,500). If Centralia decided not to establish a manufacturing facility in Spain, the €750,000 should be repatriated to the parent firm. It would be required to pay additional taxes in the United States in the amount of $185,625 = (.35 − .20)$1,237,500. If the manufacturing facility is built, the €750,000 should not be remitted to the parent firm. Thus, freed-up funds of $185,625 result from the current tax savings, which can be applied to cover a portion of the equity investment in the capital expenditure.[10]

The APV = $5,374,685 + 1,892,502 + 392,689 + 183,807 + 185,625
           − 7,260,000
         = $769,308.

There appears little doubt that the proposed manufacturing facility will be a profitable venture for Centralia. Had the APV been negative or closer to zero, we would want to consider the present value of the after-tax terminal cash flow. We are quite uncertain as to what this amount might be, and, fortunately, in this case we do not have to base a decision on this cash flow, which is difficult at best to forecast.

Risk Adjustment in the Capital Budgeting Analysis

The APV model we presented and demonstrated is suitable for use in analyzing a capital expenditure that is of average riskiness in comparison to the firm as a whole. Some projects may be more or less risky than average, however. The *risk-adjusted discount method* is the standard way to handle this situation. This approach requires adjusting the discount rate upward or downward for increases or decreases, respectively, in the systematic risk of the project relative to the firm as a whole. In the APV model presented in Equation 18.7, only the cash flows discounted at K_{ud} incorporate systematic risk; thus, only K_{ud} needs to be adjusted when project risk differs from that of the firm as a whole.[11]

A second way to adjust for risk in the APV framework is the *certainty equivalent method*. This approach extracts the risk premium from the expected cash flows to convert them into equivalent riskless cash flows, which are then discounted at the risk-free rate of interest. This is accomplished by multiplying the risky cash flows by a certainty-equivalent factor that is unity or less. The more risky the cash flow, the smaller is the certainty-equivalent factor. In general, cash flows tend to be more risky the further into the future they are expected to be received. We favor the risk-adjusted discount rate method over the certainty-equivalent approach because we find that it is easier to adjust the discount rate than it is to estimate the appropriate certainty-equivalent factors.[12]

---

[10]At the termination date, when all excess funds are repatriated to the parent firm, additional taxes will then be due on the accumulated funds. These are taken into consideration in the terminal value TV_T term.

[11]See Ross, Westerfield, and Jaffe (2008, Chapter 12) for a treatment of capital budgeting using discount rates adjusted for project systematic risk.

[12]See Brealey, Myers and Allen (2008, Chapter 10) for a more detailed discussion of the certainty equivalent method of risk adjustment.

Sensitivity Analysis

The way we have approached the analysis of Centralia's expansion into Spain is to obtain a point estimate of the APV through using expected values of the relevant cash flows. The expected values of these inputs are what the financial manager expects to obtain given the information he had at his disposal at the time the analysis was performed. However, each cash flow does have its own probability distribution. Hence, the realized value that may result for a particular cash flow may be different than expected. To examine these possibilities, the financial manager typically performs a sensitivity analysis. In a *sensitivity analysis*, different scenarios are examined by using different exchange rate estimates, inflation rate estimates, and cost and pricing estimates in the calculation of the APV. In essence, the sensitivity analysis allows the financial manager a means to analyze the business risk, economic exposure, exchange rate uncertainty, and political risk inherent in the investment. Sensitivity analysis puts financial managers in a position to more thoroughly understand the implications of planned capital expenditures. It also forces them to consider in advance actions that can be taken should an investment not develop as anticipated. Excel-based programs, such as Crystal Ball, can be easily used to conduct a Monte Carlo simulation of various probability assumptions.

Purchasing Power Parity Assumption

The APV methodology we developed assumes that PPP holds and that future expected exchange rates can be forecasted accordingly. As noted, relying on the PPP assumption is a common and conceptually satisfying way to forecast future exchange rates. Assuming no differential in marginal tax rates, when PPP holds and all foreign cash flows can be legally repatriated to the parent firm, it does not make any difference if the capital budgeting analysis is done from the perspective of the parent firm or from the perspective of the foreign subsidiary. To see this, consider the following simple example.

> ### EXAMPLE | 18.2: The PPP Assumption in Foreign Capital Expenditure Analysis
>
> A capital expenditure of FC30 by a foreign subsidiary of a U.S. MNC with a one-year economic life is expected to earn a cash flow in local currency terms of FC80. Assume inflation in the foreign host country is forecast at 4 percent per annum and at 2 percent in the United States. If the U.S. MNC's cost of capital is 7.88 percent, the Fisher equation determines that the appropriate cost of capital for the foreign subsidiary is 10 percent: $1.10 = (1.0788)(1.04)/(1.02)$. Consequently, the project NPV in foreign currency terms is $NPV_{FC} = FC80/(1.10) - FC30 = FC42.73$. If the current spot exchange rate is $FC2.00/\$1.00$, $\bar{S}_1 (FC/\$) = 2.00 (1.04)/(1.02) = 2.0392$ by PPP. In U.S. dollar terms, $NPV_\$ = (FC80/2.0392)/(1.0788) - FC30/2.00 = \$21.37$. Note that according to the *law of one price*, $NPV_{FC}/S_0 (FC/\$) = NPV_\$ = FC42.73/2.00 = \$21.37$. This is the expected result because both the exchange rate forecast and the discount rate conversion incorporate the same differential in expected inflation rates. Suppose, however, that $\bar{S}_1(FC/\$)$ actually turns out to be $FC5.00/\$1.00$, that is, the foreign currency depreciates in real terms versus the dollar, then $NPV_\$ = -\$0.17$ and the project is unprofitable from the parent's perspective.

Real Options

Throughout this chapter, we have recommended the APV framework for evaluating capital expenditures in real assets. The APV was determined by making certain assumptions about revenues, operating costs, exchange rates, and the like. This approach treats risk through the discount rate. When evaluated at the appropriate discount rate, a positive APV implies that a project should be accepted and a negative APV implies that it should be rejected. A project is accepted under the assumption that all future operating decisions will be optimal. Unfortunately, the firm's management does not know at the inception date of a project what future decisions it will be confronted with because complete information concerning the project has not yet been learned. Consequently, the firm's management has alternative paths, or options, that it can take as new information is discovered. Options pricing theory is useful for evaluating investment opportunities in real assets as well as financial assets, such as foreign exchange that we considered in Chapter 7. The application of options pricing theory to the evaluation of investment options in real projects is known as **real options**.

The firm is confronted with many possible real options over the life of a capital asset. For example, the firm may have a *timing option* about when to make the investment; it may have a *growth option* to increase the scale of the investment; it may have a *suspension option* to temporarily cease production; and, it may have an *abandonment option* to quit the investment early. All of these situations can be evaluated as real options.

In international capital expenditures, the MNC is faced with the political uncertainties of doing business in a foreign host country.[13] For example, a stable political environment for foreign investment may turn unfavorable if a different political party wins power by election—or worse, by political coup. Moreover, an unexpected change in a host country's monetary policy may cause a depreciation in its exchange rate versus the parent firm's home currency, thus adversely affecting the return to the shareholders of the parent firm. These and other political uncertainties make real options analysis ideal for use in evaluating international capital expenditures. Real options analysis, however, should be thought of as an extension of discounted cash flow analysis, not as a replacement of it, as the following example makes clear.

EXAMPLE | 18.3: Centralia's Timing Option

Suppose that the sales forecast for the first year for Centralia in the case application had been for only 22,000 units instead of 25,000. At the lower figure, the APV would have been −$55,358. It is doubtful that Centralia would have entered into the construction of a manufacturing facility in Spain in this event. Suppose further that it is well known that the European Central Bank has been contemplating either tightening or loosening the economy of the European Union through a change in monetary policy that would cause the euro to either appreciate to $1.45/€1.00 or depreciate to $1.20/€1.00 from its current level of $1.32/€1.00. Under a restrictive monetary policy, the APV would be $86,674, and Centralia would begin operations. On the other hand, an expansionary policy would cause the APV to become an even more negative −$186,464.

Centralia believes that the effect from any change in monetary policy will be known in a year's time. Thus it decides to put its plans on hold until it learns what the ECB decides to do. In the meantime, Centralia can obtain a purchase option for a year on the parcel of land in Zaragoza on which it would build the manufacturing facility by paying the current landowner a fee of €5,000, or $6,600.

---

[13]It may be helpful to review the discussion on political risk in Chapter 16.

The situation described is a classic example in which real options analysis is useful in evaluating a capital expenditure. In this situation, the purchase option of €5,000 represents the option premium of the real option and the initial investment of €5,500,000 represents the exercise price of the option. Centralia will only exercise its real option if the ECB decides to follow a restrictive policy that would cause the APV to be a positive $86,674. The €5,000 seems like a small amount to allow Centralia the flexibility to postpone making a costly capital expenditure until more information is learned. The following example explicitly values the timing option using the binomial options pricing model.

EXAMPLE | 18.4: Valuing Centralia's Timing Option

In this example, we value the timing option described in the preceding example using the binomial options pricing model developed in Chapter 7. We use Centralia's 8 percent borrowing cost in dollars and 7 percent borrowing cost in euros as our estimates of the domestic and foreign risk-free rates of interest. Depending upon the action of the ECB, the euro will either appreciate 10 percent to $1.45/€1.00 or depreciate 9 percent to $1.20/€1.00 from its current level of $1.32/$1.00. Thus, $u = 1.10$ and $d = 1/1.10. = .91$. This implies that the risk-neutral probability of an appreciation is $q = [(1 + i_d)/(1 + i_f) - d]/(u - d) = [(1.08)/(1.07) - .91]/(1.10 - .91) = .52$ and the probability of a depreciation is $1 - q = .48$. Since the timing option will only be exercised if the APV is positive, the value of the timing option is $C = .52(\$86,674)/(1.08) = \$41,732$. Since this amount is in excess of the $6,600 cost of the purchase option on the land, Centralia should definitely take advantage of the timing option it is confronted with to wait and see what monetary policy the ECB decides to pursue.

SUMMARY

This chapter presents a review of the NPV capital budgeting framework and expands the methodology into the APV model that is suitable for analyzing capital expenditures of a MNC in a foreign land.

1. The NPV capital budgeting framework in a domestic context is reviewed. The NPV is the difference between the present value of the cash inflows and outflows. If NPV ≥ 0 for a capital project, it should be accepted.

2. The annual after-tax cash flow formula was thoroughly defined and presented in a number of variations. This was necessary to expand the NPV model into the APV model.

3. The APV model of capital budgeting was developed by analogy to the Modigliani-Miller formula for the value of a levered firm. The APV model separates the operating cash flows from the cash flows due to financing. Additionally, each cash flow is discounted at a rate of discount commensurate with the inherent risk of the individual cash flow.

4. The APV model was further expanded to make it amenable for use by a MNC parent analyzing a capital project of a foreign subsidiary. The cash flows were converted into the parent firm's home currency, and additional terms were added to the model to handle cash flows that are frequently encountered in international capital projects.

5. A case application showing how to apply the APV model was presented and solved.

KEY WORDS

adjusted present value (APV), *460*
all-equity cost of capital, *465*
all-equity cost of equity, *459*

borrowing capacity, *463*
concessionary loan, *462*
incremental cash flow, *458*

lost sales, *462*
net present value (NPV), *458*
real option, *470*
restricted funds, *462*
value-additivity, *461*

QUESTIONS

1. Why is capital budgeting analysis so important to the firm?

2. What is the intuition behind the NPV capital budgeting framework?

3. Discuss what is meant by the *incremental* cash flows of a capital project.

4. Discuss the nature of the equation sequence, Equations 18.2a to 18.2f.

5. What makes the APV capital budgeting framework useful for analyzing foreign capital expenditures?

6. Relate the concept of *lost sales* to the definition of incremental cash flows.

7. What problems can enter into the capital budgeting analysis if project debt is evaluated instead of the *borrowing capacity* created by the project?

8. What is the nature of a *concessionary* loan and how is it handled in the APV model?

9. What is the intuition of discounting the various cash flows in the APV model at specific discount rates?

10. In the Modigliani-Miller equation, why is the market value of the levered firm greater than the market value of an equivalent unlevered firm?

11. Discuss the difference between performing the capital budgeting analysis from the parent firm's perspective as opposed to the subsidiary's perspective.

12. Define the concept of a real option. Discuss some of the various real options a firm can be confronted with when investing in real projects.

13. Discuss the conditions under which the capital expenditure of a foreign subsidiary might have a positive NPV in local currency terms but be unprofitable from the parent firm's perspective.

PROBLEMS

1. The Alpha Company plans to establish a subsidiary in Hungary to manufacture and sell fashion wristwatches. Alpha has total assets of $70 million, of which $45 million is equity financed. The remainder is financed with debt. Alpha considered its current capital structure optimal. The construction cost of the Hungarian facility in forints is estimated at HUF2,400,000,000, of which HUF1,800,000,000 is to be financed at a below-market borrowing rate arranged by the Hungarian government. Alpha wonders what amount of debt it should use in calculating the tax shields on interest payments in its capital budgeting analysis. Can you offer assistance?

2. The current spot exchange rate is HUF250/$1.00. Long-run inflation in Hungary is estimated at 10 percent annually and 3 percent in the United States. If PPP is expected to hold between the two countries, what spot exchange rate should one forecast five years into the future?

3. The Beta Corporation has an optimal debt ratio of 40 percent. Its cost of equity capital is 12 percent and its before-tax borrowing rate is 8 percent. Given a marginal tax rate of 35 percent, calculate (a) the weighted-average cost of capital, and (b) the cost of equity for an equivalent all-equity financed firm.

4. Zeda, Inc., a U.S. MNC, is considering making a fixed direct investment in Denmark. The Danish government has offered Zeda a concessionary loan of

DKK 15,000,000 at a rate of 4 percent per annum. The normal borrowing rate for Zeda is 6 percent in dollars and 5.5 percent in Danish krone. The load schedule calls for the principal to be repaid in three equal annual installments. What is the present value of the benefit of the concessionary loan? The current spot rate is DKK5.60/$1.00 and the expected inflation rate is 3 percent in the United States and 2.5 percent in Denmark.

5. Delta Company, a U.S. MNC, is contemplating making a foreign capital expenditure in South Africa. The initial cost of the project is ZAR10,000. The annual cash flows over the five year economic life of the project in ZAR are estimated to be 3,000, 4,000, 5,000, 6,000, and 7,000. The parent firm's cost of capital in dollars is 9.5 percent. Long run inflation is forecasted to be 3 percent per annum in the United States and 7 percent in South Africa. The current spot foreign exchange rate is ZAR/USD = 3.75. Determine the NPV for the project in USD by:

  a. Calculating the NPV in ZAR using the ZAR equivalent cost of capital according to the Fisher effect and then converting to USD at the current spot rate.

  b. Converting all cash flows from ZAR to USD at purchasing power parity forecasted exchange rates and then calculating the NPV at the dollar cost of capital.

  c. Are the two dollar NPVs different or the same? Explain.

  d. What is the NPV in dollars if the actual pattern of ZAR/USD exchange rates is: $S(0) = 3.75, S(1) = 5.7, S(2) = 6.7, S(3) = 7.2, S(4) = 7.7,$ and $S(5) = 8.2$?

6. Suppose that in the case application in the chapter the APV for Centralia had been $-\$60,000$. How large would the after-tax terminal value of the project need to be before the APV would be positive and Centralia would accept the project?

7. With regard to the Centralia case application in the chapter, how would the APV change if:

  a. The forecast of $\overline{\pi}_d$ and/or $\overline{\pi}_f$ is incorrect?

  b. Depreciation cash flows are discounted at K_{ud} instead of i_d?

  c. The host country did not provide the concessionary loan?

INTERNET EXERCISES

Many articles on the importance of concessionary financing can be found on the Internet by searching under the keywords *concessionary financing*.

MINI CASE 1

Dorchester, Ltd.

Dorchester, Ltd. is an old-line confectioner specializing in high-quality chocolates. Through its facilities in the United Kingdom, Dorchester manufactures candies that it sells throughout Western Europe and North America (United States and Canada). With its current manufacturing facilities, Dorchester has been unable to supply the U.S. market with more than 225,000 pounds of candy per year. This supply has allowed its sales affiliate, located in Boston, to be able to penetrate the U.S. market no farther west than St. Louis and only as far south as Atlanta. Dorchester believes that a separate manufacturing facility located in the United States would allow it to supply the entire U.S. market and Canada (which presently accounts for 65,000 pounds per year). Dorchester currently estimates initial demand in the North American market at 390,000 pounds, with growth at a 5 percent annual rate. A separate manufacturing

CHAPTER

19 Multinational Cash Management

OUR PRIMARY CONCERN in this chapter is with the efficient management of cash within a MNC. We are concerned with the size of cash balances, their currency denominations, and where these cash balances are located among the MNC's affiliates. Efficient cash management techniques can reduce the investment in cash balances and foreign exchange transaction expenses, and it can provide for maximum return from the investment of excess cash. Additionally, efficient cash management techniques result in borrowing at the lowest rate when a temporary cash shortage exists. The chapter begins with a case application that develops a centralized cash management system for a MNC. The system we develop includes interaffiliate netting and a centralized cash depository. The benefits of a centralized system are clearly detailed.

The Management of International Cash Balances

Cash management refers to the investment the firm has in **transaction balances** to cover scheduled outflows of funds during a cash budgeting period and the funds the firm has tied up in precautionary cash balances. **Precautionary cash balances** are necessary in case the firm has underestimated the amount needed to cover transactions. Good cash management also encompasses investing excess funds at the most favorable rate and borrowing at the lowest rate when there is a temporary cash shortage.

Many of the skills necessary for effective cash management are the same regardless of whether the firm has only domestic operations or if it operates internationally. For example, the cash manager of a domestic firm should source funds internationally to obtain the lowest borrowing cost and to place excess funds wherever the greatest return can be earned. Firms with multinational operations, however, regularly deal in more than one currency, and hence the cost of foreign exchange transactions is an important factor in efficient cash management. Moreover, multinational operations require the firm to decide on whether the cash management function should be centralized at corporate headquarters (or elsewhere) or decentralized and handled locally by each affiliate. In this chapter, we make a strong case for centralized cash management.

CASE APPLICATION

Teltrex's Cash Management System

We use a case problem for a company named Teltrex International to illustrate how a centralized cash management system works. Teltrex is a U.S. multinational firm with headquarters in California's Silicon Valley. It manufactures low-priced quartz watches which it markets throughout North America and Europe. In addition to its manufacturing facilities in California, Teltrex has three sales affiliates in Canada, Germany, and the United Kingdom.

EXHIBIT 19.1 Cash Receipts and Disbursements Matrix for Teltrex ($000)

		Disbursements					
Receipts	U.S.	Canada	Germany	U.K.	External	Total Internal	Total Receipts
U.S.	—	30	35	60	140	125	265
Canada	20	—	10	40	135	70	205
Germany	10	25	—	30	125	65	190
U.K.	40	30	20	—	130	90	220
External	120	165	50	155	—	—	490
Total Internal	70	85	65	130	—	350	
Total Disbursements	190	250	115	285	550	—	1,370

[a]Total cash disbursed by the U.S. parent firm and its affiliates to external parties.
[b]Total cash received by the U.S. parent firm and its affiliates from external parties.
[c]Balancing check figure.

Note: $350,000 is shifted among the various affiliates; $530,000 − $490,000 = $40,000 = increase in cash balances for Teltrex during the week.

The foundation of any cash management system is its cash budget. The **cash budget** is a plan detailing the time and the size of expected cash receipts and disbursements. Teltrex prepares a cash budget in advance for the fiscal year (updating it periodically as the year progresses), using a weekly time interval as the planning frequency. Exhibit 19.1 presents a payments matrix for one week during the cash budget planning horizon; it summarizes all interaffiliate cash receipts and disbursements of Teltrex *and* the receipts from and disbursements to external parties with which Teltrex does business. Exhibit 19.1 is denominated in U.S. dollars, the reporting currency of the parent firm. However, the functional currency of each foreign affiliate is the local currency.

Exhibit 19.1 shows, for example, that the U.S. parent expects to receive the equivalent of $30,000 in Canadian dollars from its Canadian affiliate, the equivalent of $35,000 in euros from its German affiliate, and the equivalent of $60,000 in British pounds sterling from its affiliate in the United Kingdom. In total, it expects to receive $125,000 from interaffiliate transactions. Additionally, the U.S. parent expects to receive $140,000 from external parties, say, from sales in the United States. In total, the parent expects to receive $265,000 in cash during the week. On the disbursements side, the U.S. parent expects to make payments in dollars in the amounts of $20,000 to its Canadian affiliate, $10,000 to its German affiliate, and $40,000 to its British affiliate. It also expects to make external disbursements of $120,000 to, say, suppliers for component parts and to cover other operating costs. Analogous cash flows exist for the three affiliates.

Exhibit 19.1 shows that the equivalent of $350,000 in interaffiliate cash flows are expected to flow among the parent and its three affiliates. Note that no increase in cash in the MNC occurs as a result of interaffiliate transactions. Interaffiliate transactions effectively represent taking money out of one pocket of the MNC and putting it into another. However, Teltrex expects to receive the equivalent of $530,000 from external parties and to make payments of $490,000 to other external parties. From these external transactions, a net increase of $40,000 in cash among the affiliates is expected during the week.

Netting Systems

Let's first consider the interaffiliate transactions that make up part of Exhibit 19.1. Later we will examine the transactions Teltrex expects to have with external parties. Exhibit 19.2 presents only the portion of Teltrex's receipts and disbursements matrix from Exhibit 19.1 that concerns interaffiliate cash flows.

Exhibit 19.2 shows the amount that each affiliate is to pay and receive from the other. Without a netting policy, 12 foreign exchange transactions will take place among the four affiliates. In general, if there are N affiliates, there will be a maximum of $N(N − 1)$ transactions; in our case $4(4 − 1) = 12$. Exhibit 19.3 diagrams these 12 transactions.

EXHIBIT 19.2	Teltrex's Interaffiliate Cash Receipts and Disbursements Matrix ($000)					
	Disbursements					
Receipts	**U.S.**	**Canada**	**Germany**	**U.K.**	**Total Receipts**	**Net**[a]
U.S.	—	30	35	60	125	55
Canada	20	—	10	40	70	(15)
Germany	10	25	—	30	65	0
U.K.	40	30	20	—	90	(40)
Total Disbursements	70	85	65	130	350	0

[a]Net denotes the difference between total receipts and total disbursements for each affiliate.

EXHIBIT 19.3

Teltrex's Interaffiliate
Foreign Exchange
Transactions Without
Netting ($000)

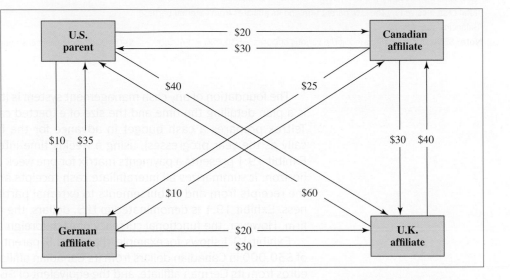

Exhibit 19.3 indicates that the equivalent of $350,000 in funds flows among the four affiliates in 12 foreign exchange transactions. This represents a needless use of administrative time in arranging the transactions and a waste of corporate funds in making the transactions. The cost of transferring funds is in the range of .25 percent to 1.5 percent of the transaction; this includes transaction expenses and the opportunity cost of funds tied up in interaffiliate float. If we assume a cost of .5 percent, the cost for transferring $350,000 is $1,750 for the week.

The 12 transactions can be reduced at least by half through bilateral netting. Under a **bilateral netting** system, each pair of affiliates determines the net amount due between them, and only the net amount is transferred. For example, the U.S. parent and the Canadian affiliate would net the $30,000 and the $20,000 to be received from one another. The result is that only one payment is made; the Canadian affiliate pays the U.S. parent an amount equivalent to $10,000. Exhibit 19.4 shows the results of bilateral netting among Teltrex's four affiliates.

From Exhibit 19.4, it can be seen that a total of $90,000 flows among the four affiliates of Teltrex in six transactions. Bilateral netting can reduce the number of foreign exchange transactions among the affiliates to $N(N-1)/2$, or less. The equivalent of $260,000 in foreign exchange transactions is eliminated through bilateral netting. At .5 percent, the cost of netting interaffiliate foreign exchange transactions is $450, a savings of $1,300 (= $1,750 − 450) over a non-netting system.

Exhibit 19.2 implies a way to limit interaffiliate transfers to no more than $(N-1)$ separate foreign exchange transactions. Rather than stop at bilateral netting, the MNC can establish a multilateral netting system. Under a **multilateral netting** system, each affiliate nets all its interaffiliate receipts against all its disbursements. It then

EXHIBIT 19.4

Bilateral Netting of
Teltrex's Interaffiliate
Foreign Exchange
Transactions ($000)

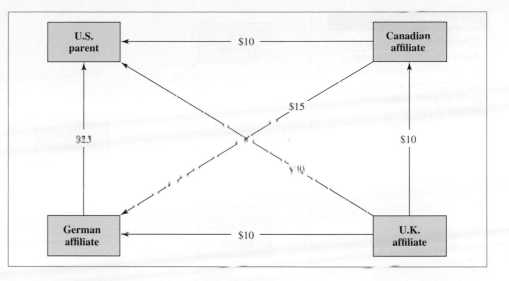

EXHIBIT 19.5

Multilateral Netting of
Teltrex's Interaffiliate
Foreign Exchange
Transactions ($000)

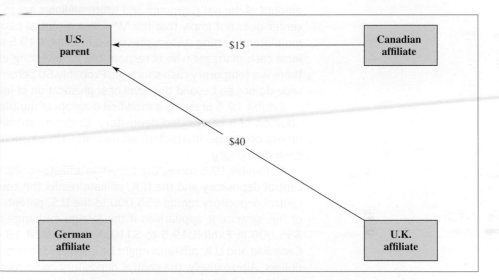

transfers or receives the balance, respectively, if it is a net payer or receiver. Recall from Exhibit 19.1 that total interaffiliate receipts will always equal total interaffiliate disbursements. Thus, under a multilateral netting system, the net funds to be received by the affiliates will equal the net disbursements to be made by the affiliates.

Exhibit 19.5 illustrates a multilateral netting system for Teltrex. Because the German affiliate's net receipts equal zero, only two foreign exchange transactions are necessary. The Canadian and U.K. affiliates, respectively, pay the equivalent of $15,000 and $40,000 to the U.S. parent firm. At .5 percent, the cost of transferring $55,000 is only $275 for the week, a savings of $1,475 (= $1,750 − 275) with a multilateral netting system. Moreover, multilateral netting reduces foreign exchange risk because currency flows are reduced. In a typical multilateral netting operation, it is common to cut FX volume and expense by up to 70 percent.

Centralized Cash Depository

A multilateral netting system requires a certain degree of administrative structure. At the minimum, there must be a netting center manager who has an overview of the inter-affiliate cash flows from the cash budget. The **netting center** manager determines the

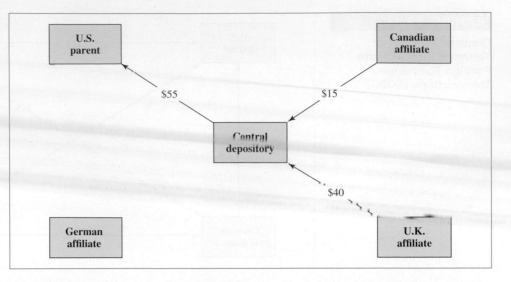

amount of the net payments and which affiliates are to make or receive them. A netting center does not imply that the MNC has a central cash manager, however. Indeed, the multilateral netting system presented in Exhibit 19.5 suggests that each affiliate has a local cash manager who is responsible for investing excess cash and borrowing when there is a temporary cash shortage. Probably 50 percent of all netting operations world-wide do not go beyond this level of sophistication of international cash management.

Exhibit 19.6 presents a modified diagram of multilateral netting for Teltrex with the addition of a centralized depository. Under a centralized cash management system, unless otherwise instructed, all interaffiliate payments will flow through the *central cash depository.*

As Exhibit 19.6 shows, the Canadian affiliate remits the equivalent of $15,000 to the central depository and the U.K. affiliate remits the equivalent of $40,000. In turn, the central depository remits $55,000 to the U.S. parent. One might question the wisdom of this system. It appears as if the foreign exchange transactions have doubled from $55,000 in Exhibit 19.5 to $110,000 in Exhibit 19.6. But that is not the case. The Canadian and U.K. affiliates might be instructed to remit to the central depository in U.S. dollars. Alternatively, the central depository could receive the remittances in Canadian dollars and British pounds sterling and exchange them for dollars before transferring the funds to the U.S. parent. (There is the expense of an additional wire transfer, however.)

The benefits of a central cash depository derive mainly from the business transactions the affiliates have with external parties. Exhibit 19.7 presents a table showing the net amount of external receipts and disbursements each affiliate of Teltrex is expected to have during the week, as originally presented in Exhibit 19.1.

As Exhibit 19.7 shows, the U.S. parent expects to have net receipts of $20,000 by the end of the week. Analogously, in dollars, the German affiliate expects net receipts of $75,000. The Canadian affiliate expects a cash shortage of $30,000, and the U.K. affiliate expects a cash shortage of $25,000. In total, $40,000 of net receipts are expected for the MNC as a whole.

Affiliate	Receipts	Disbursements	Net
United States	$140,000	$120,000	$20,000
Canada	135,000	165,000	(30,000)
Germany	125,000	50,000	75,000
United Kingdom	130,000	155,000	(25,000)
			$40,000

EXHIBIT 19.8

Flow of Teltrex's Net
Cash Receipts from
Transactions with
External Parties with a
Centralized Depository
($000)

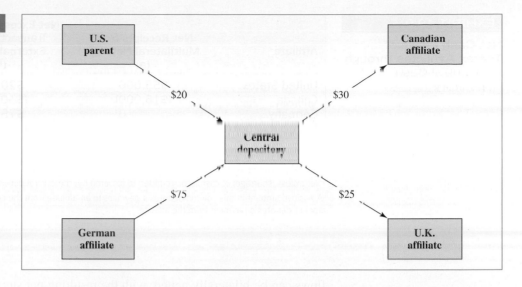

With a **centralized cash depository**, excess cash is remitted to the central cash pool. Analogously, the central cash manager arranges to cover shortages of cash. The central cash manager has a global view of the MNC's overall cash position and needs. Consequently, there is less of a chance for *mislocated funds;* that is, there is less chance for funds to be denominated in the wrong currency. Moreover, because of his global perspective, the central cash manager will know the best borrowing and investing rates. A centralized system facilitates *funds mobilization,* where systemwide cash excesses are invested at the most advantageous rates and cash shortages are covered by borrowing at the most favorable rates. Without a centralized cash depository, one affiliate might end up borrowing locally at an unfavorable rate, while another is investing temporary surplus funds locally at a disadvantageous rate. Exhibit 19.8 diagrams the cash payments for Teltrex depicted in Exhibit 19.7, showing the flows to and from the central cash pool.

Exhibit 19.8 shows that the U.S. parent will remit $20,000 of excess cash from transactions with external parties to the central cash pool, and similarly, the German affiliate will remit the $75,000 it has obtained. Both the Canadian and U.K. affiliates will have their cash shortages of $30,000 and $25,000, respectively, covered by the central pool. In total, a net increase of $40,000 is expected at the central cash depository at the end of the week. The diagram shows that a total of $150,000 of cash is expected to flow to ($95,000) and from ($55,000) the cash depository.

www.treasury-
management.com

This is the website of the online magazine *Treasury Management International.* *TMI* articles are written by corporate treasurers. Many articles on international cash management can be found at this site.

In More Depth

Bilateral Netting of Internal and External Net Cash Flows

Up to this point, we have handled the multilateral netting of interaffiliate cash flows (Exhibit 19.6) *and* the net receipts of the affiliates from the transactions with external parties (Exhibit 19.8) as two separate sets of cash flows through the central cash depository. While it was easier to develop the concepts in that manner, it is not necessary, practical, or efficient to do it that way in practice. Instead, the two sets of net cash

Affiliate	Net Receipts from Multilateral Netting[a] (a)	Net Excess Cash from Transactions with External Parties[b] (b)	Net Flow[c] (a − b)
United States	$55,000	$20,000	$35,000
Canada	($15,000)	($30,000)	$15,000
Germany	0	$75,000	($75,000)
United Kingdom	($40,000)	($25,000)	($15,000)
			($40,000)

[a]Net receipt from (payment to) the central depository resulting from multilateral netting, as shown in Exhibit 19.6.
[b]Net excess (shortage) of cash to be remitted to (covered by) the central depository, as shown in Exhibit 19.7.
[c]A positive amount in this column denotes a payment to an affiliate from the central cash depository; a negative amount denotes a payment from the affiliate.

flows can be bilaterally netted, with the resulting net sums going through the central depository. This will further reduce the number, size, and expense of foreign exchange transactions for the MNC. Exhibit 19.9 calculates the net amount of funds from Teltrex affiliates to flow through the central depository.

Exhibit 19.9 shows the result of netting the cash receipts that would flow through the central cash depository via multilateral netting with the net cash flows that would flow through the central depository as a result of external transactions. As the exhibit shows, the U.S. parent will receive a single payment from the cash pool of $35,000 and the Canadian affiliate will receive $15,000. The German affiliate will remit to the central depository $75,000 and the U.K. affiliate will remit $15,000. In total, the central depository receives $90,000 and disburses $50,000, for an expected net increase in cash of $40,000 for the week. Instead of two separate sets of cash flows totaling $55,000 from the multilateral netting and $150,000 from transactions with external parties, there is only one set of cash flows after the netting totaling $140,000. Thus, there is a savings on foreign exchange transactions of $65,000 for the week. Exhibit 19.10 diagrams the resulting $140,000 of cash flows for Teltrex that are calculated in Exhibit 19.9.

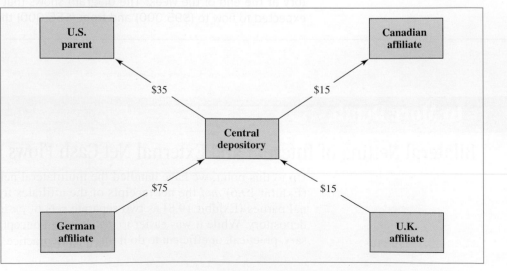

Reduction in Precautionary Cash Balances

An additional benefit of a centralized cash depository is that the MNC's investment in precautionary cash balances can be substantially reduced without a reduction in its ability to cover unforeseen expenses. To see how this is accomplished, consider the receipts and disbursements each affiliate of Teltrex expected to make with external parties during the week. Assume, for simplicity, that each affiliate will have to make all its planned payments to external parties before it receives any cash from other external sources. For example, from Exhibit 19.7, the Canadian affiliate expects to have to pay to external parties the equivalent of $165,000 before it receives any of the expected $135,000 in receipts. Thus, the Canadian affiliate will need a transactions balance of $165,000 to cover expected transactions.

As previously mentioned, a firm keeps a precautionary cash balance to cover unexpected transactions during the budget period. The size of this balance depends on how safe the firm desires to be in its ability to meet unexpected transactions. The larger the precautionary cash balance, the greater is the firm's ability to meet unexpected expenses, and the less is the risk of financial embarrassment and loss of credit standing. Assume that cash needs are normally distributed and that the cash needs of one affiliate are independent from the others. If Teltrex follows a conservative policy, it might keep three standard deviations of cash for precautionary purposes, in addition to the cash needed to cover expected transactions for the planning period. Thus, the probability that Teltrex would experience a cash shortage is only .13 of 1 percent; it will have sufficient cash to cover transactions 99.87 percent of the time.

Under a decentralized cash management system, each affiliate would hold its own transaction balance and precautionary cash. Exhibit 19.11 shows the total cash held for transactions and precautionary purposes by each affiliate and by Teltrex as a whole.

As can be seen from Exhibit 19.11, Teltrex needs the equivalent of $490,000 in cash to cover expected transactions and an additional $615,000 in precautionary balances to cover unexpected expenses, for a total of $1,105,000. A centralized cash management system will greatly reduce the investment in precautionary cash balances. Under a centralized system, the amount of cash held by the MNC is viewed as a portfolio. Each affiliate will continue to hold cash sufficient to cover its expected cash transactions, but the precautionary cash balances are held by the central cash manager at the central cash depository. In the event one of the affiliates experiences a cash shortage, funds are wired from precautionary cash held in the central cash pool.

From portfolio theory, the standard deviation of the portfolio of cash held by the centralized depository for N affiliates is calculated as:[1]

$$\text{Portfolio Std. Dev.} = \sqrt{(\text{Std. Dev. Affiliate 1})^2 + \ldots + (\text{Std. Dev. Affiliate } N)^2}$$

EXHIBIT 19.11	Affiliate	Expected Transactions (a)	Standard Deviation (b)	Expected Needs plus Precautionary (a + 3b)
Transaction and Precautionary Cash Balances Held by Each Teltrex Affiliate under a Decentralized Cash Management System	United States	$120,000	$50,000	$ 270,000
	Canada	165,000	70,000	375,000
	Germany	50,000	20,000	110,000
	United Kingdom	155,000	65,000	350,000
	Total	$490,000		$1,105,000

[1]The standard deviation formula assumes that interaffiliate cash flows are uncorrelated with one another.

For our example,

$$\text{Portfolio Std. Dev.} = \sqrt{(\$50,000)^2 + (\$70,000)^2 + (\$20,000)^2 + (\$65,000)^2}$$
$$= \$109,659.$$

Thus under a centralized system, only $328,977 (= 3 \times \$109,659$) needs to be held for precautionary purposes by Teltrex's central cash manager. A total of $818,977 (= \$490,000 + \$328,977$) is held by Teltrex. The reduction in precautionary cash balances under the centralized system is $286,023 (= \$1,105,000 - \$818,977$), a sum that most likely can be used more profitably elsewhere, rather than standing by as a potential safety net.

Cash Management Systems in Practice

Multilateral netting is an efficient and cost-effective mechanism for handling interaffiliate foreign exchange transactions. Not all countries allow MNCs the freedom to net payments, however. Some countries allow interaffiliate transactions to be settled only on a gross basis. That is, all receipts for a settlement period must be grouped into a single large receipt and all disbursements must be grouped into a single large payment. The reason for requiring gross settlement is precisely the opposite of the reason that MNCs desire to net. By limiting netting, more needless foreign exchange transactions flow through the local banking system, thus generating income for the local banks that handle them.

A study by Collins and Frankle (1985) surveyed the cash management practices of the *Fortune* 1000 firms. The researchers received a 22 percent response rate from their questionnaire. Of the responding firms, 163 were involved in international operations. Thirty-five percent of the international respondents reported using some type of intracorporate netting and 23 percent had centralized funds concentration.

In another study, Bokos and Clinkard (1983) found that the most frequently cited benefits of a multilateral netting system were:

1. The decrease in the expense associated with funds transfer, which in some cases can be over $1,000 for a large international transfer of foreign exchange.

2. The reduction in the number of foreign exchange transactions and the associated cost of making fewer but larger transactions.

3. The reduction in intracompany float, which is frequently as high as five days even for wire transfers.

4. The savings in administrative time.

5. The benefits that accrue from the establishment of a formal information system, which serves as the foundation for centrally managing transaction exposure and the investment of excess funds.

www.euronetting.com

This is the website of EuroNetting, an online netting company that enables companies worldwide to manage their intercompany netting activities.

There are several commercial multilateral netting packages available that offer full international cash management services. For example, EuroNetting is a 100 percent web browser-based system for both the netting center and the participants. It is used by approximately 50 companies with about 8,000 associated users worldwide to manage their interaffiliate reconcilement and netting activities. The EuroNetting system facilitates both balance and invoice-level netting with participant settlement in any currency. The system incorporates a comprehensive set of hedging capabilities and interfaces with most popular bank settlement systems and treasury workstations. Wall Street Systems' Wallstreet Treasura is another international cash management system that allows the corporation to achieve global cash visibility by connecting to all the firm's banks to position cash and reconcile daily cash and liquidity. It allows the firm to make daily, weekly, and monthly cash forecasts, facilitates interaffiliate loans, and can accommodate foreign exchange transactions. Bank of America Merril

Lynch's CashPro Accelerate is a similar cash management system that integrates with the firm's general ledger. It provides for streamline cash position reporting in multiple bank accounts around the globe. Daily currency exchange rates are built into the system to allow viewing cash balances in different currencies. It is capable of providing updated cash balances every five minutes.

SUMMARY

This chapter discussed cash management in the multinational firm. Special attention was given to the topic of multilateral netting. A case application was used to show the benefits of centralized cash management.

1. A multilateral netting system is beneficial in reducing the number of and the expense associated with interaffiliate foreign exchange transactions.

2. A centralized cash pool assists in reducing the problem of mislocated funds and in funds mobilization. A central cash manager has a global view of the most favorable borrowing rates and most advantageous investment rates.

3. A centralized cash management system with a cash pool can reduce the investment the MNC has in precautionary cash balances, saving the firm money.

KEY WORDS

bilateral netting, *478*
cash budget, *477*
cash management, *476*
centralized cash
   depository, *481*
multilateral
   netting, *478*
netting center, *479*
precautionary cash
   balances, *476*
transaction balances, *476*

QUESTIONS

1. Describe the key factors contributing to effective cash management within a firm. Why is the cash management process more difficult in a MNC?

2. Discuss the pros and cons of a MNC having a centralized cash manager handle all investment and borrowing for all affiliates of the MNC versus each affiliate having a local manager who performs the cash management activities of the affiliate.

PROBLEMS

1. Assume that interaffiliate cash flows are uncorrelated with one another. Calculate the standard deviation of the portfolio of cash held by the centralized depository for the following affiliate members:

Affiliate	Expected Transactions	Standard Deviation
U.S.	$100,000	$40,000
Canada	$150,000	$60,000
Mexico	$175,000	$30,000
Chile	$200,000	$70,000

INTERNET EXERCISES

1. EuroNetting, an online netting company, offers a multilateral service that enables companies to run their netting efficiently over the Internet. See their website at www.euronetting.com to view their product offerings. EuroNetting is used by approximately 50 companies with about 8,000 associated users worldwide to manage their intercompany reconcilement and netting activities.

2. Students interested in a professional designation in international cash management should explore the online program leading to a Certificate in International Cash Management (CertICM) at the Association of Corporate Treasurers website, www.treasurers.org. The six-month program requires 200 hours of self-study, after which there is a three-hour written exam.

MINI CASE 1

Efficient Funds Flow at Eastern Trading Company

The Eastern Trading Company of Singapore purchases spices in bulk from around the world, packages them into consumer-size quantities, and sells them through sales affiliates in Hong Kong, the United Kingdom, and the United States. For a recent month, the following payments matrix of interaffiliate cash flows, stated in Singapore dollars, was forecast. Show how Eastern Trading can use multilateral netting to minimize the foreign exchange transactions necessary to settle interaffiliate payments. If foreign exchange transactions cost the company 5 percent, what savings result from netting?

Eastern Trading Company Payments Matrix (S$000)

Receipts	Disbursements				
	Singapore	Hong Kong	U.K.	U.S.	Total Receipts
Singapore	—	40	75	55	170
Hong Kong	8	—	—	22	30
U.K.	15	—	—	17	32
U.S.	11	25	9	—	45
Total disbursements	34	65	84	94	277

MINI CASE 2

Eastern Trading Company's New MBA

The Eastern Trading Company of Singapore presently follows a decentralized system of cash management where it and its affiliates each maintain their own transaction and precautionary cash balances. Eastern Trading believes that it and its affiliates' cash needs are normally distributed and independent from one another. It is corporate policy to maintain two and one-half standard deviations of cash as precautionary holdings. At this level of safety there is a 99.37 percent chance that each affiliate will have enough cash holdings to cover transactions.

A new MBA hired by the company claims that the investment in precautionary cash balances is needlessly large and can be reduced substantially if the firm converts to a centralized cash management system. Use the projected information for the current month, which is presented below, to determine the amount of cash Eastern Trading needs to hold in precautionary balances under its current decentralized system and the level of precautionary cash it would need to hold under a centralized system. Was the new MBA a good hire?

Affiliate	Expected Transactions	One Standard Deviation
Singapore	S$125,000	S$40,000
Hong Kong	60,000	25,000
United Kingdom	95,000	40,000
United States	70,000	35,000

REFERENCES & SUGGESTED READINGS

Bokos, W. J., and Anne P. Clinkard. "Multilateral Netting." *Journal of Cash Management* 3 (1983), pp. 24–34.

Collins, J. Markham, and Alan W. Frankle. "International Cash Management Practices of Large U.S. Firms." *Journal of Cash Management* 5 (1985), pp. 42–48.

20 International Trade Finance

IN MODERN TIMES, it is virtually impossible for a country to produce domestically everything its citizens need or demand. Even if it could, it is unlikely that it could produce all items more efficiently than producers in other countries. Without international trade, scarce resources are not put to their best uses.

International trade is more difficult and risky, however, than domestic trade. In foreign trade, the exporter may not be familiar with the buyer, and thus may not know if the importer is a good credit risk. If merchandise is exported abroad and the buyer does not pay, it may prove difficult, if not impossible, for the exporter to have any legal recourse. Additionally, political instability makes it risky to ship merchandise abroad to certain parts of the world. From the importer's perspective, it is risky to make advance payment for goods that may never be shipped by the exporter.

The present chapter deals with these issues and others. The chapter begins with an example of a simple yet typical foreign trade transaction. The mechanics of the trade are discussed, delineating the institutional arrangements that have been developed over time to facilitate international trade in light of the risks we have identified. The three basic documents needed in a foreign trade transaction—a letter of credit, a time draft, and a bill of lading—are discussed in detail. It is shown how a time draft becomes a banker's acceptance, a negotiable money market instrument.

The second part of the chapter discusses the role of the Export-Import Bank, an independent government agency founded to offer competitive assistance to U.S. exporters through loans, financial guarantees, and credit insurance. The chapter concludes with a discussion of various types of countertrade transactions. Countertrade transactions can collectively be defined as foreign trade transactions in which the seller provides the buyer with goods or services in return for a reciprocal promise from the seller to purchase goods or services from the buyer.

A Typical Foreign Trade Transaction

To understand the mechanics of a typical foreign trade transaction, it is best to use an illustration. Consider a U.S. importer, who is an automobile dealer, and who desires to purchase automobiles from a Japanese exporter, the manufacturer. The two do not know one another and are obviously separated by a great distance. If the Japanese manufacturer could have his way, he would have the U.S. importer pay *cash in advance* for the shipment, since he is unfamiliar with the creditworthiness of the auto dealer.

If the auto dealer could have his way, he ideally would prefer to receive the cars on consignment from the auto manufacturer. In a *consignment* sale, the exporter retains title to the merchandise that is shipped. The importer only pays the exporter once he sells the merchandise. If the importer cannot sell the merchandise, he returns it to the exporter. Obviously, the exporter bears all the risk in a consignment sale. Second best for the auto dealer would be to receive the car shipment on credit and then to make payment, thus not paying in advance for an order that might not ever be received.

How can the situation be reconciled so that the foreign trade transaction is satisfactory for both the exporter and the importer? Fortunately for the auto dealer and the auto manufacturer, they are not the first two parties who have faced such a dilemma. Over the years, an elaborate process has evolved for handling just this type of foreign commerce transaction. Exhibit 20.1 presents a schematic of the process that is typically followed in foreign trade. Working our way through Exhibit 20.1 in a narrative fashion will allow us to understand the mechanics of a trade and also the three major documents involved.

Exhibit 20.1 begins with (1) the U.S. importer placing an order with the Japanese exporter, asking if he will ship automobiles under a letter of credit. If the auto

EXHIBIT 20.1   Process of a Typical Foreign Trade Transaction

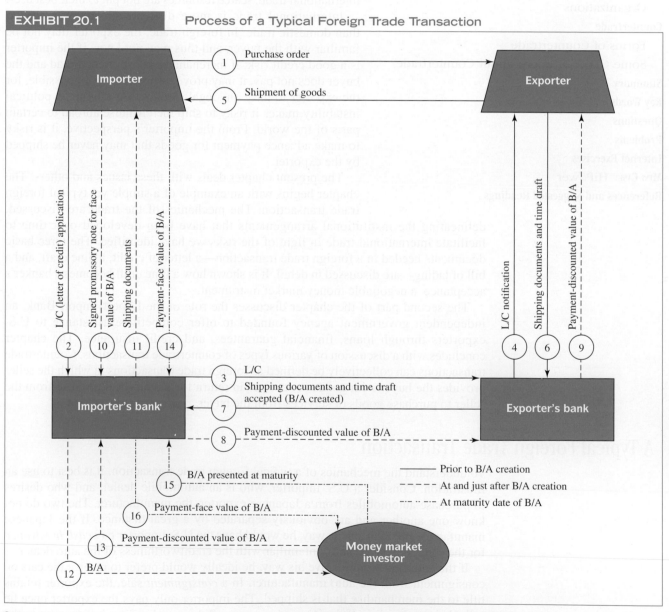

Source: Adapted from *Instruments of the Money Market*, Federal Reserve Bank of Richmond, 1986. Used by permission.

manufacturer agrees to this, he will inform the U.S. importer of the price and the other terms of sale, including the credit terms. For discussion purposes, we will assume the length of the credit period is 60 days. The U.S. importer will (ii) apply to his bank for a letter of credit for the merchandise he desires to purchase, providing his bank with the terms of the sale.

A **letter of credit (L/C)** is a guarantee from the importer's bank that it will act on behalf of the importer and pay the exporter for the merchandise if all relevant documents specified in the L/C are presented according to the terms of the L/C. In essence, the importer's bank is substituting its creditworthiness for that of the unknown U.S. importer.

The L/C is (iii) sent via the importer's bank to the exporter's bank. Once the L/C is received, the exporter's bank will (iv) notify the exporter. The Japanese exporter will (v) then ship the cars.

After shipping the automobiles, the Japanese exporter will (vi) present to his bank a (60-day) time draft, drawn according to the instructions in the L/C, the bill of lading, and any other shipping documents that are required, such as the invoice and a packing list. A **time draft** is a written order instructing the importer or his agent, the importer's bank, to pay the amount specified on its face on a certain date (that is, the end of the credit period in a foreign trade transaction). A **bill of lading (B/L)** is a document issued by the common carrier specifying that it has received the goods for shipment; it can serve as title to the goods. The exporter's bank (vii) presents the shipping documents and the time draft to the importer's bank. After taking title to the goods via the bill of lading, the importer's bank accepts the time draft, creating at this point a **banker's acceptance (B/A)**, a negotiable money market instrument for which a secondary market exists. The importer's bank charges an acceptance commission, which is deducted at the time of final settlement. The acceptance commission is based on the term-to-maturity of the time draft and the creditworthiness of the importer.

One of several things can happen with the B/A. It can be returned to the Japanese exporter, who will hold it for 60 days and then present it for payment to the importer's bank at maturity. Should the exporter suddenly find he needs funds prior to the maturity date, the B/A can be sold at a discount in the money market. Since their risks are similar, banker's acceptances trade at rates similar to rates for negotiable bank certificates of deposit. Alternatively, as in Exhibit 20.1, the Japanese exporter could instruct its bank to have the B/A (viii) discounted by the importer's bank and (ix) pay that amount to it. Analogously, the exporter's bank may decide to hold the B/A to maturity as an investment, and pay the Japanese exporter the discounted equivalent.

The U.S. importer (x) signs a (60-day) promissory note with his bank for the face value of the banker's acceptance, due on the maturity date of the B/A. In return, the exporter's bank (xi) provides the auto dealer with the shipping documents needed to take possession of the automobiles from the common carrier.

If the B/A is not held by the Japanese exporter or the exporter's bank, the importer's bank may hold it for 60 days until maturity when it will collect the face value from the U.S. importer via the promissory note. Alternatively, as in Exhibit 20.1, the importer's bank may (xii) sell the B/A in the money market to an investor at a (xiii) discount from face value. At maturity, the importer's bank will (xiv) collect the face value of the B/A via the promissory note from the U.S. importer, the money market investor will (xv) present the B/A for payment to the importer's bank, and the importer's bank will (xvi) pay the face value of the B/A to the investor. In the event of default by the U.S. importer, the importer's bank will seek recourse against the importer. B/As usually have maturities ranging from 30 days to 180 days; as such they are only short-term sources of trade financing.

EXHIBIT 21.1   Corporate Percentage Income Tax Rates from Certain Countries[a]

Country	Tax Rate	Country	Tax Rate	Country	Tax Rate	Country	Tax Rate
Albania	10	Czech Republic	19	Kuwait	0	Qatar	10
Angola	35	Denmark	25	Kyrgyzstan	10	Romania	16
Antigua & Barbuda	25	Dominica, Commonwealth of	30	Lao, People's Democratic Republic	28	Russian Federation	20
Argentina	35	Dominican Republic	25	Latvia	15	Rwanda	30
Armenia	20	Ecuador	23	Lebanon	15	St. Kitts and Nevis	35
Aruba	28	Egypt	25	Libya	20	St. Lucia	30
Australia	30	El Salvador	30	Liechtenstein	12.5	Saudi Arabia	20
Austria	25	Equatorial Guinea	35	Lithuania	15	Senegal	25
Azerbaijan	20	Estonia	21	Luxembourg	22.05	Serbia	10
Bahrain	0	Fiji	20	Macau	12	Singapore	17
Barbados	25	Finland	24.5	Macedonia	10	Sint Maarten	34.5
Belarus	24	France	36.1	Madagascar	21	Slovak Republic	19
Belgium	33.99	Gabon	35	Malawi	30	Slovenia	18
Bermuda	0	Georgia	15	Malaysia	25	South Africa	28
Bolivia	25	Germany	33	Malta	35	Spain	30
Bosnia Herzegovina	10	Ghana	25	Mauritius	15	Sri Lanka	28
Botswana	22	Gibraltar	10	Mexico	30	Swaziland	30
Brazil	34	Greece	20	Moldova	12	Sweden	26.3
Bulgaria	10	Guatemala	31	Mongolia	25	Switzerland	11.5–24.2
Cambodia	20	Guyana	40	Montenegro	9	Syria	28
Cameroon	38.5	Honduras	25	Morocco	30	Taiwan	17
Canada	15	Hong Kong	16.5	Mozambique	32	Tajikistan	15
Cape Verde	25	Hungary	19	Namibia	34	Tanzania	30
Caribbean Netherlands	0	Iceland	20	Netherlands	25	Thailand	23
Cayman Islands	0	India	34.5	New Zealand	28	Timor-este	10
Chad	40	Indonesia	25	Nicaragua	30	Trinidad & Tobago	25
Channel Islands, Guernsey	0	Iraq	15	Nigeria	30	Tunisia	30
Channel Islands, Jersey	0	Ireland	12.5	Norway	28	Turkey	20
Chile	17	Isle of Man	0	Oman	12	Turkmenistan	8
China	25	Israel	25	Pakistan	35	Uganda	30
Colombia	33	Italy	27.5	Panama	27.5	Ukraine	21
Congo, Democratic Republic of	40	Ivory Coast	25	Papua New Guinea	30	United Arab Emirates	≤ 55
Congo, Republic of	34	Jamaica	33.33	Paraguay	10	United Kingdom	24
Costa Rica	30	Japan	42	Peru	30	United States	35
Croatia	20	Jordan	14	Philippines	30	Uruguay	25
Curacao	27.5	Kazakhstan	20	Poland	19	Uzbekistan	9
Cyprus	10	Kenya	30	Portugal	25	Venezuela	34
		Korea	22	Puerto Rico	30	Vietnam	25
						Zimbabwe	25.75

[a]The table lists normal, standard, or representative upper-end marginal tax rates for nonfinancial corporations.

Source: Derived from PriceWaterhouseCoopers. *Corporate Taxes: Worldwide Summaries*, www.pwc.com, 2012/13.

derived from the PriceWaterhouseCoopers summaries. It lists the normal, standard, or representative upper-end marginal income tax rates for domestic nonfinancial corporations for 152 countries for tax year 2012. As the exhibit shows, national tax rates vary from a low of zero percent in such tax haven countries as Bahrain, and the Cayman Islands, to 40 percent or more in some countries. The current U.S. marginal tax rate of 35 percent is positioned toward the upper end of the rates assessed by the majority of countries.

Withholding Tax

A **withholding tax** is a tax generally levied on passive income earned by an individual or corporation of one country within the tax jurisdiction of another country. **Passive income** includes dividends and interest income, and income from royalties, patents, or copyrights paid to the taxpayer by a corporation. A withholding tax is an **indirect tax** that is borne by a taxpayer who did not directly generate the income. The tax is withheld from payments the corporation makes to the taxpayer and turned over to the local tax authority. The withholding tax assures the local tax authority that it will receive the tax due on the passive income earned within its tax jurisdiction.

www.taxsites.com/ international.html

www.worldwide-tax.com

These websites provide tax and accounting information by country.

Many countries have **tax treaties** with one another specifying the withholding tax rate applied to various types of passive income. Exhibit 21.2 lists the *basic* withholding tax rates the U.S. imposes on other countries through its tax treaties with them for 2012. For specific types of passive income, the tax rates may be different from those presented in the exhibit.[1] Withholding tax rates imposed through tax treaties are bilateral; that is, through negotiation two countries agree as to what tax rates apply to various categories of passive income.

Note from Exhibit 21.2 that withholding tax rates vary by category of passive income from zero to 30 percent. It is also noteworthy that withholding tax rates vary significantly among countries within an income category. For example, the United States withholds 0 percent on interest income from taxpayers residing in most Western European countries, but 30 percent from taxpayers residing in Pakistan. The exhibit also shows that the United States withholds 30 percent of passive income from taxpayers that reside in countries with which it does not have withholding tax treaties. Exhibit 21.2 also indicates that according to the withholding tax treaty with a country, the *general* tax rate on dividends paid to foreign payees from portfolio investment in a U.S. firm is frequently higher than the *direct* dividend rate applied to investors with a substantial ownership share.

Value-Added Tax

http://ec.europa.eu/taxation_ customs/taxation/vat

Use the site map at this website to find a discussion of the practical aspects of value-added taxation in the European Union.

A **value-added tax (VAT)** is an indirect national tax levied on the value added in the production of a good (or service) as it moves through the various stages of production. There are several ways to implement a VAT. The "subtraction method" is frequently followed in practice.

EXAMPLE | 21.1: Value-Added Tax Calculation

As an example of the subtraction method of calculating VAT, consider a VAT of 15 percent charged on a consumption good that goes through three stages of production. Suppose that Stage 1 is the sale of raw materials to the manufacturer at a cost of €100 per unit of production. Stage 2 results in a finished good shipped to retailers at a price of €300. Stage 3 is the retail sale to the final consumer at a price of €380. €100 of value has been added in Stage 1, resulting in a VAT of €15. In Stage 2 the VAT is 15 percent of €300, or €45, with a credit of €15 given against the value added in Stage 1. In Stage 3, an additional VAT of €12 is due on the €80 of value added by the retailer. Since the final consumer pays a price of €380, he effectively pays the total VAT of €57 (= €15 + €30 + €12), which is 15 percent of €380. Obviously, a VAT is the equivalent of imposing a national sales tax. Exhibit 21.3 summarizes the VAT calculation.

---

[1]See the United States Internal Revenue Service website at www.irs.gov for exceptions to the basic withholding tax rates.

Glossary

A

Active Income Income that results from production or services provided by an individual or corporation.

Adjusted Present Value (APV) A present value technique that discounts a firm's cash flows at different rates depending on the risk of the cash flows.

Agency Market A market in which the broker takes the client's order through the agent, who matches it with another public order.

Agency Problem Managers who are hired as the agents working for shareholders may actually pursue their own interests at the expense of shareholders, causing conflicts of interest. Agency problems are especially acute for firms with diffused share ownership.

All-Equity Cost of Capital The required return on a company's stock in the absence of debts.

All-in-Cost All costs of a swap, which are interest expense, transaction cost, and service charges.

American Depository Receipt (ADR) A certificate of ownership issued by a U.S. bank representing a multiple of foreign shares that are deposited in a U.S. bank. ADRs can be traded on the organized exchanges in the United States or in the OTC market.

American Option An option that can be exercised at any time during the option contract.

Appreciate In the context of a domestic currency, a decrease (an increase) in a foreign exchange rate relative to another currency when stated in terms of the domestic (foreign) currency.

Arbitrage The act of simultaneously buying and selling the same or equivalent assets or commodities for the purpose of making certain, guaranteed profits.

Ask Price *See* Offer Price.

B

Balance of Payments A country's record of international transactions presented in a double-entry bookkeeping form.

Balance Sheet Hedge Intended to reduce translation exposure of a MNC by eliminating the mismatch of exposed net assets and exposed net liabilities denominated in the same currency.

Bank Capital Adequacy The amount of equity capital and other securities a bank holds as reserves against risky assets to reduce the probability of a bank failure.

Banker's Acceptance (B/A) A negotiable money market instrument for which a secondary market exists and is issued by the Importer's Bank once the bill of lading and time draft are accepted. It is essentially a promise that the bank will pay the draft when it matures.

Basel Accord Established in 1988 by the Bank for International Settlements, this act established a framework to measure bank capital adequacy for banks in the Group of Ten and Luxembourg.

Bearer Bond A bond in which ownership is demonstrated through possession of the bond.

Bid Price The price at which dealers will buy a financial asset.

Bilateral Netting A system in which a pair of affiliates determines the net amount due between them and only this amount is transferred.

Bill of Lading (B/L) In exporting, a document issued by a common carrier specifying that it has received goods for shipment and that can also serve as title to the goods.

Bimetallism A double standard maintaining free coinage for both gold and silver.

Brady Bonds Loans converted into collateralized bonds with a reduced interest rate devised to resolve the international debt crisis in the late 1980s. Named after the U.S. Treasury Secretary Nicholas Brady.

Bretton Woods System An international monetary system created in 1944 to promote postwar exchange rate stability and coordinate international monetary policies. Otherwise known as the gold-exchange system.

C

Cadbury Code The Cadbury Committee appointed by the British government issued the *Code of Best Practice* in corporate governance for British companies, recommending, among other things, appointing at least three outside board directors and having the positions of CEO and board chairman held by two different individuals.

Call Market A market in which market and limit orders are accumulated and executed at specific intervals during the day.

Call Option An option to "buy" an underlying asset at a specified price.

Capital Account Balance-of-payment entry capturing all sales and purchases of financial assets, real estate, and businesses.

Capital-Export Neutrality The idea that an ideal tax is one which is effective in raising revenue for the government and, at the same time, does not prevent economic resources from being deployed most efficiently no matter where in the world the highest return can be earned.

Capital-Import Neutrality The idea that an ideal tax burden imposed by a host country on a foreign subsidiary of a MNC should be the same regardless of which country the MNC is incorporated in and should be the same burden as placed on domestic firms.

Cash Budget In cash management, a plan that details the time and size of expected receipts and disbursements.

Cash Management The handling of cash within a firm such as the investment a firm has in transaction balances, funds tied up in precautionary cash balances, investment of excess funds at the most favorable rate, and borrowing at the lowest rate when there is a temporary cash shortage.

Centralized Cash Depository In a MNC, it is a central cash pool in which excess cash from affiliates is collected and invested or used to cover system-wide shortages of cash.

Closed-End Country Fund (CECF) A country fund (fund invested exclusively in the securities of one country) that issues a given number of shares that are traded on the host country exchange as if it were an individual stock. These shares are not redeemable at the underlying net asset value set in the home market.

Comparative Advantage David Ricardo used the notion of comparative advantage to justify international trade. Specifically, if countries specialize production in those industries where they can produce goods and services more efficiently (in relative terms) than other countries, and engage in trade, all countries will be better off.

Competitive Effect Refers to the effect of exchange rate changes on the firm's competitive position, which, in turn, affects the firm's operating cash flows.

Complete Contract Refers to the contract that specifies exactly what each party will do under all possible future contingencies.

Concessionary Loan A loan below the market interest rate offered by the host country to a parent MNC to encourage capital expenditures in the host country.

Contingent Claim Security *See* Derivative Security.

Contingent Exposure The risk due to uncertain situations in which a firm does not know if it will face exchange risk exposure in the future.

Continuous Market A market in which market and limit orders can be executed any time during business hours.

Controlled Foreign Corporation (CFC) A foreign subsidiary in which U.S. shareholders own more than 50 percent of the voting equity stock.

Conversion Effect Refers to the fact that the dollar amount converted from a given cash flow from foreign operation will be affected by exchange rate changes.

Convertible Bond A bond that can be exchanged for a predetermined number of equity shares of the issuer.

Corporate Governance The economic, legal, and institutional framework in which corporate control and cash flow rights are distributed among shareholders, managers, and other stakeholders of the company.

Counterparty One of the two parties involved in financial contracts who agrees to exchange cash flows on particular terms.

Countertrade Transactions in which parties exchange goods or services. If these transactions do not involve an exchange of money, they are a type of barter.

Country Risk In banking and investment, it is the probability that unexpected events in a country will influence its ability to repay loans and repatriate dividends. It includes political and credit risks.

Covered Interest Arbitrage A situation that occurs when IRP does not hold, thereby allowing certain arbitrage profits to be made without the arbitrageur investing any money out of pocket or bearing any risk.

Cross-Currency Interest Rate Swap Typically called a "currency swap." One counterparty exchanges the debt service obligations of a bond denominated in one currency for the debt service obligations of the other counterparty that are denominated in another currency.

Cross-Exchange Rate An exchange rate between a currency pair where neither currency is the U.S. dollar.

Cross-Hedging Involves hedging a position in one asset by taking a position in another asset.

Cross-Listing The act of directly listing securities on foreign financial exchanges. Cross-listing will require meeting the listing and disclosure standards of foreign exchanges.

Cumulative Translation Adjustment (CTA) Used in the current rate method of translating foreign currency financial statements, this equity account allows balancing of the balance sheet by accounting for translation gains and losses.

Currency Board An extreme form of the fixed exchange rate regime under which local currency is fully backed by the U.S. dollar or another chosen standard currency.

Currency Swap One counterparty exchanges the debt service obligations of a bond denominated in one currency for the debt service obligations of the other counterparty denominated in another currency.

Current Account Balance-of-payment entry representing the exports and imports of goods and services, and unilateral transfer.

Current/Noncurrent Method In dealing with foreign currency translation, the idea that current assets and liabilities are converted at the current exchange rate while noncurrent assets and liabilities are translated at the historical exchange rates.

Current Rate Method In dealing with foreign currency translation, the idea that all balance sheet accounts are translated at the current exchange rate except stockholder's equity, which is translated at the exchange rate on the date of issuance.

D

Dealer Market A market in which the broker takes the trade through the dealer, who participates in trades as a principal.

Debt-for-Equity Swap The sale of sovereign debt for U.S. dollars to investors desiring to make equity investment in the indebted nation.

Depreciate In the context of a domestic currency, an increase (a decrease) in a foreign exchange rate relative to another currency when stated in terms of the domestic (foreign) currency.

Derivative Security A security whose value is contingent upon the value of the underlying security. Examples are futures, forward, and options contracts.

Direct Tax A tax paid directly by the taxpayer on whom the tax is levied.

Diversification of the Market A strategy for managing operating exposure in which a firm diversifies the market for its product. Thus, exchange rate changes in one country may be offset by opposite exchange rate changes in another.

Dodd-Frank Act The Dodd-Frank Wall Street Reform and Consumer Protection Act of 2010 aims to identify and reduce the systemic risk of the entire financial system by regulating Wall Street and big banks.

Draft A written order instructing the importer or his agent to pay the amount specified on its face at a certain date.

Dual-Currency Bond A straight fixed-rate bond that pays coupon interest in the issue currency, but at maturity pays the principal in a currency other than the issue currency.

E

Economic Exposure The possibility that cash flows and the value of the firm may be affected by unanticipated changes in the exchange rates.

Market Completeness A market is complete if each state of the economy is matched by security payoff.

Market Imperfections Various frictions, such as transaction costs and legal restrictions, that prevent the markets from functioning perfectly.

Market Order An order executed at the best price available (market price) when the order is received in the market.

Marked-to-Market The process of establishing daily price gains and losses in the futures market by the change in the settlement price of the futures contract.

Merchant Bank A bank that performs traditional commercial banking as well as investment banking activities.

Monetary/Nonmonetary Method In dealing with foreign currency translation, the idea that monetary balance sheet accounts such as accounts receivable are translated at the current exchange rate while nonmonetary balance sheet accounts such as stockholder's equity are converted at the historical exchange rate.

Money Market Hedge A method of hedging transaction exposure by borrowing and lending in the domestic and foreign money markets.

Multilateral Netting A system in which all affiliates each net their individual interaffiliate receipts against all their disbursements and transfer or receive the balance, respectively, if they are net payers or net receivers.

Multinational Corporation (MNC) Refers to a firm that has business activities and interests in multiple countries.

N

National Neutrality The idea that an ideal tax on taxable income would tax all income in the same manner by the taxpayer's national tax authority regardless of where in the world it is earned.

Negotiable Certificate of Deposit (NCD) A negotiable bank time deposit.

Net Present Value (NPV) A capital budgeting method in which the present value of cash outflows is subtracted from the present value of expected future cash inflows to determine the net present value of an investment project.

Netting Center In multilateral netting, it determines the amount of net payments and which affiliates are to make or pay them.

North American Free Trade Agreement (NAFTA) Created in 1994, it includes the United States, Canada, and Mexico as members in a free trade area. NAFTA aimed to eliminate tariffs and import quotas over a 15-year period.

Notional Principal A reference amount of principal used for determining payments under various derivative contracts.

O

Offer Price The price at which a dealer will sell a financial asset.

Offshore Banking Center A country in which the banking system is organized to allow external accounts beyond the normal economic activity of the country. Their primary function is to seek deposits and grant loans in currencies other than the host country currency.

Open Interest The total number of short or long contracts outstanding for a particular delivery month in the derivative markets.

Operating Exposure The extent to which the firm's operating cash flows will be affected by random changes in the exchange rates.

Operational Hedging Long-term, operational approaches to hedging exchange exposure that include diversification of the market and flexible sourcing.

Optimum Currency Area A geographical area that is suitable for sharing a common currency by virtue of a high degree of factor mobility within the area.

Option A contract giving the owner the right, but not the obligation, to buy or sell a given quantity of an asset at a specified price at some date in the future.

Options Market Hedge Use of put and call options to limit the downside risk of transaction exposure while preserving the upside potential. The price of such flexibility is the option premium.

Over-the-Counter (OTC) Market Trading market in which there is no central marketplace; instead, buyers and sellers are linked via a network of telephones, telex machines, computers, and automated dealing systems.

P

Par Value The nominal or face value of stocks or bonds.

Passive Income Income not directly generated by an individual or corporation, such as interest income, royalty income, and copyright income.

Plaza Accord G-5 agreement in 1985 that depreciation of the dollar is desirable to correct the U.S. trade deficits.

Political Risk Potential losses to the parent firm resulting from adverse political developments in the host country.

Portfolio Risk Diversification Portfolio risk is minimized by investing in multiple securities that do not have strong correlations between one another.

Precautionary Cash Balance Emergency funds a firm maintains in case it has underestimated its transaction cash balance.

Price-Specie-Flow Mechanism Under the gold standard, it is the automatic correction of payment imbalances between countries. This is based on the fact that, under the gold standard, the domestic money stock rises or falls as the country experiences inflows or outflows of gold.

Primary Market The market in which new security issues are sold to investors. In selling the new securities, investment bankers can play the role of either broker or dealer.

Privatization Act of a country divesting itself of ownership and operation of business ventures by turning them over to the free market system.

Product Differentiation Creating a perception among consumers that a firm's product(s) are different from those offered by competitors, thereby reducing price sensitivity of demand.

Purchasing Power Parity (PPP) A theory stating that the exchange rate between currencies of two countries should be equal to the ratio of the countries' price levels of a commodity basket.

Put An option to sell an underlying asset at a prespecified price.

Q

Quality Spread Differential (QSD) The difference between the fixed interest rate spread differential and the floating interest rate spread differential of the debt of two counterparties of different creditworthiness. A positive QSD is a necessary condition for an interest swap to occur that ensures that the swap will be beneficial to both parties.

Quantity Theory of Money An identity stating that for each country, the general price level times aggregate output should be equal to the money supply times the velocity of money.

R

Random Walk Hypothesis A hypothesis stating that in an efficient market, asset prices change randomly (i.e., independently of historical trends), or follow a "random walk." Thus, the expected future exchange rate is equivalent to the current exchange rate.

Real Exchange Rate Measures the degree of deviation from PPP over a period of time, assuming PPP held at the beginning of the period.

Real Option The application of options pricing theory to the evaluation of investment options in real projects.

Registered Bond A bond whose ownership is demonstrated by associating the buyer's name with the bond in the issuer's records.

Reinvoice Center A central financial subsidiary of a multinational corporation where intrafirm transaction exposure is netted, and the residual exposure is managed.

Reporting Currency The currency in which a MNC prepares its consolidated financial statements. Typically this is the currency in which the parent firm keeps its books.

Residential Taxation See Worldwide Taxation.

Residual Control Rights Refers to the right to make discretionary decisions under those contingencies that are not specifically covered by the contract.

Reversing Trade A trade in either the futures or forward market that will neutralize a position.

S

Sarbanes-Oxley Act The U.S. Congress passed this law in 2002 to strengthen corporate governance. The act requires the creation of a public accounting oversight board. It also requires that the CEO and the CFO sign off on the company's financial statements.

Secondary Market A market in which investors buy and sell securities to other investors, the original issuer is not involved in these trades. This market provides marketability and valuation of the securities.

Shareholder Wealth Maximization This represents the most important objective of corporate management that managers of companies should keep in mind when they make important corporate decisions. Managers can maximize shareholder wealth by maximizing the market value of the firm.

Sharpe Performance Measure (SHP) A risk-adjusted performance measure for a portfolio that gives the excess return (above the risk-free interest rate) per standard deviation risk.

Shelf Registration Allows a bond issuer to pre-register a securities issue that will occur at a later date.

Single-Currency Interest Rate Swap Typically called an "interest rate swap." There are many variants; however, all involve swapping interest payments on debt obligations that are denominated in the same currency.

Smithsonian Agreement In December 1971, the G-10 countries agreed to devalue the U.S. dollar against gold and most major currencies in an attempt to save the Bretton Woods system.

Snake European version of fixed exchange rate system that appeared as the Bretton Woods system declined.

Source Taxation See Territorial Taxation.

Special Drawing Rights (SDRs) An artificial international reserve created by the International Monetary Fund (IMF) that is a currency basket currently composed of four major currencies.

Specialist On exchange markets in the United States, each stock is represented by a specialist who makes a market by holding an inventory of the security.

Speculator One who attempts to profit from a favorable, but uncertain, price change in an asset by acquiring a position in it.

Spot (Exchange) Rate Price at which foreign exchange can be sold or purchased for immediate (within two business days) delivery.

Straight Fixed-Rate Bond Bonds with a specified maturity date that have fixed coupon payments.

Striking Price See Exercise Price.

Stripped Bond A synthetic zero coupon bond created by an investment bank by selling the rights to a specific coupon payment or the bond principal of a coupon bond, typically a U.S. Treasury bond.

Subpart F Income Income of controlled foreign corporations that is subject to immediate U.S. taxation; includes income that is relatively easy to transfer between countries and is subject to a low foreign tax levy.

Swap Bank A generic term to describe a financial institution that facilitates currency and interest rate swaps between counterparties.

Swap Broker Function of a swap bank in which it matches counterparties but does not assume any risk of the swap; however, it does receive a commission for this service.

Swap Dealer Function of a swap bank in which it makes a market in one or the other side of a currency or interest rate swap.

Swap Transaction The simultaneous spot sale (purchase) of an asset against a forward purchase (sale) of an approximately equal amount of the asset.

Syndicate A group of Eurobanks banding together to share the risk of lending Eurocredits.

Systemic Risk The risk of collapse of the entire financial system, as opposed to the risk associated with any one individual component, market, or sector.